Sb
Shojo Beat

GENTLEMEN'S ✝ ALLIANCE CROSS

Story & Art by
Arina Tanemura

Vol. 6

CONTENTS

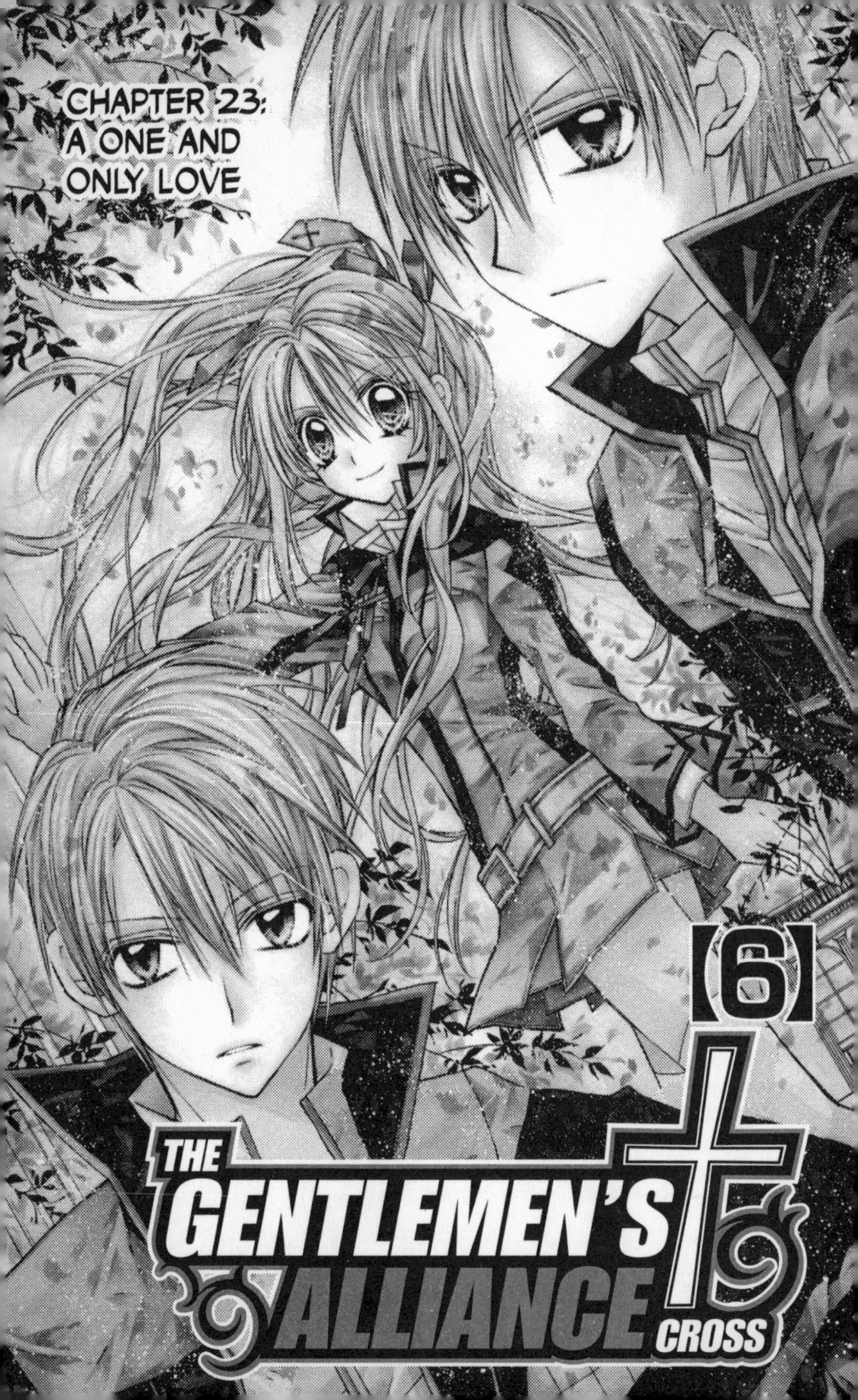
CHAPTER 23:
A ONE AND
ONLY LOVE
(6)
THE
GENTLEMEN'S
ALLIANCE
CROSS

CHARACTER INTRODUCTIONS

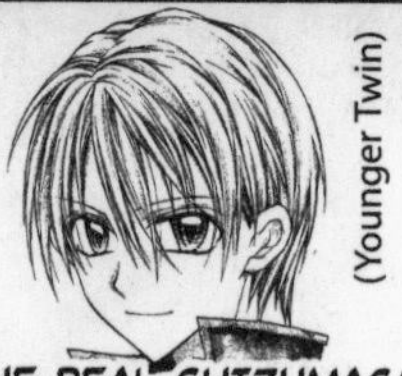

(Younger Twin)

THE REAL SHIZUMASA

An illness prevents him from attending school. He helped Haine mend her yanki ways.

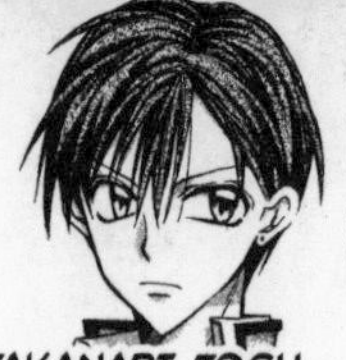

(Elder Twin)

TAKANARI TOGU

Student Council President

The double. Referred to as "the Emperor" and is the highest authority in school. Wrote Haine's favorite picture book.

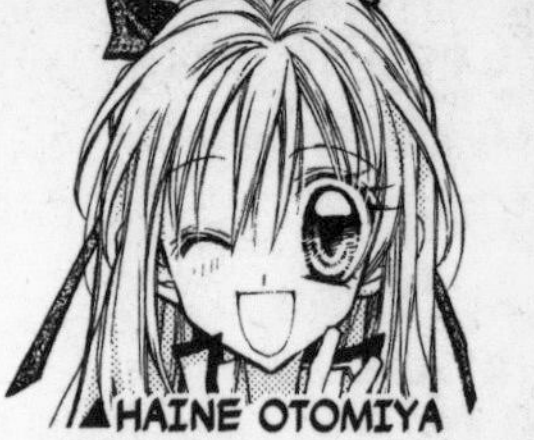

HAINE OTOMIYA

Bodyguard & General Affairs

A cheerful girl who is in love with Shizumasa-sama. Former juvenile delinquent. Adopted into the Otomiya family in fourth grade.

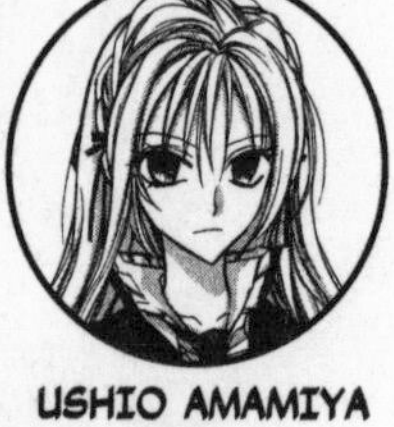

USHIO AMAMIYA

Clerk

Haine's friend. She's beautiful.

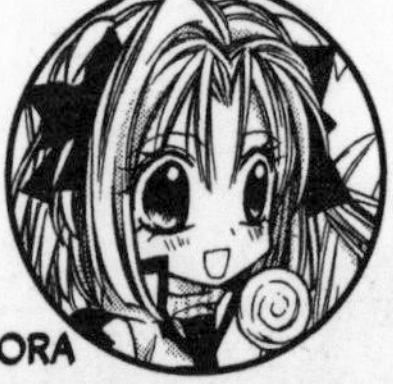

MAORA

Planning Events & Accounting

Childhood friend of Maguri.

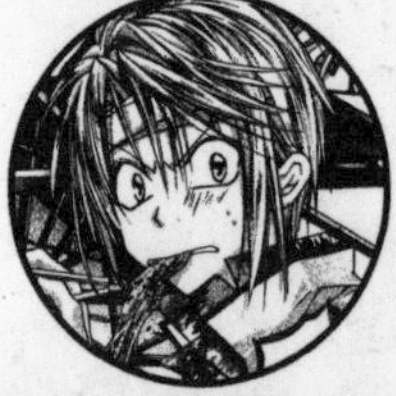

MAGURI TSUJIMIYA

Vice President

In love with the Emperor.

THE GENTLEMEN'S ALLIANCE CROSS

Haine Otomiya is a former juvenile delinquent who attends Imperial Academy. She is appointed the rank of "Platinum" as Emperor Shizumasa Togu's fake girlfriend in order to ward off the other girls.

But—there are two Shizumasas! The fake Shizumasa takes away Haine's Platinum status after finding out she kissed the real Shizumasa. Haine, not knowing there are two Shizumasas, is befuddled by the situation...

Around the same time, Haine is forcefully brought to Kamiya mansion. There, she is reunited with her mother, Maika, but Maika has lost her memory and doesn't recognize Haine. Shizumasa and the others rescue Haine from the mansion. With Shizumasa's apology (?) she is reinstated as the Platinum.

Shizumasa tells Haine he has something important to talk to her about, but during their date, she accidentally sees the other Shizumasa. As the fake Shizumasa kisses her, the other appears and tells her the shocking truth: "That guy isn't me. He's my older twin brother"...

STORY THUS FAR

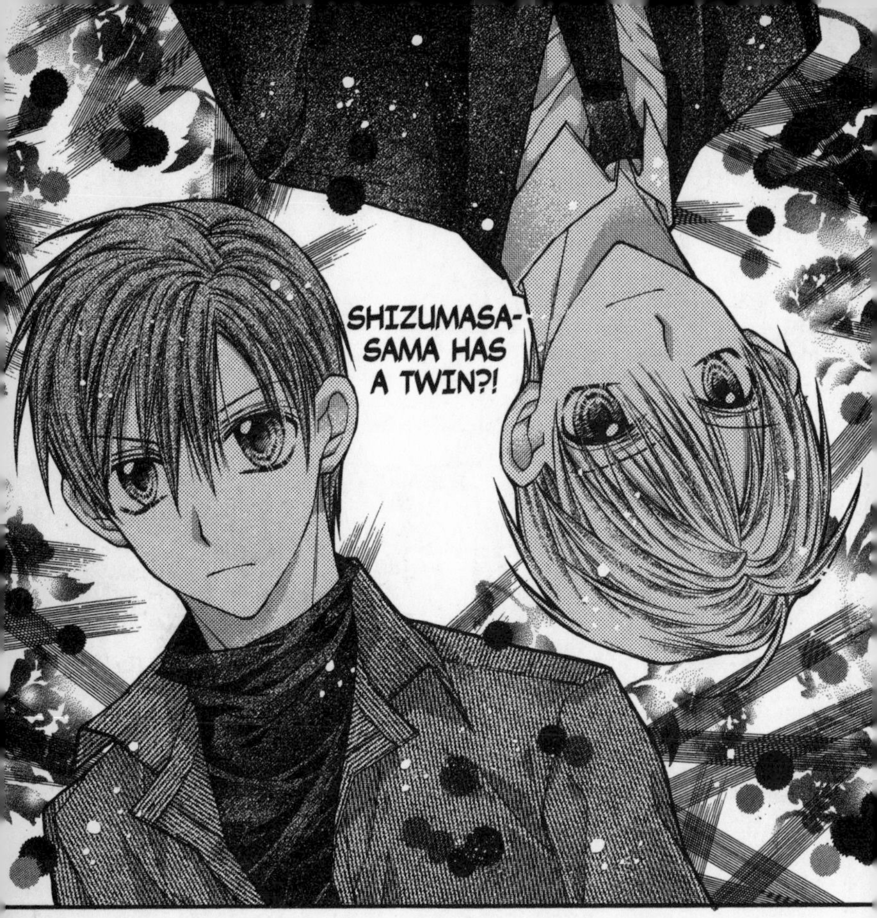
SHIZUMASA-SAMA HAS A TWIN?!

Chapter 23: A One and Only Love

Lead-in I thought being in love with all one's heart and soul was a good thing...

※·I'm giving away the story. (It may be better to read this after you read all of vol. 6.)

This chapter is packed with all the characters' idiosyncrasies, and that's what I like about it. Though I've already forgotten some parts. (Hey!)
My supervisor was O-shi, but during this chapter Y-san became my supervisor, and I got comments like, "That chapter was really exciting!" Takanari's popularity was also skyrocketing, so it was a very memorable time for me.

I guess the spotlight is on Toya-kun. I'm surprised at how dark he can become to secure Takanari's happiness. He probably approves of Haine as Takanari's love, but if she wasn't Shizumasa's love interest, I'm sure he wouldn't have tried this hard to try and bring Haine and Takanari together.

I'm often asked, "So who is Haine going to get together with in the end?!" I really have no idea about that at this point. My vague goal for *Gentlemen's Alliance †* is to try to create it in a different way (for me, anyway). I usually create my manga after I determine the whole story, but for this series I'm attempting to go with the flow.

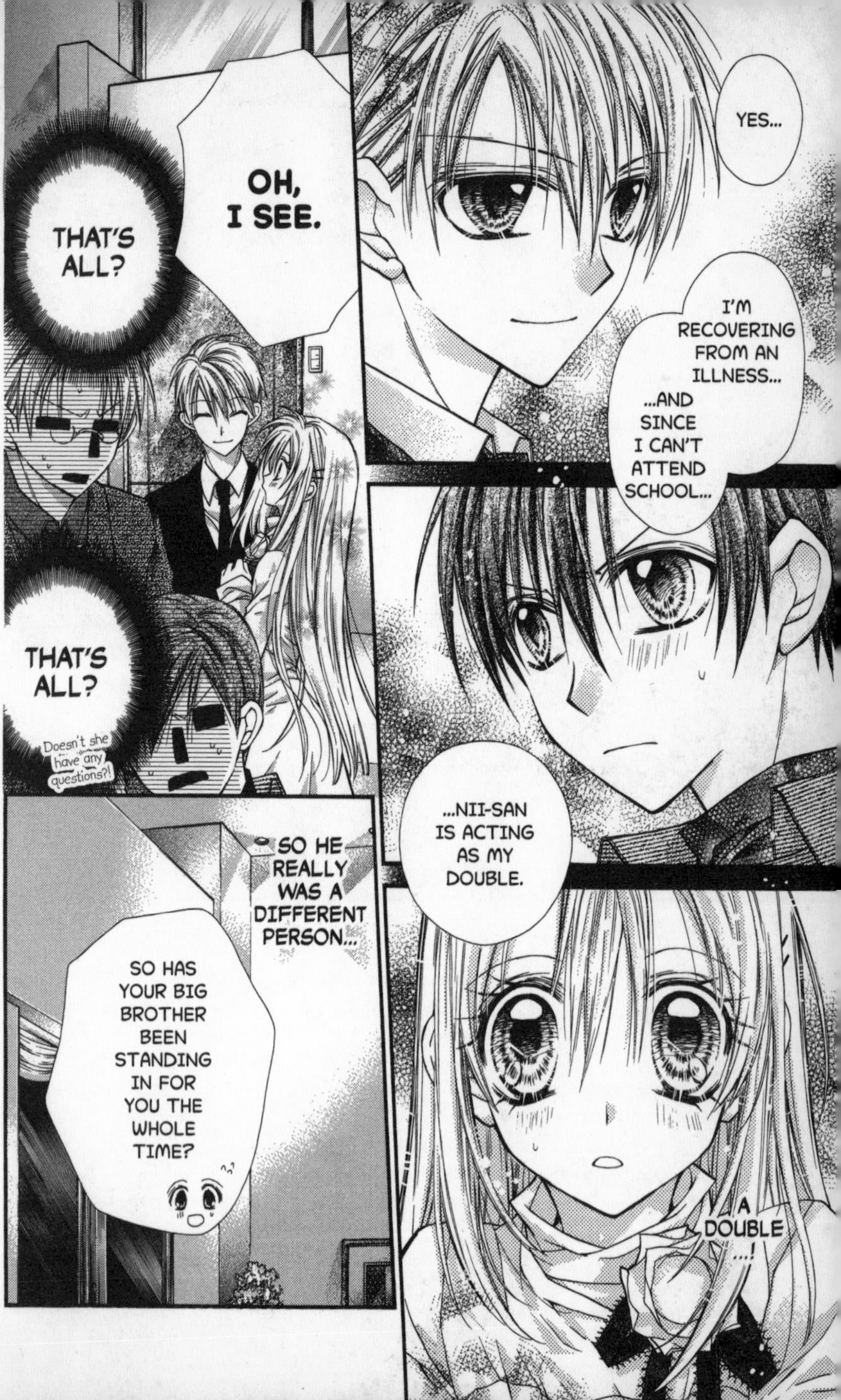
YES...
I'M RECOVERING FROM AN ILLNESS...
...AND SINCE I CAN'T ATTEND SCHOOL...
...NII-SAN IS ACTING AS MY DOUBLE.
A DOUBLE ...!
OH, I SEE.
THAT'S ALL?
THAT'S ALL?
Doesn't she have any questions?!
SO HE REALLY WAS A DIFFERENT PERSON...
SO HAS YOUR BIG BROTHER BEEN STANDING IN FOR YOU THE WHOLE TIME?

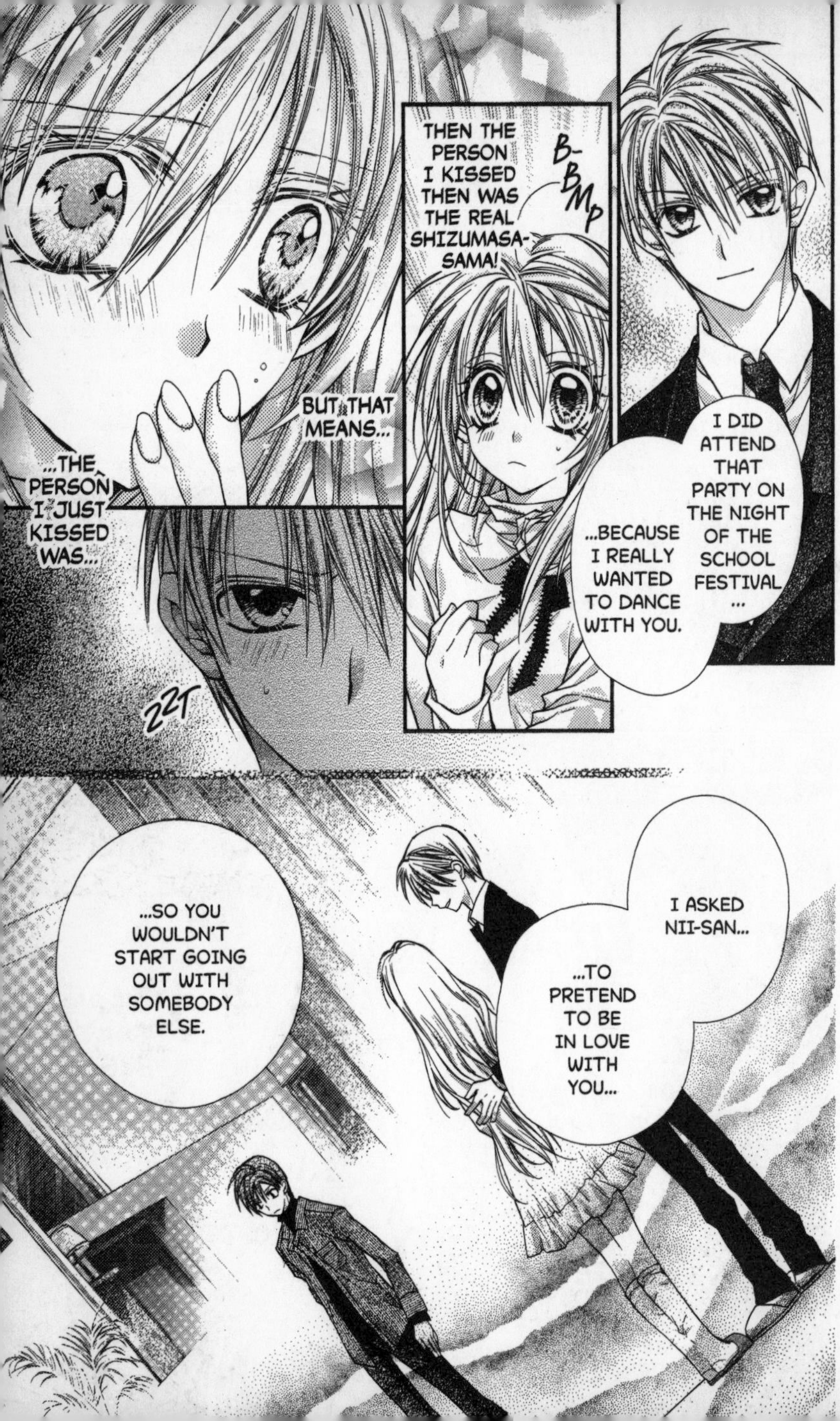
I DID ATTEND THAT PARTY ON THE NIGHT OF THE SCHOOL FESTIVAL...
...BECAUSE I REALLY WANTED TO DANCE WITH YOU.
THEN THE PERSON I KISSED THEN WAS THE REAL SHIZUMASA-SAMA!
B-BMP
BUT THAT MEANS...
...THE PERSON I JUST KISSED WAS...
ZZT
I ASKED NII-SAN...
...TO PRETEND TO BE IN LOVE WITH YOU...
...SO YOU WOULDN'T START GOING OUT WITH SOMEBODY ELSE.

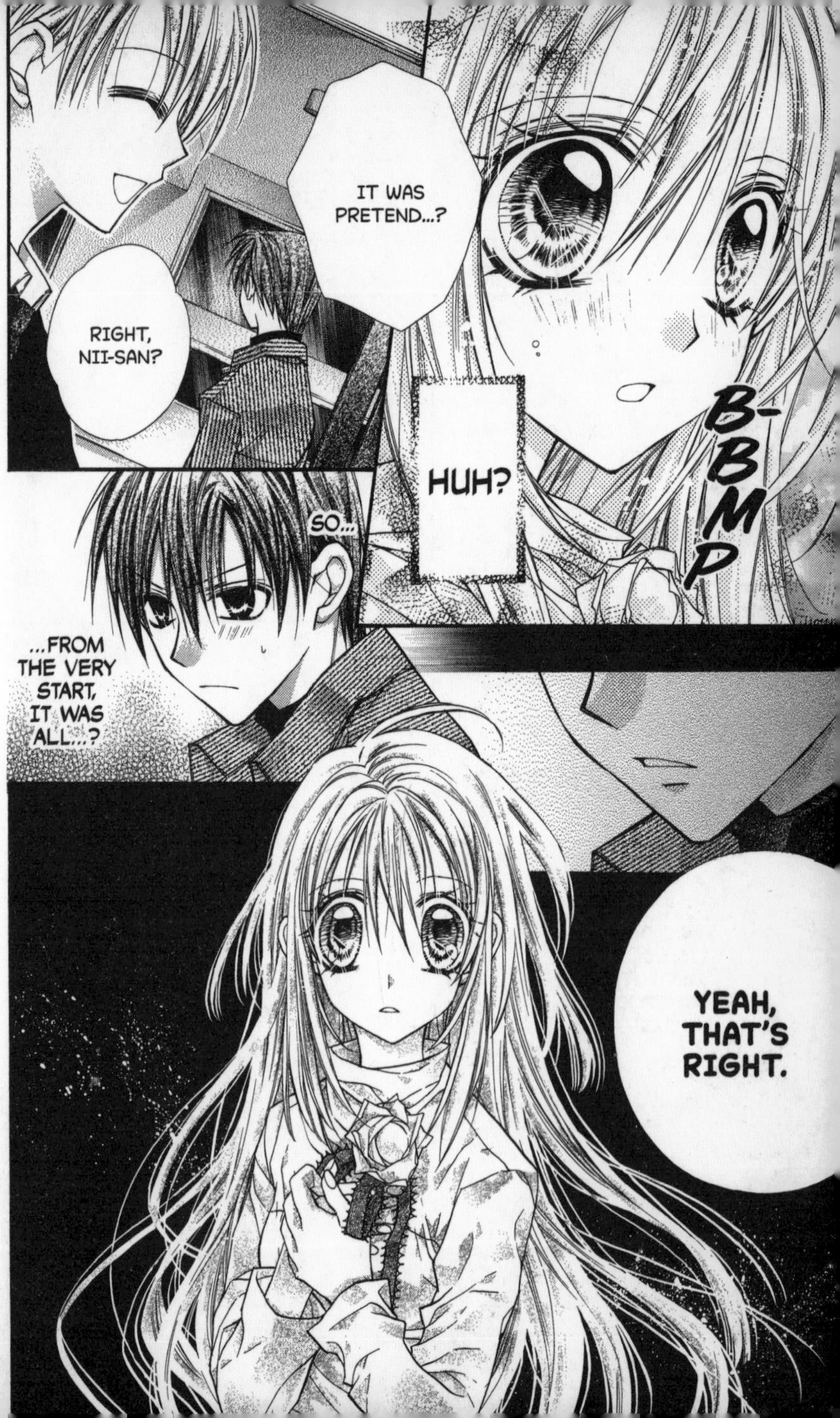
IT WAS PRETEND...?
HUH?
B-BBMP
RIGHT, NII-SAN?
SO...
...FROM THE VERY START, IT WAS ALL...?
YEAH, THAT'S RIGHT.

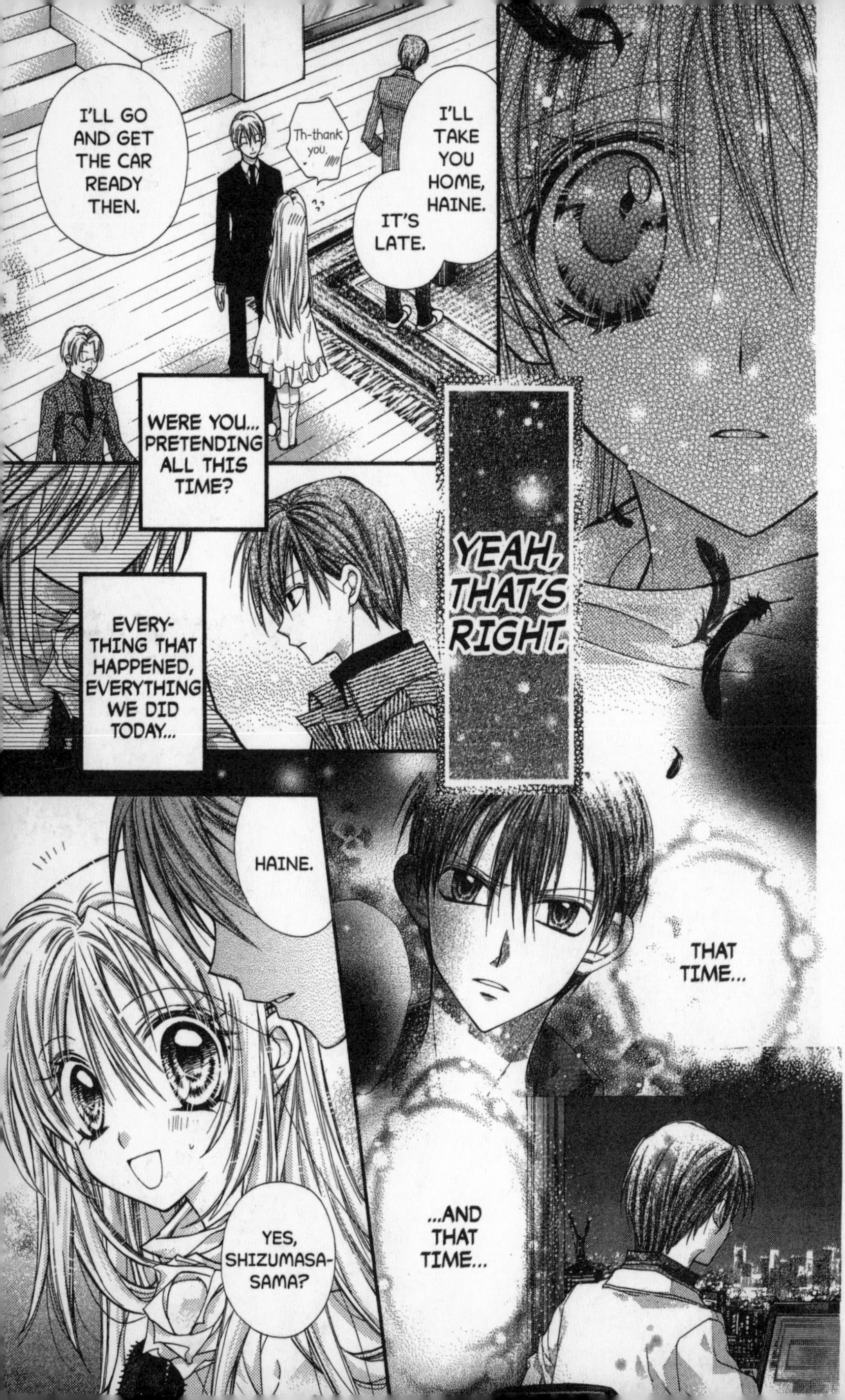

I'LL TAKE YOU HOME, HAINE.
IT'S LATE.
Th-thank you.
I'LL GO AND GET THE CAR READY THEN.
WERE YOU... PRETENDING ALL THIS TIME?
EVERY-THING THAT HAPPENED, EVERYTHING WE DID TODAY...
YEAH, THAT'S RIGHT.
THAT TIME...
...AND THAT TIME...
HAINE.
YES, SHIZUMASA-SAMA?

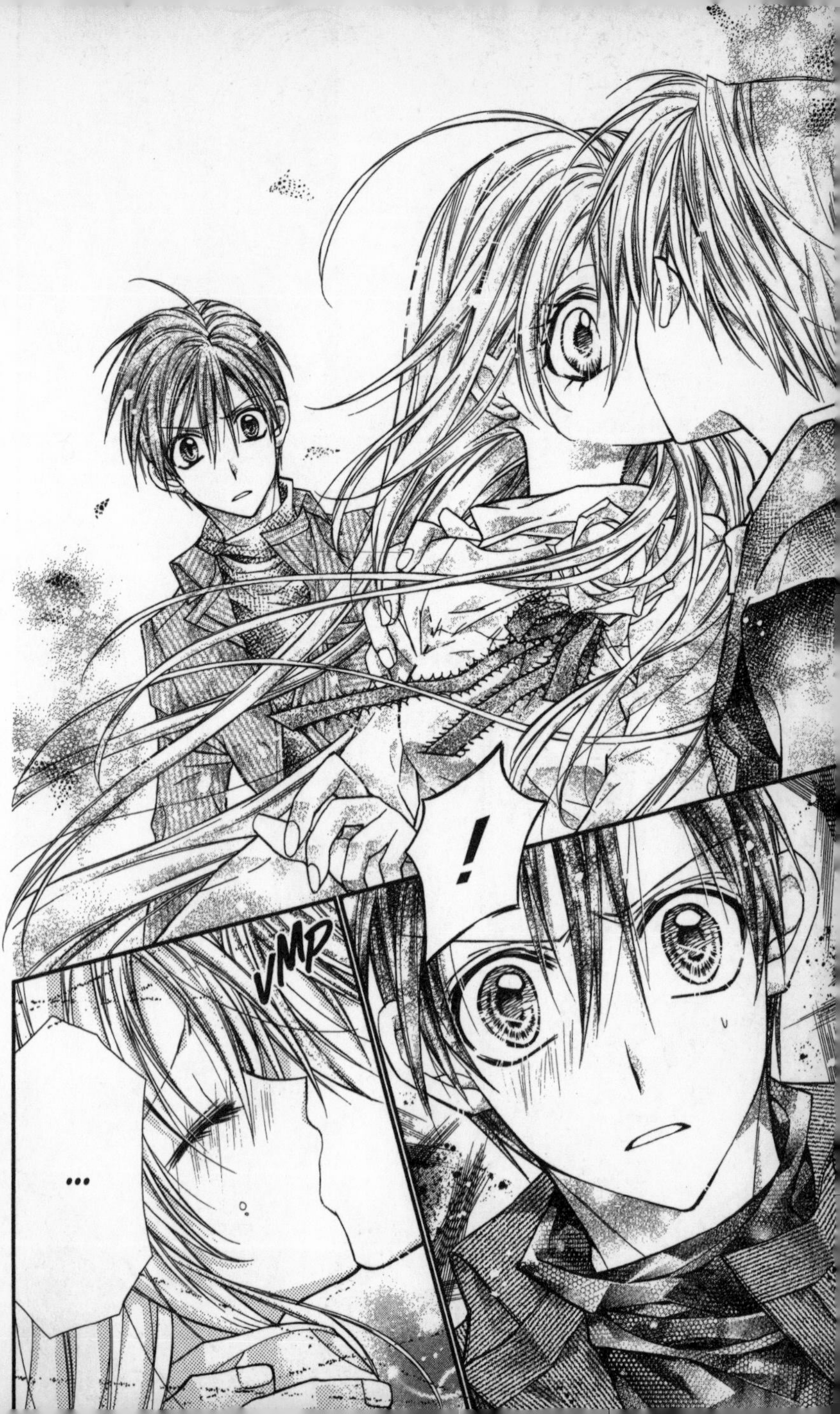
!
VMP
...

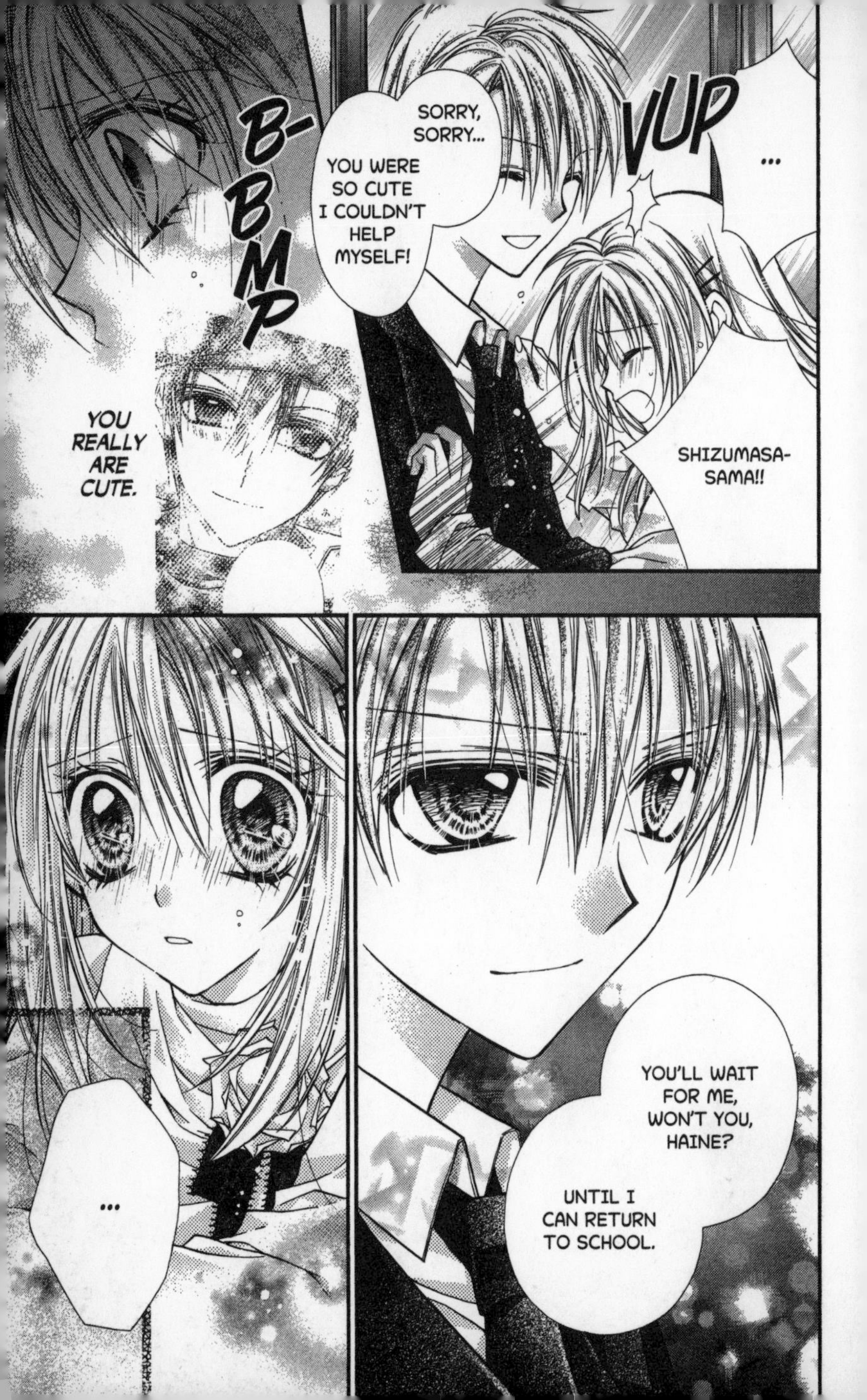
VUP
...
SHIZUMASA-SAMA!!
SORRY, SORRY...
YOU WERE SO CUTE I COULDN'T HELP MYSELF!
B-BMP
YOU REALLY ARE CUTE.
YOU'LL WAIT FOR ME, WON'T YOU, HAINE?
UNTIL I CAN RETURN TO SCHOOL.
...

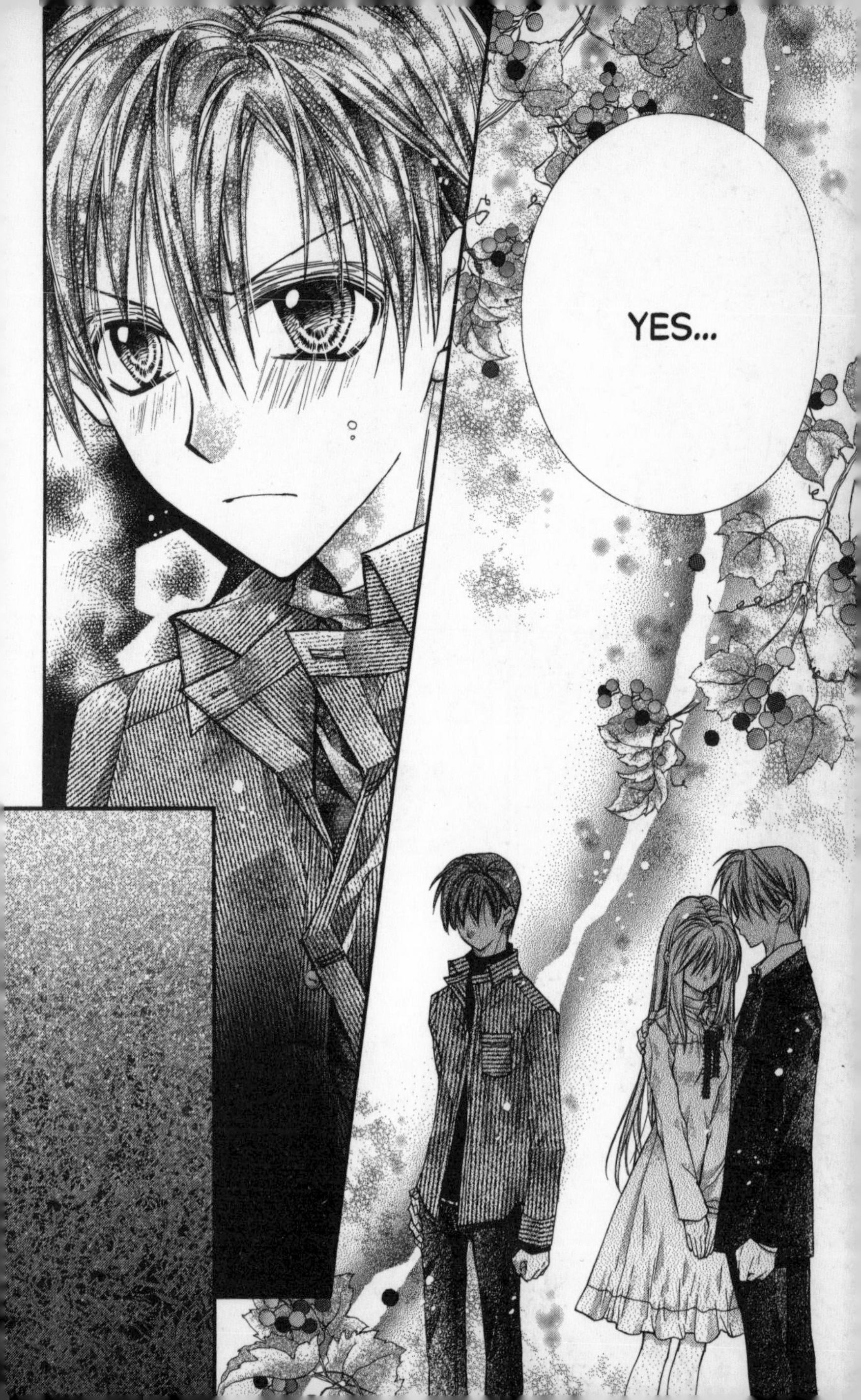
YES...

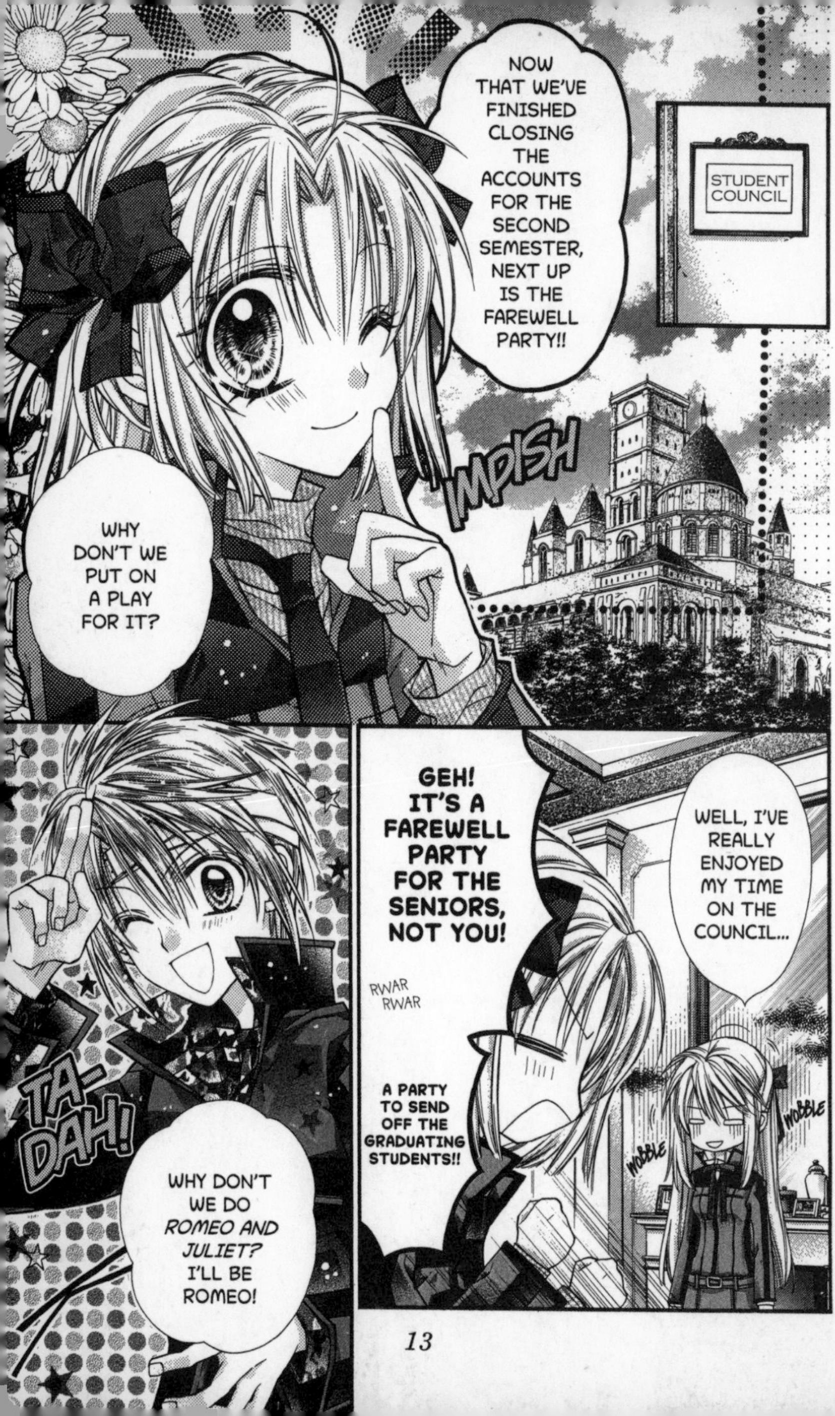
STUDENT COUNCIL
NOW THAT WE'VE FINISHED CLOSING THE ACCOUNTS FOR THE SECOND SEMESTER, NEXT UP IS THE FAREWELL PARTY!!
IMPISH
WHY DON'T WE PUT ON A PLAY FOR IT?
WELL, I'VE REALLY ENJOYED MY TIME ON THE COUNCIL...
GEH! IT'S A FAREWELL PARTY FOR THE SENIORS, NOT YOU!
RWAR RWAR
WOBBLE
WOBBLE
A PARTY TO SEND OFF THE GRADUATING STUDENTS!!
TA-DAH!
WHY DON'T WE DO *ROMEO AND JULIET?* I'LL BE ROMEO!

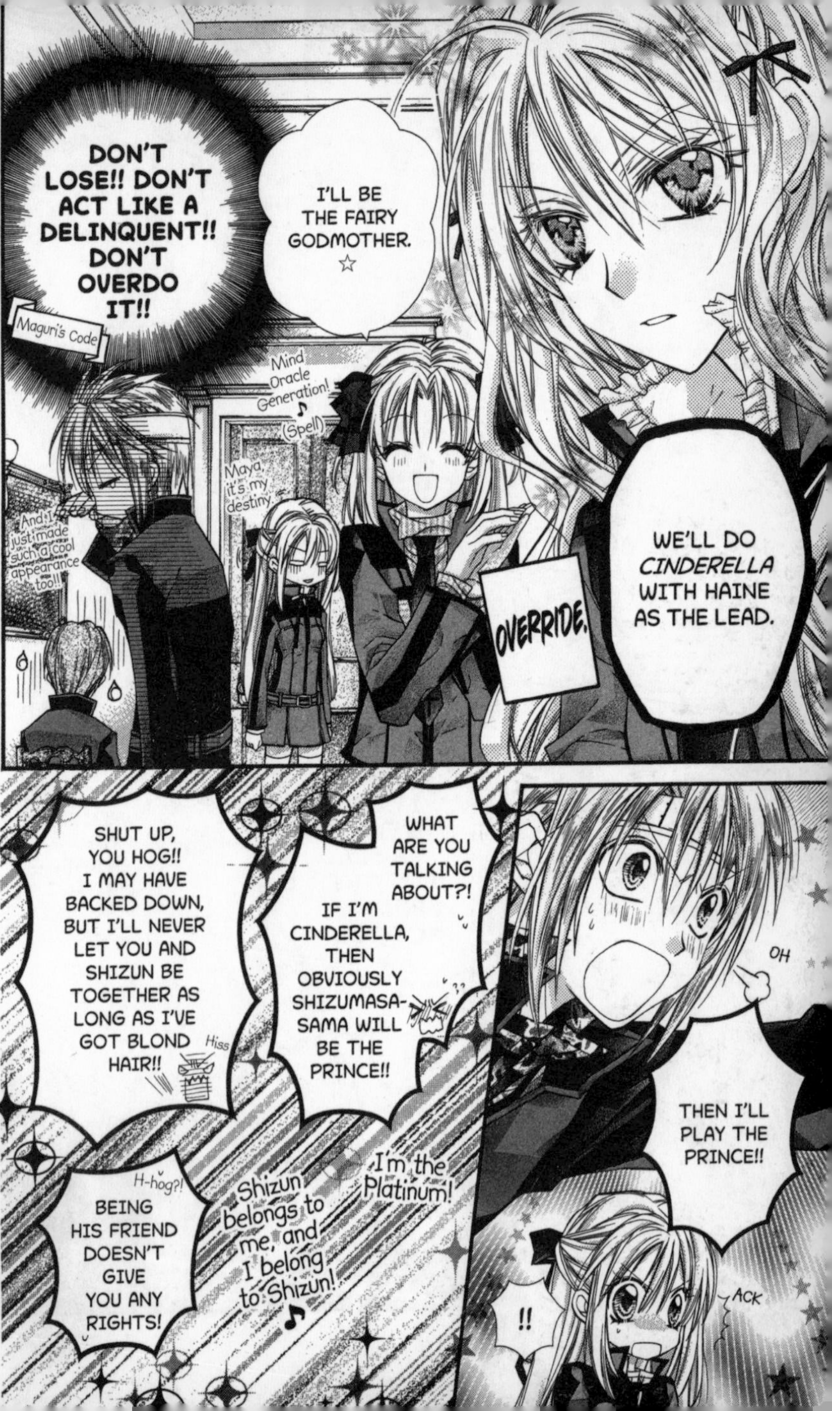
WE'LL DO *CINDERELLA* WITH HAINE AS THE LEAD.
OVERRIDE.
I'LL BE THE FAIRY GODMOTHER. ☆
Mind Oracle Generation! ♪
(Spell)
Maya, it's my destiny.
DON'T LOSE!! DON'T ACT LIKE A DELINQUENT!! DON'T OVERDO IT!!
Maguri's Code
And I just made such a cool appearance too!!
OH
THEN I'LL PLAY THE PRINCE!!
ACK
!!
WHAT ARE YOU TALKING ABOUT?!
IF I'M CINDERELLA, THEN OBVIOUSLY SHIZUMASA-SAMA WILL BE THE PRINCE!!
SHUT UP, YOU HOG!! I MAY HAVE BACKED DOWN, BUT I'LL NEVER LET YOU AND SHIZUN BE TOGETHER AS LONG AS I'VE GOT BLOND HAIR!!
Hiss
I'm the Platinum!
Shizun belongs to me, and I belong to Shizun! ♪
H-hog?!
BEING HIS FRIEND DOESN'T GIVE YOU ANY RIGHTS!

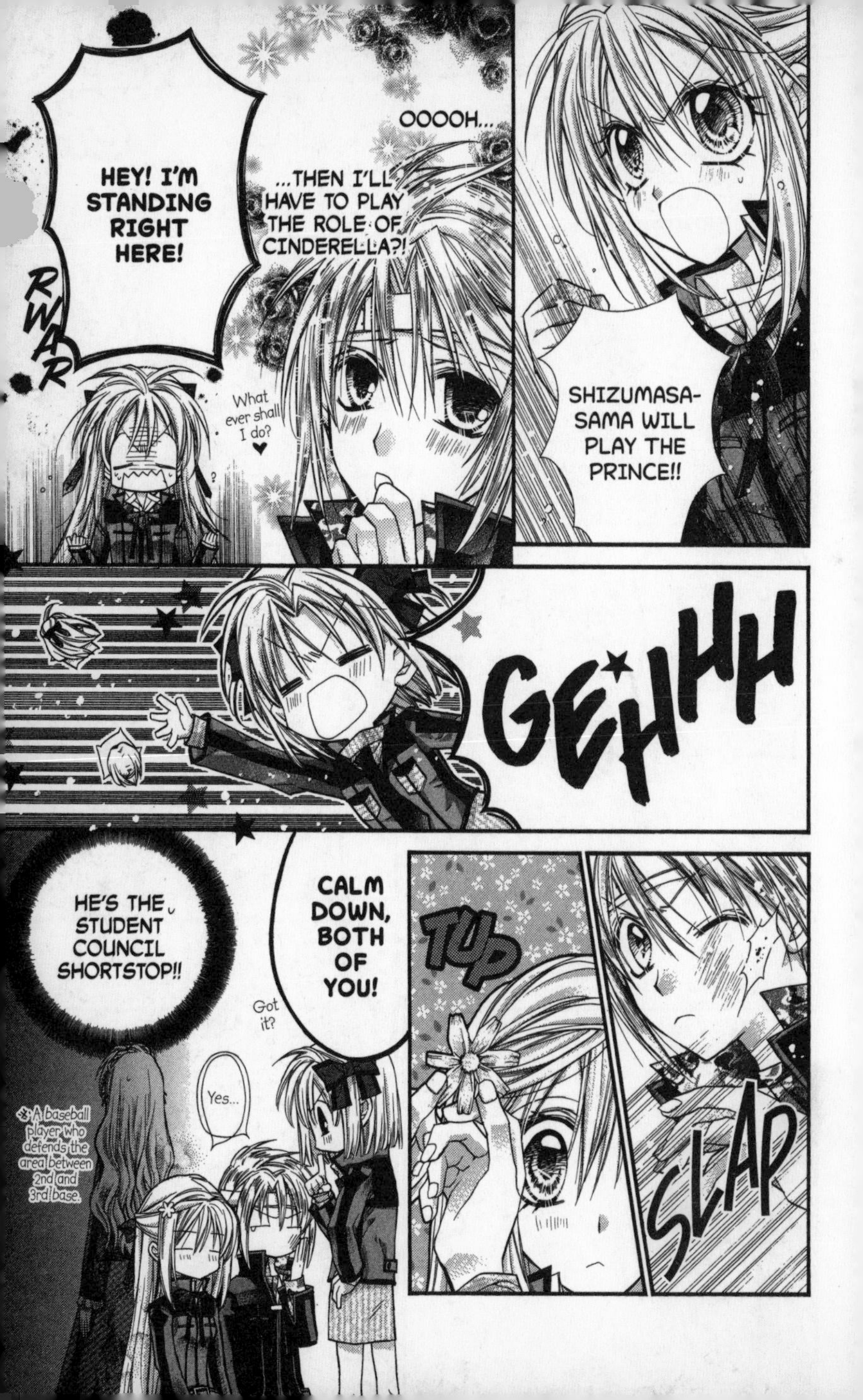
SHIZUMASA-SAMA WILL PLAY THE PRINCE!!
OOOOH...
...THEN I'LL HAVE TO PLAY THE ROLE OF CINDERELLA?!
What ever shall I do?
HEY! I'M STANDING RIGHT HERE!
RWAR
GEHHH
SLAP
TUP
CALM DOWN, BOTH OF YOU!
Got it?
Yes...
HE'S THE STUDENT COUNCIL SHORTSTOP!!
A baseball player who defends the area between 2nd and 3rd base.

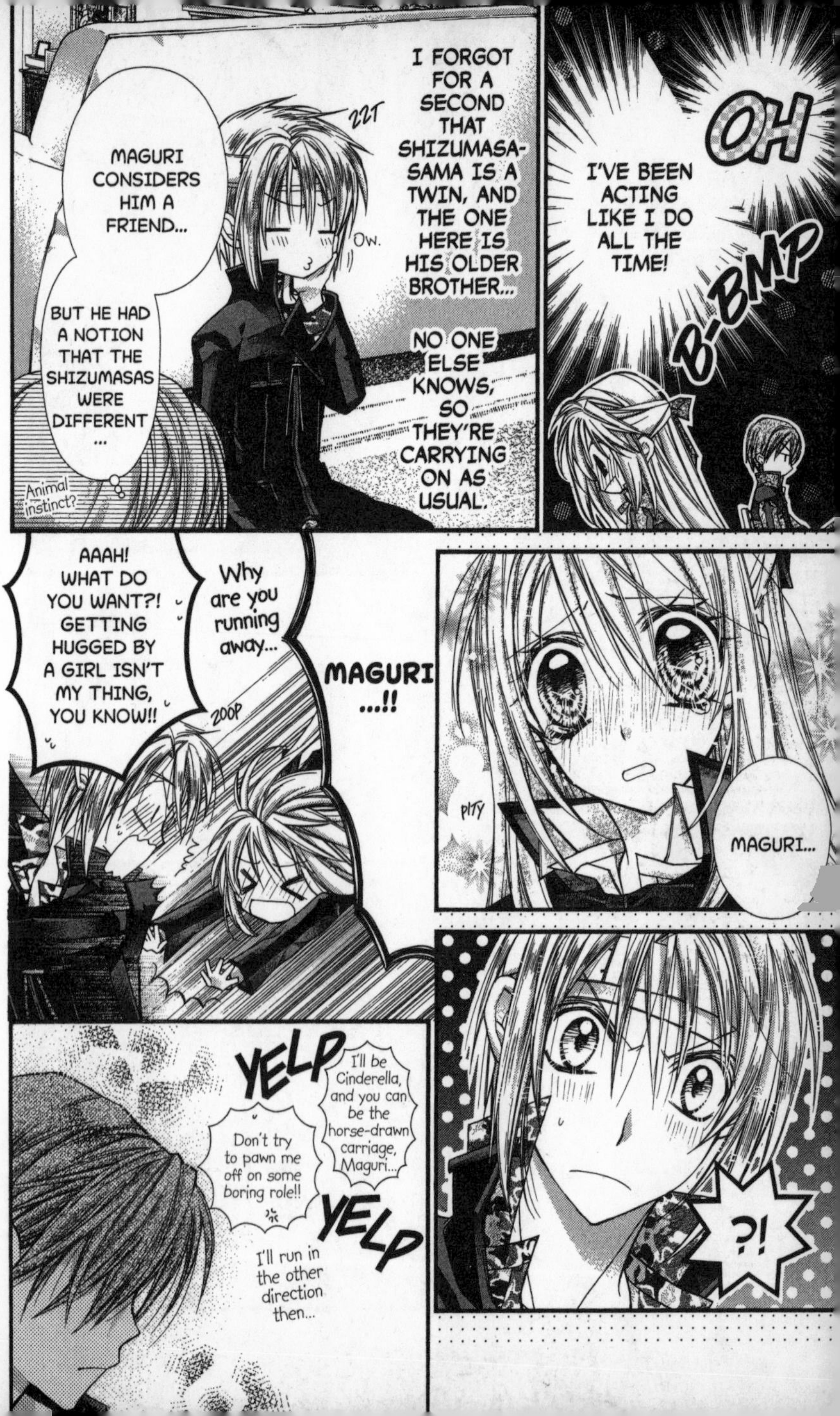
OH
I'VE BEEN ACTING LIKE I DO ALL THE TIME!
B-BMP
I FORGOT FOR A SECOND THAT SHIZUMASA-SAMA IS A TWIN, AND THE ONE HERE IS HIS OLDER BROTHER...
ZZT
MAGURI CONSIDERS HIM A FRIEND...
OW.
NO ONE ELSE KNOWS, SO THEY'RE CARRYING ON AS USUAL.
BUT HE HAD A NOTION THAT THE SHIZUMASAS WERE DIFFERENT ...
Animal instinct?
MAGURI...
PITY
MAGURI ...!!
Why are you running away...
AAAH! WHAT DO YOU WANT?! GETTING HUGGED BY A GIRL ISN'T MY THING, YOU KNOW!!
ZOOP
?!
YELP
I'll be Cinderella, and you can be the horse-drawn carriage, Maguri...
Don't try to pawn me off on some boring role!!
YELP
I'll run in the other direction then...

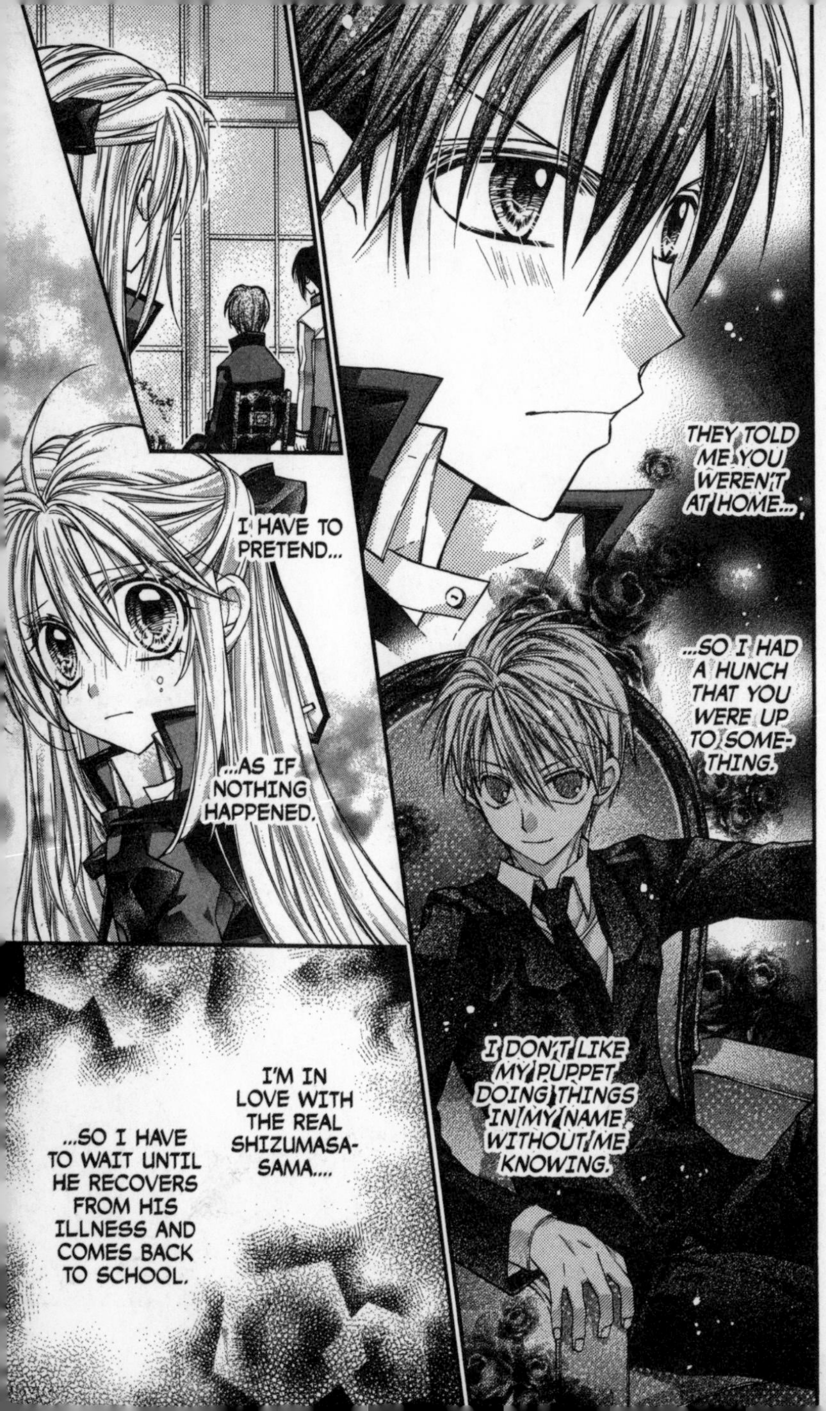
THEY TOLD ME YOU WEREN'T AT HOME...
...SO I HAD A HUNCH THAT YOU WERE UP TO SOME-THING.
I DON'T LIKE MY PUPPET DOING THINGS IN MY NAME WITHOUT ME KNOWING.
I HAVE TO PRETEND...
...AS IF NOTHING HAPPENED.
I'M IN LOVE WITH THE REAL SHIZUMASA-SAMA....
...SO I HAVE TO WAIT UNTIL HE RECOVERS FROM HIS ILLNESS AND COMES BACK TO SCHOOL.

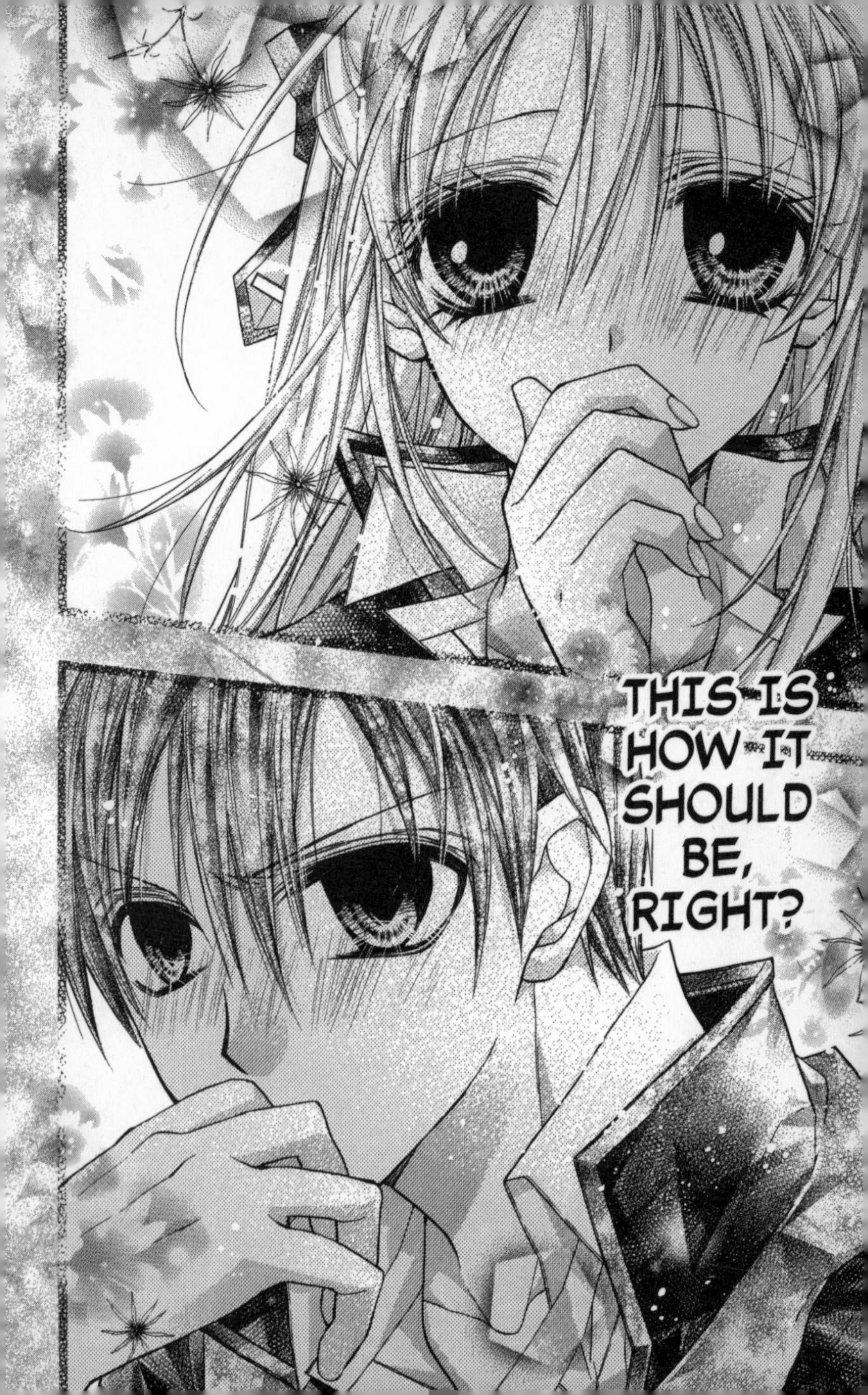
THIS IS HOW IT SHOULD BE, RIGHT?

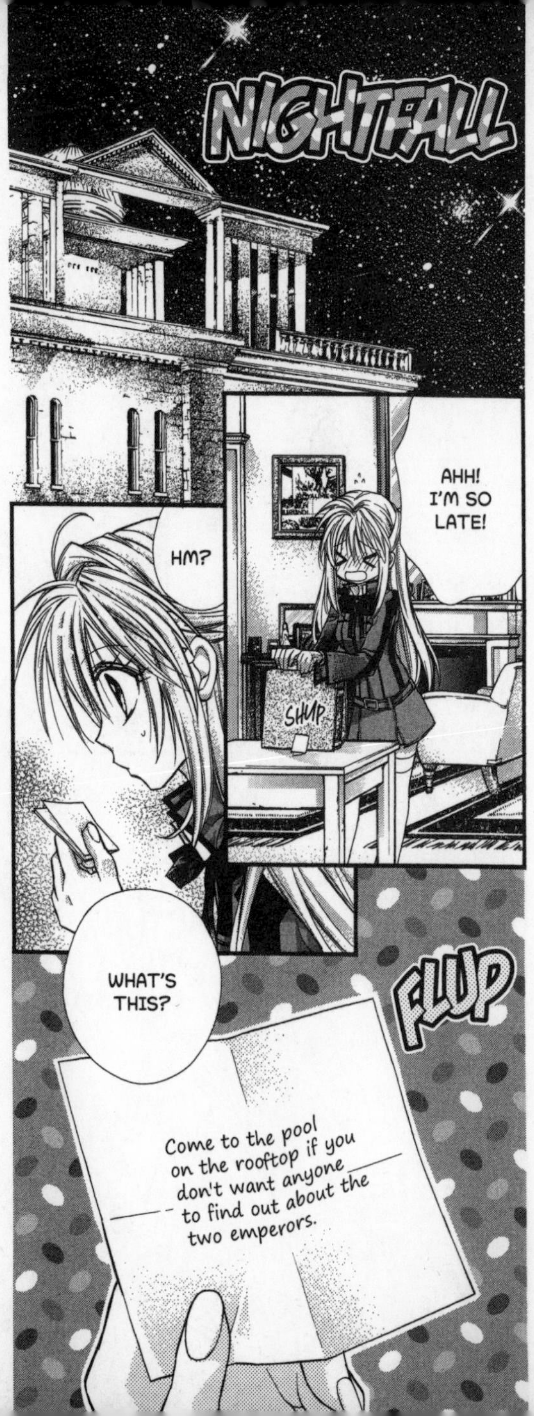
NIGHTFALL
AHH! I'M SO LATE!
SHUP
HM?
WHAT'S THIS?
FLUP
Come to the pool on the rooftop if you don't want anyone to find out about the two emperors.

Coo

Hello.♥ I'm Arina Tanemura. Here is *The Gentlemen's Alliance* † 6.

The cover for this volume ended up being the postman and the warden... For those who have been looking forward to finding out who was on the cover, how do you like it? I thought it would convey an Imperial Academy feeling if I drew those two together...

I'll announce who will be on the cover of the next volume in the last sidebar!
Please look forward to it!

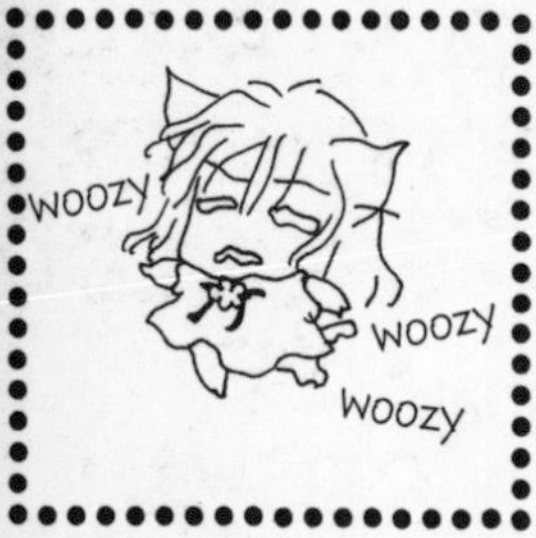
WOOZY
WOOZY
WOOZY

↰ I'm feeling woozy from all the work I've been doing recently.

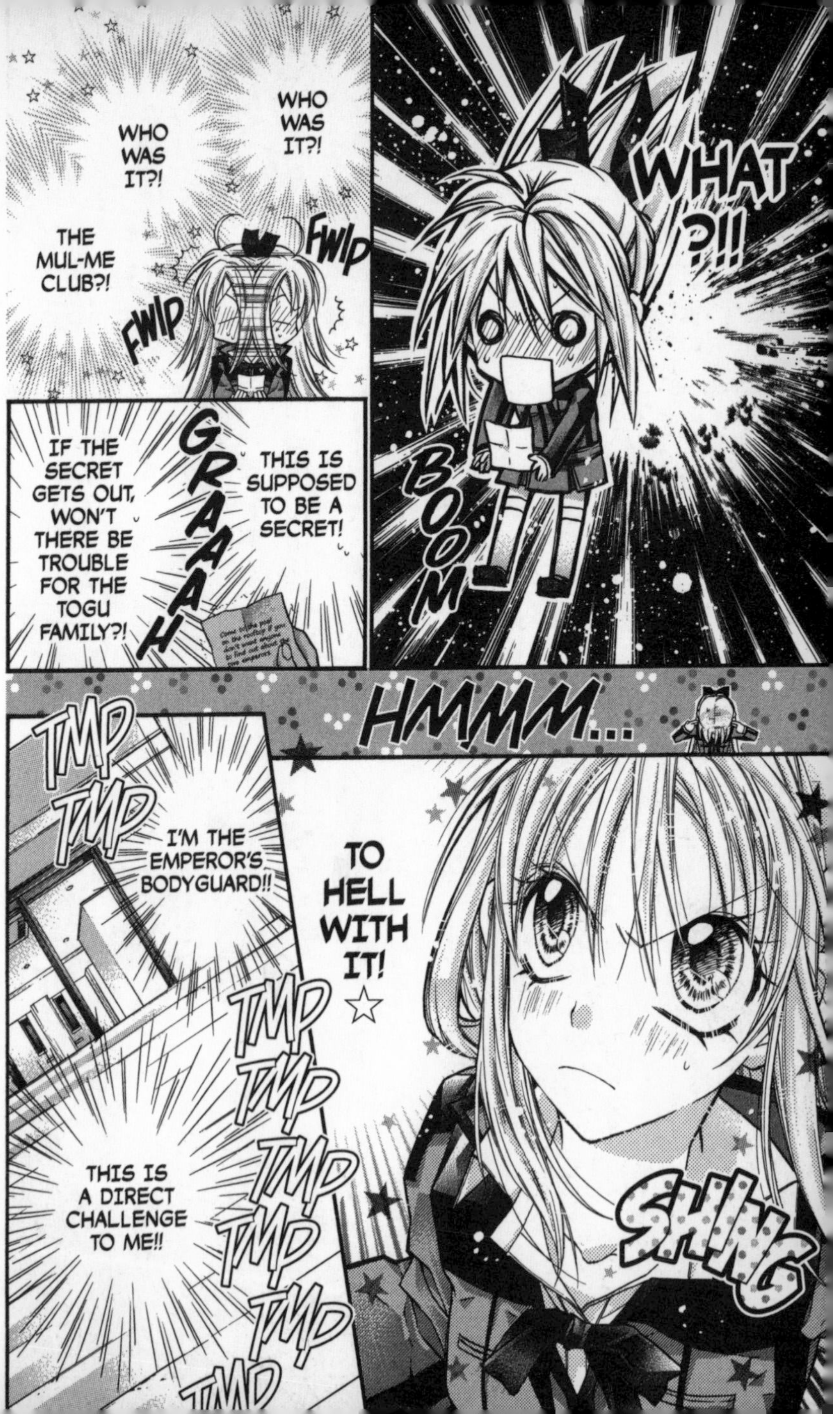
WHAT ?!!
BOOM
WHO WAS IT?!
WHO WAS IT?!
FWIP
THE MUL-ME CLUB?!
FWIP
THIS IS SUPPOSED TO BE A SECRET!
GRAAAAH
IF THE SECRET GETS OUT, WON'T THERE BE TROUBLE FOR THE TOGU FAMILY?!
HMMMM...
TO HELL WITH IT! ☆
SHING
TMP TMP
I'M THE EMPEROR'S BODYGUARD!!
THIS IS A DIRECT CHALLENGE TO ME!!
TMP TMP TMP TMP TMP TMP

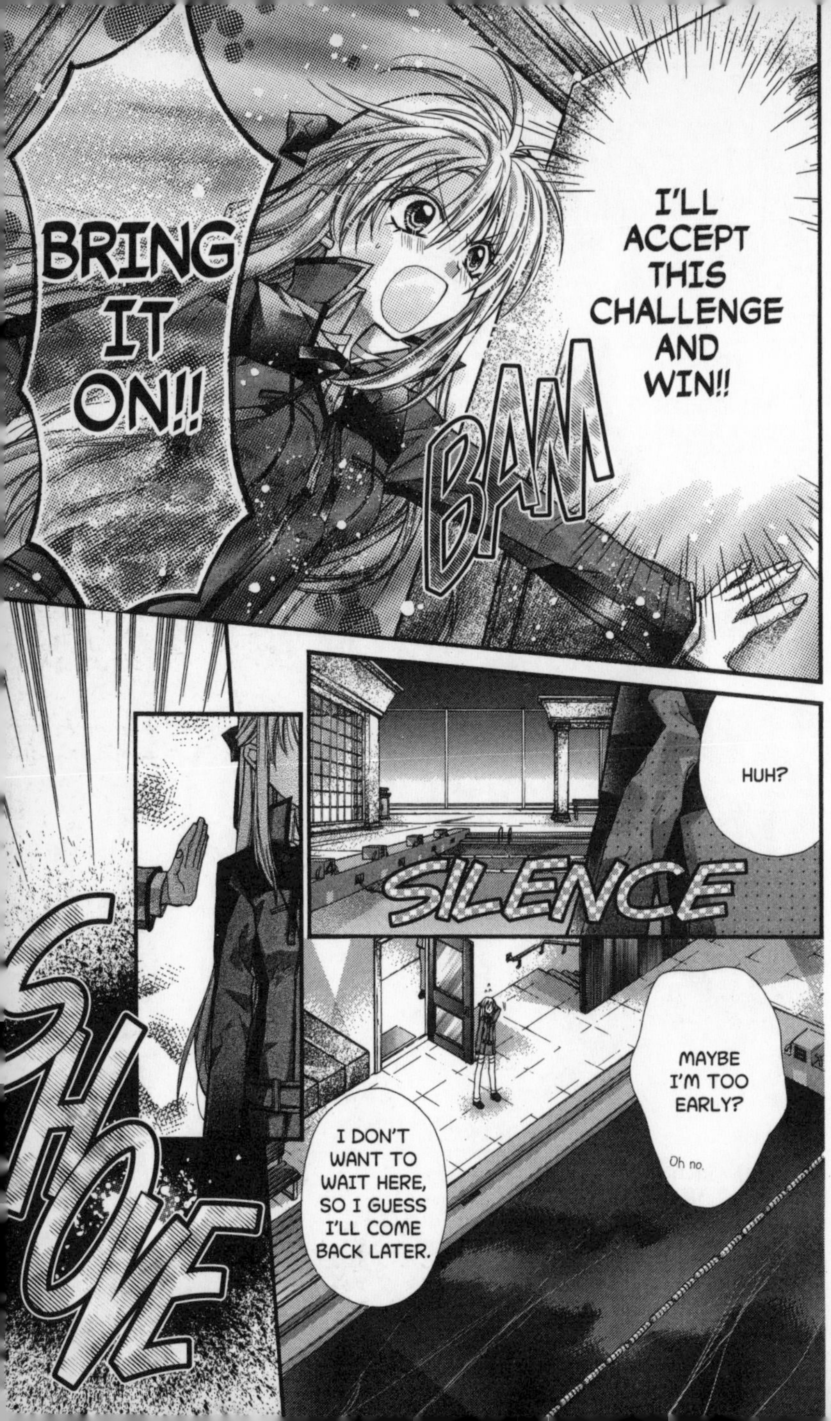
I'LL ACCEPT THIS CHALLENGE AND WIN!!
BAM
BRING IT ON!!
HUH?
SILENCE
MAYBE I'M TOO EARLY?
Oh no.
I DON'T WANT TO WAIT HERE, SO I GUESS I'LL COME BACK LATER.
SHOVE

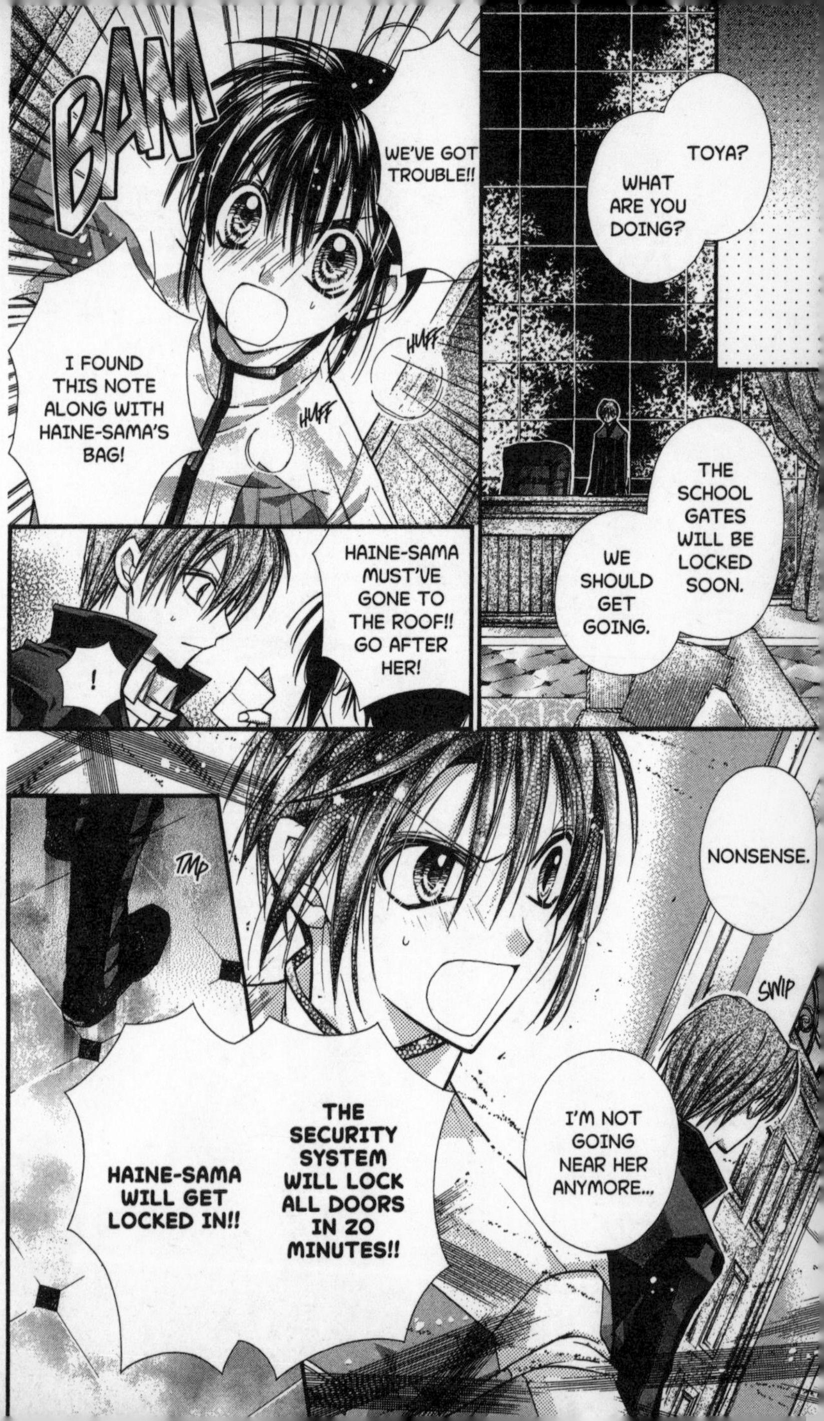
TOYA?
WHAT ARE YOU DOING?
THE SCHOOL GATES WILL BE LOCKED SOON.
WE SHOULD GET GOING.
BAM
WE'VE GOT TROUBLE!!
HUFF
HUFF
I FOUND THIS NOTE ALONG WITH HAINE-SAMA'S BAG!
HAINE-SAMA MUST'VE GONE TO THE ROOF!! GO AFTER HER!
!
NONSENSE.
SWIP
I'M NOT GOING NEAR HER ANYMORE...
THE SECURITY SYSTEM WILL LOCK ALL DOORS IN 20 MINUTES!!
HAINE-SAMA WILL GET LOCKED IN!!
TMP

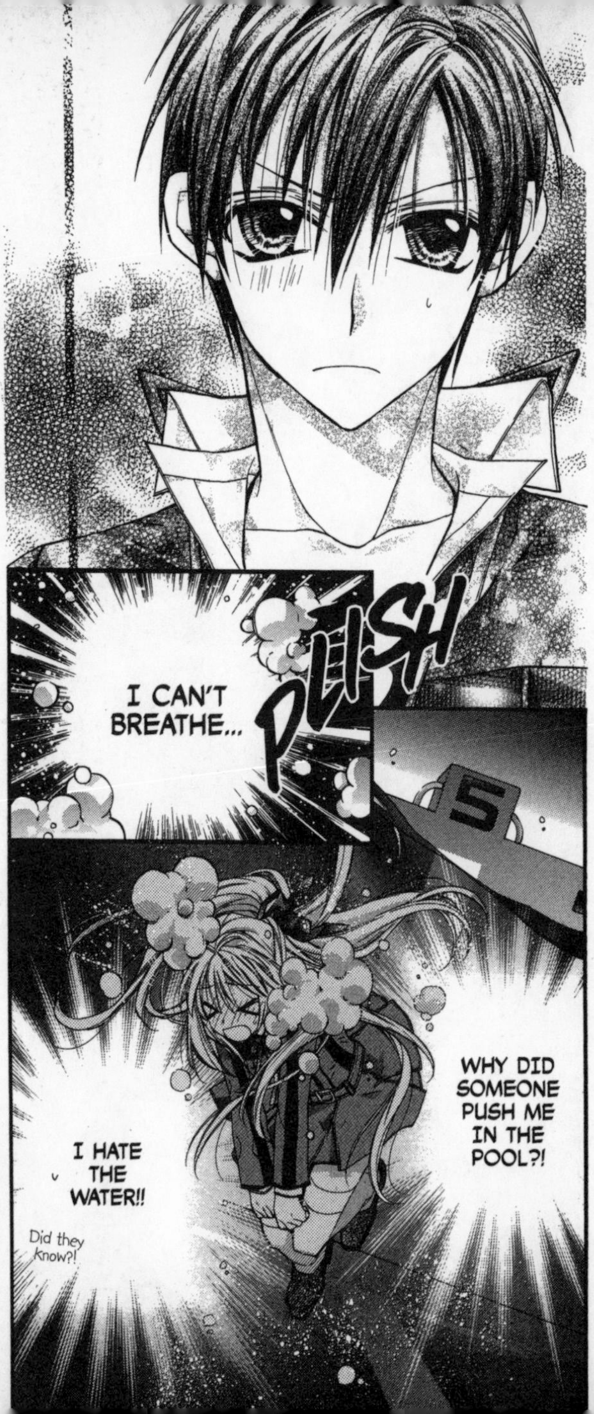
PLISH
I CAN'T BREATHE...
WHY DID SOMEONE PUSH ME IN THE POOL?!
I HATE THE WATER!!
Did they know?!

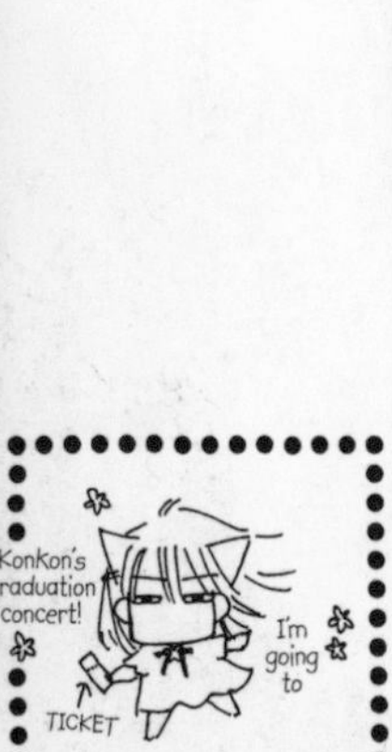
KonKon's graduation concert!
I'm going to
TICKET

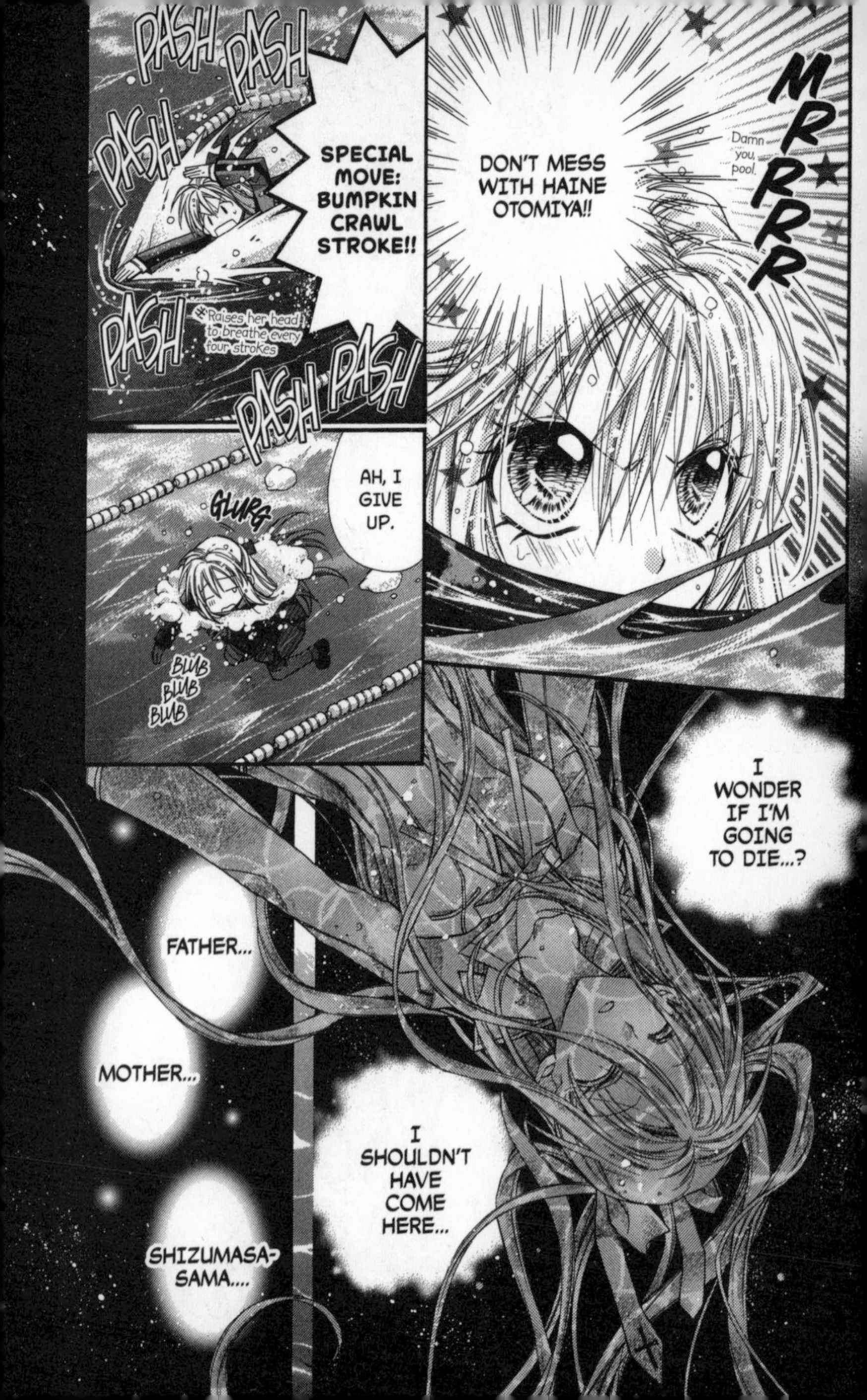
MRRR
Damn you, pool.
DON'T MESS WITH HAINE OTOMIYA!!
SPECIAL MOVE: BUMPKIN CRAWL STROKE!!
PASH PASH
PASH
PASH
Raises her head to breathe every four strokes
PASH PASH
AH, I GIVE UP.
GLURG
BLUB BLUB BLUB
I WONDER IF I'M GOING TO DIE...?
I SHOULDN'T HAVE COME HERE...
FATHER...
MOTHER...
SHIZUMASA-SAMA....

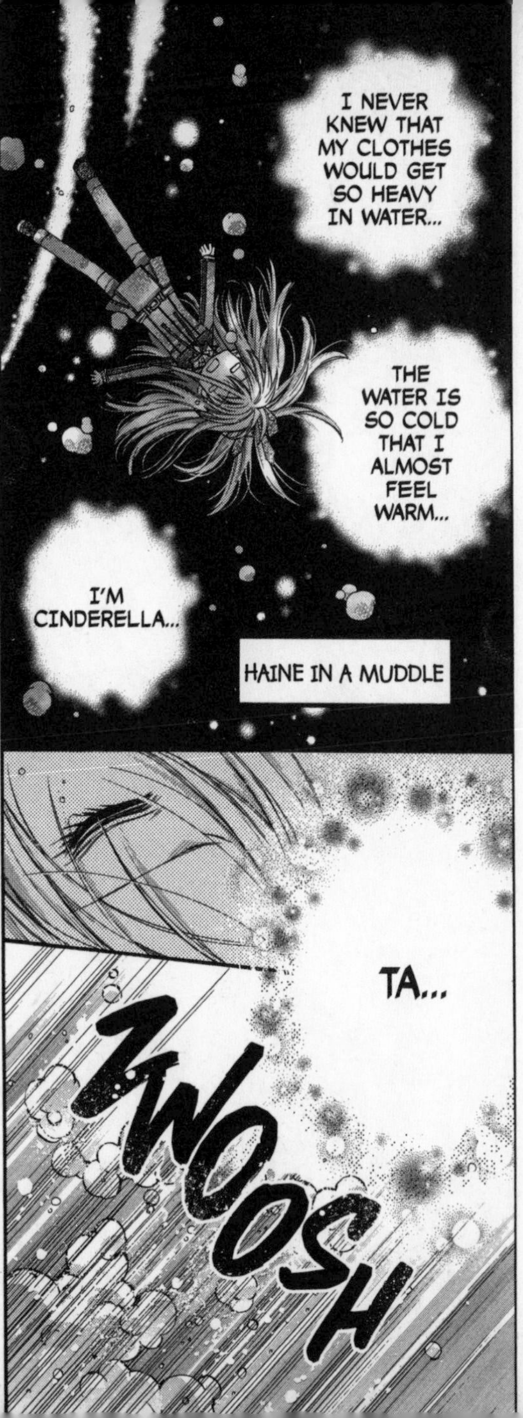
I NEVER KNEW THAT MY CLOTHES WOULD GET SO HEAVY IN WATER...
THE WATER IS SO COLD THAT I ALMOST FEEL WARM...
I'M CINDERELLA...
HAINE IN A MUDDLE
TA...
WHOOSH

Blog

Starting with this volume, I'll show the illustrations I drew and uploaded on my blog.

Ribon is targeted mainly at elementary and middle school girls, and even though the Internet is widespread now, there are some people who still don't have their own computers or cell phones. I thought I'd introduce the illustrations here, but I hope the people who have already seen them will also enjoy them again.

http://rikukai.arinalolipop.jp/

↑ Here is the address. You can see it from your cell phone too.

Currently, I get a hundred thousand hits a day!
Thank you very much!!!
(But the counter doesn't seem to count people hitting the site on their cell phones.)

I'll fix it sooner or later...
To tell you the truth, I'm not sure how it works yet.

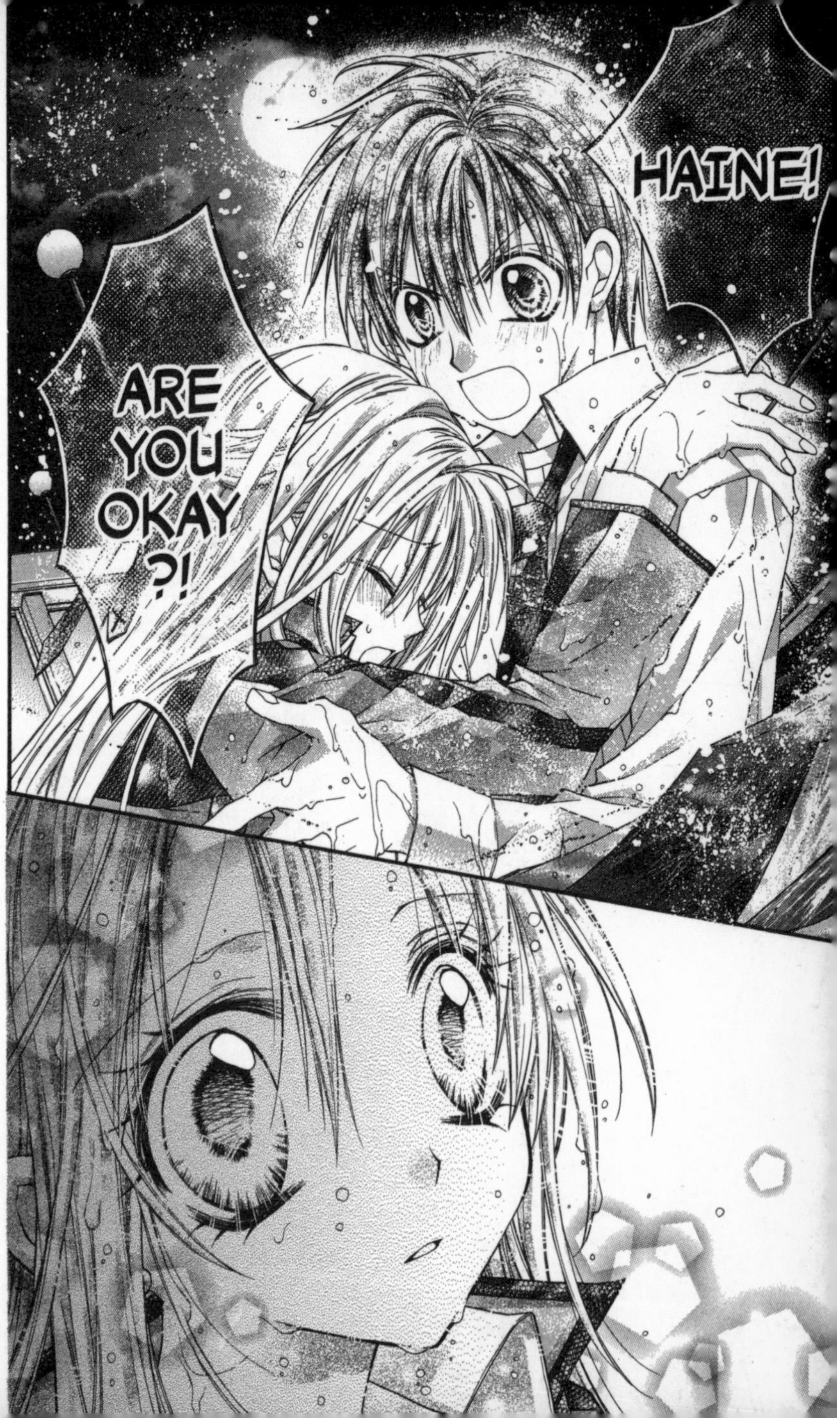
HAINE!
ARE YOU OKAY ?!

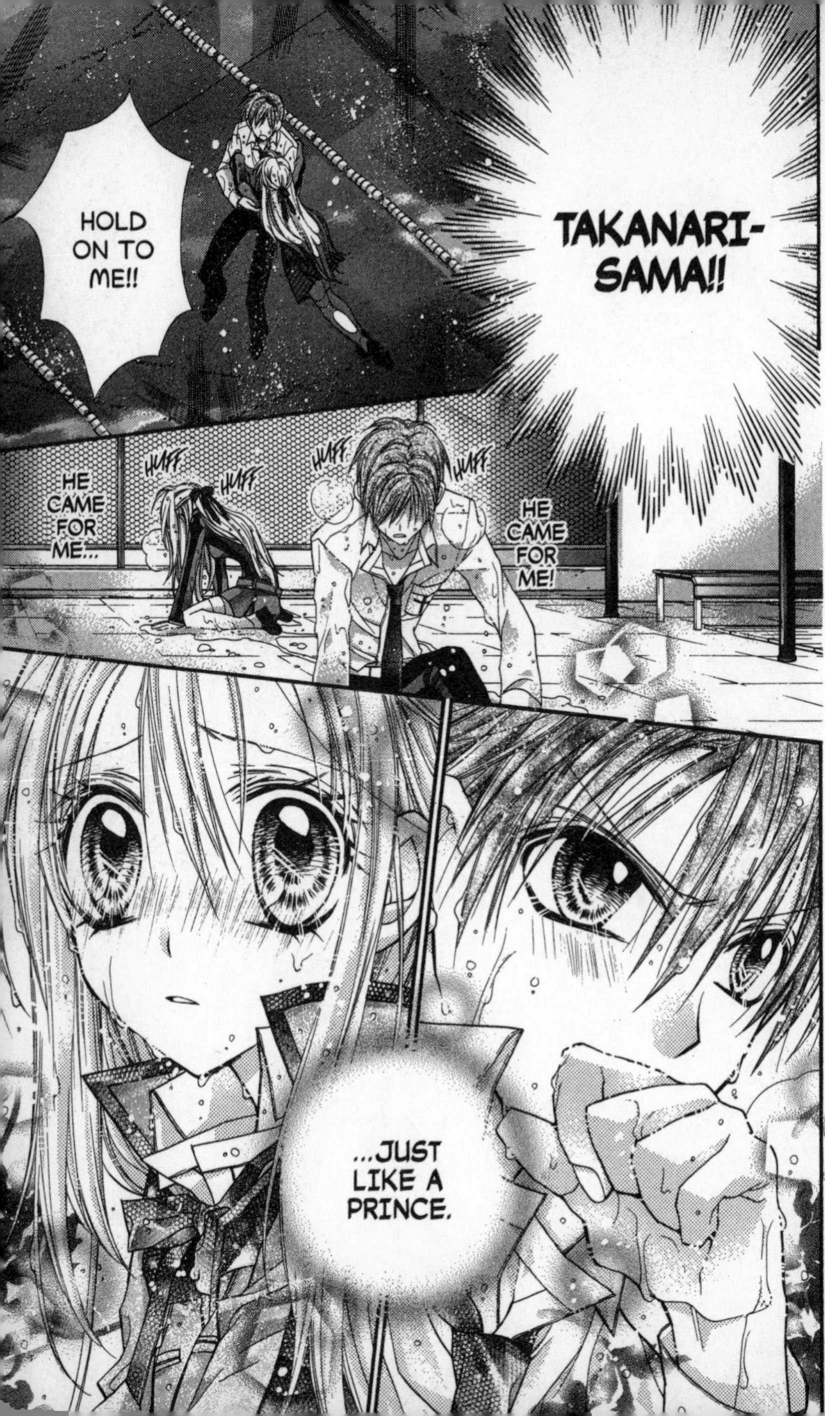
TAKANARI-SAMA!!
HOLD ON TO ME!!
HUFF
HE CAME FOR ME!
HUFF
HUFF
HUFF
HE CAME FOR ME...
...JUST LIKE A PRINCE.

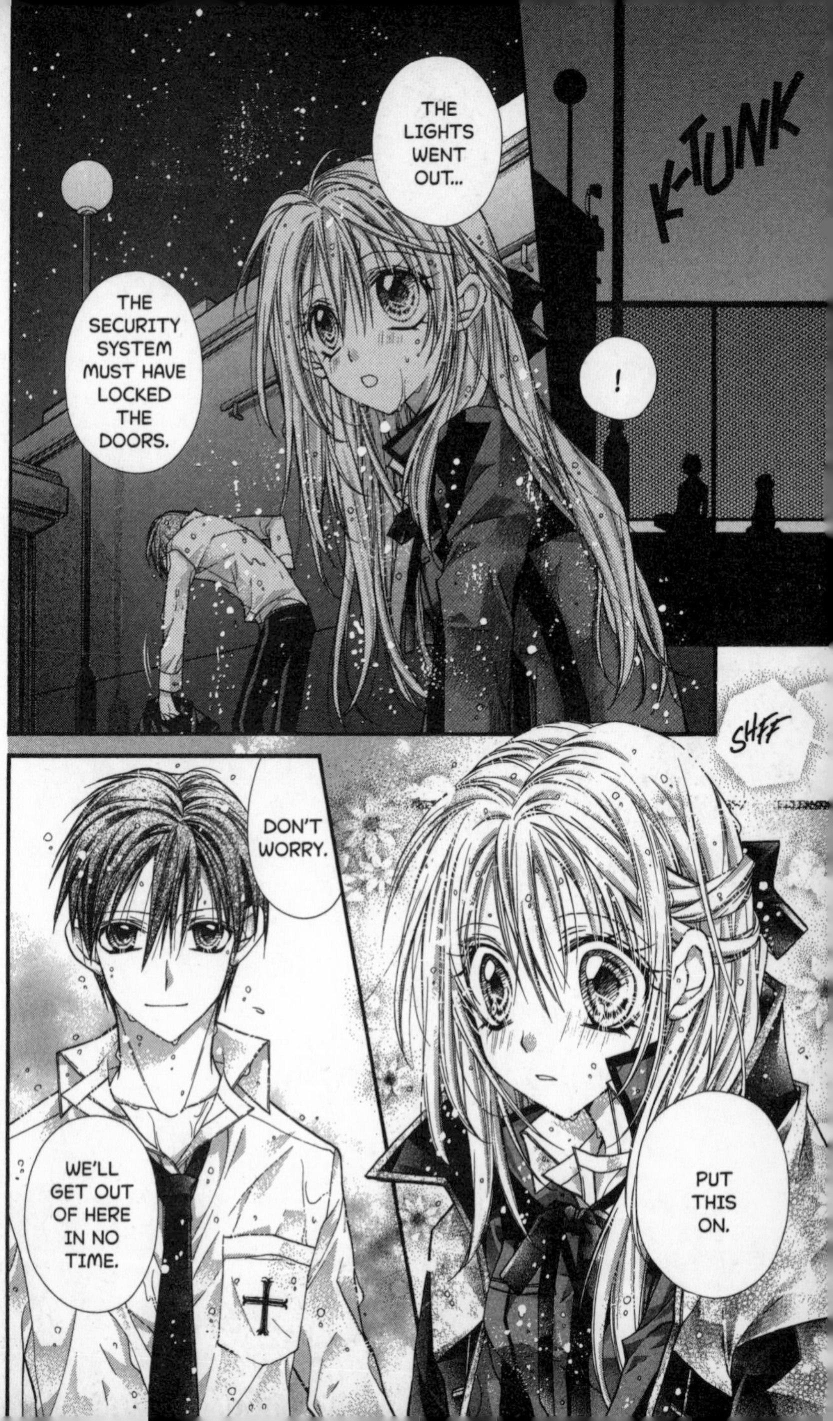
K-TUNK
!
THE LIGHTS WENT OUT...
THE SECURITY SYSTEM MUST HAVE LOCKED THE DOORS.
SHFF
PUT THIS ON.
DON'T WORRY.
WE'LL GET OUT OF HERE IN NO TIME.

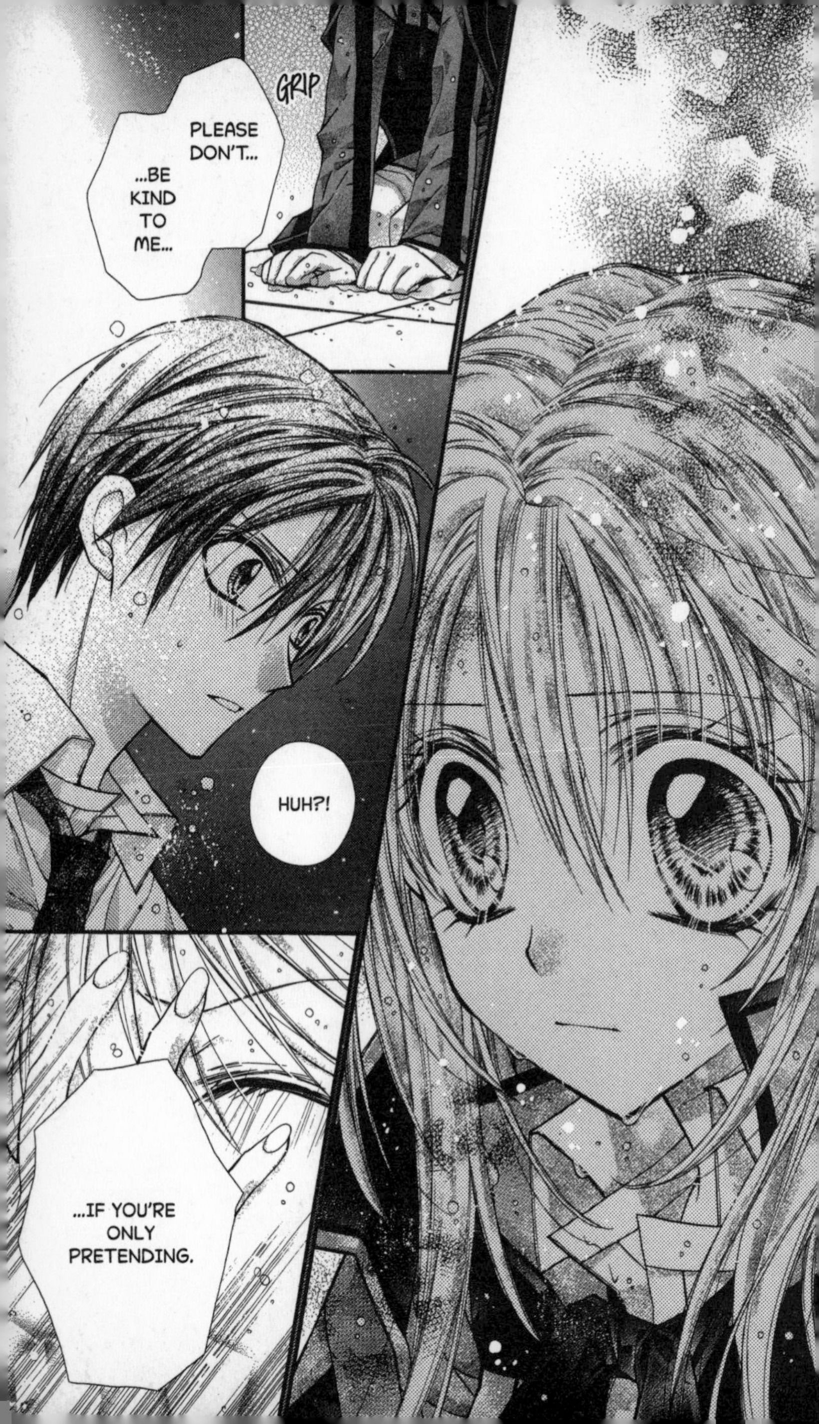
GRIP
PLEASE DON'T... ...BE KIND TO ME...
HUH?!
...IF YOU'RE ONLY PRETENDING.

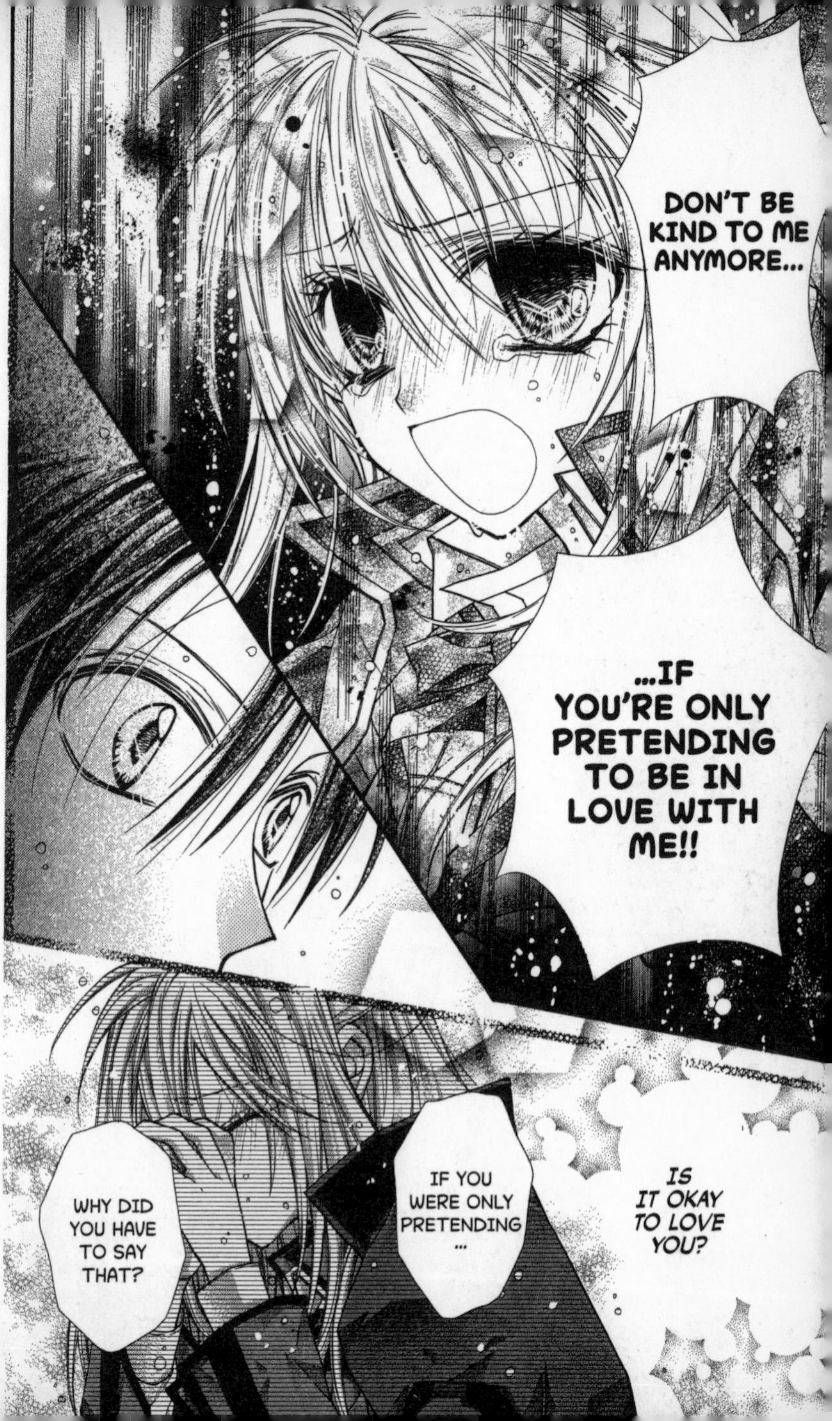
DON'T BE KIND TO ME ANYMORE...
...IF YOU'RE ONLY PRETENDING TO BE IN LOVE WITH ME!!
IS IT OKAY TO LOVE YOU?
IF YOU WERE ONLY PRETENDING ...
WHY DID YOU HAVE TO SAY THAT?

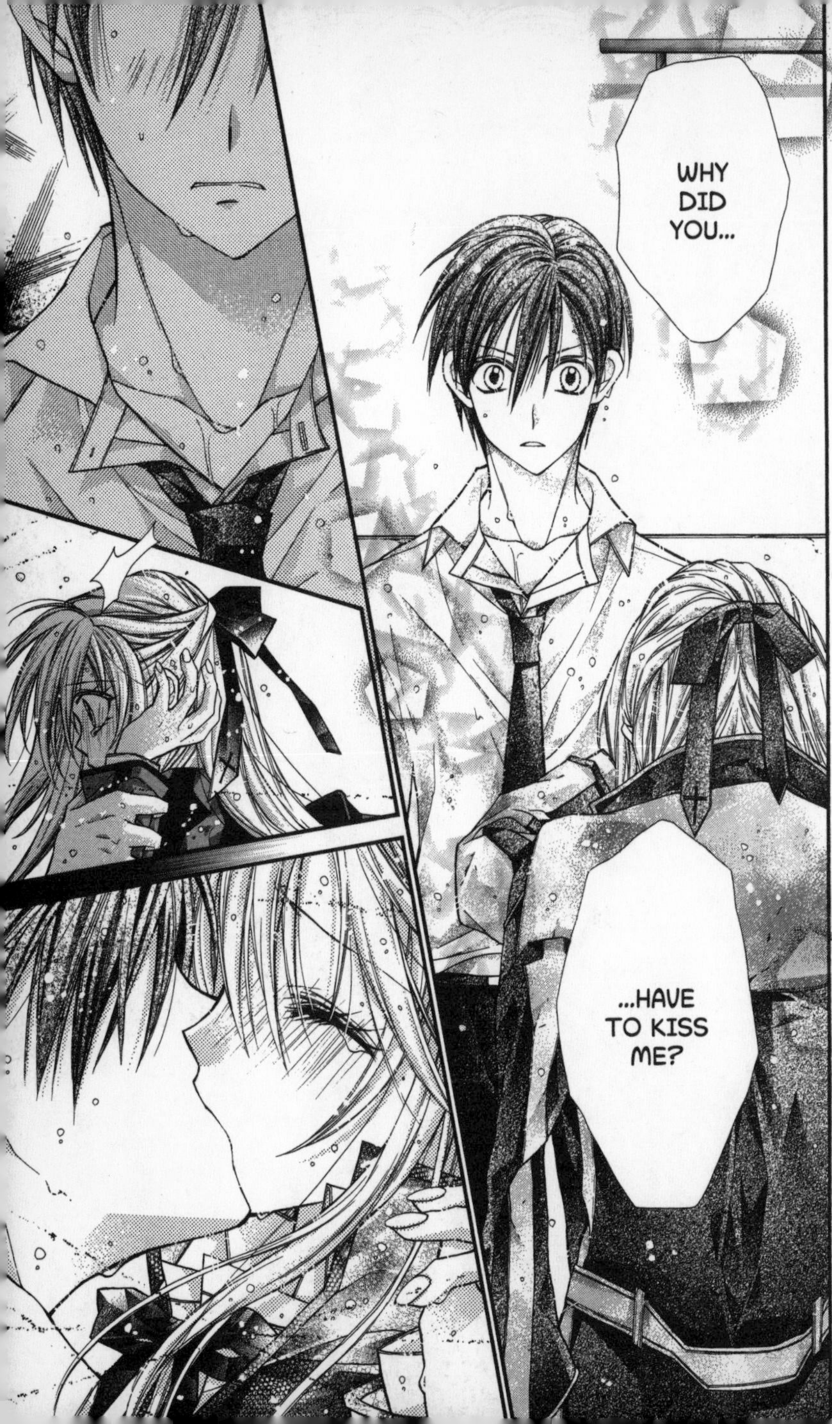
WHY DID YOU...
...HAVE TO KISS ME?

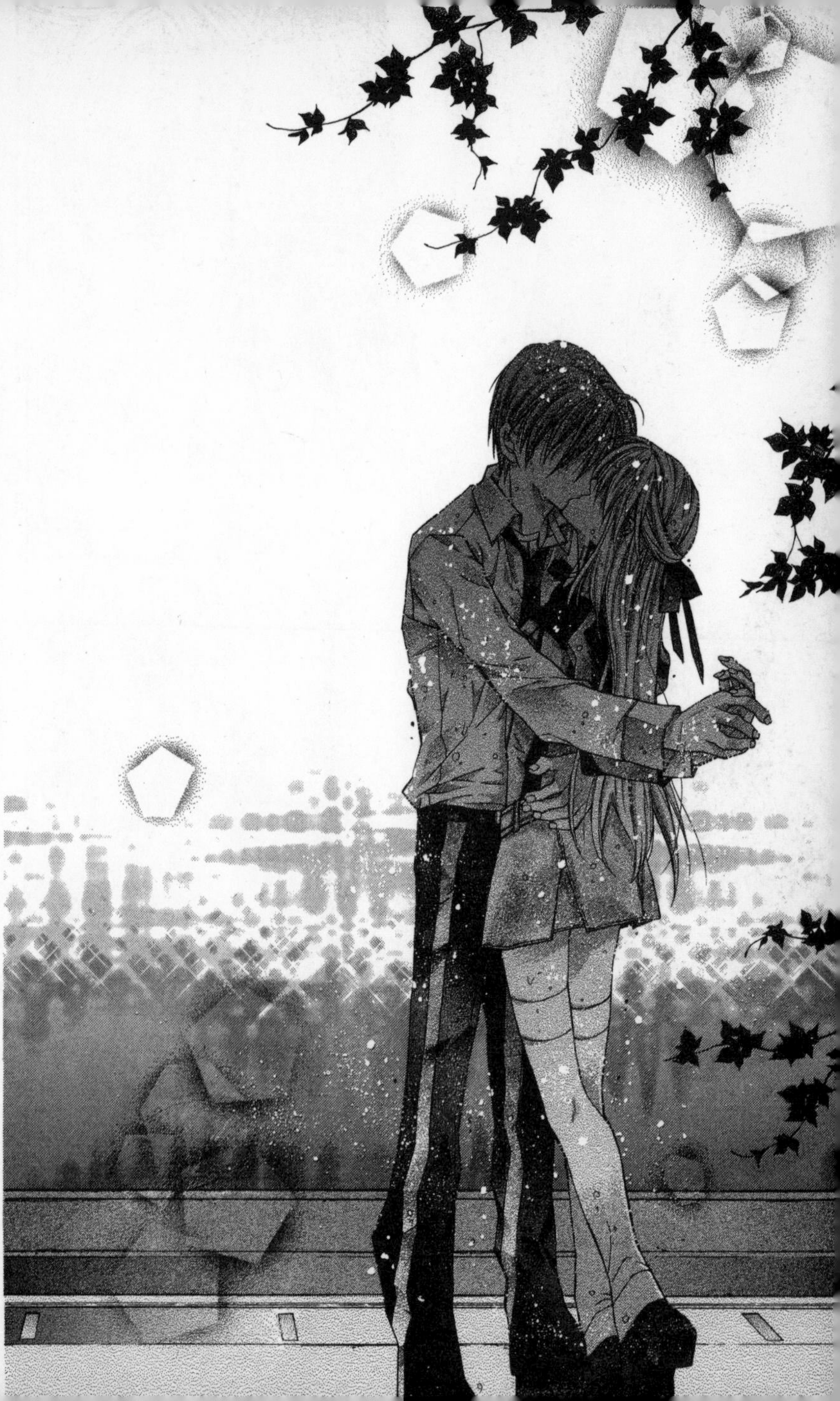

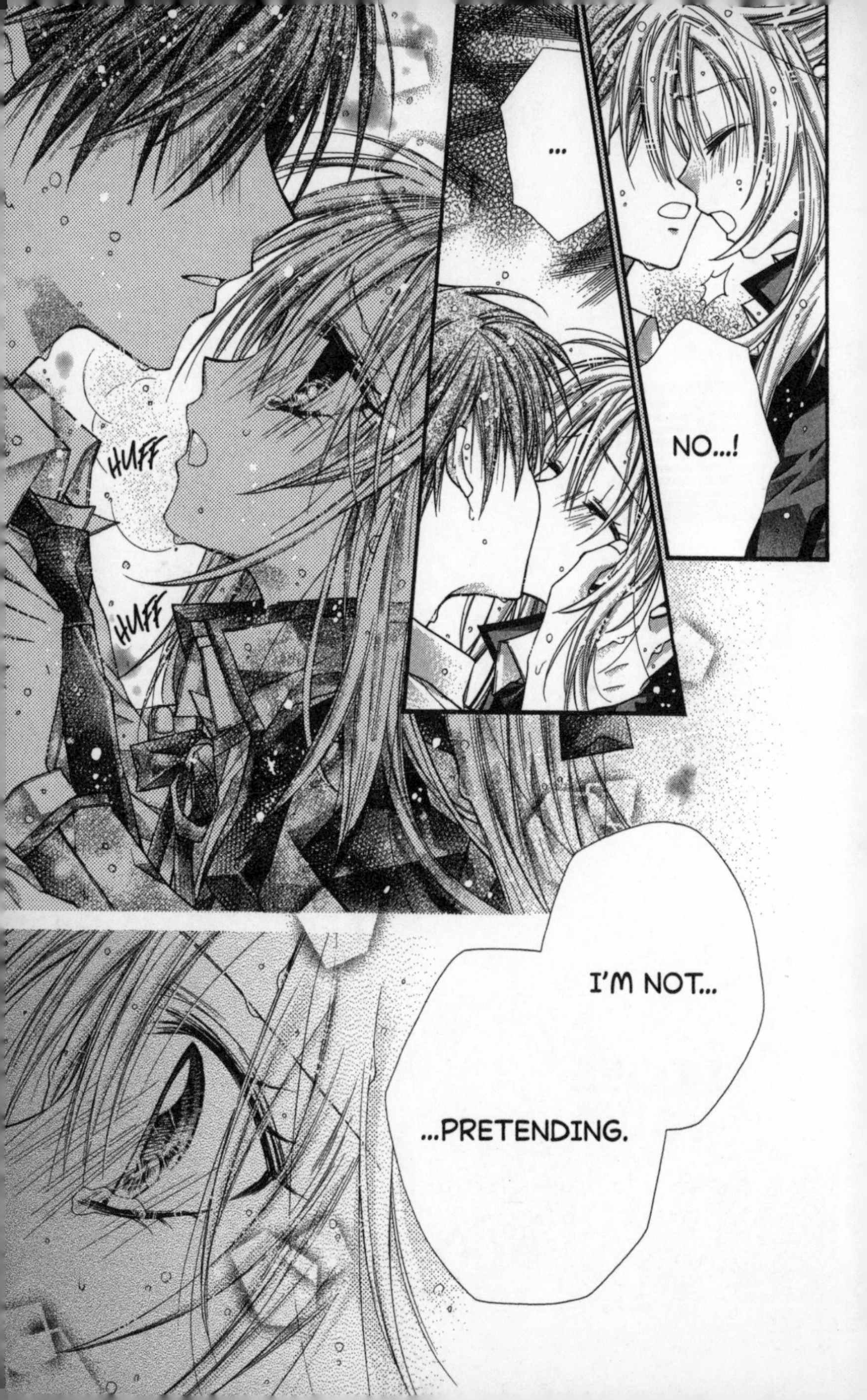
NO...!
...
HUFF
HUFF
I'M NOT...
...PRETENDING.

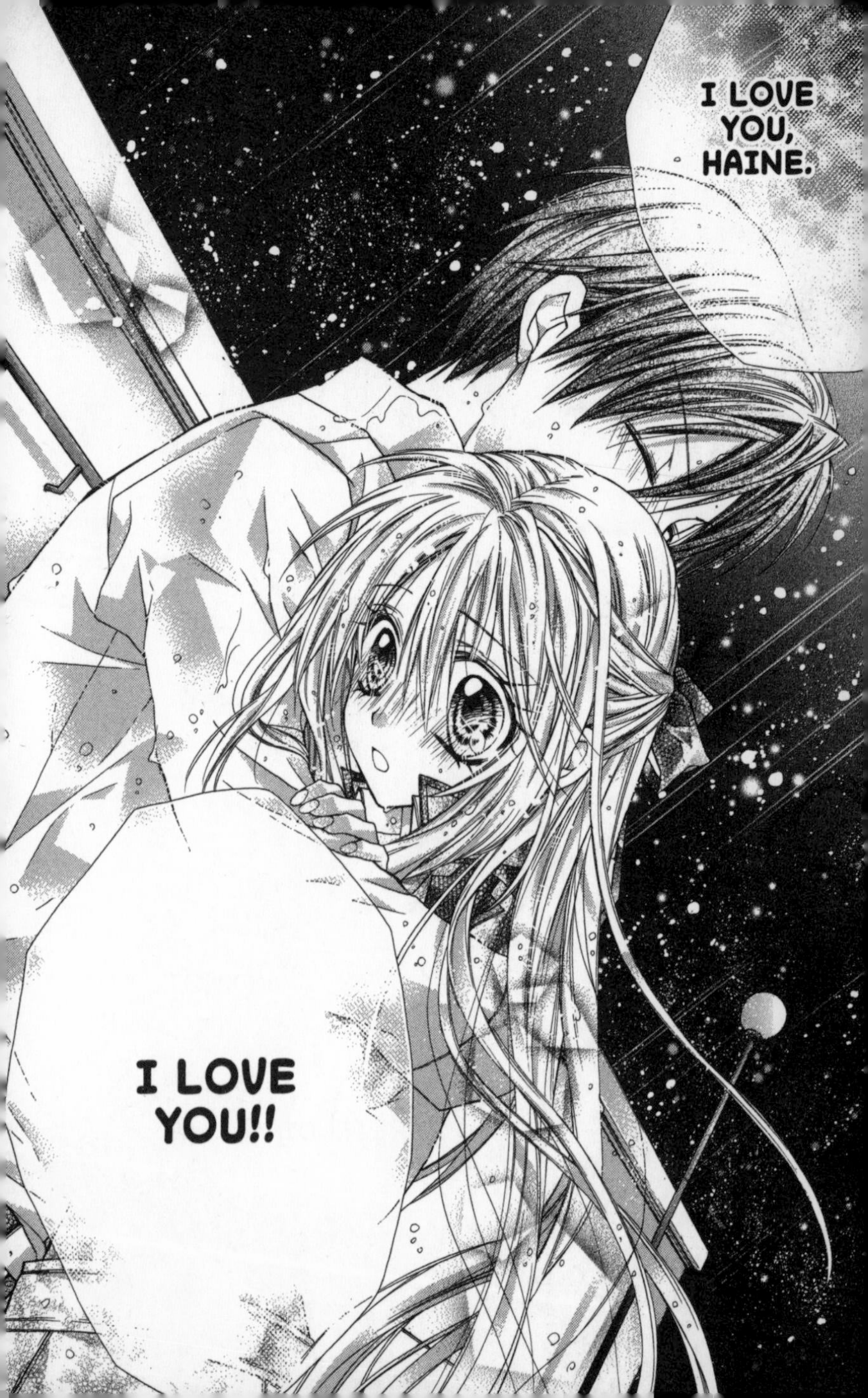
I LOVE YOU, HAINE.
I LOVE YOU!!

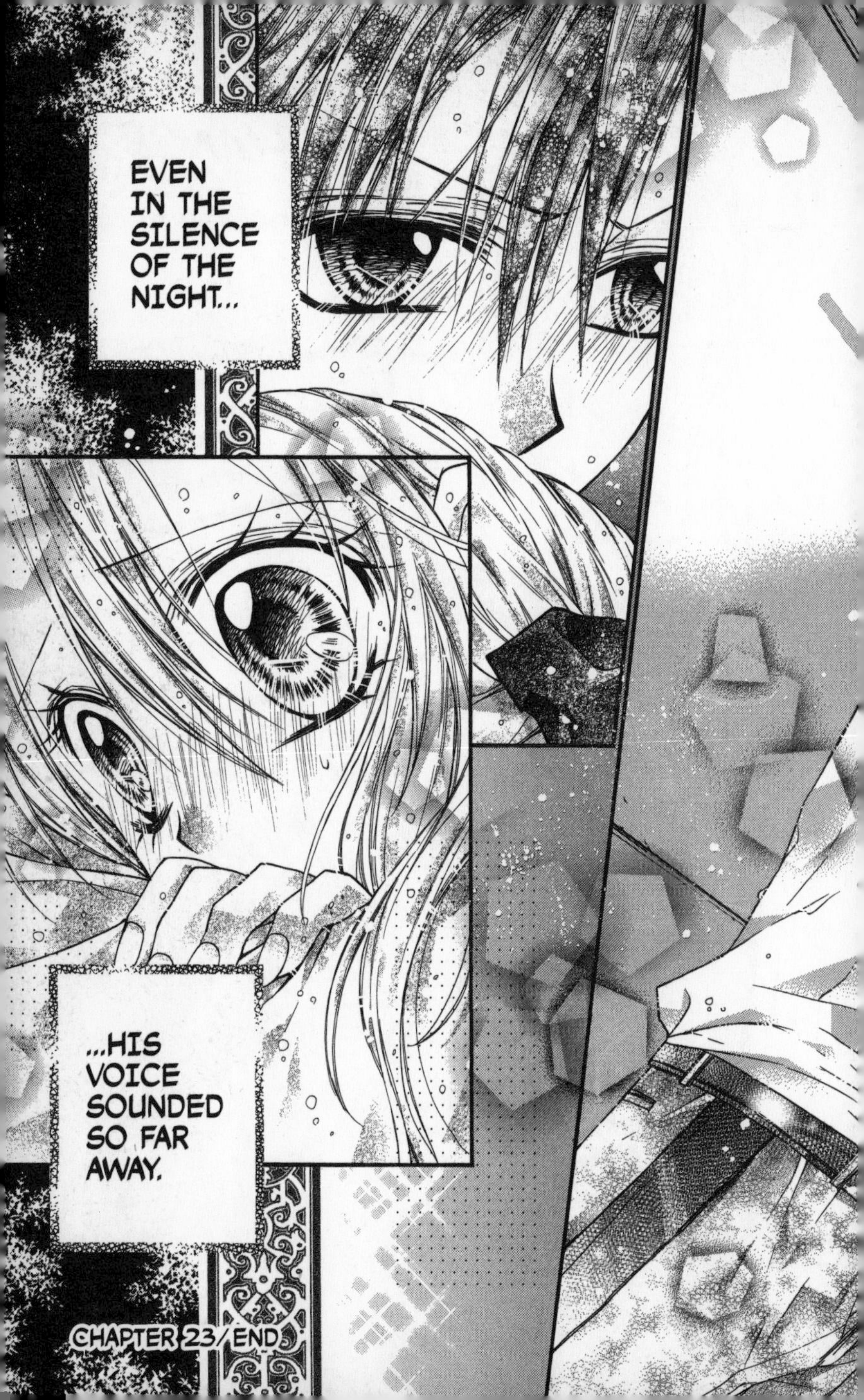
EVEN IN THE SILENCE OF THE NIGHT...
...HIS VOICE SOUNDED SO FAR AWAY.
CHAPTER 23/END

THE GENTLEMEN'S ALLIANCE CROSS
POPULARITY POLL: CHARACTER SURVEYS

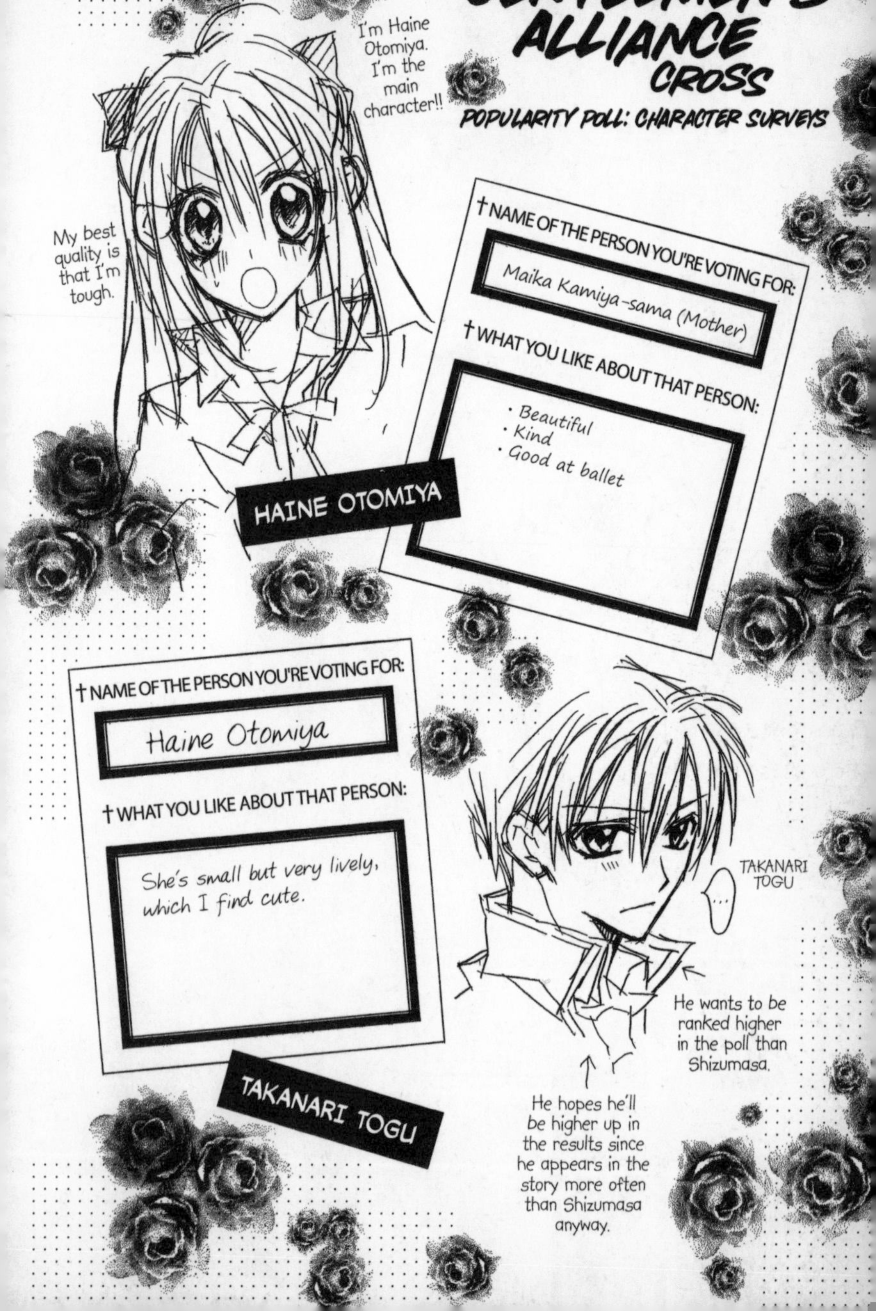

I'm Haine Otomiya. I'm the main character!!
My best quality is that I'm tough.
HAINE OTOMIYA
† NAME OF THE PERSON YOU'RE VOTING FOR:
Maika Kamiya-sama (Mother)
† WHAT YOU LIKE ABOUT THAT PERSON:
· Beautiful
· Kind
· Good at ballet
TAKANARI TOGU
...
He wants to be ranked higher in the poll than Shizumasa.
He hopes he'll be higher up in the results since he appears in the story more often than Shizumasa anyway.
† NAME OF THE PERSON YOU'RE VOTING FOR:
Haine Otomiya
† WHAT YOU LIKE ABOUT THAT PERSON:
She's small but very lively, which I find cute.
TAKANARI TOGU

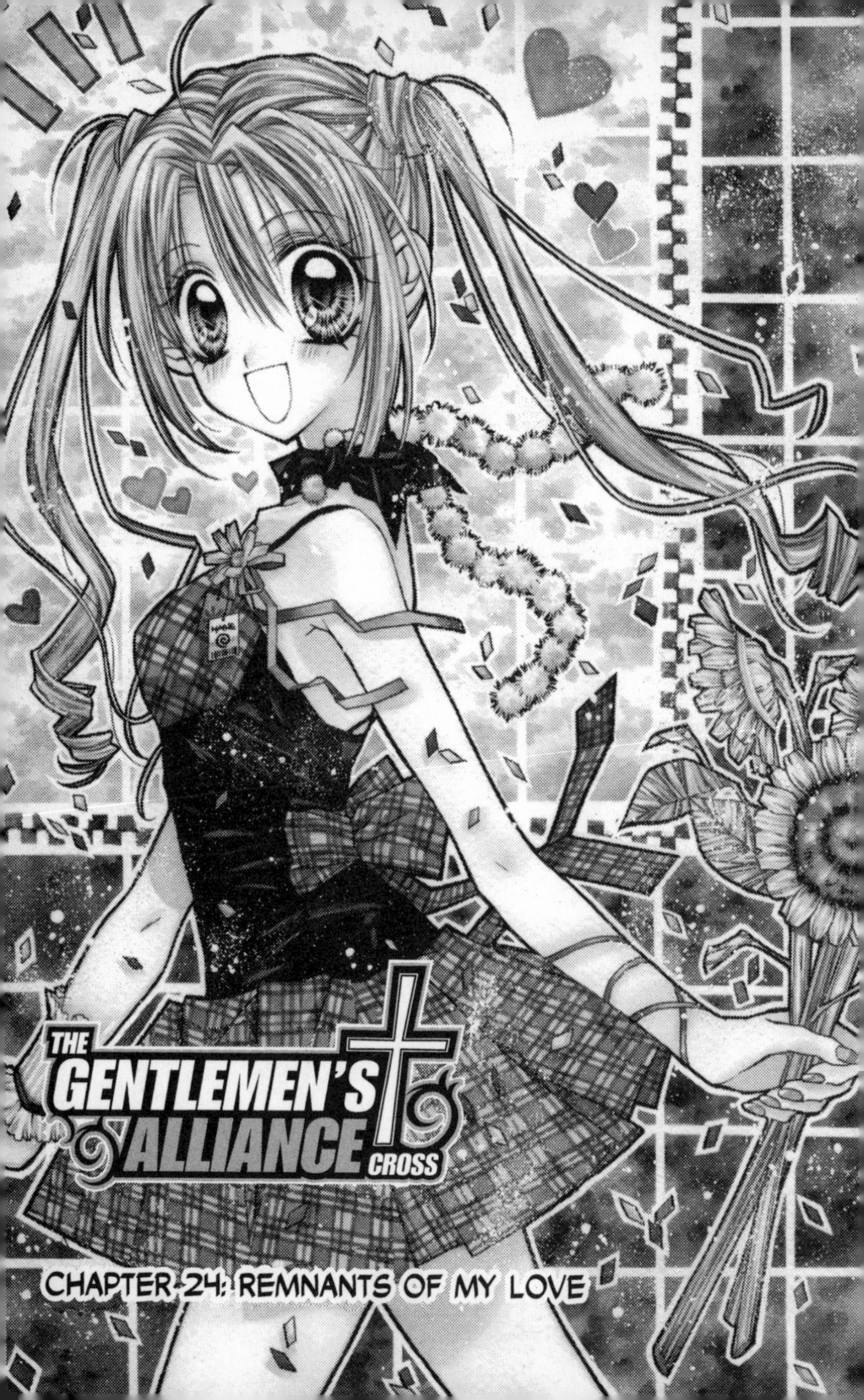
THE GENTLEMEN'S ALLIANCE CROSS
CHAPTER 24: REMNANTS OF MY LOVE

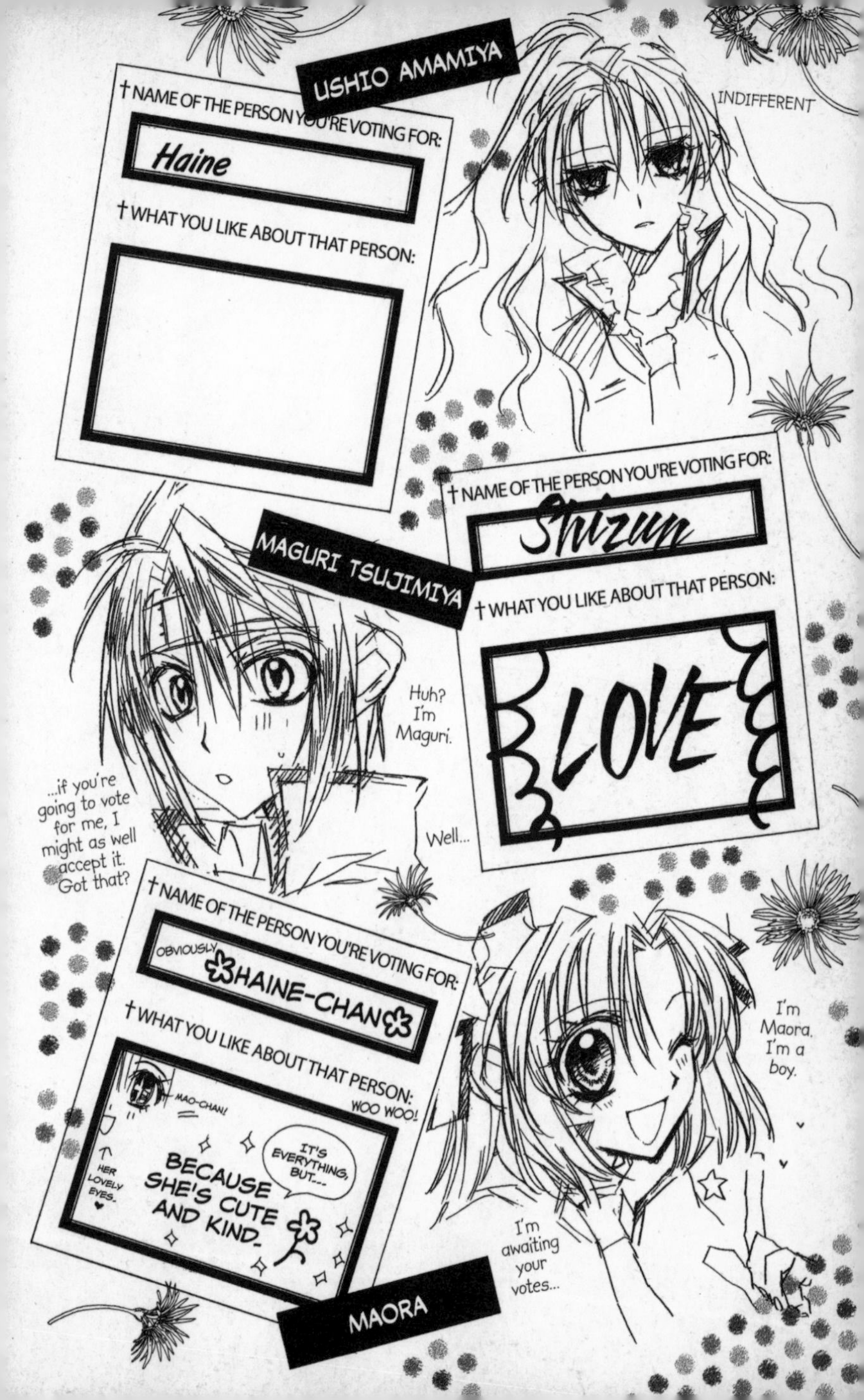
USHIO AMAMIYA
INDIFFERENT
† NAME OF THE PERSON YOU'RE VOTING FOR:
Haine
† WHAT YOU LIKE ABOUT THAT PERSON:
† NAME OF THE PERSON YOU'RE VOTING FOR:
Shizun
† WHAT YOU LIKE ABOUT THAT PERSON:
LOVE
MAGURI TSUJIMIYA
Huh? I'm Maguri.
Well...
...if you're going to vote for me, I might as well accept it. Got that?
I'm Maora. I'm a boy.
I'm awaiting your votes...
† NAME OF THE PERSON YOU'RE VOTING FOR:
OBVIOUSLY
HAINE-CHAN
† WHAT YOU LIKE ABOUT THAT PERSON:
WOO WOO!
MAO-CHAN!
HER LOVELY EYES.
IT'S EVERYTHING, BUT...
BECAUSE SHE'S CUTE AND KIND.
MAORA

AS ALWAYS...
...YOU HIDE YOUR EMOTIONS BEHIND THAT PASSIVE FACE...
BUT TONIGHT I CAN FEEL YOUR PASSIONATE HEARTBEAT.

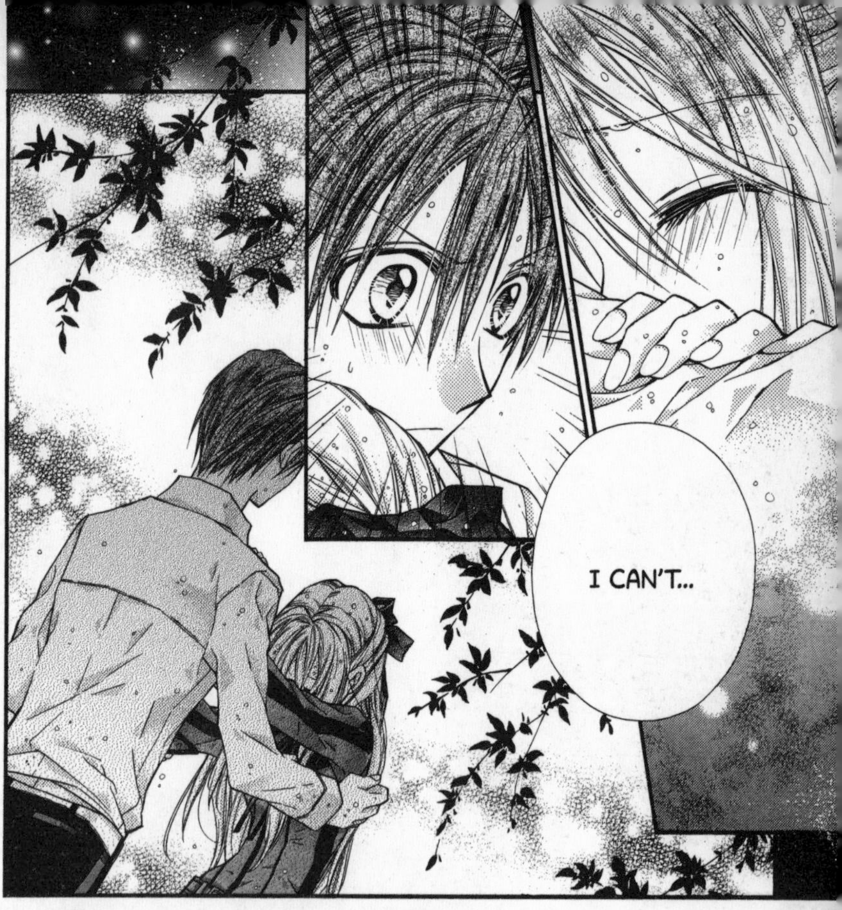
I CAN'T...

Chapter 24: Remnants of My Love Lead-in You'll truly love me, won't you?

※I'm giving away the story.
I love how Takanari-sama defiantly declares himself...
This chapter is basically "filler" in the middle of a large story, but I actually enjoy creating filler chapters. (I like reading them too. It helps you to enjoy the everyday life of the characters.)

I try to draw Haine with a different hairstyle when she's not in her school uniform, but her hairstyle when she's wearing the jersey has actually appeared before. Do you remember when the first time was??
Beeep! (It was when she went shopping during the excursion for planning the school festival.)

I'm getting a little off-track, but whenever I draw Haine in her regular clothes, I often draw her in trousers, and that is pretty rare for me.
(I hardly ever wear jeans and whatnot, so I don't think about having my characters wear them that often.)

I'm working hard on my goal of "trying to draw differently than usual."

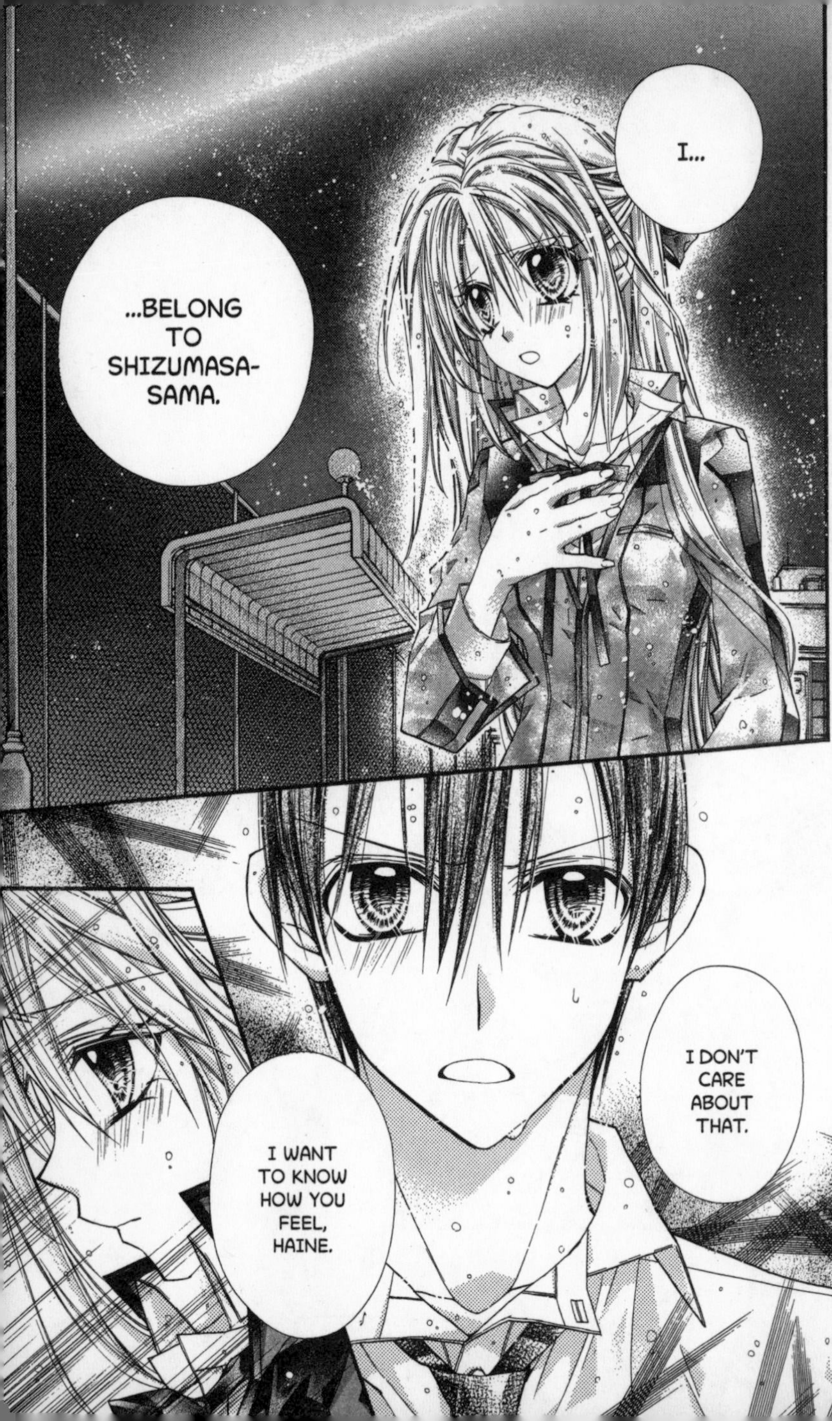
I...
...BELONG TO SHIZUMASA-SAMA.
I DON'T CARE ABOUT THAT.
I WANT TO KNOW HOW YOU FEEL, HAINE.

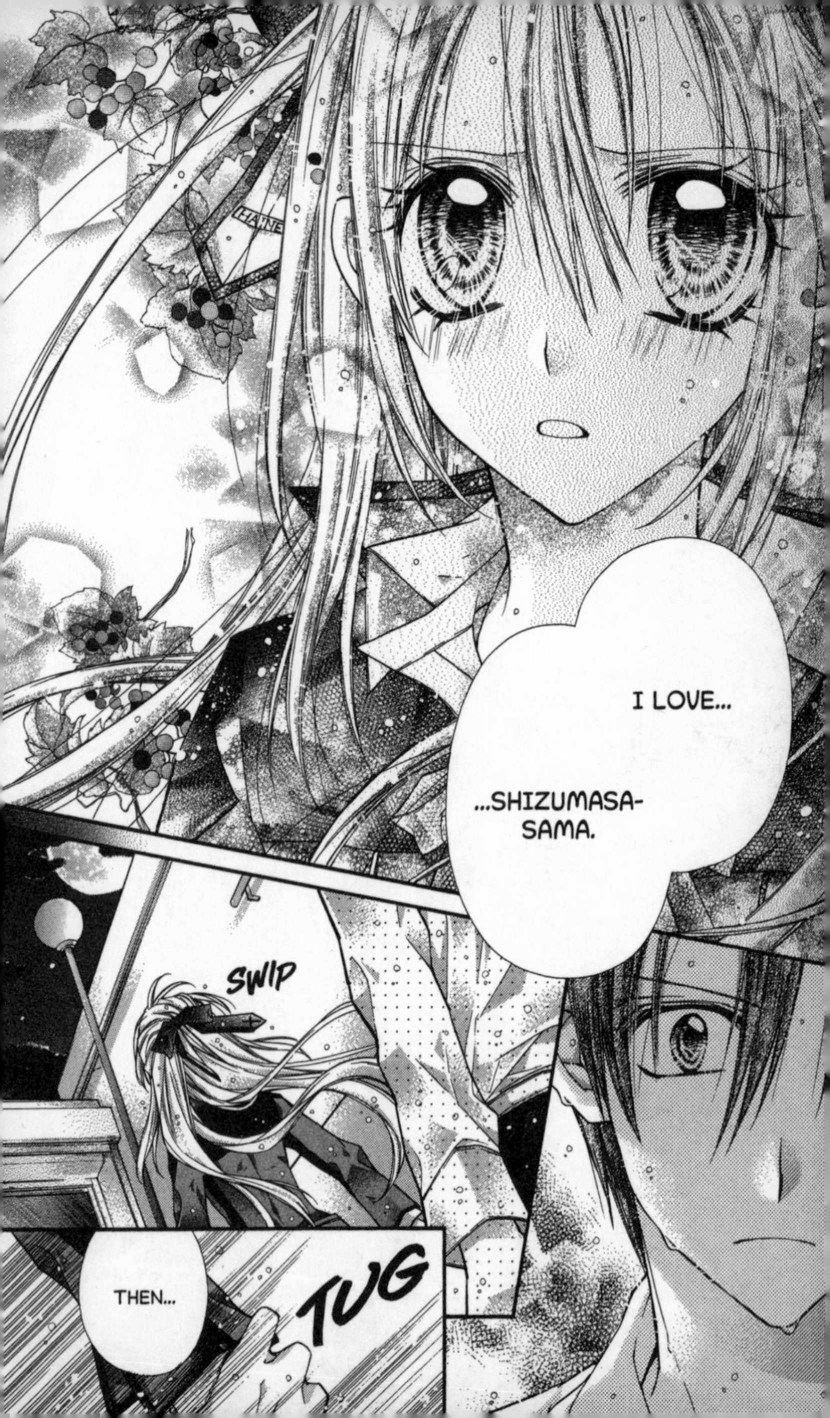
I LOVE...
...SHIZUMASA-SAMA.
SWIP
THEN...
TUG

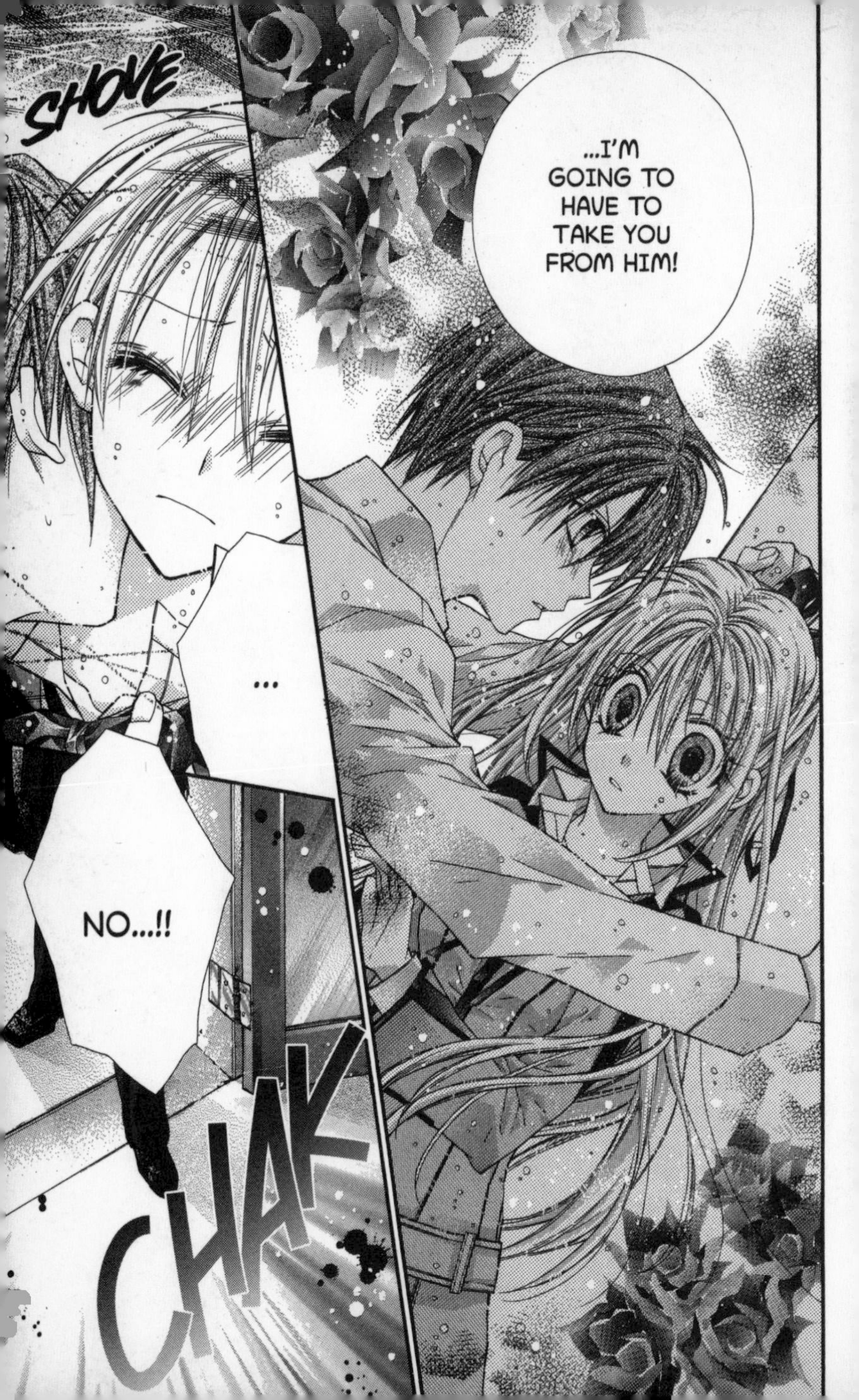
...I'M GOING TO HAVE TO TAKE YOU FROM HIM!
SHOVE
...
NO...!!
CHAK

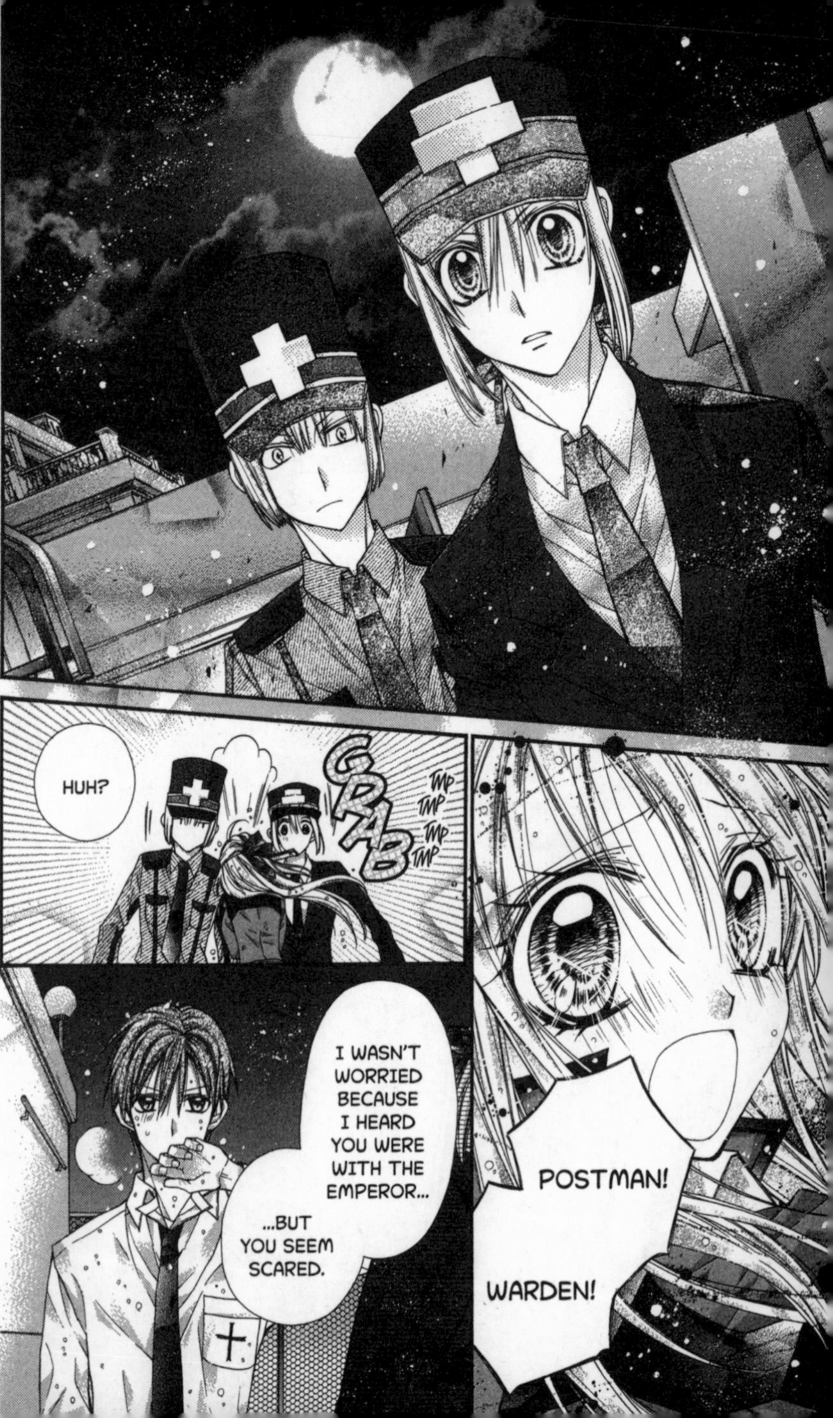
POSTMAN!
WARDEN!
TMP TMP TMP TMP
GRAB
HUH?
I WASN'T WORRIED BECAUSE I HEARD YOU WERE WITH THE EMPEROR...
...BUT YOU SEEM SCARED.

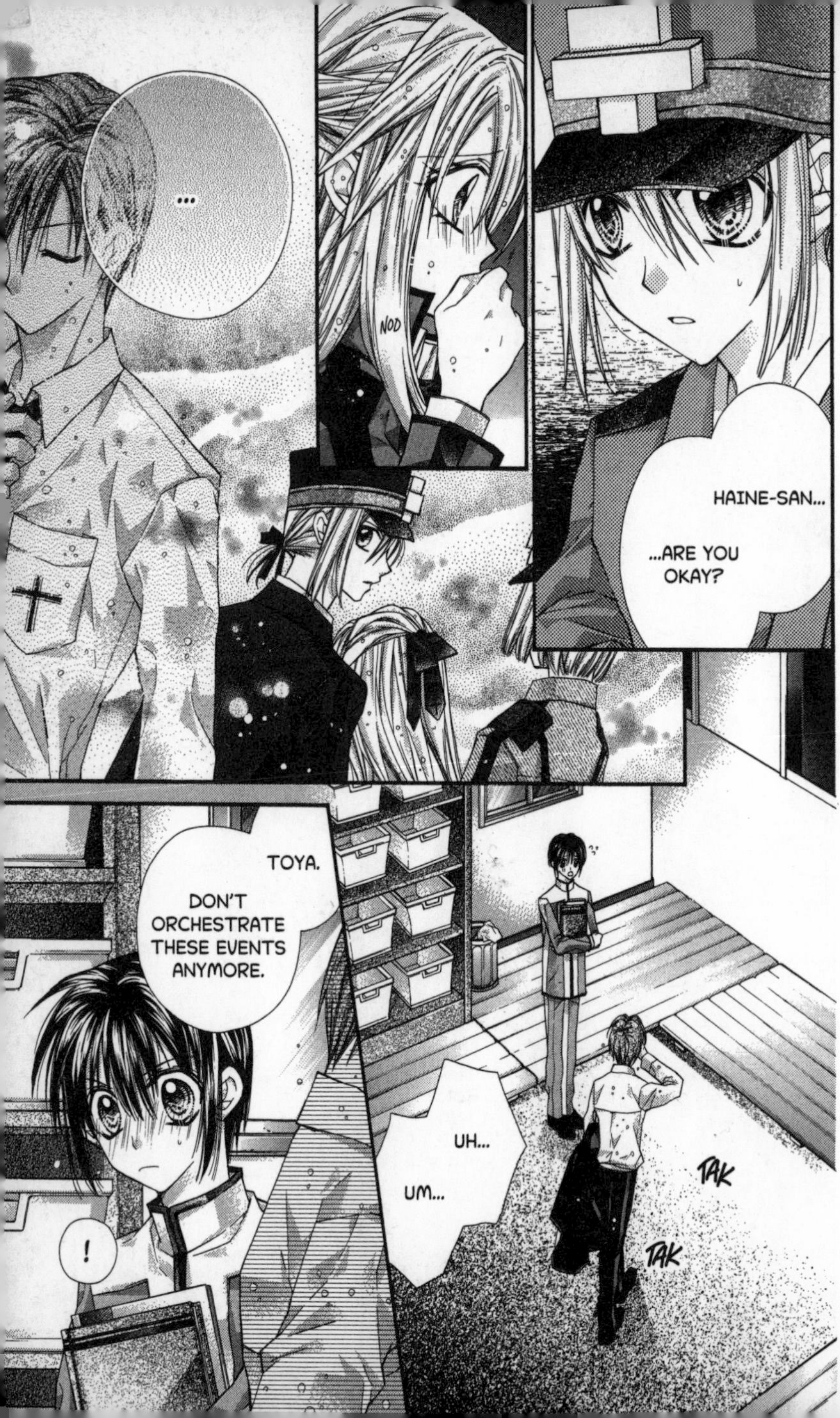
HAINE-SAN...
...ARE YOU OKAY?
NOD
...
UH...
UM...
TAK
TAK
TOYA.
DON'T ORCHESTRATE THESE EVENTS ANYMORE.
!

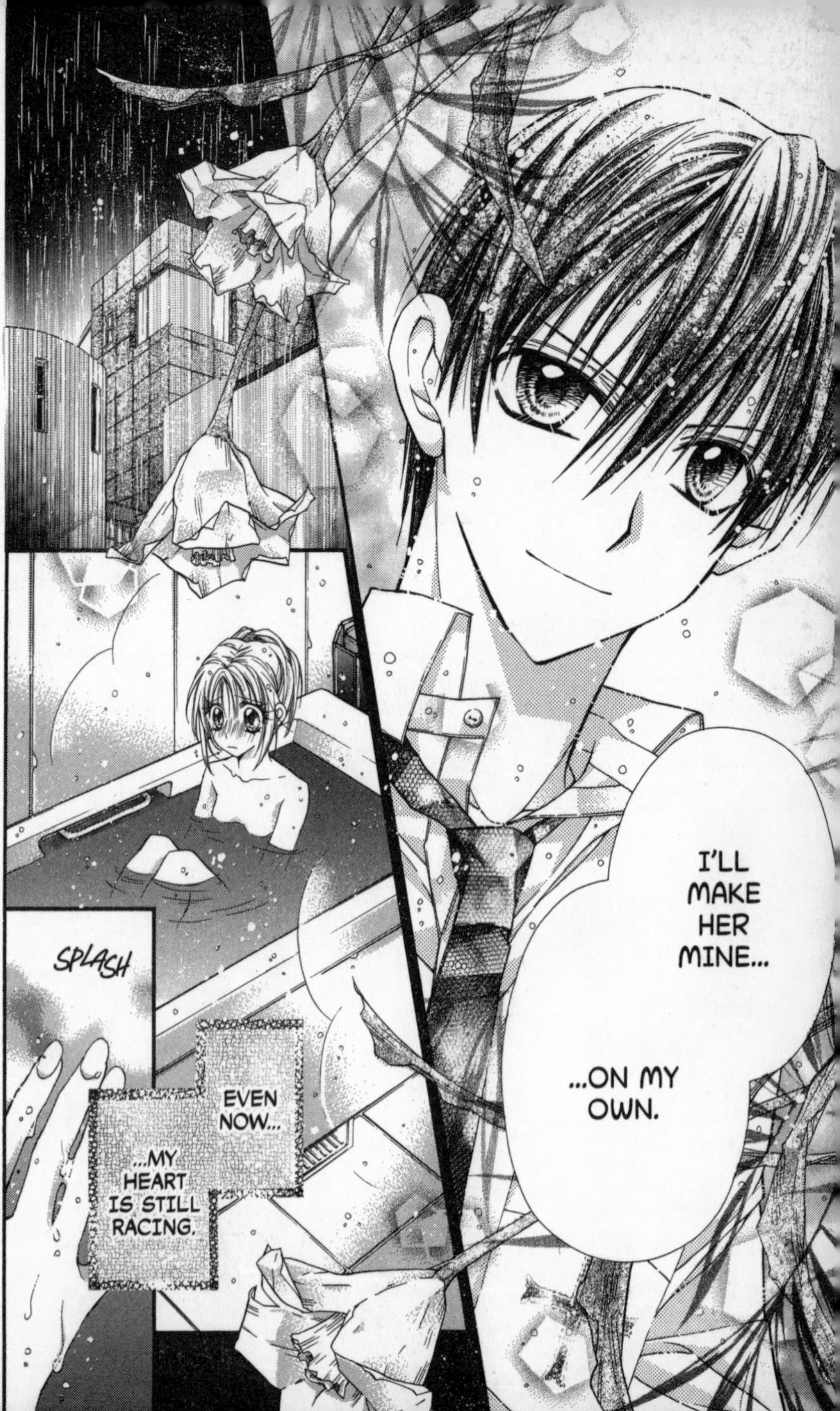
I'LL MAKE HER MINE...
...ON MY OWN.
SPLASH
EVEN NOW...
...MY HEART IS STILL RACING.

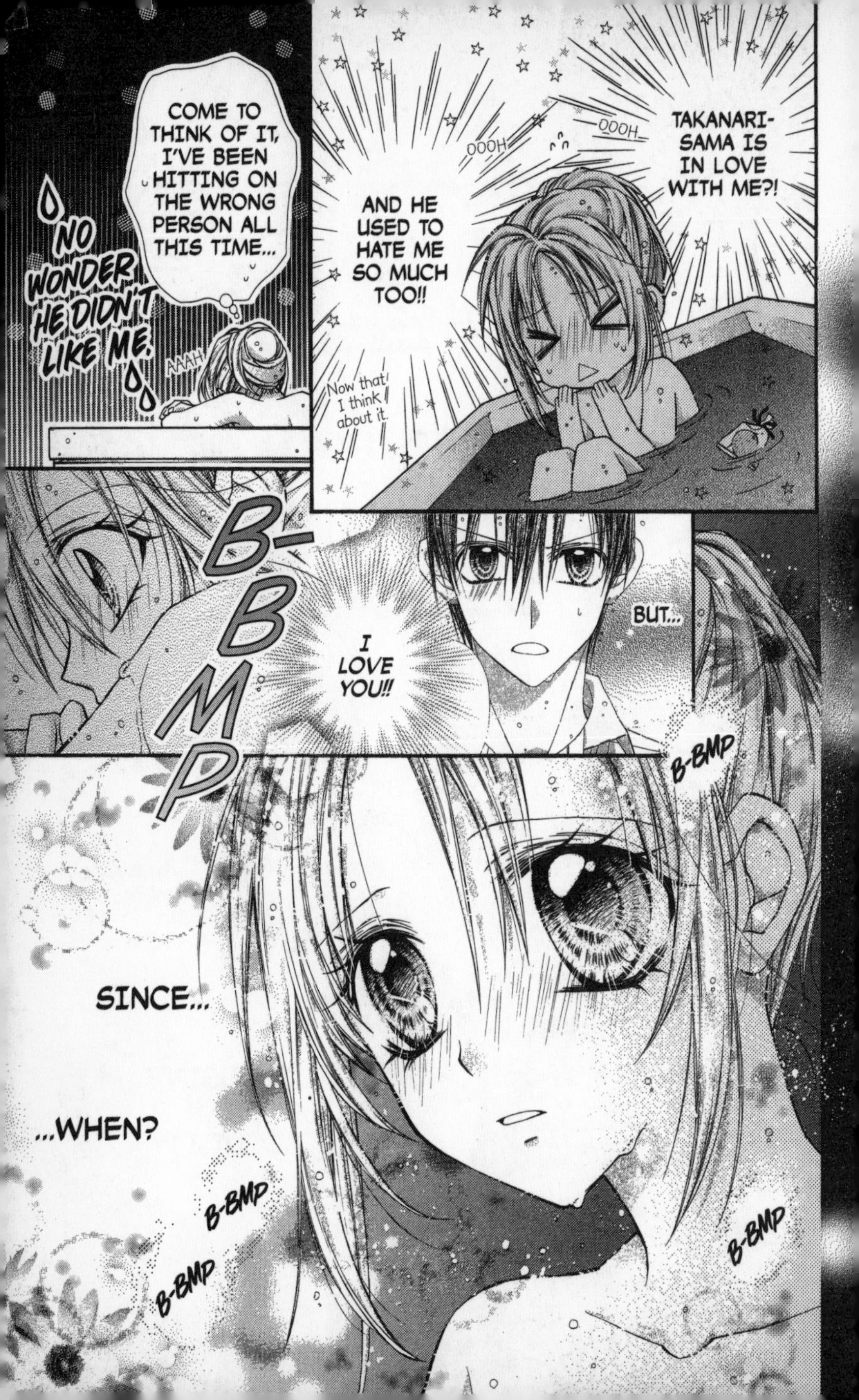
TAKANARI-SAMA IS IN LOVE WITH ME?!
OOOH
OOOH
AND HE USED TO HATE ME SO MUCH TOO!!
Now that I think about it.
COME TO THINK OF IT, I'VE BEEN HITTING ON THE WRONG PERSON ALL THIS TIME...
NO WONDER HE DIDN'T LIKE ME.
AAAH
BUT...
I LOVE YOU!!
B-BMP
B-BMP
SINCE...
...WHEN?
B-BMP
B-BMP
B-BMP

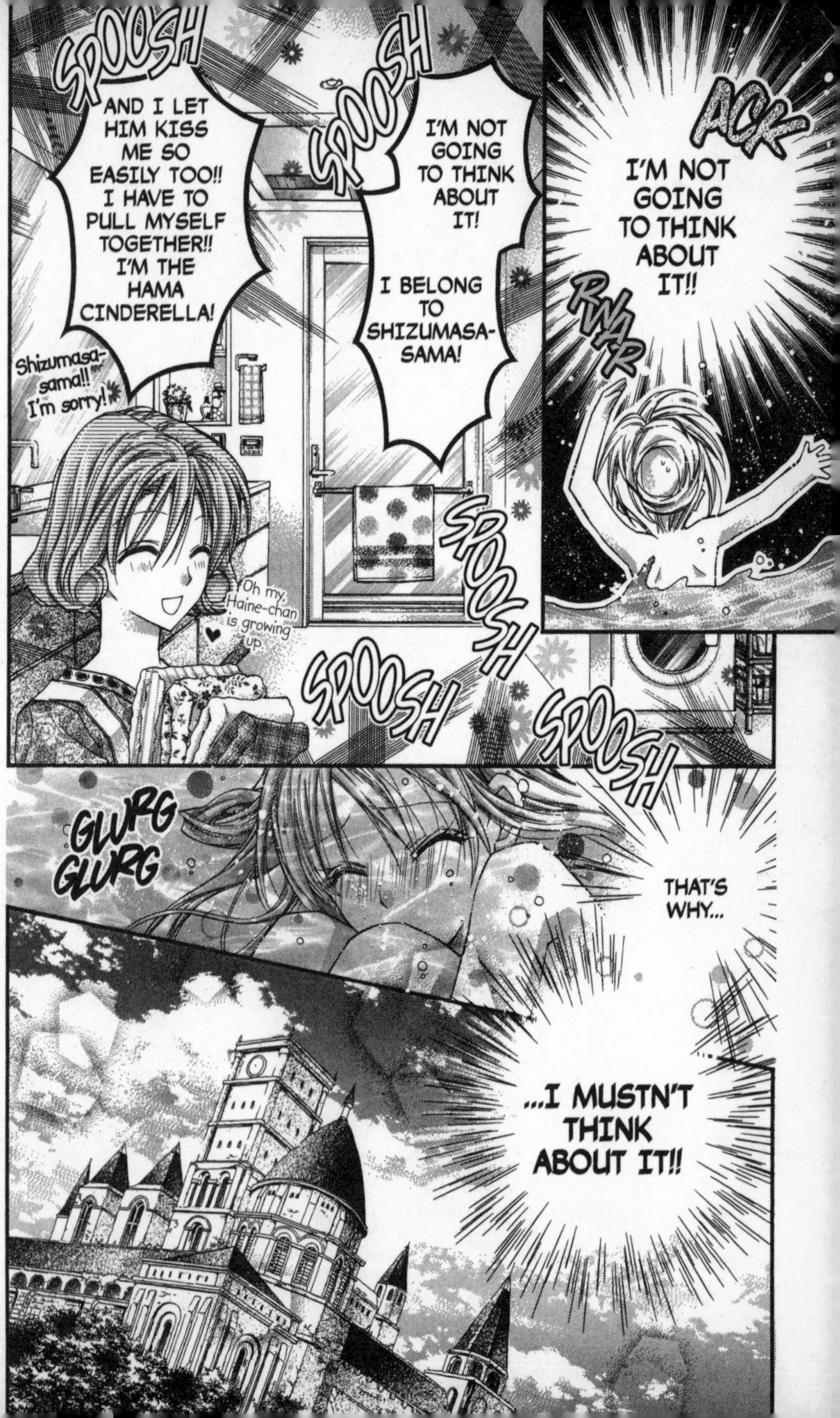
ACK
I'M NOT GOING TO THINK ABOUT IT!!
RWAR
SPOOSH
I'M NOT GOING TO THINK ABOUT IT!
I BELONG TO SHIZUMASA-SAMA!
SPOOSH
AND I LET HIM KISS ME SO EASILY TOO!! I HAVE TO PULL MYSELF TOGETHER!! I'M THE HAMA CINDERELLA!
Shizumasa-sama!! I'm sorry!
Oh my, Haine-chan is growing up
SPOOSH
SPOOSH
SPOOSH
THAT'S WHY...
GLURG GLURG
...I MUSTN'T THINK ABOUT IT!!

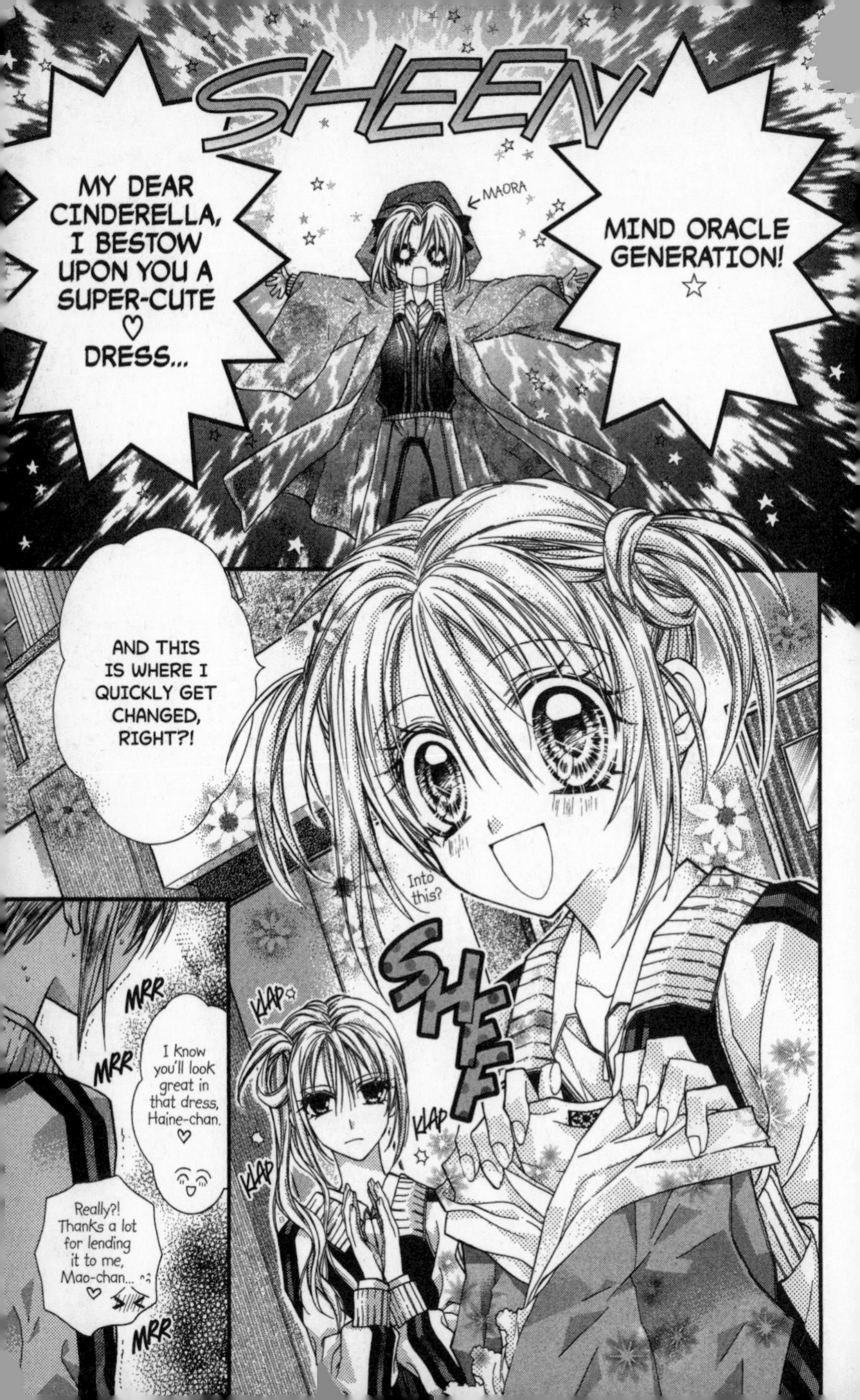
SHEEN
MIND ORACLE GENERATION! ☆
MAORA
MY DEAR CINDERELLA, I BESTOW UPON YOU A SUPER-CUTE ♡ DRESS...
AND THIS IS WHERE I QUICKLY GET CHANGED, RIGHT?!
Into this?
SHFF
KLAP
KLAP
KLAP
I know you'll look great in that dress, Haine-chan. ♡
MRR
MRR
Really?! Thanks a lot for lending it to me, Mao-chan... ♡
MRR

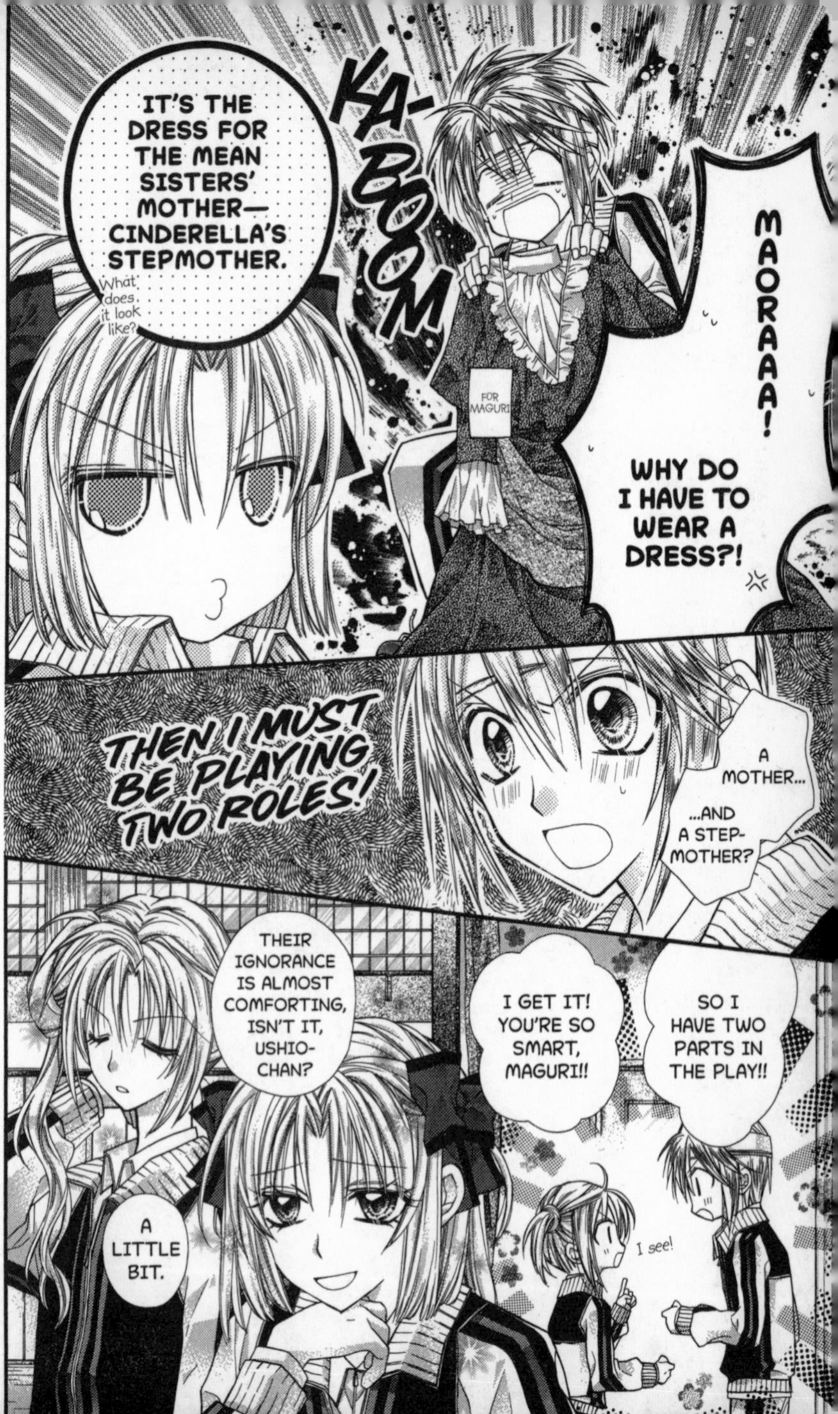
MAORAAA!
WHY DO I HAVE TO WEAR A DRESS?!
KA-BOOM
FOR MAGURI
IT'S THE DRESS FOR THE MEAN SISTERS' MOTHER—CINDERELLA'S STEPMOTHER.
What does it look like?
A MOTHER...
...AND A STEP-MOTHER?
THEN I MUST BE PLAYING TWO ROLES!
SO I HAVE TWO PARTS IN THE PLAY!!
I see!
I GET IT! YOU'RE SO SMART, MAGURI!!
THEIR IGNORANCE IS ALMOST COMFORTING, ISN'T IT, USHIO-CHAN?
A LITTLE BIT.

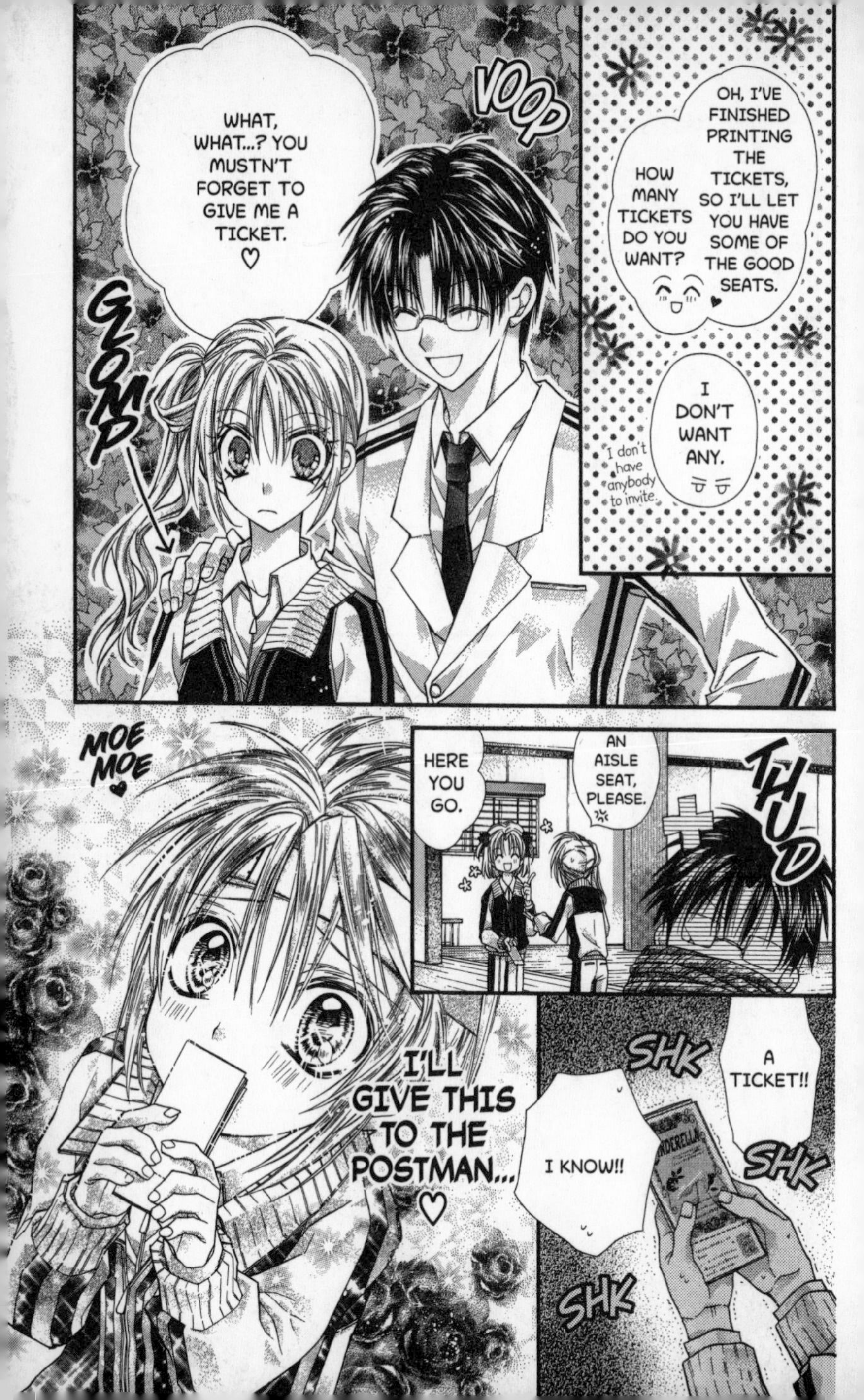
OH, I'VE FINISHED PRINTING THE TICKETS, SO I'LL LET YOU HAVE SOME OF THE GOOD SEATS.
HOW MANY TICKETS DO YOU WANT?
I DON'T WANT ANY.
I don't have anybody to invite.
VOOP
WHAT, WHAT...? YOU MUSTN'T FORGET TO GIVE ME A TICKET. ♡
GLOMP
THUD
AN AISLE SEAT, PLEASE.
HERE YOU GO.
SHK
A TICKET!!
SHK
I KNOW!!
SHK
MOE MOE
I'LL GIVE THIS TO THE POSTMAN... ♡

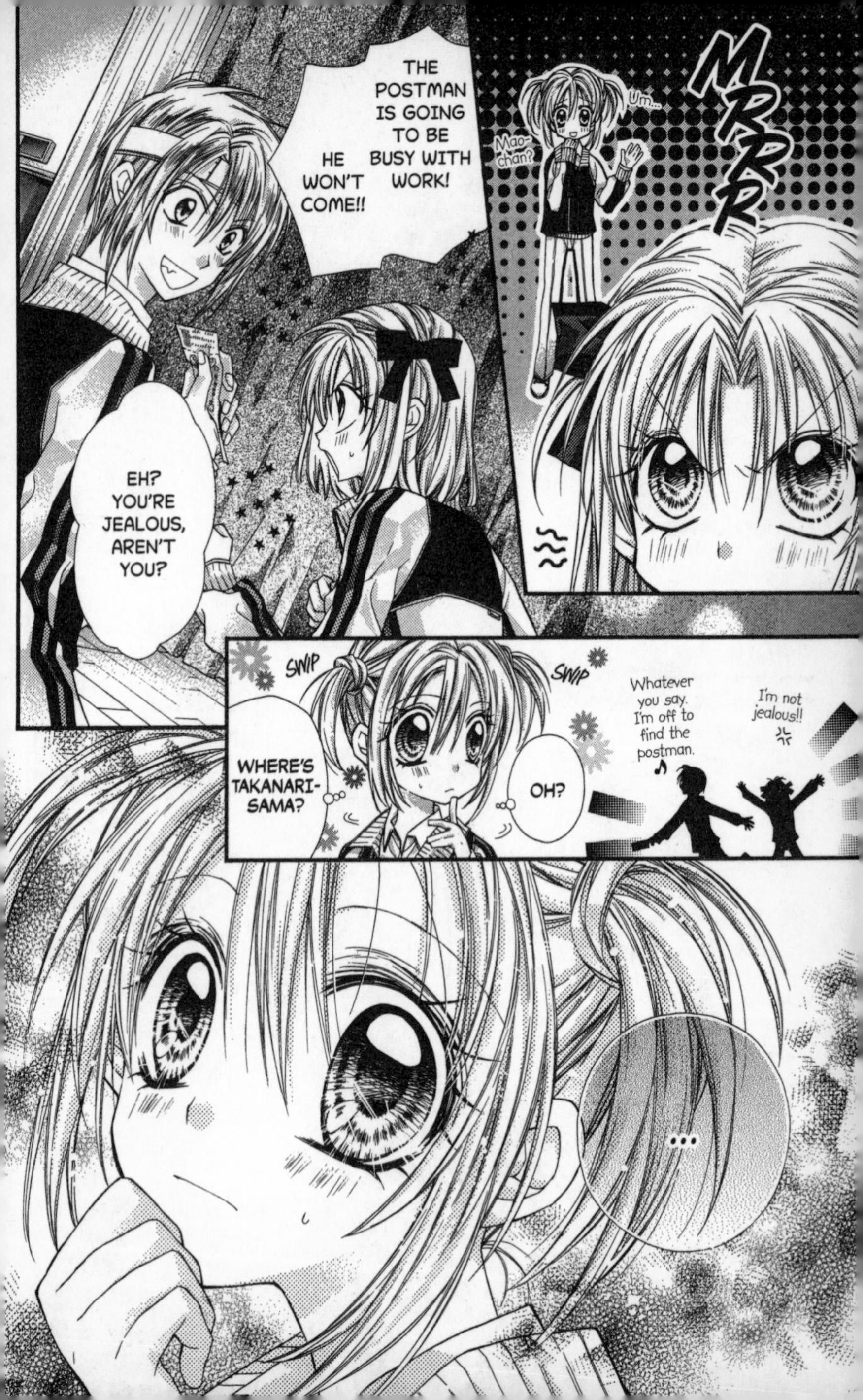
MRRR
Um...
Mao-chan?
THE POSTMAN IS GOING TO BE BUSY WITH WORK!
HE WON'T COME!!
EH? YOU'RE JEALOUS, AREN'T YOU?
I'm not jealous!!
Whatever you say. I'm off to find the postman.
SWIP
OH?
SWIP
WHERE'S TAKANARI-SAMA?
...

Games: Baten Kaitos Origins

To tell you the truth, I played *Baten Kaitos I* immediately after its release on the Game Cube, but back then I was, well... I didn't get the fun of it, even though it had some characters I liked, so I didn't write a review... (By the way, I loved Lyude!! And Ladekahn. ♥♥♥)

I decided to give the sequel a try after hearing it was set 20 years before the first game... And it was wonderful!! Really!!

You fight the battles using cards called Magnuses. You make certain card combinations, but you must be a fast thinker as well as a good guesser. The more you play it, the more addicting it gets!!

There are only three characters—the main character plus two others—but they're all really nice people, making it really enjoyable to watch their conversations and such.

(Sagi is sooo cute... ////)

Oh... Until this I've never been that interested in cute-looking boys...

So I highly recommend this for both those who haven't played the first one and those who have.

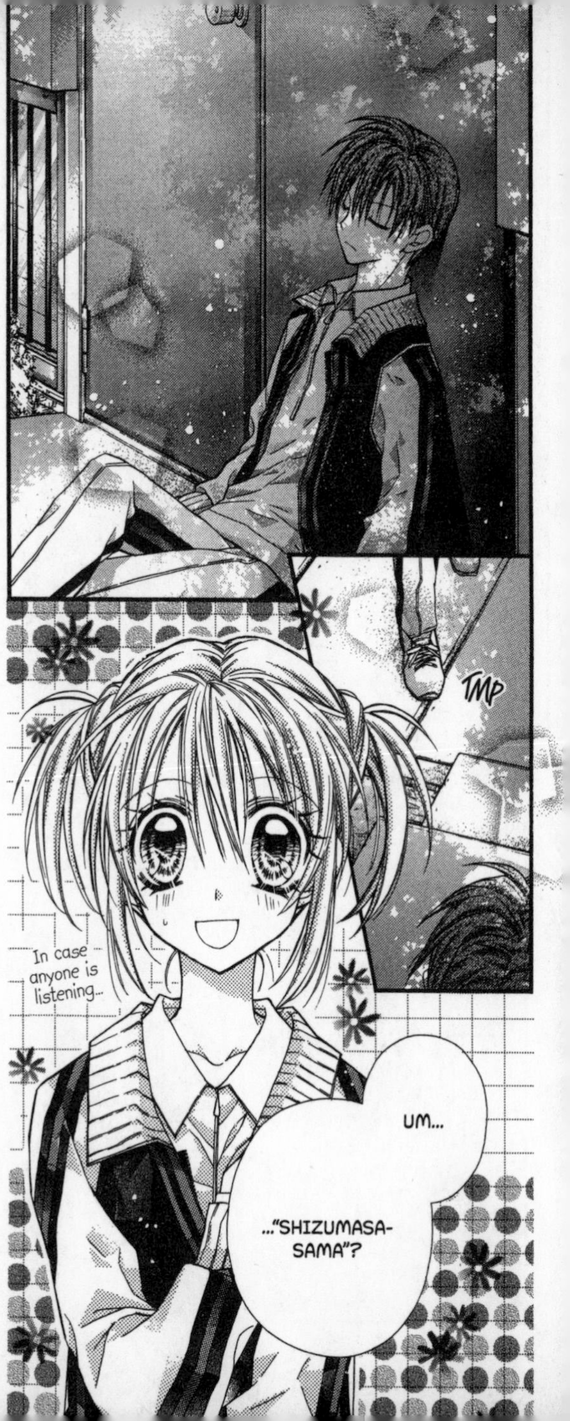
TMP
UM...
..."SHIZUMASA-SAMA"?
In case anyone is listening...

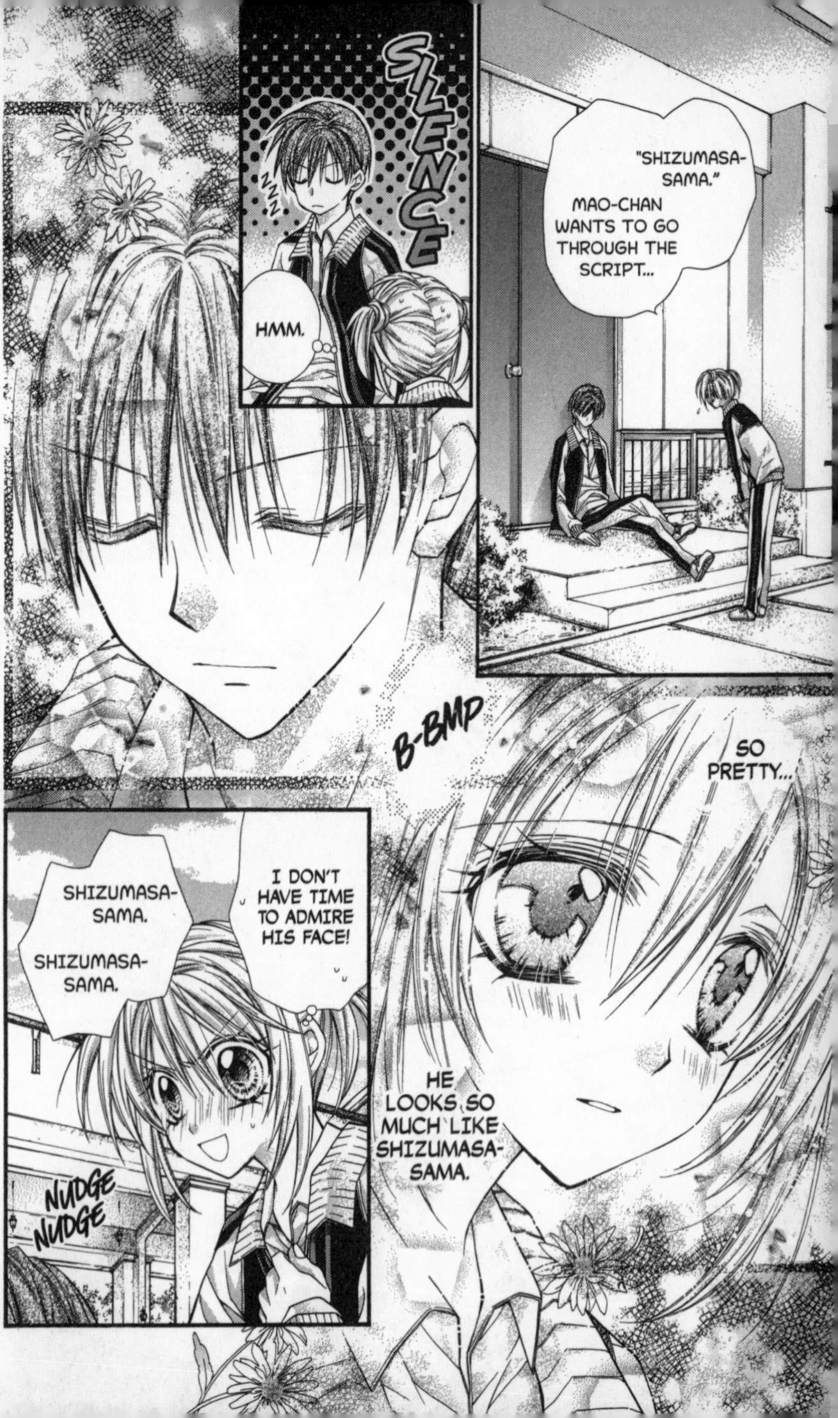
"SHIZUMASA-SAMA."
MAO-CHAN WANTS TO GO THROUGH THE SCRIPT...
SILENCE
ZZZ
HMM.
B-BMP
SO PRETTY...
HE LOOKS SO MUCH LIKE SHIZUMASA-SAMA.
I DON'T HAVE TIME TO ADMIRE HIS FACE!
SHIZUMASA-SAMA.
SHIZUMASA-SAMA.
NUDGE NUDGE

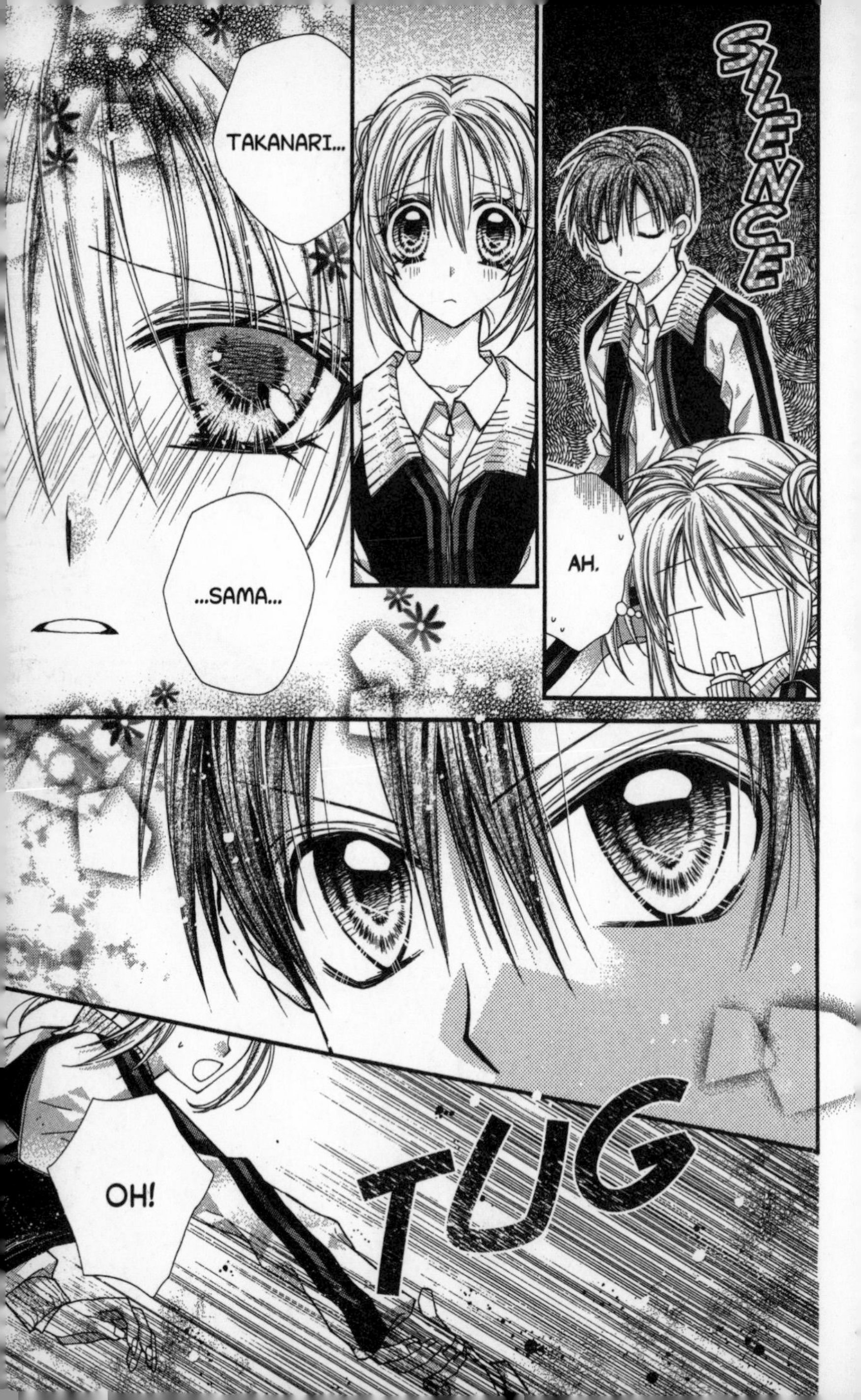
SILENCE
AH.
TAKANARI...
...SAMA...
TUG
OH!

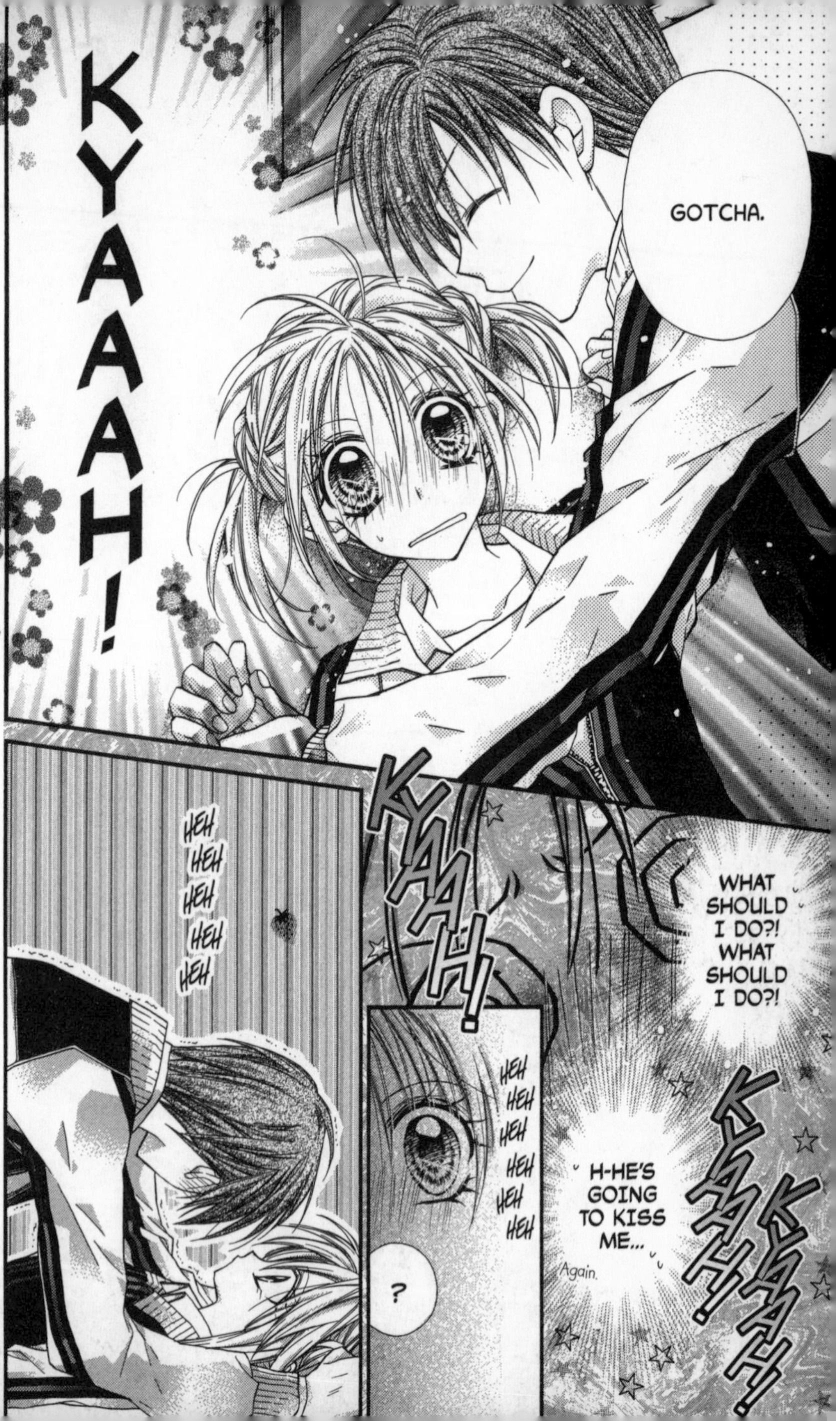
KYAAAH!
GOTCHA.
KYAAAH!
WHAT SHOULD I DO?! WHAT SHOULD I DO?!
H-HE'S GOING TO KISS ME...
Again.
KYAAAH!
KYAAAH!
HEH HEH HEH HEH HEH HEH
?
HEH HEH HEH HEH HEH

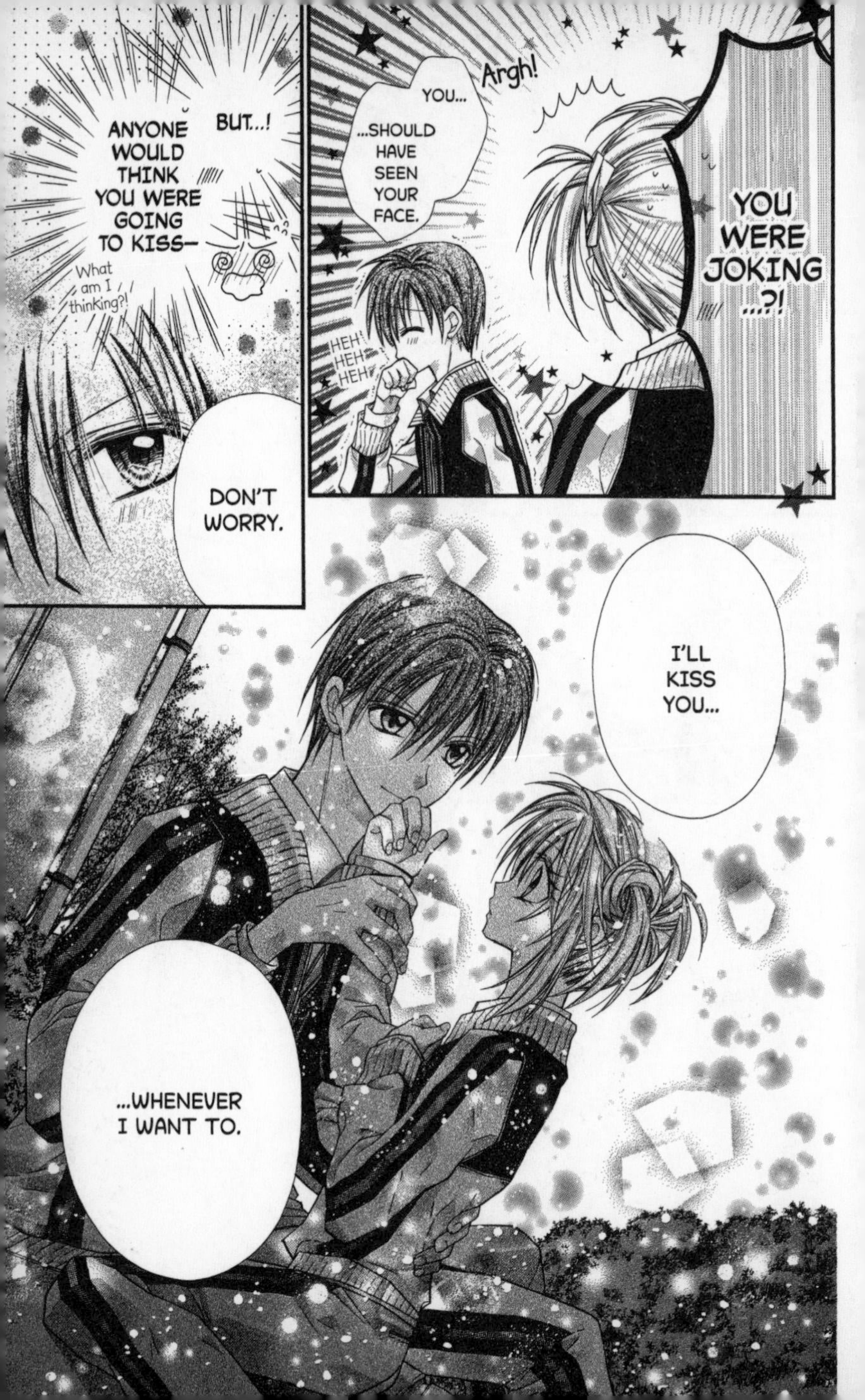
YOU WERE JOKING ...?!
Argh!
YOU...
...SHOULD HAVE SEEN YOUR FACE.
HEH HEH HEH
BUT...!
ANYONE WOULD THINK YOU WERE GOING TO KISS—
What am I thinking?!
DON'T WORRY.
I'LL KISS YOU...
...WHENEVER I WANT TO.

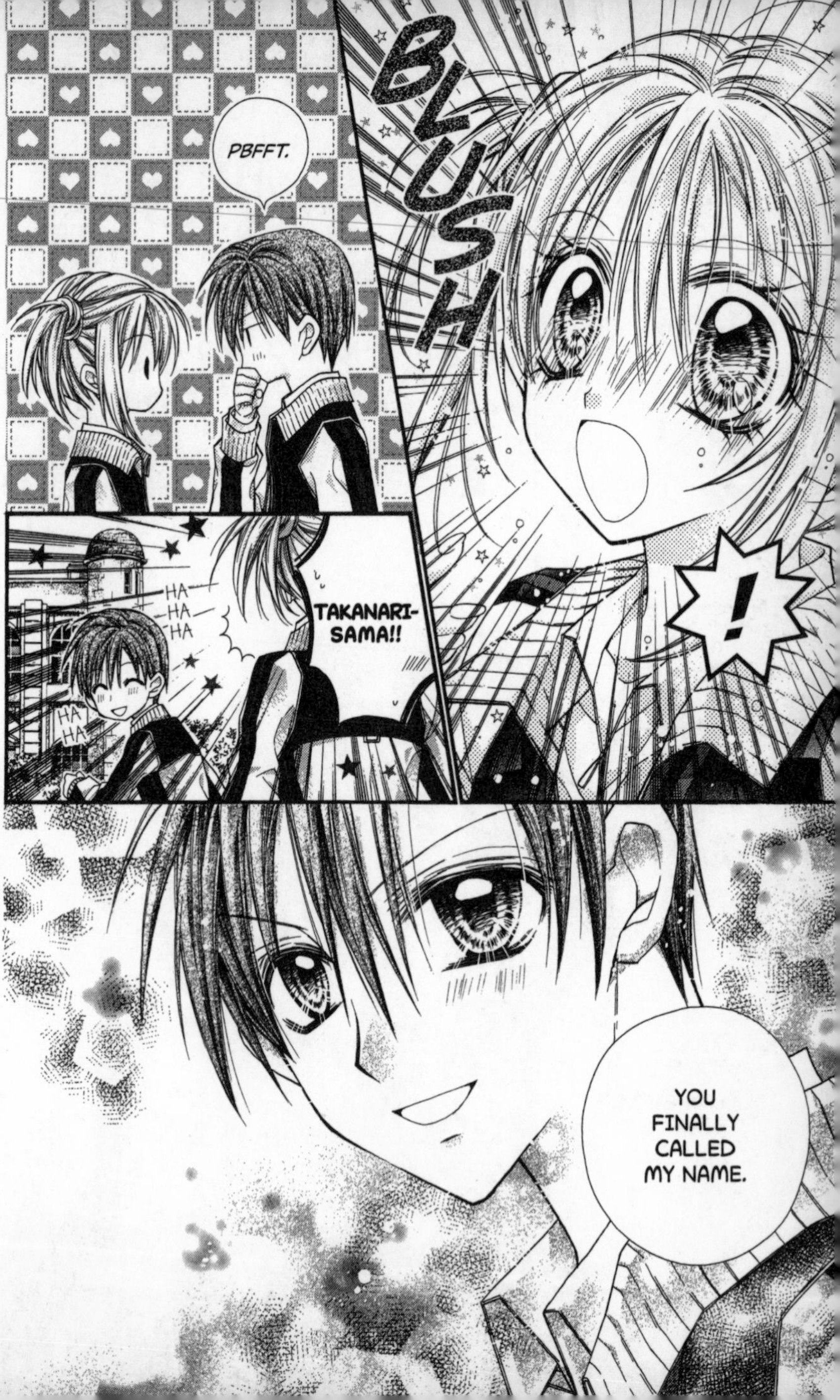
BLUSH
!
PBFFT.
TAKANARI-SAMA!!
HA HA HA
HA HA
YOU FINALLY CALLED MY NAME.

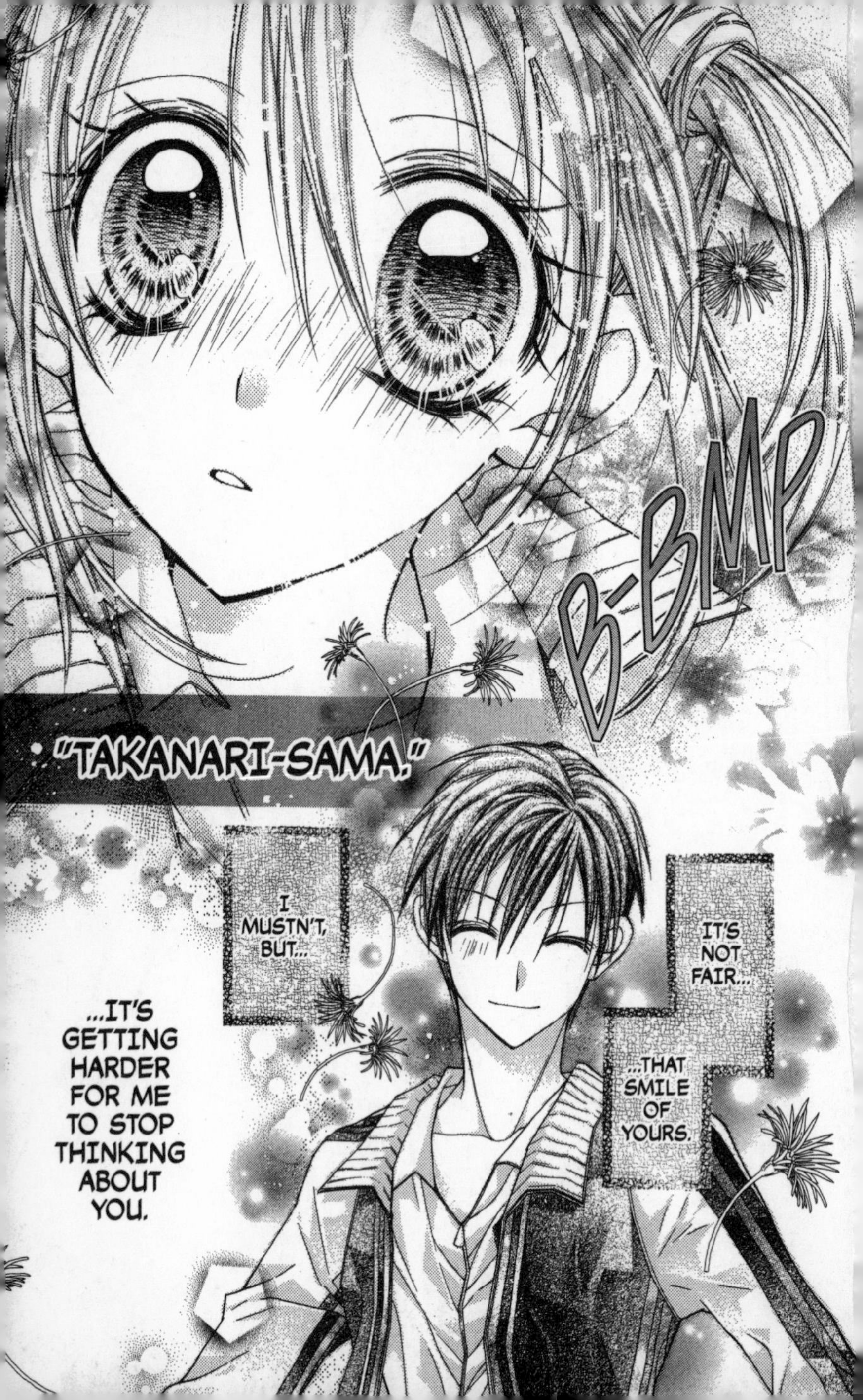
B-BMP
"TAKANARI-SAMA."
IT'S NOT FAIR...
...THAT SMILE OF YOURS.
I MUSTN'T, BUT...
...IT'S GETTING HARDER FOR ME TO STOP THINKING ABOUT YOU.

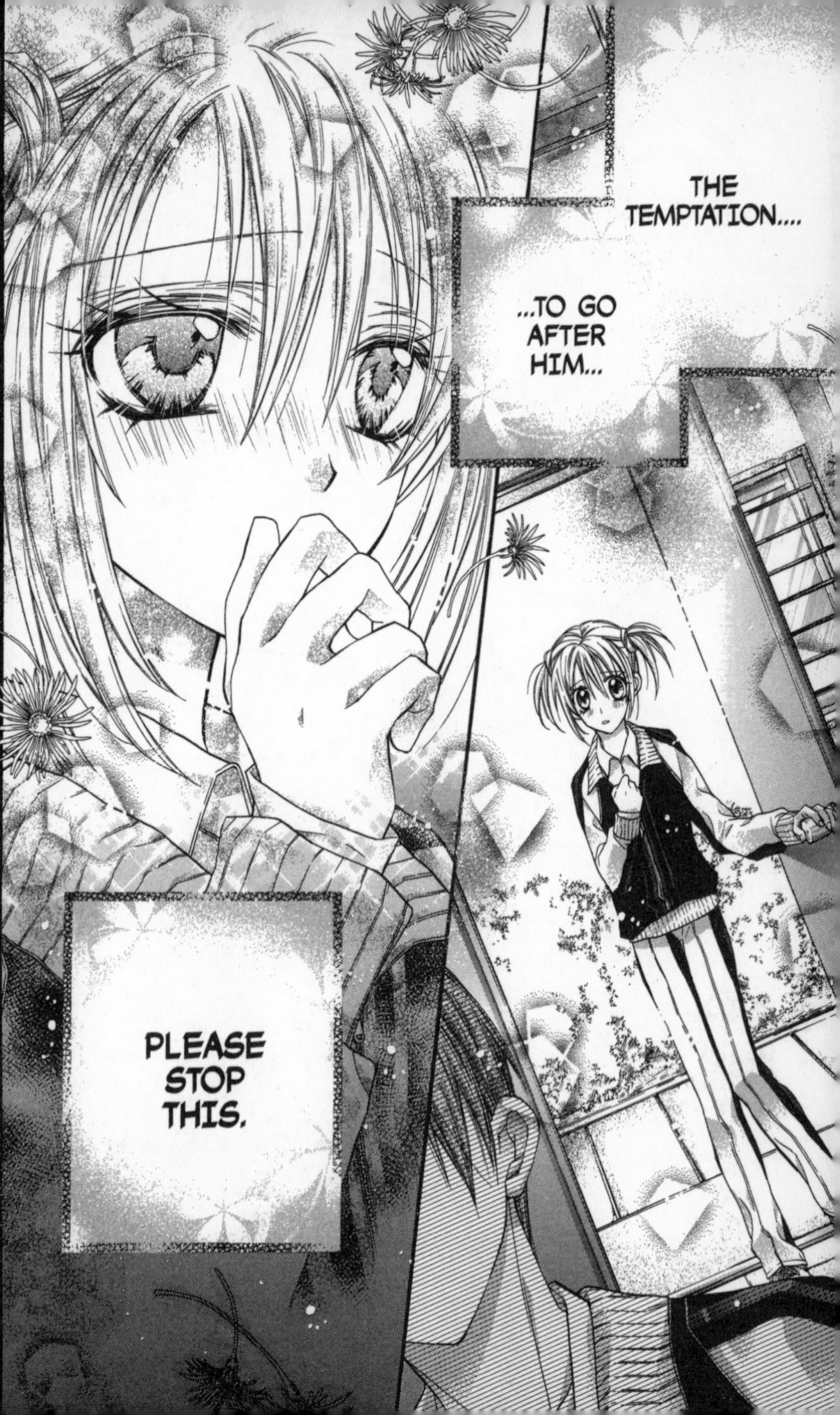
THE TEMPTATION....
...TO GO AFTER HIM...
PLEASE STOP THIS.

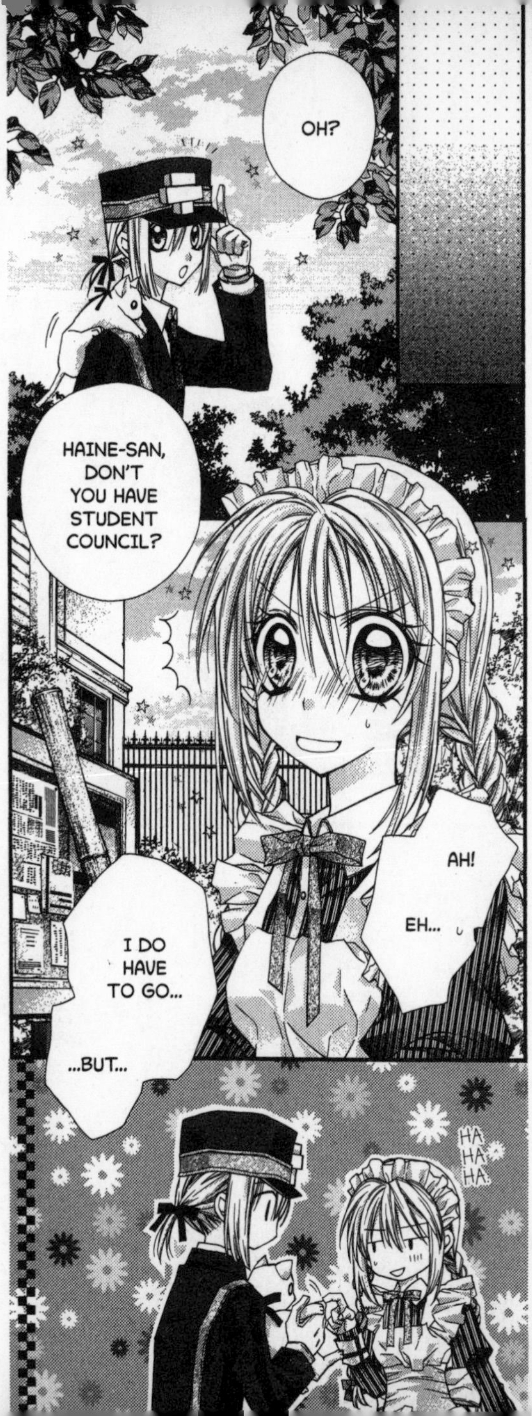
OH?
HAINE-SAN, DON'T YOU HAVE STUDENT COUNCIL?
AH!
EH...
I DO HAVE TO GO...
...BUT...
HA HA HA

Popularity Poll☆

By the time this manga is out, the poll will be over, but we did a "*The Gentlemen's Alliance †* character popularity poll" in *Ribon* magazine!

We announced the results in the March edition of *Ribon*.

As the author, I wanted Haine-chan to be in first place...

Saori ordered an iced tea at the Hamburg steak shop we went to just a while ago.

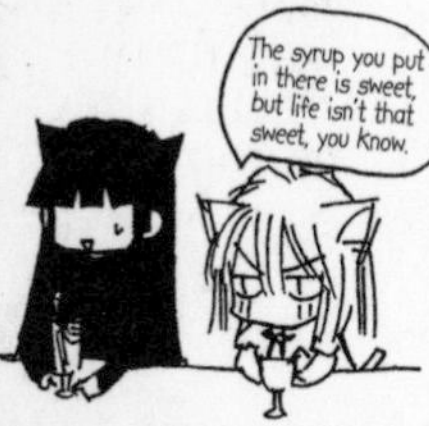
The syrup you put in there is sweet, but life isn't that sweet, you know.

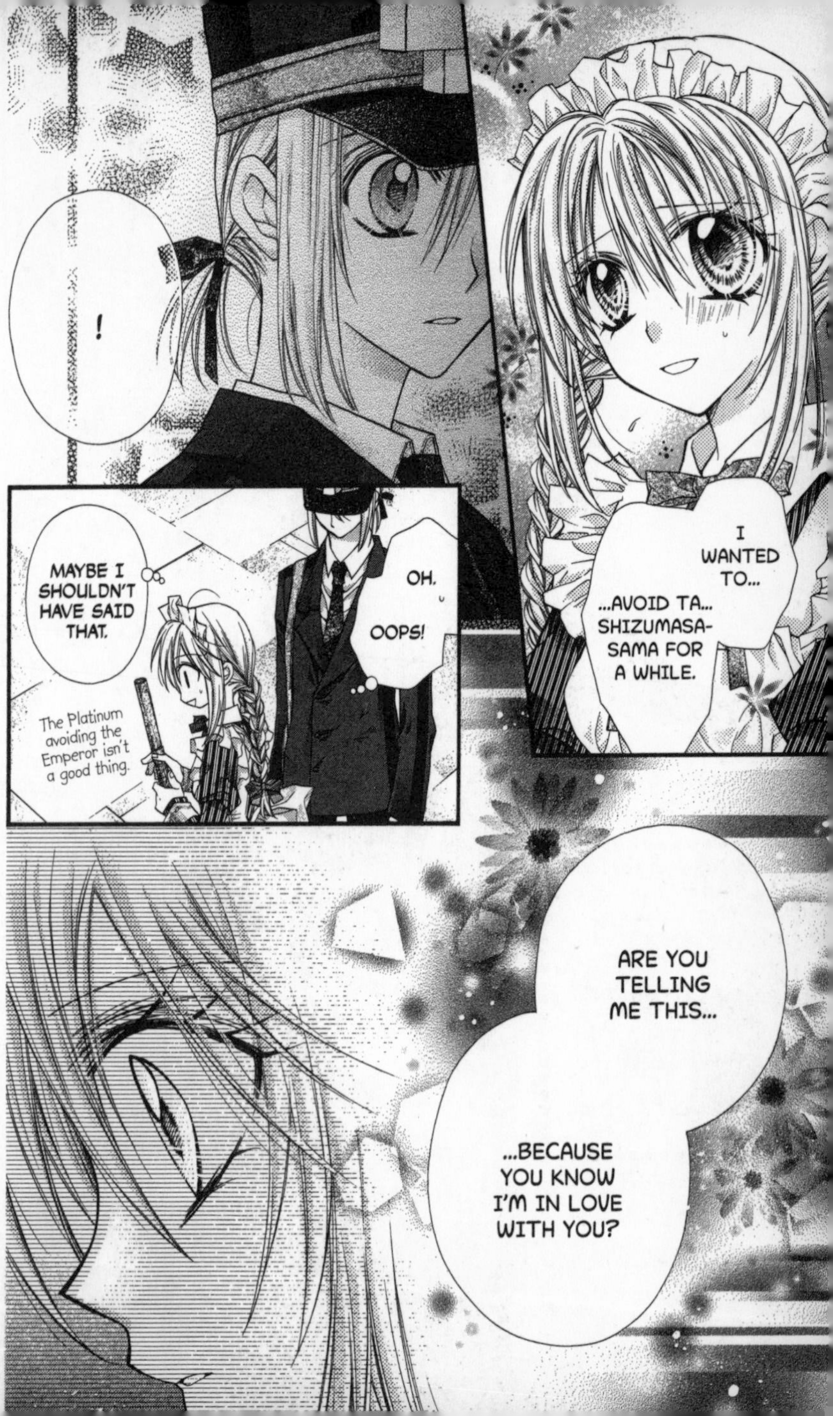
I WANTED TO...
...AVOID TA... SHIZUMASA-SAMA FOR A WHILE.
!
OH.
OOPS!
MAYBE I SHOULDN'T HAVE SAID THAT.
The Platinum avoiding the Emperor isn't a good thing.
ARE YOU TELLING ME THIS...
...BECAUSE YOU KNOW I'M IN LOVE WITH YOU?

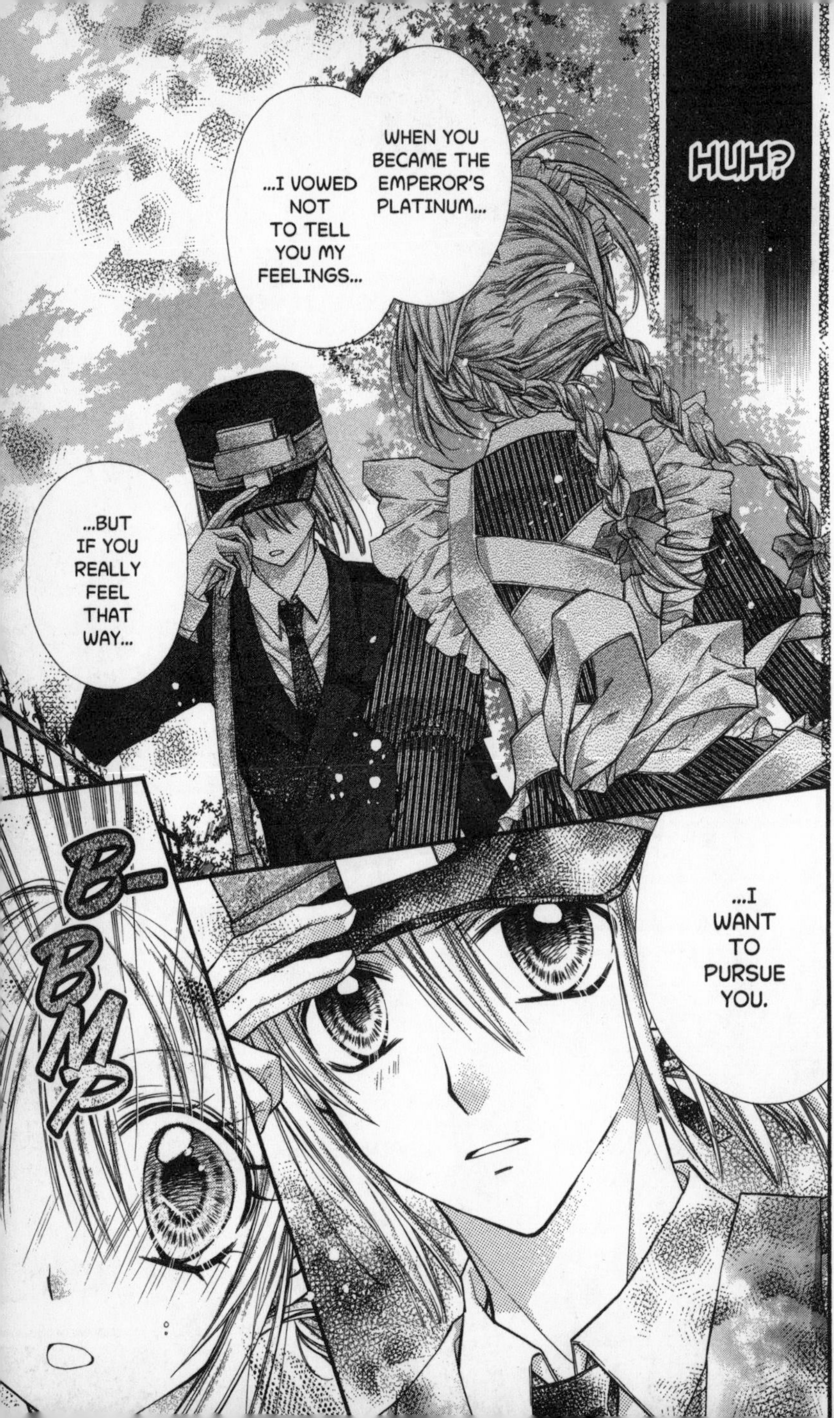
HUH?
WHEN YOU BECAME THE EMPEROR'S PLATINUM...
...I VOWED NOT TO TELL YOU MY FEELINGS...
...BUT IF YOU REALLY FEEL THAT WAY...
...I WANT TO PURSUE YOU.
B-BMP

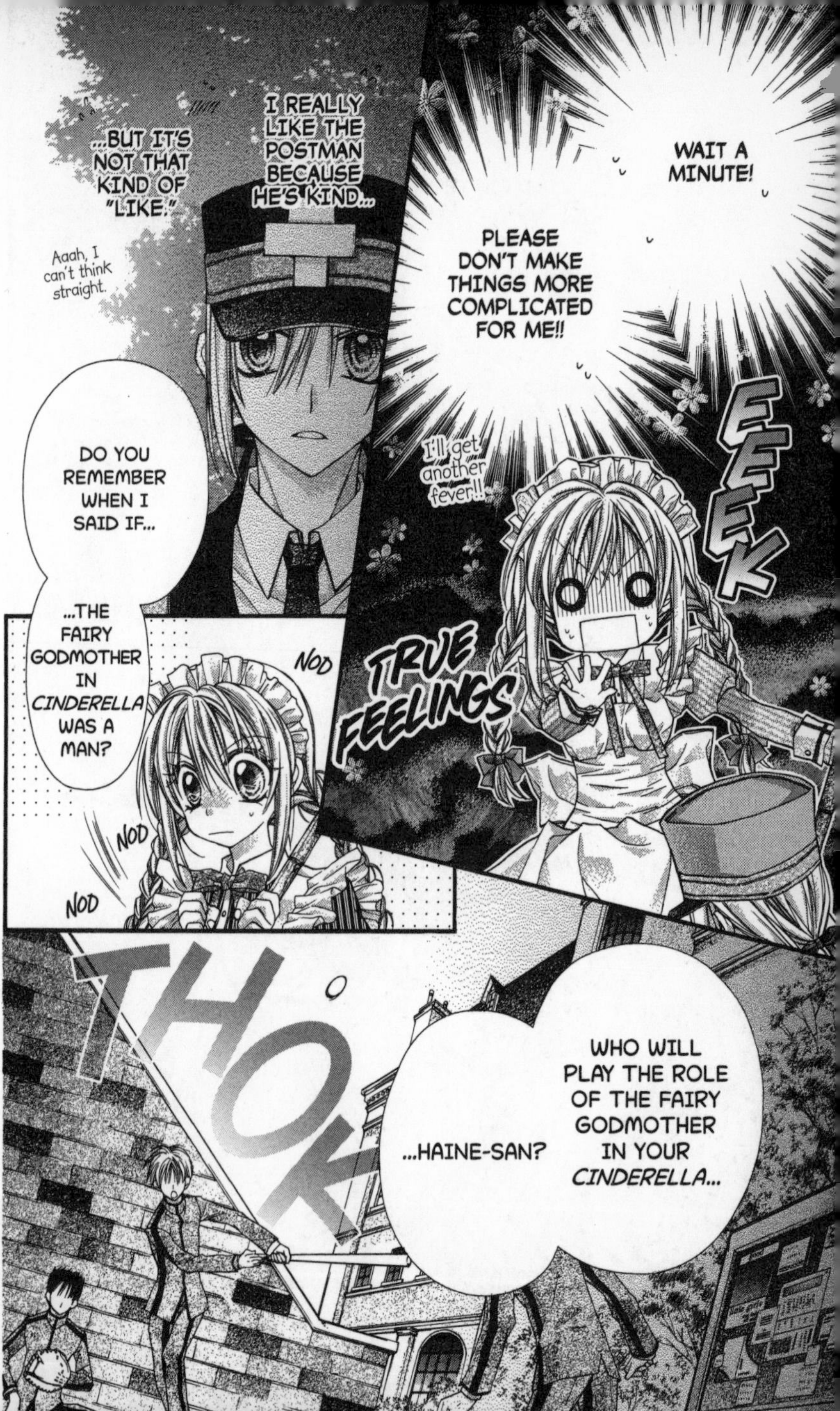
WAIT A MINUTE!
PLEASE DON'T MAKE THINGS MORE COMPLICATED FOR ME!!
EEEK
I'll get another fever!!
TRUE FEELINGS
I REALLY LIKE THE POSTMAN BECAUSE HE'S KIND...
...BUT IT'S NOT THAT KIND OF "LIKE."
Aaah, I can't think straight.
DO YOU REMEMBER WHEN I SAID IF...
...THE FAIRY GODMOTHER IN *CINDERELLA* WAS A MAN?
NOD
NOD
NOD
THOK
WHO WILL PLAY THE ROLE OF THE FAIRY GODMOTHER IN YOUR *CINDERELLA*...
...HAINE-SAN?

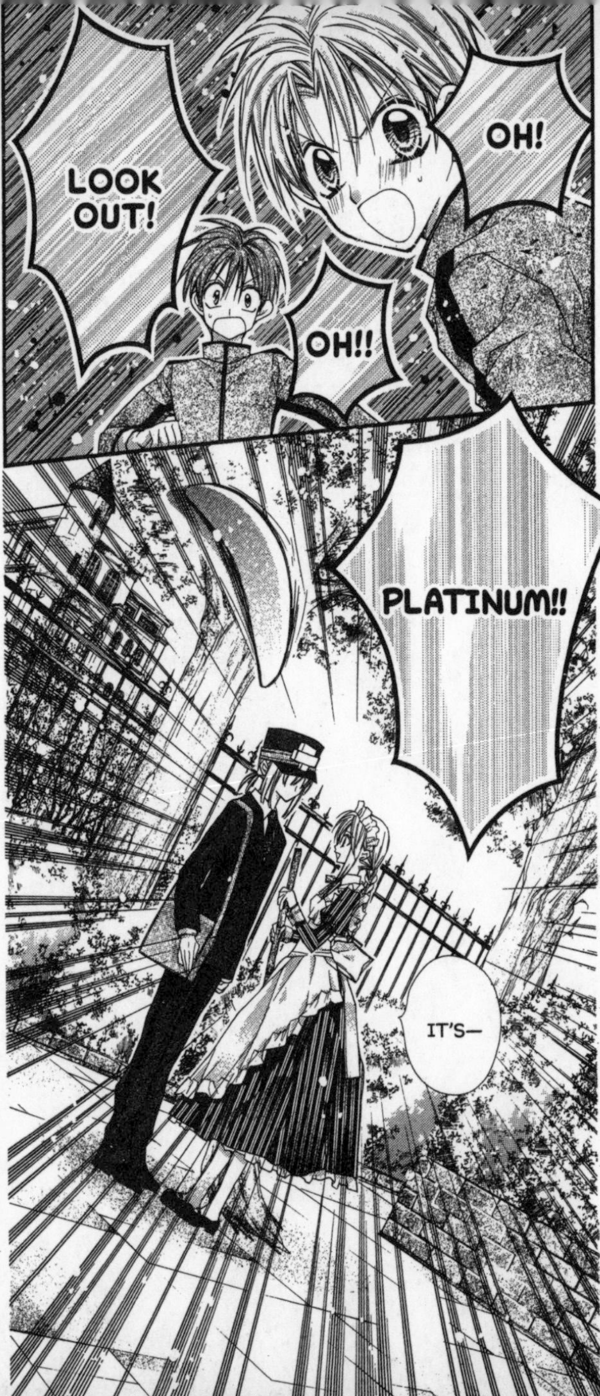
OH!
LOOK OUT!
OH!!
PLATINUM!!
IT'S—

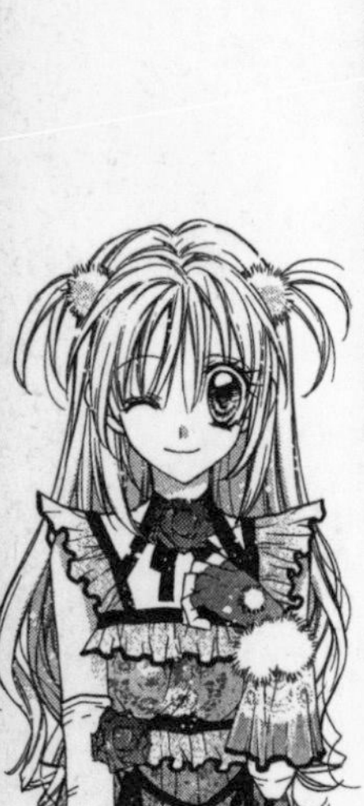

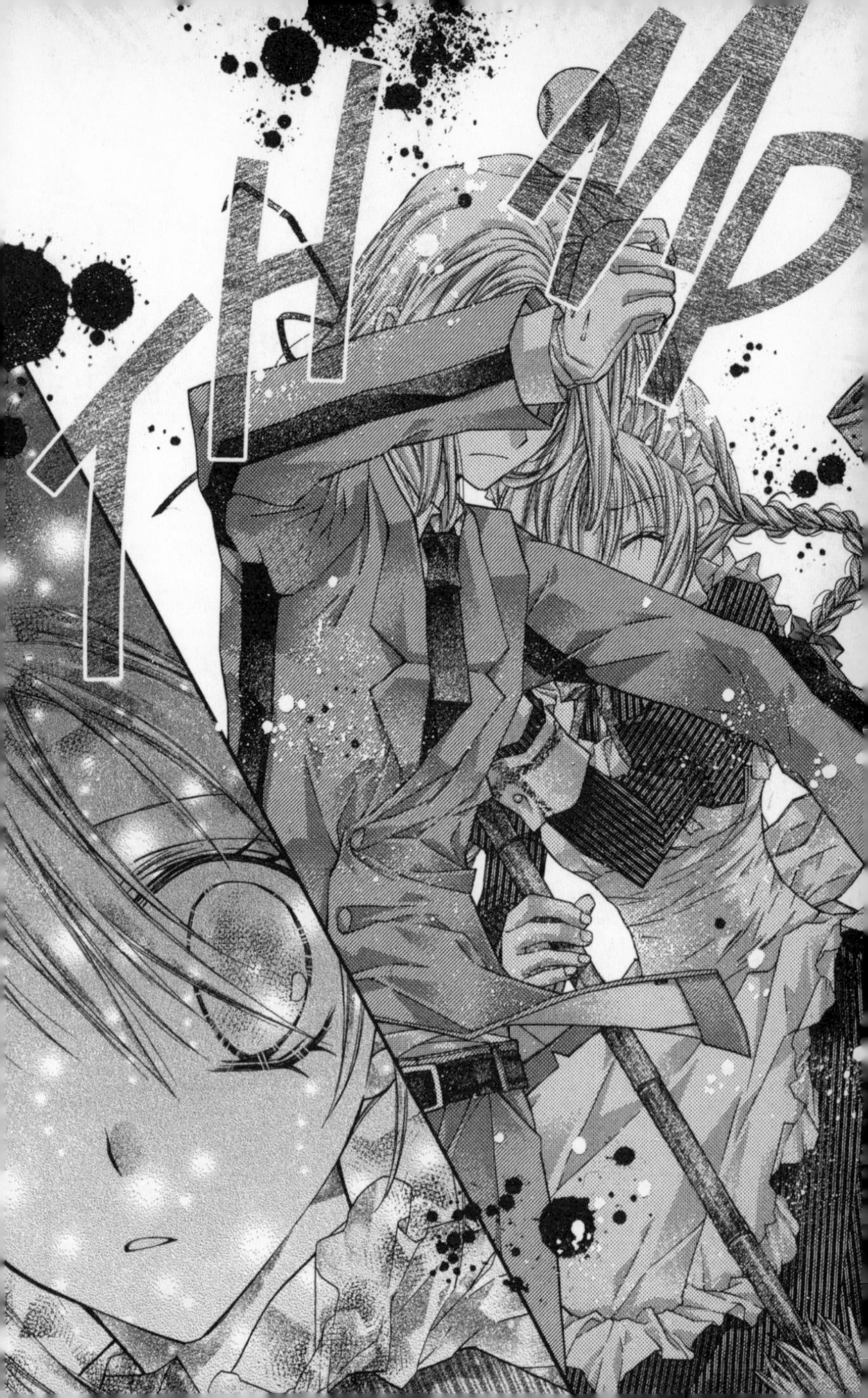
THAMP

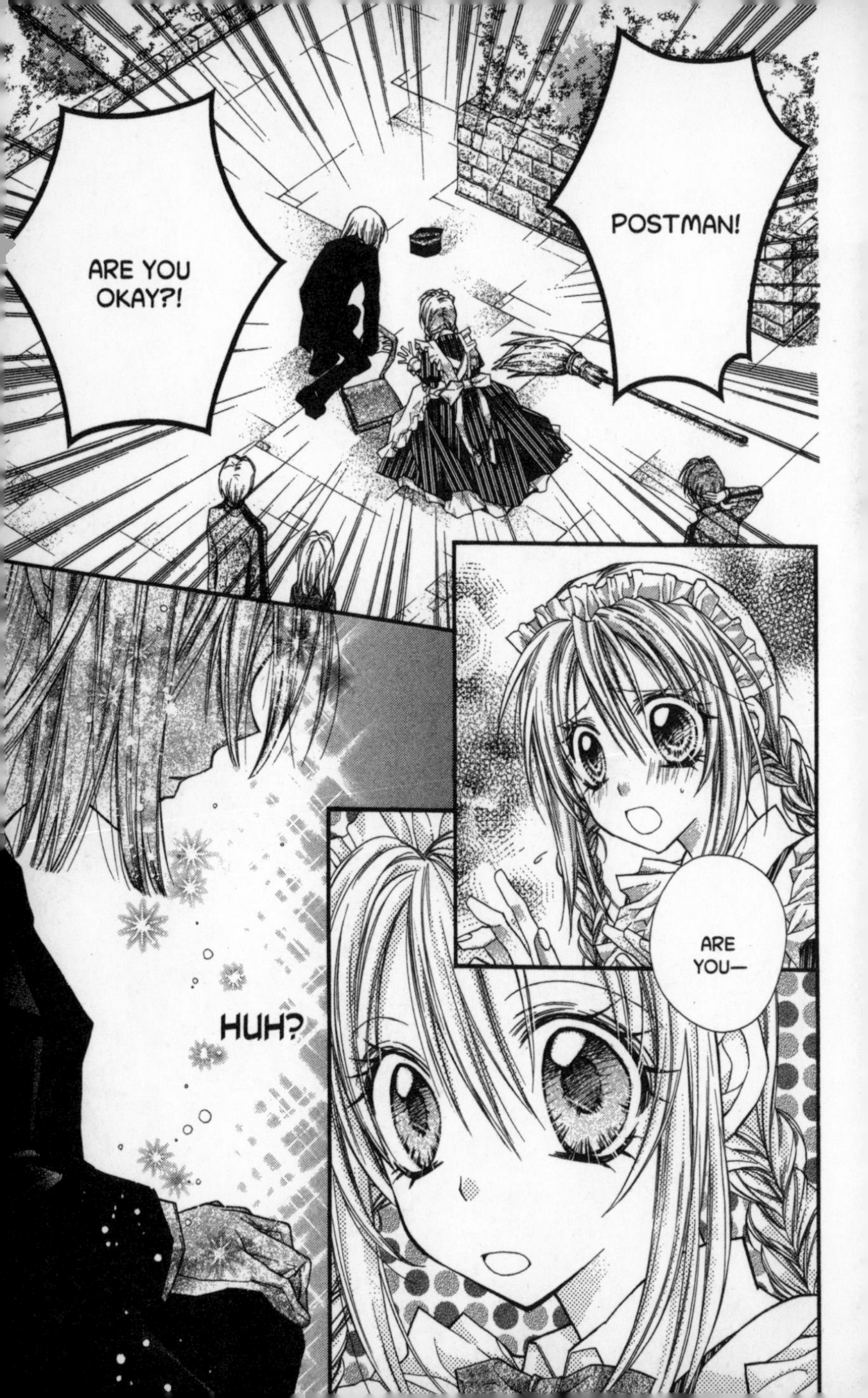
POSTMAN!
ARE YOU OKAY?!
ARE YOU—
HUH?

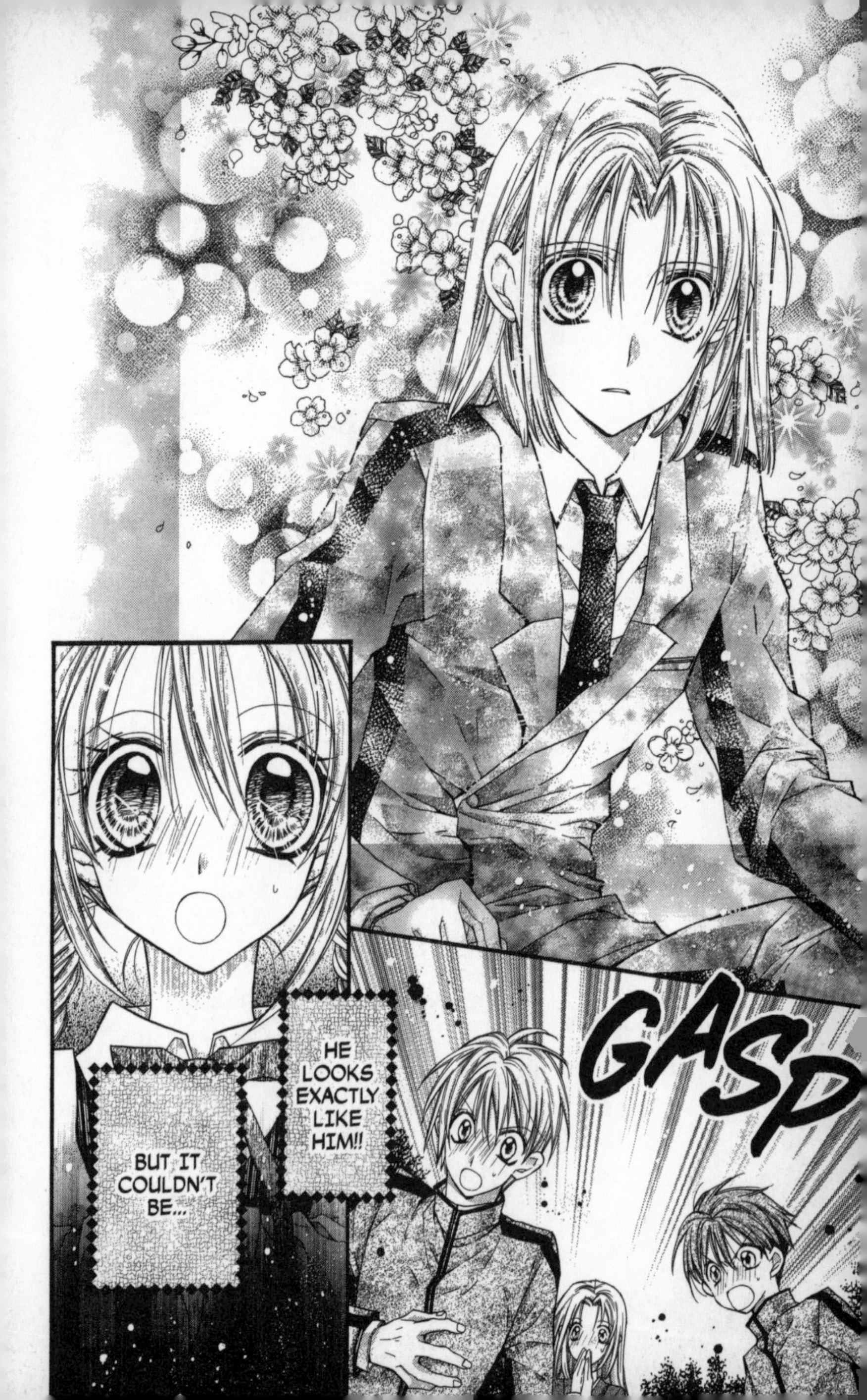
GASP
HE LOOKS EXACTLY LIKE HIM!!
BUT IT COULDN'T BE...

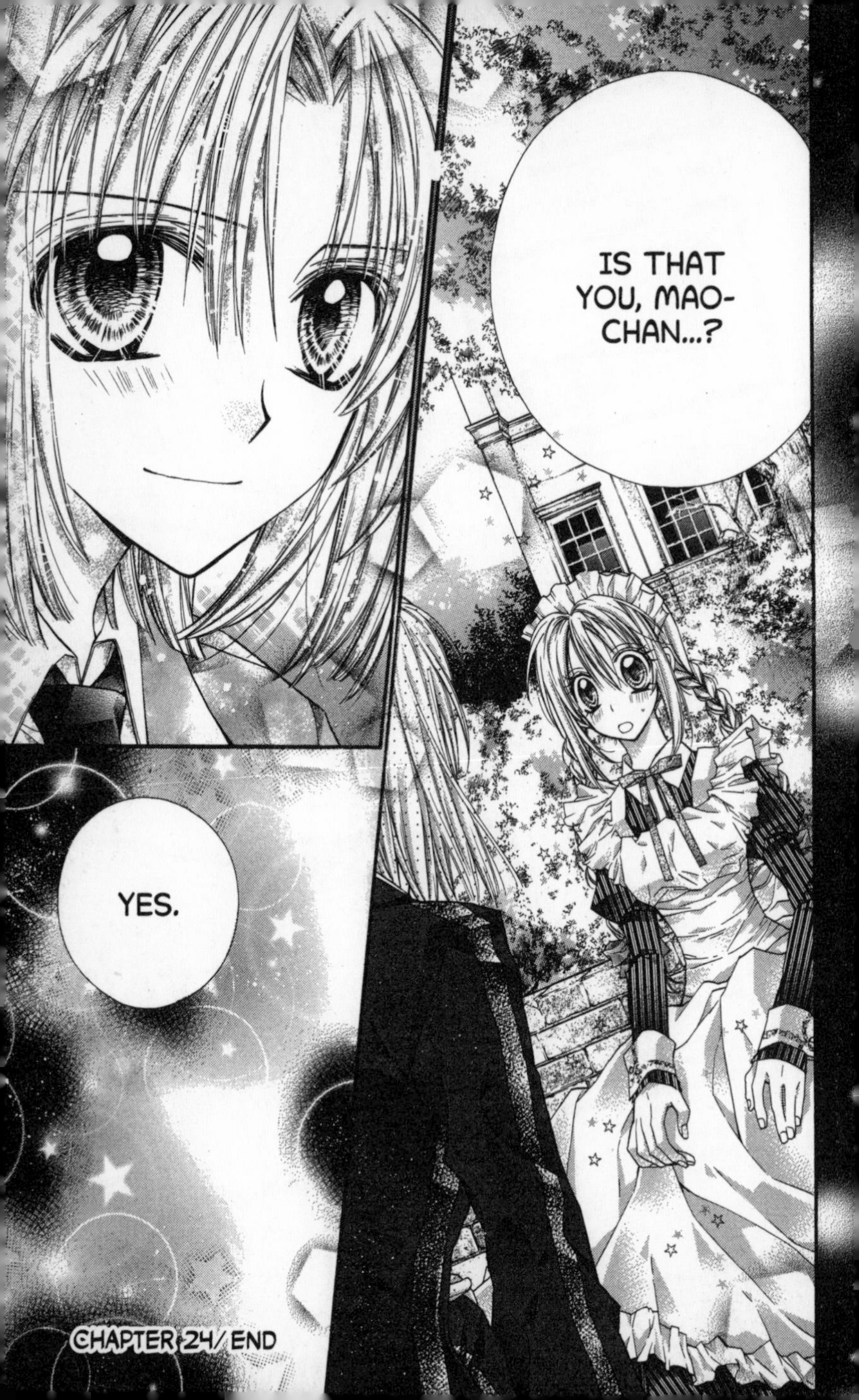
IS THAT YOU, MAO-CHAN...?
YES.
CHAPTER 24/ END

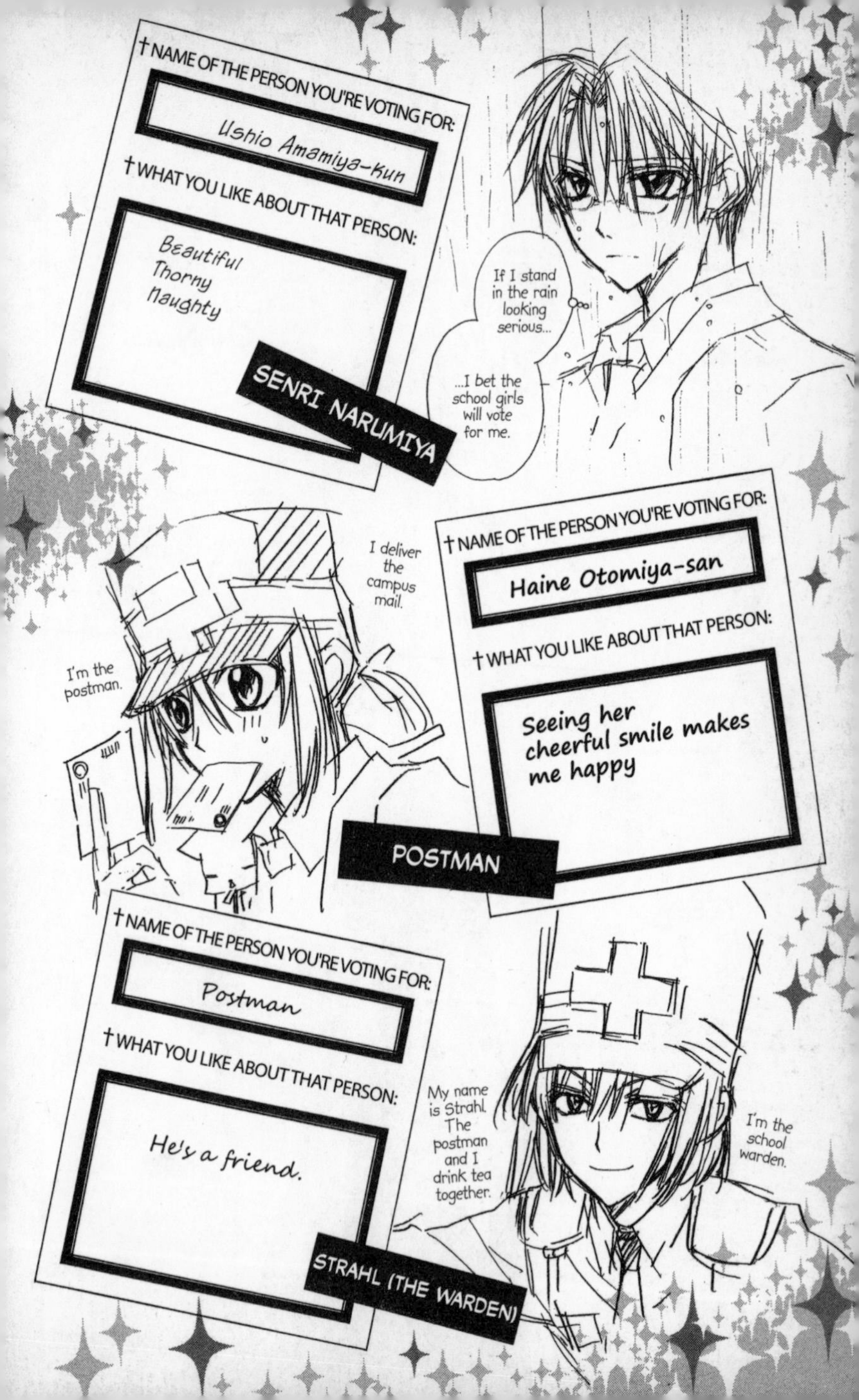
If I stand in the rain looking serious...
...I bet the school girls will vote for me.
†NAME OF THE PERSON YOU'RE VOTING FOR:
Ushio Amamiya-kun
†WHAT YOU LIKE ABOUT THAT PERSON:
Beautiful
Thorny
Naughty
SENRI NARUMIYA
†NAME OF THE PERSON YOU'RE VOTING FOR:
Haine Otomiya-san
†WHAT YOU LIKE ABOUT THAT PERSON:
Seeing her cheerful smile makes me happy
POSTMAN
I deliver the campus mail.
I'm the postman.
I'm the school warden.
My name is Strahl. The postman and I drink tea together.
†NAME OF THE PERSON YOU'RE VOTING FOR:
Postman
†WHAT YOU LIKE ABOUT THAT PERSON:
He's a friend.
STRAHL (THE WARDEN)

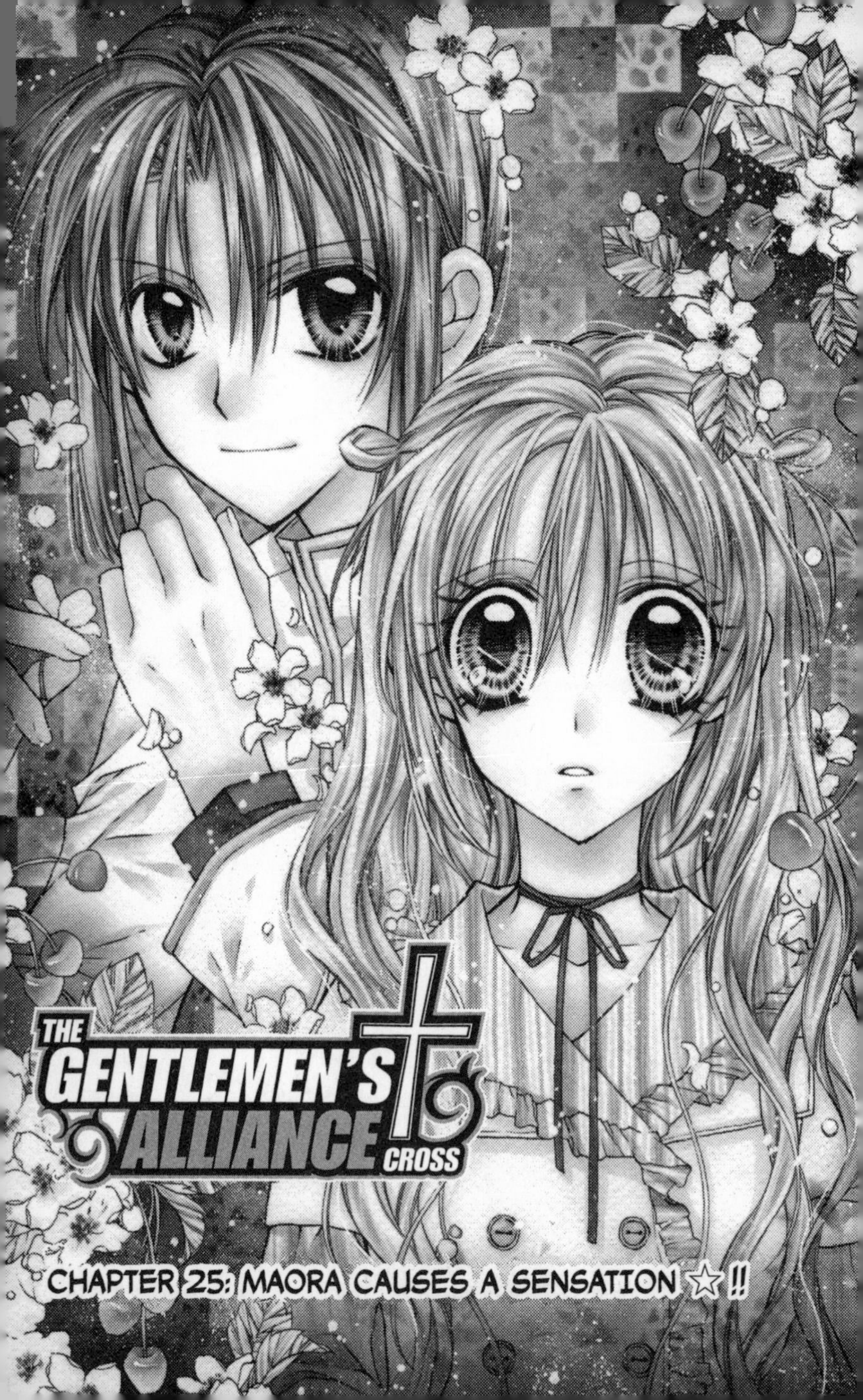
THE GENTLEMEN'S ALLIANCE CROSS
CHAPTER 25: MAORA CAUSES A SENSATION ☆ !!

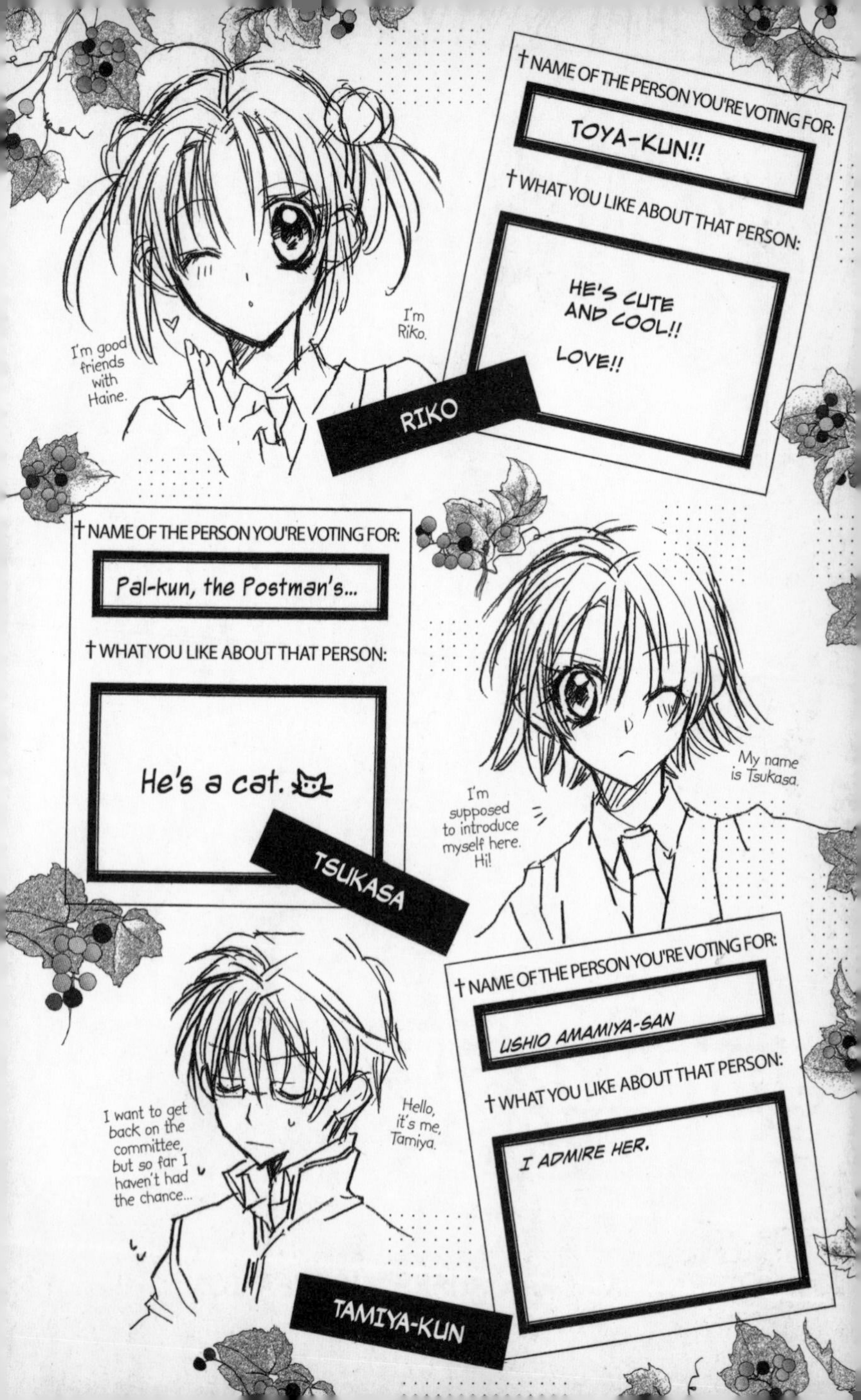
† NAME OF THE PERSON YOU'RE VOTING FOR:
TOYA-KUN!!
† WHAT YOU LIKE ABOUT THAT PERSON:
HE'S CUTE AND COOL!! LOVE!!
RIKO
I'm Riko.
I'm good friends with Haine.
My name is Tsukasa.
I'm supposed to introduce myself here. Hi!
† NAME OF THE PERSON YOU'RE VOTING FOR:
Pal-kun, the Postman's...
† WHAT YOU LIKE ABOUT THAT PERSON:
He's a cat.
TSUKASA
† NAME OF THE PERSON YOU'RE VOTING FOR:
USHIO AMAMIYA-SAN
† WHAT YOU LIKE ABOUT THAT PERSON:
I ADMIRE HER.
Hello, it's me, Tamiya.
I want to get back on the committee, but so far I haven't had the chance...
TAMIYA-KUN

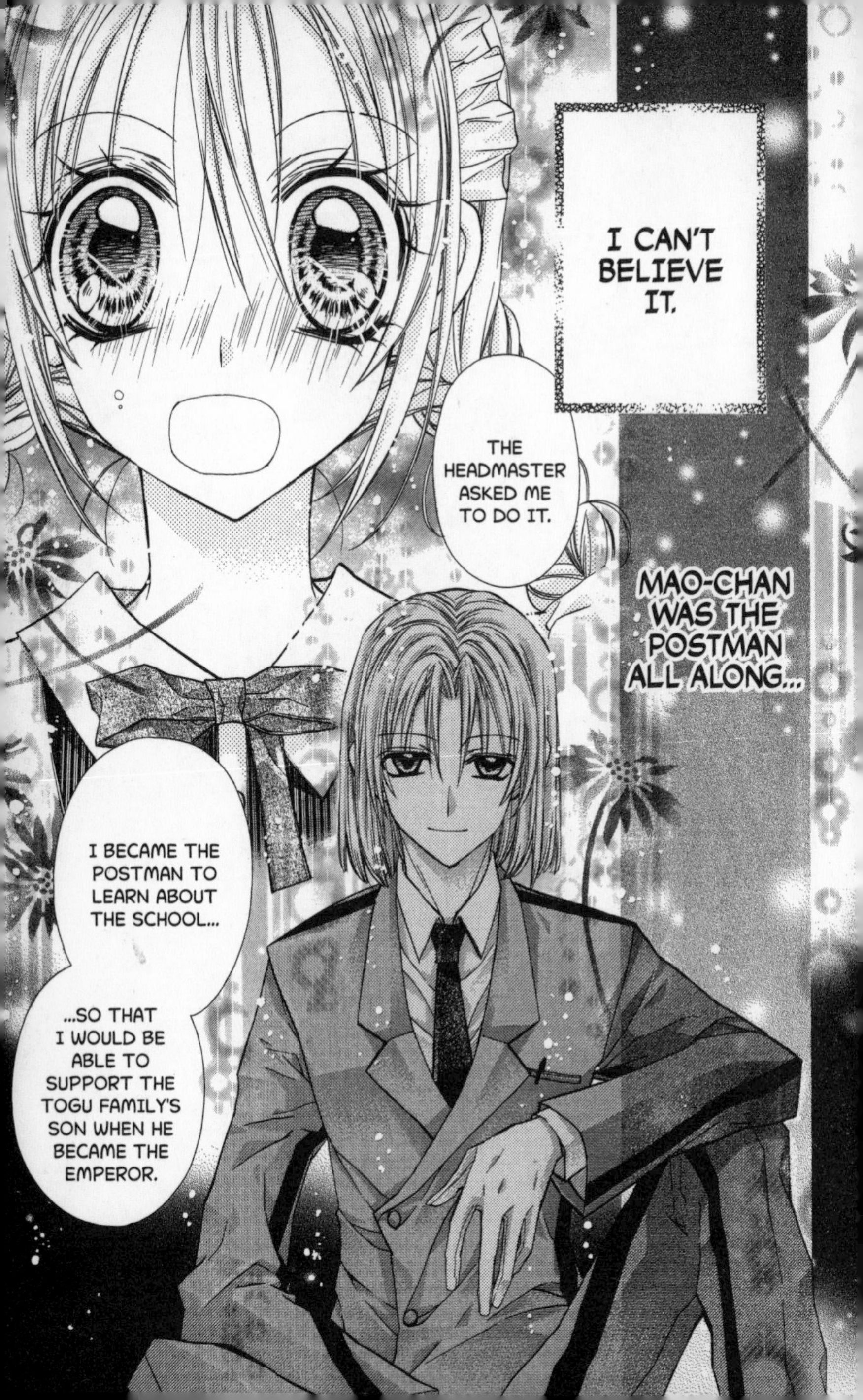
I CAN'T BELIEVE IT.
THE HEADMASTER ASKED ME TO DO IT.
MAO-CHAN WAS THE POSTMAN ALL ALONG...
I BECAME THE POSTMAN TO LEARN ABOUT THE SCHOOL...
...SO THAT I WOULD BE ABLE TO SUPPORT THE TOGU FAMILY'S SON WHEN HE BECAME THE EMPEROR.

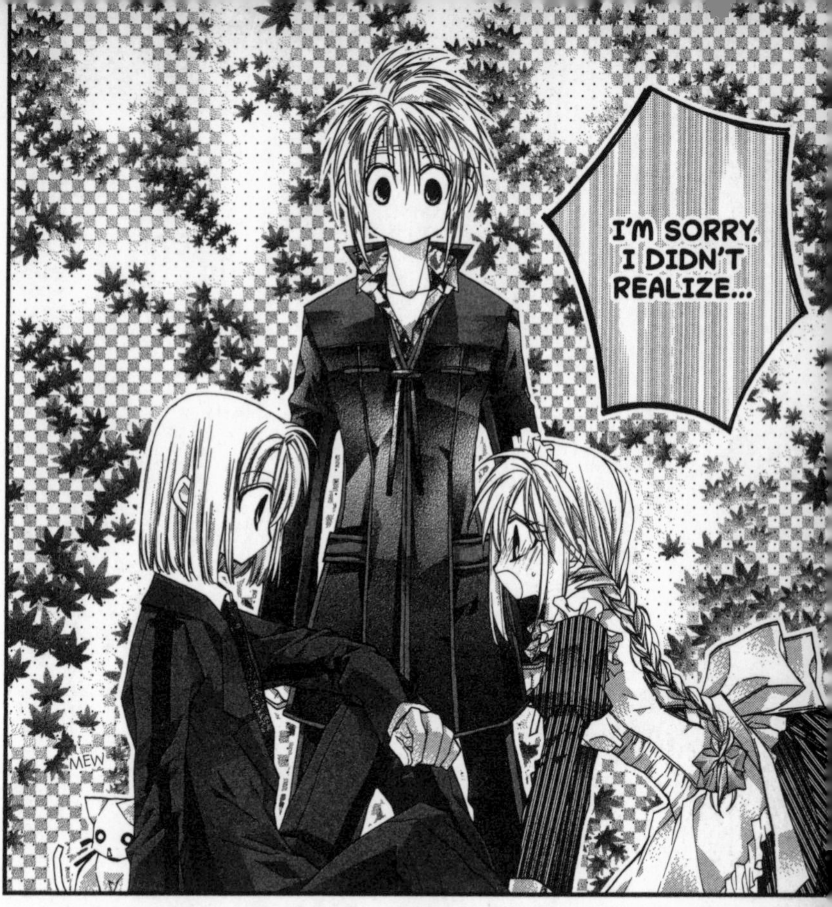
I'M SORRY. I DIDN'T REALIZE...
MEW

Chapter 25: Maora Causes a Sensation☆!! Lead-in It doesn't matter if you're a boy—I like the cute and bright Mao-chan!

☆ I'm giving the story away.

Eh...! That's right!! He happened to be Mao-chan!! You know! (Arina tries to hide it, but it's too late for that now.)

Of course, this was something I had planned from chapter 1, and the whole incident about Mao-chan actually being a boy was just camouflage. (I assumed that readers would not expect to be surprised by the same character twice.)

I really like it when Mao-chan is angry at Maguri on page 76. I think it's a lot like him to have that expression on his face. They both care (for each other) deeply. Mao-chan is trying to maintain their bond by becoming closer to Maguri, whereas Maguri is trying to strengthen their bond by keeping Mao-chan at a certain distance... And that distance must be frustrating for Mao-chan...

Mao-chan really went for broke here. I guess things must have been too much for him. He's madly in love with Maguri, so he couldn't take it when Maguri purposefully refused to consider him.

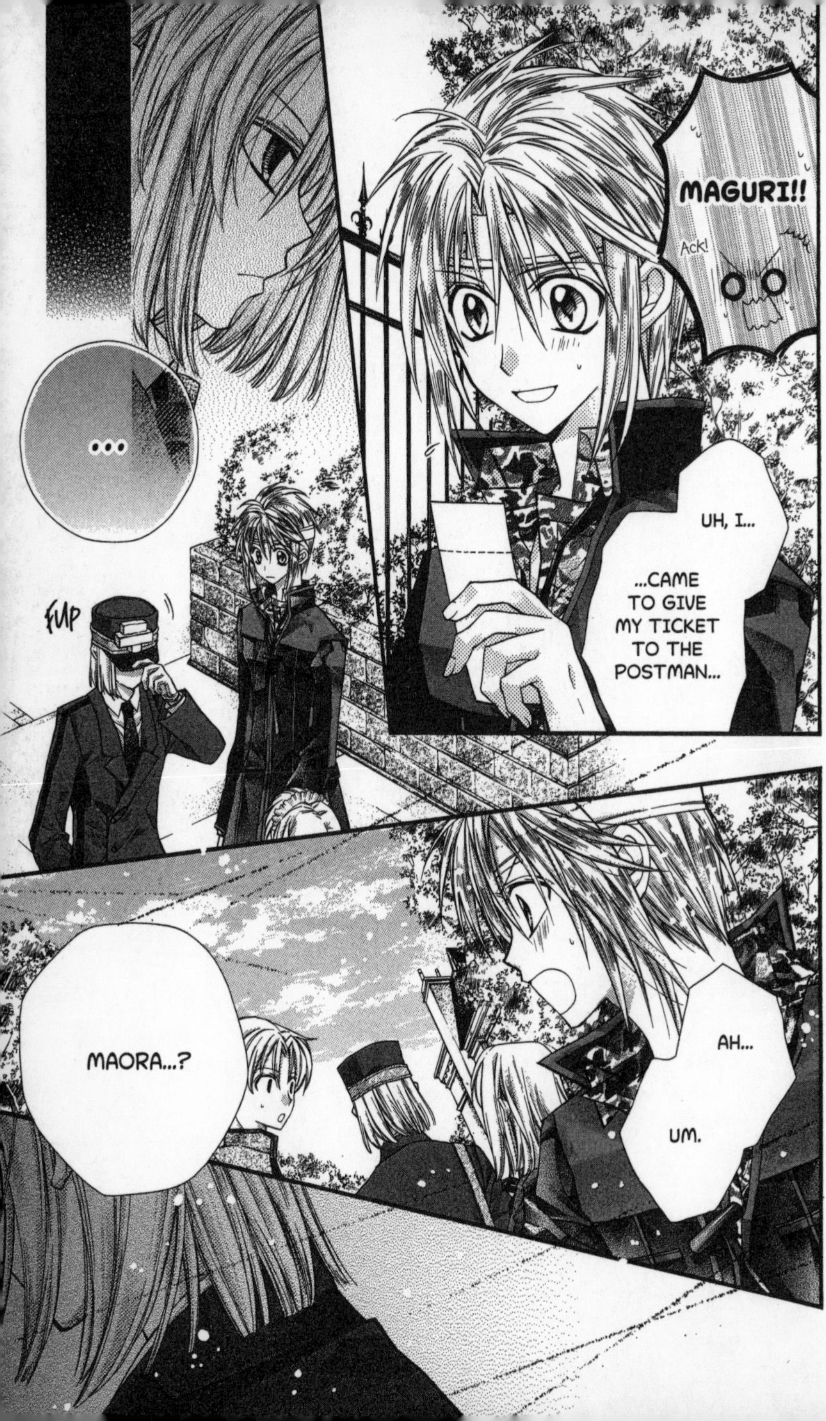
MAGURI!!
Ack!
UH, I...
...CAME TO GIVE MY TICKET TO THE POSTMAN...
...
FLIP
AH...
UM.
MAORA...?

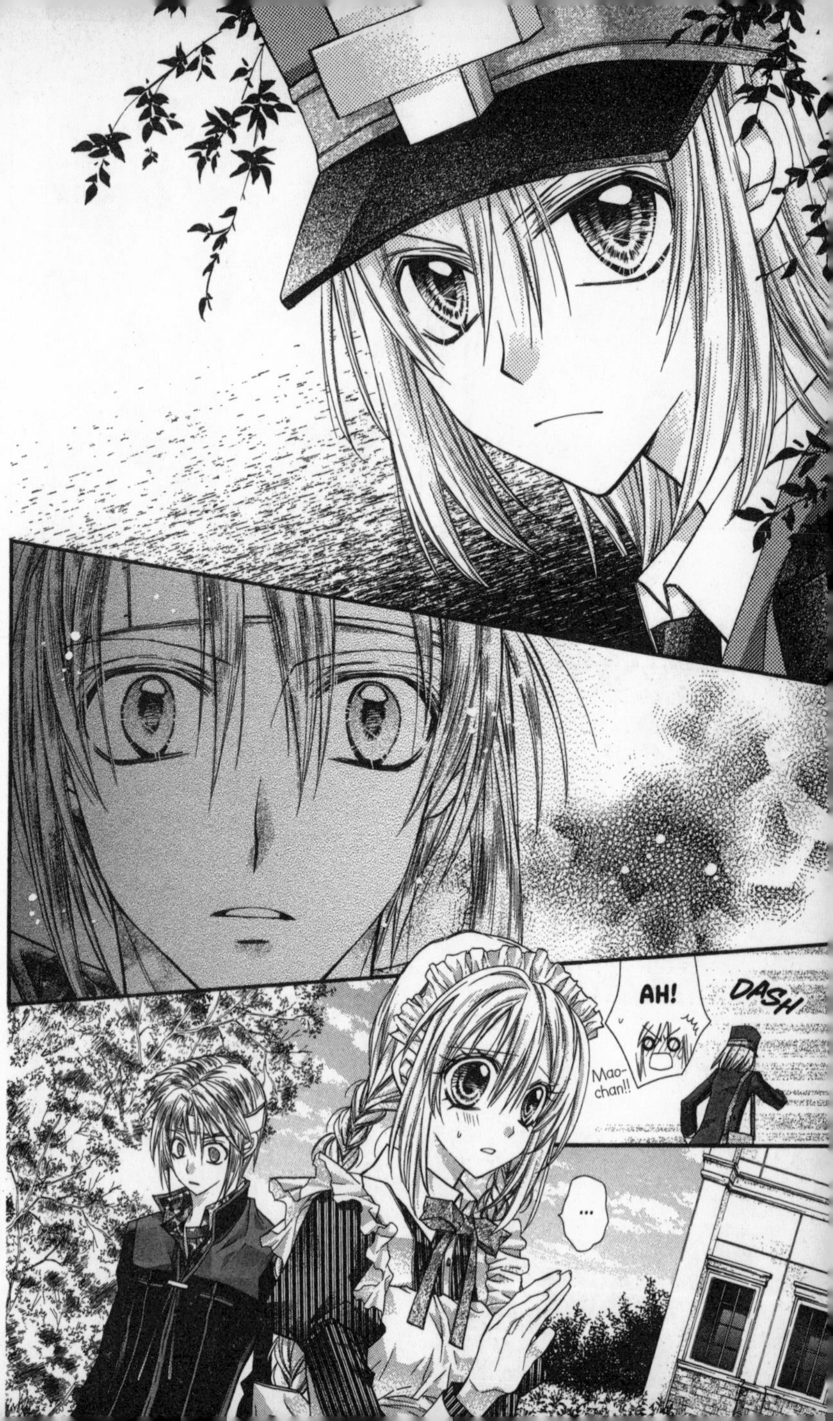
DASH
AH!
Mao-chan!!
...

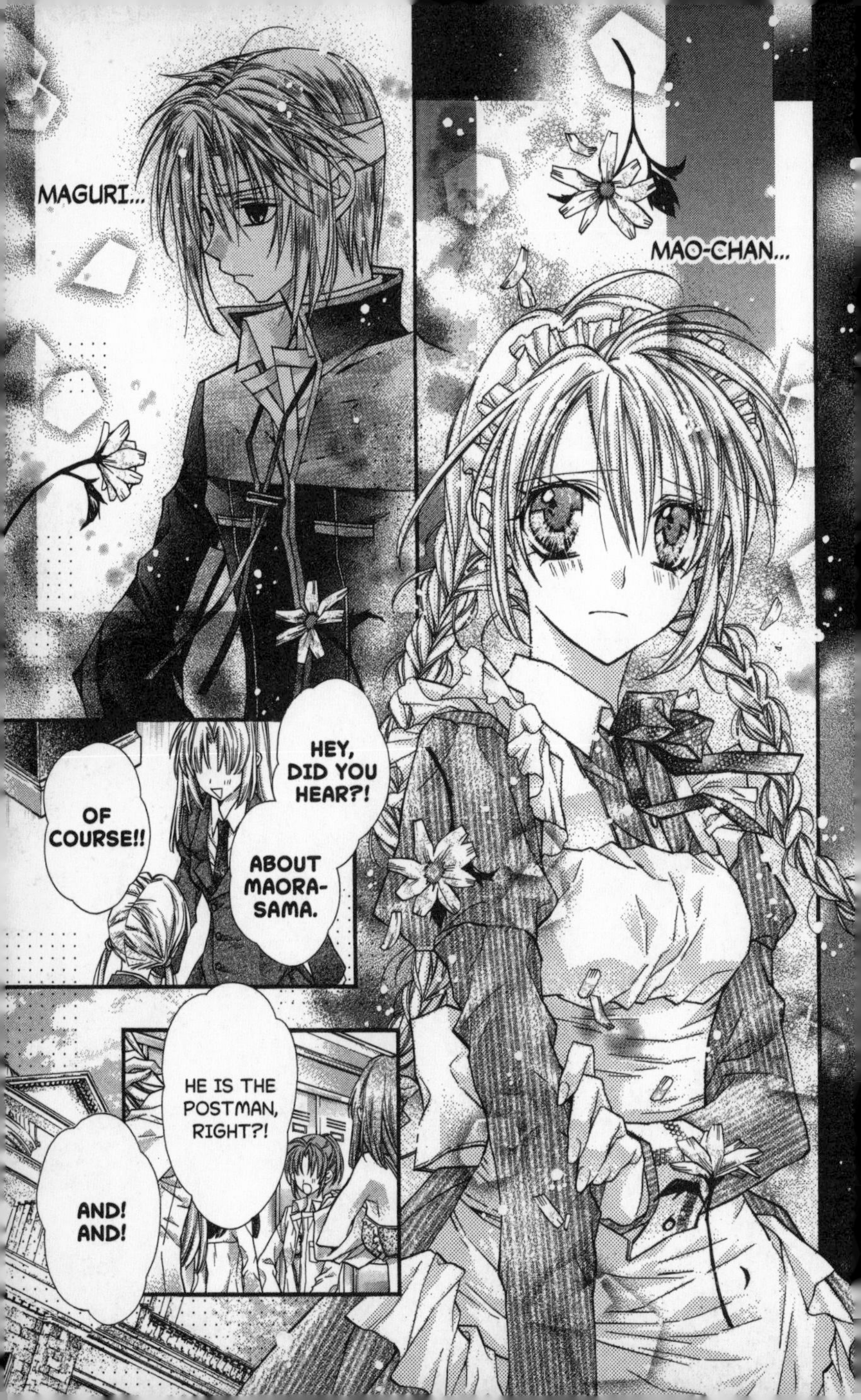
MAO-CHAN...
MAGURI...
HEY, DID YOU HEAR?!
ABOUT MAORA-SAMA.
OF COURSE!!
HE IS THE POSTMAN, RIGHT?!
AND! AND!

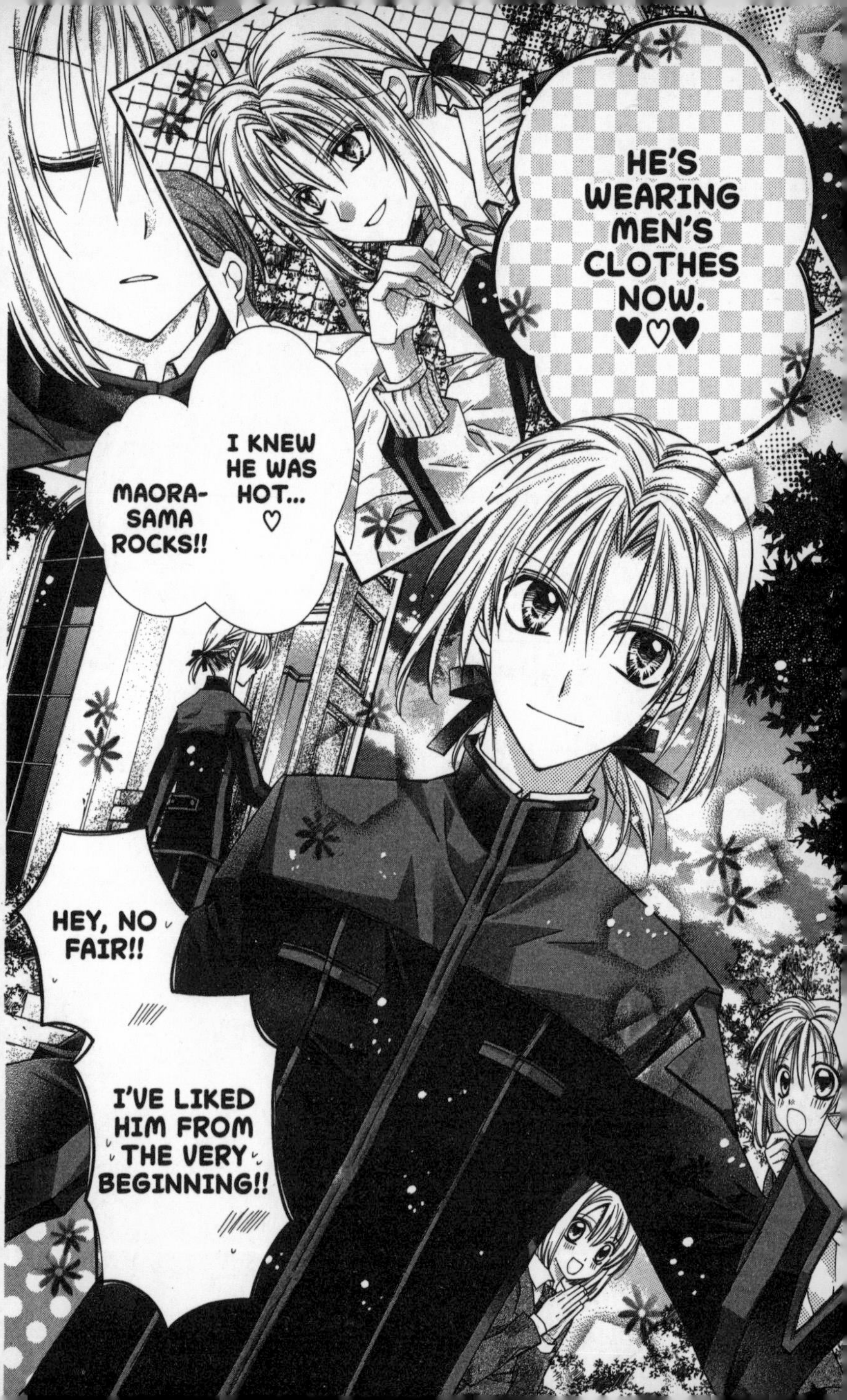
HE'S WEARING MEN'S CLOTHES NOW. ♥♡♥
I KNEW HE WAS HOT... ♡
MAORA-SAMA ROCKS!!
HEY, NO FAIR!!
I'VE LIKED HIM FROM THE VERY BEGINNING!!

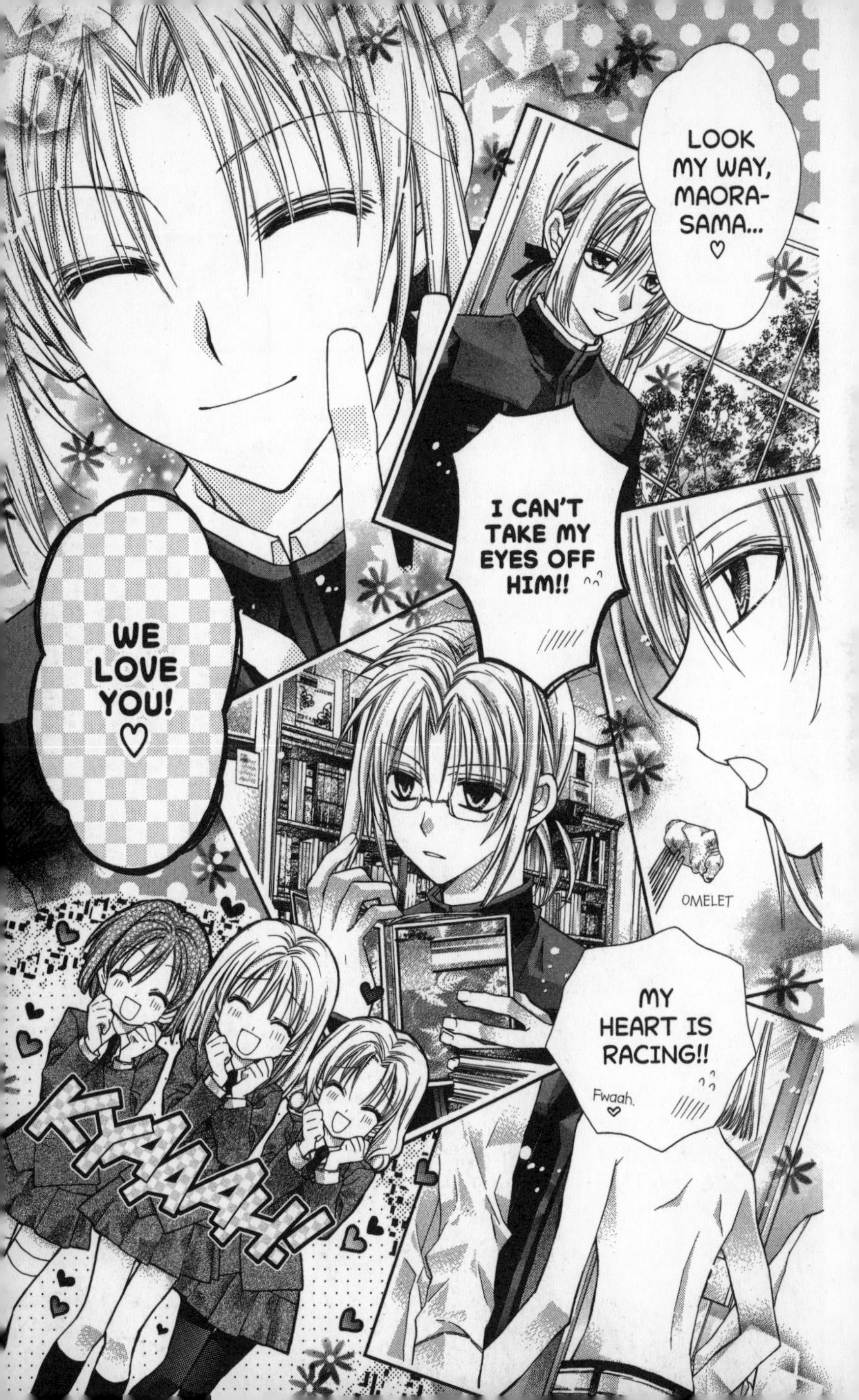
LOOK MY WAY, MAORA-SAMA... ♡
I CAN'T TAKE MY EYES OFF HIM!!
OMELET
MY HEART IS RACING!!
Fwaah. ♡
WE LOVE YOU! ♡
KYAAAH!

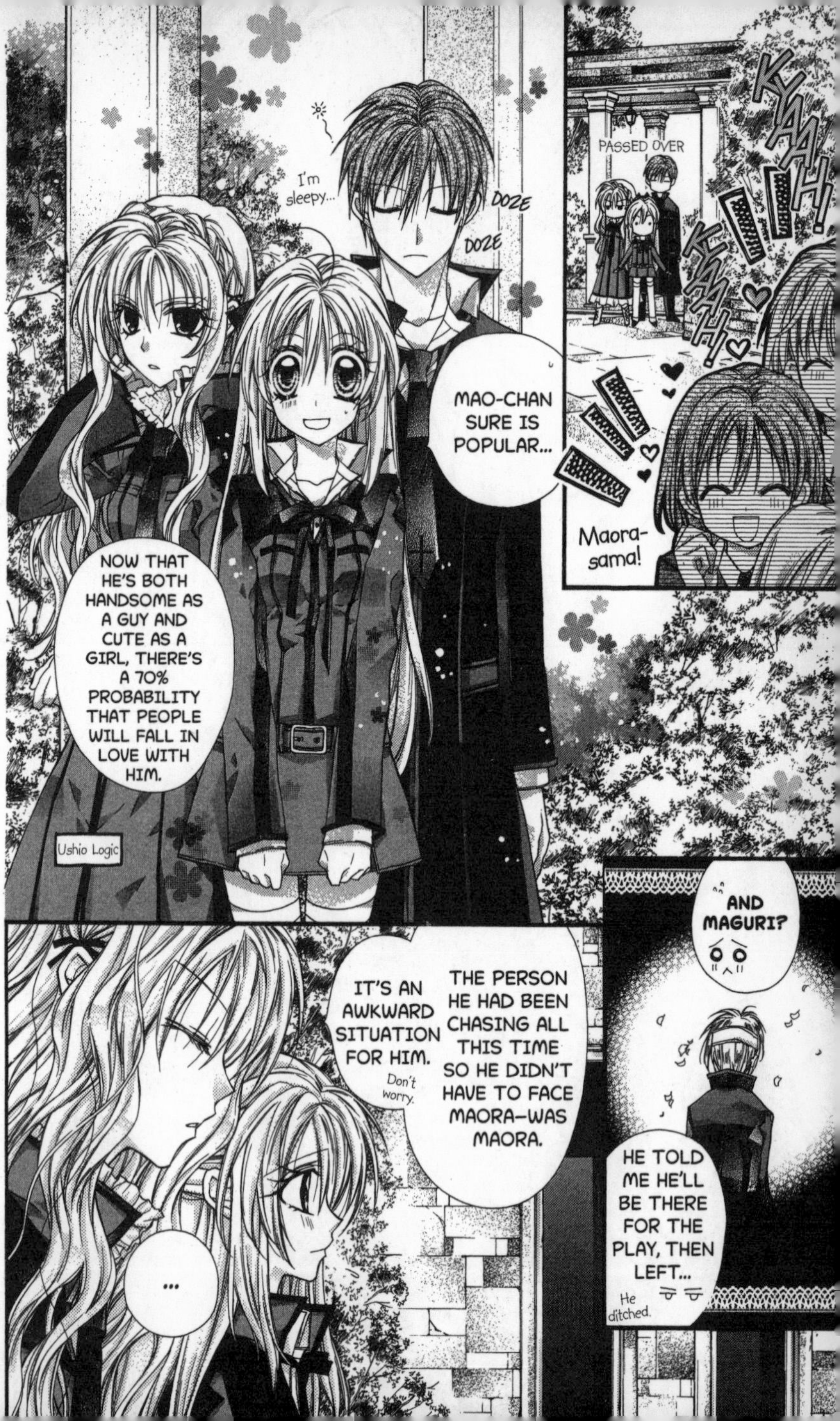
KYAAH!
KYAAH!
PASSED OVER
Maora-sama!
I'm sleepy...
DOZE
DOZE
MAO-CHAN SURE IS POPULAR...
NOW THAT HE'S BOTH HANDSOME AS A GUY AND CUTE AS A GIRL, THERE'S A 70% PROBABILITY THAT PEOPLE WILL FALL IN LOVE WITH HIM.
Ushio Logic
AND MAGURI?
HE TOLD ME HE'LL BE THERE FOR THE PLAY, THEN LEFT...
He ditched.
THE PERSON HE HAD BEEN CHASING ALL THIS TIME SO HE DIDN'T HAVE TO FACE MAORA—WAS MAORA.
IT'S AN AWKWARD SITUATION FOR HIM.
Don't worry.
...

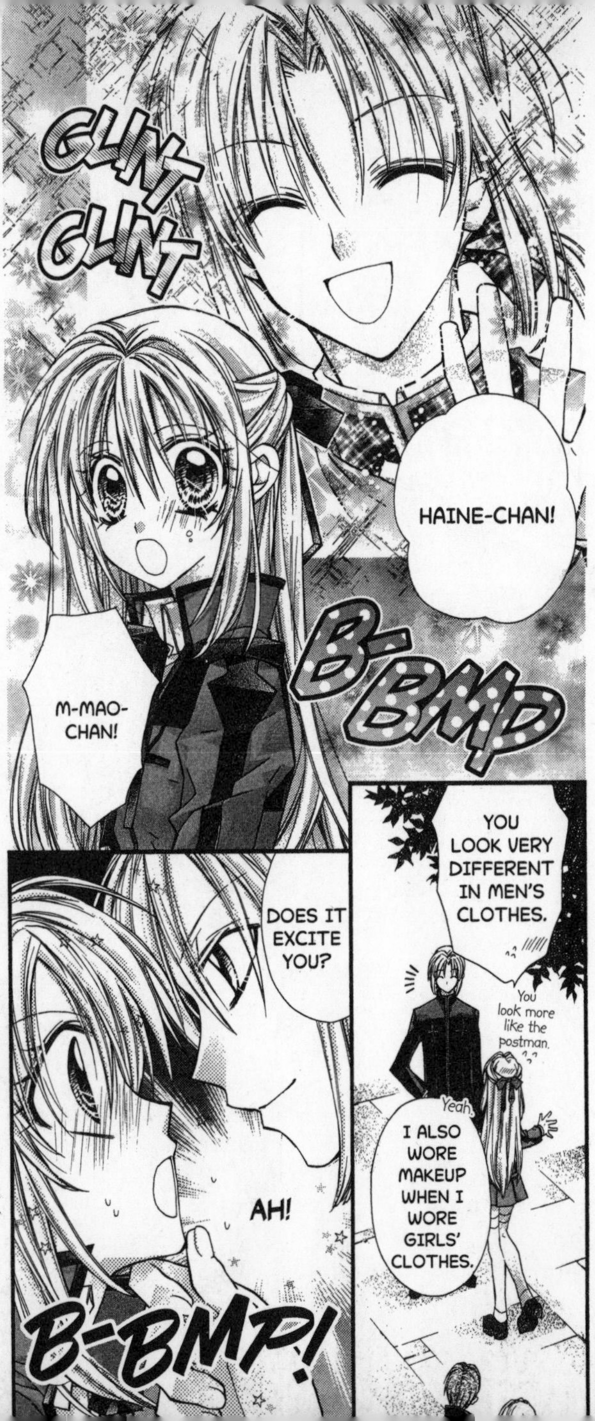
GLINT GLINT
HAINE-CHAN!
B-BMP
M-MAO-CHAN!
YOU LOOK VERY DIFFERENT IN MEN'S CLOTHES.
You look more like the postman.
Yeah.
I ALSO WORE MAKEUP WHEN I WORE GIRLS' CLOTHES.
DOES IT EXCITE YOU?
AH!
B-BMP!

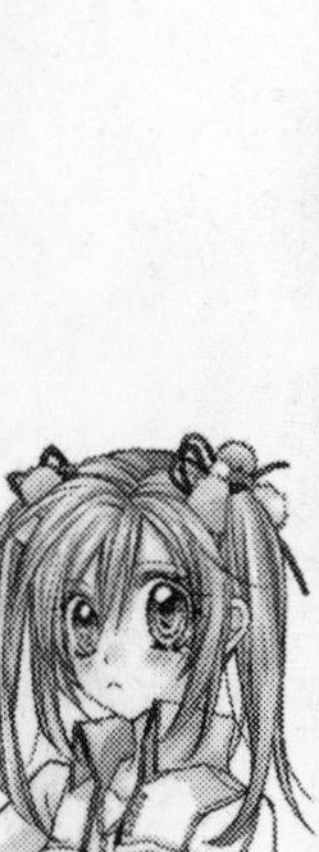

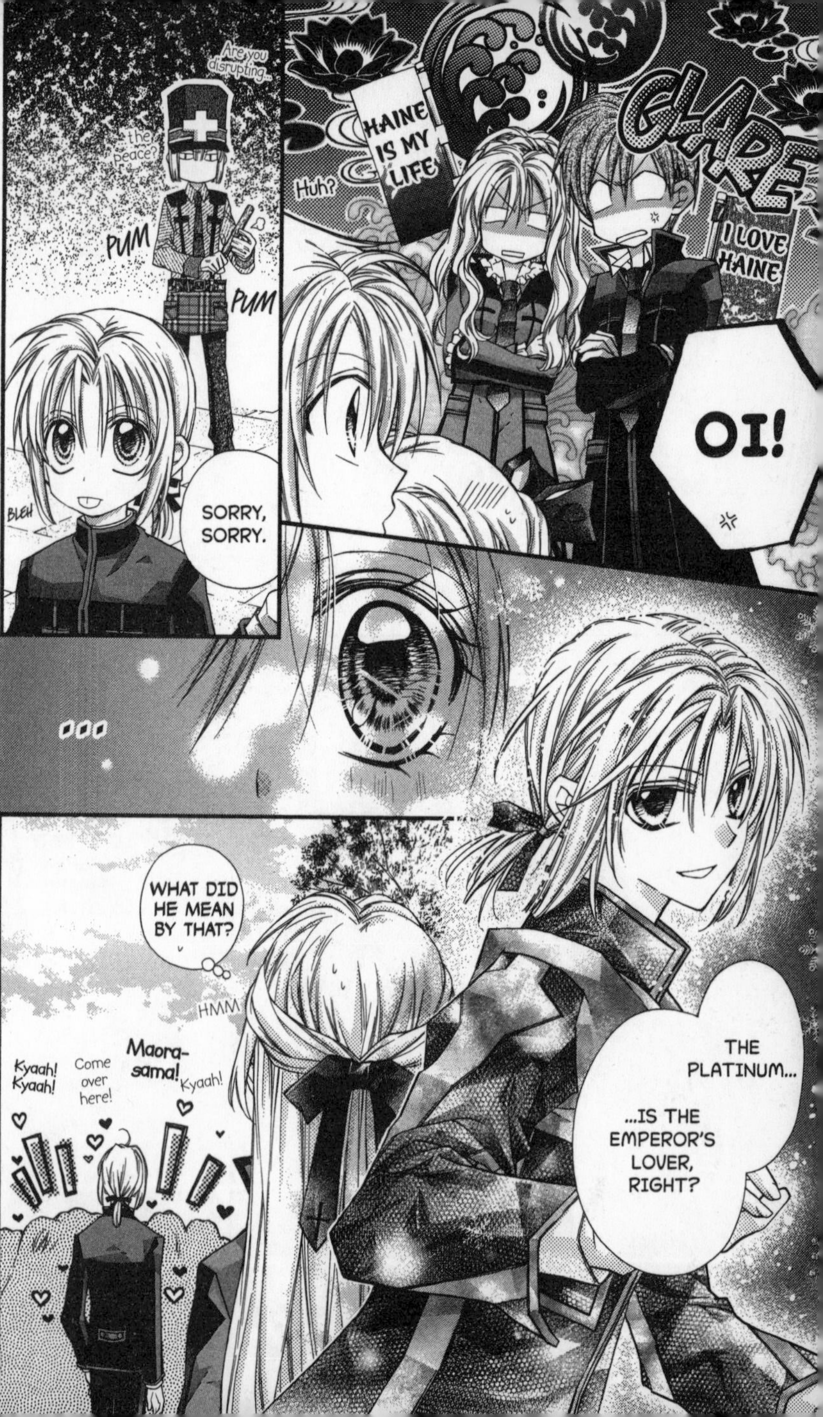
HAINE IS MY LIFE
GLARE
I LOVE HAINE
Huh?
OI!
Are you disrupting...
...the peace?
PUM
PUM
BLEH
SORRY, SORRY.
...
THE PLATINUM...
...IS THE EMPEROR'S LOVER, RIGHT?
WHAT DID HE MEAN BY THAT?
HMM
Maora-sama!
Kyaah!
Come over here!
Kyaah! Kyaah!

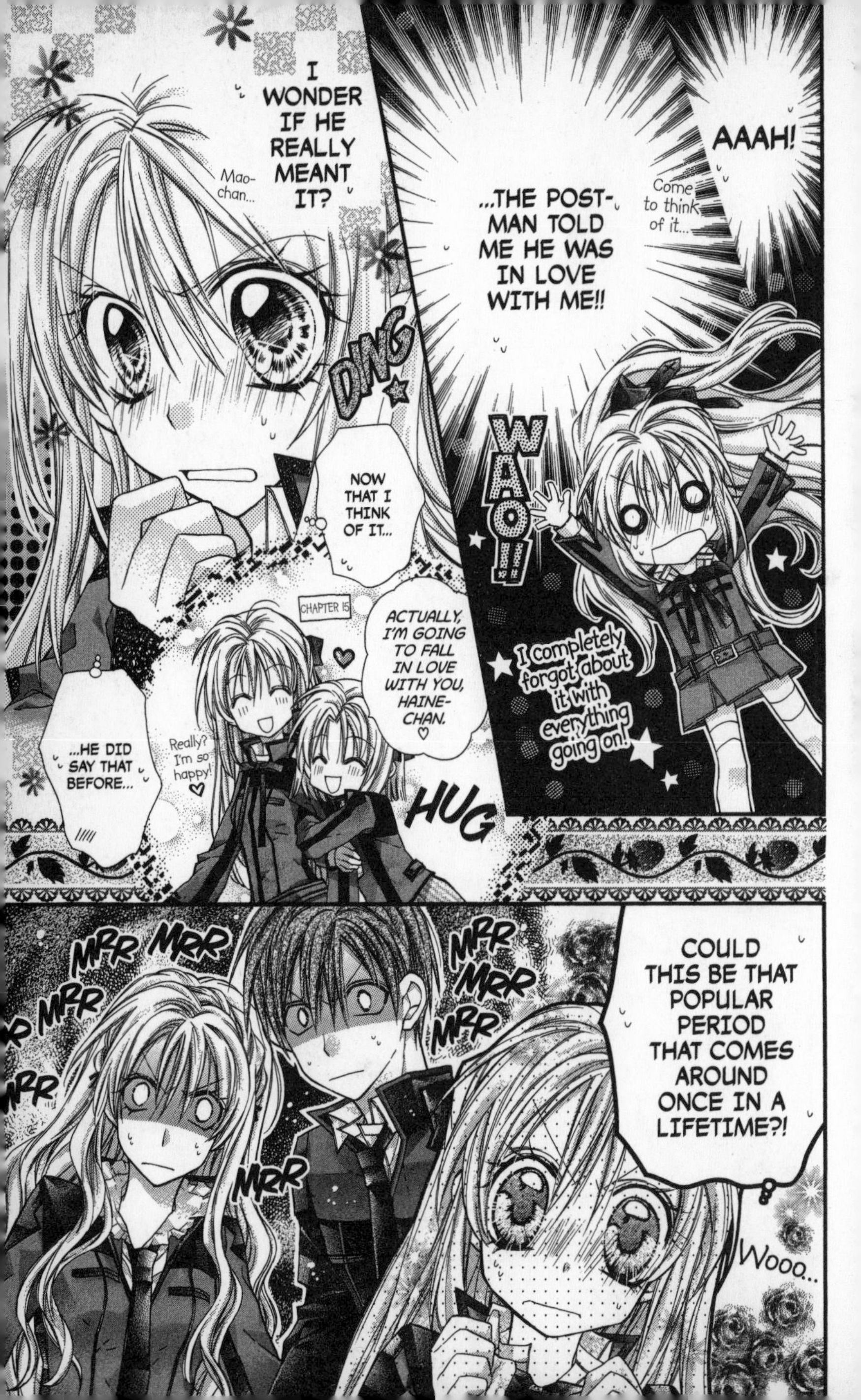
AAAH!
Come to think of it...
...THE POST-MAN TOLD ME HE WAS IN LOVE WITH ME!!
WAO!!
I completely forgot about it with everything going on!
I WONDER IF HE REALLY MEANT IT?
Mao-chan...
DING
NOW THAT I THINK OF IT...
CHAPTER 15
ACTUALLY, I'M GOING TO FALL IN LOVE WITH YOU, HAINE-CHAN.
Really? I'm so happy!
HUG
...HE DID SAY THAT BEFORE...
COULD THIS BE THAT POPULAR PERIOD THAT COMES AROUND ONCE IN A LIFETIME?!
MRR MRR MRR MRR
MRR MRR MRR MRR MRR MRR
MRR
Wooo...

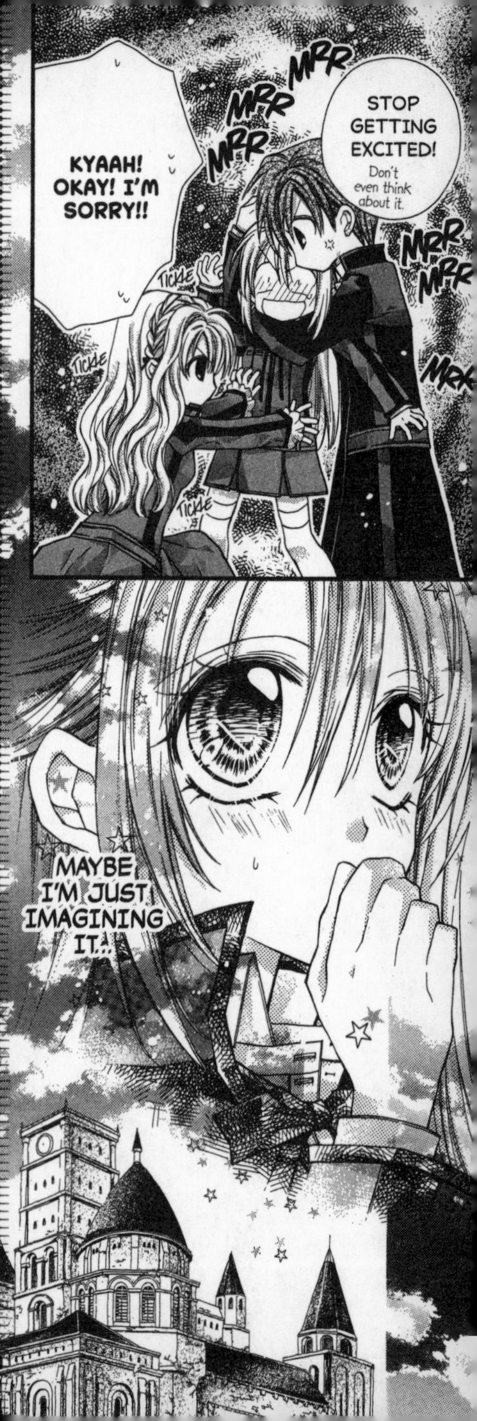
MRR
MRR
MRR
STOP GETTING EXCITED!
Don't even think about it.
KYAAH! OKAY! I'M SORRY!!
MRR
MRR
TICKLE
TICKLE
MRR
TICKLE
MAYBE I'M JUST IMAGINING IT...

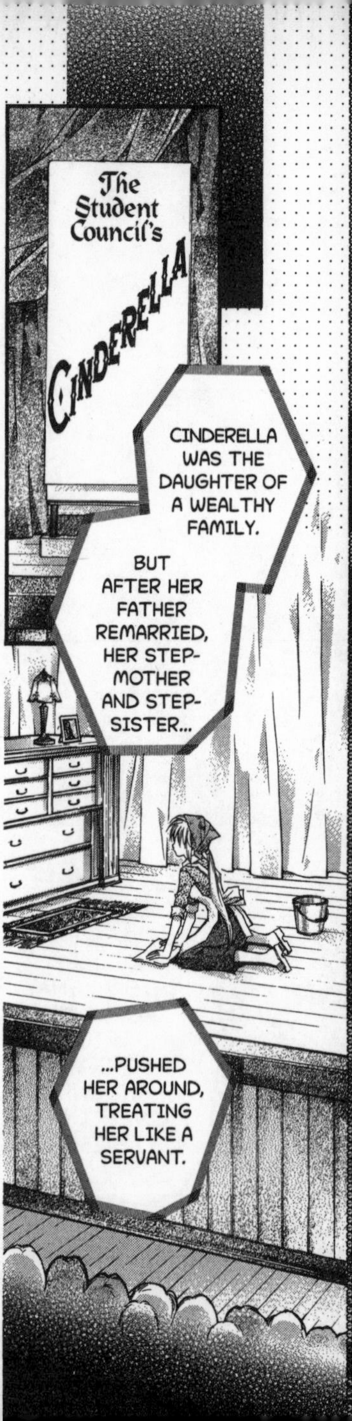
The Student Council's
CINDERELLA
CINDERELLA WAS THE DAUGHTER OF A WEALTHY FAMILY.
BUT AFTER HER FATHER REMARRIED, HER STEP-MOTHER AND STEP-SISTER...
...PUSHED HER AROUND, TREATING HER LIKE A SERVANT.

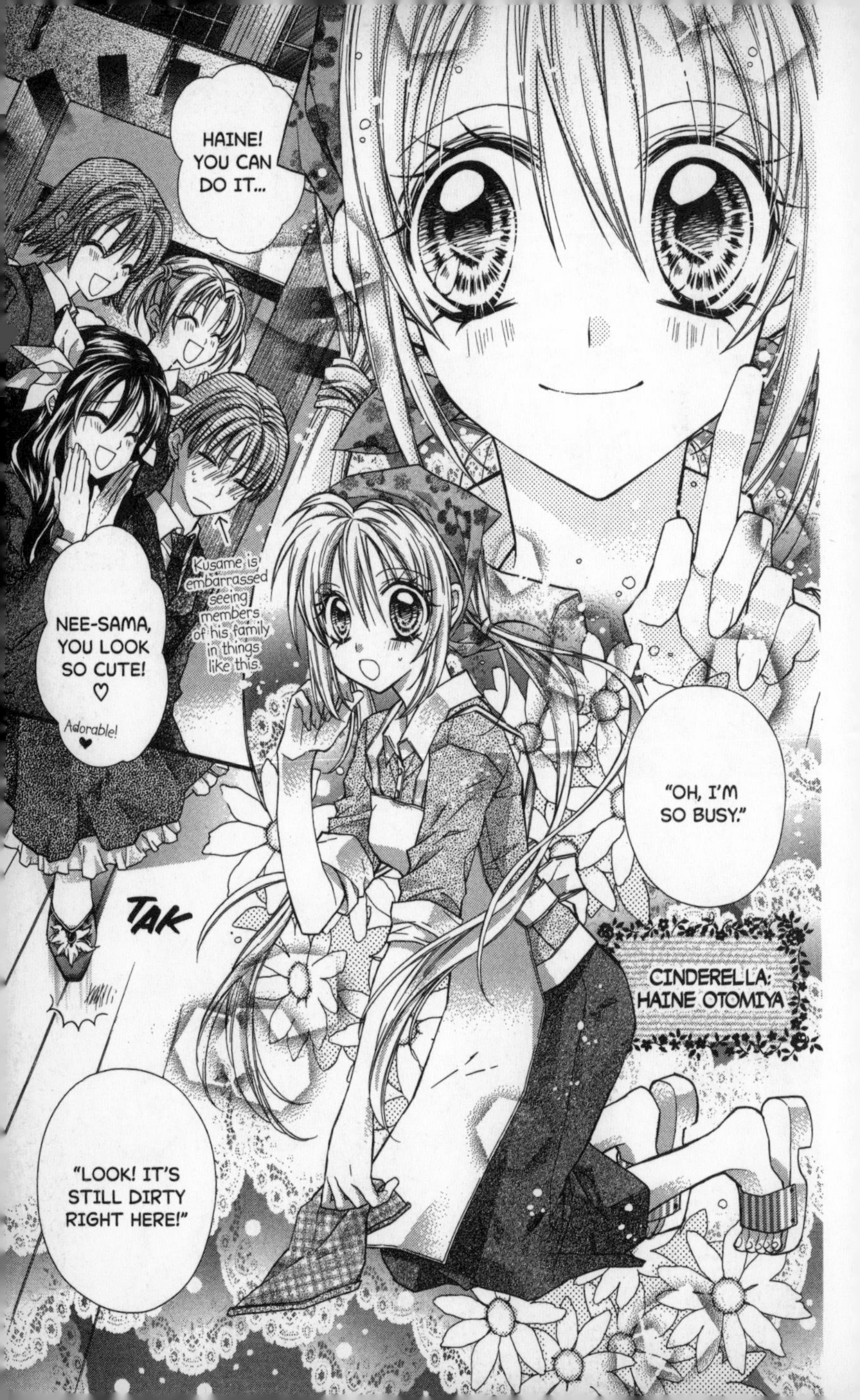
"OH, I'M SO BUSY."
CINDERELLA: HAINE OTOMIYA
HAINE! YOU CAN DO IT...
Kusame is embarrassed seeing members of his family in things like this.
NEE-SAMA, YOU LOOK SO CUTE! ♡
Adorable! ♥
TAK
"LOOK! IT'S STILL DIRTY RIGHT HERE!"

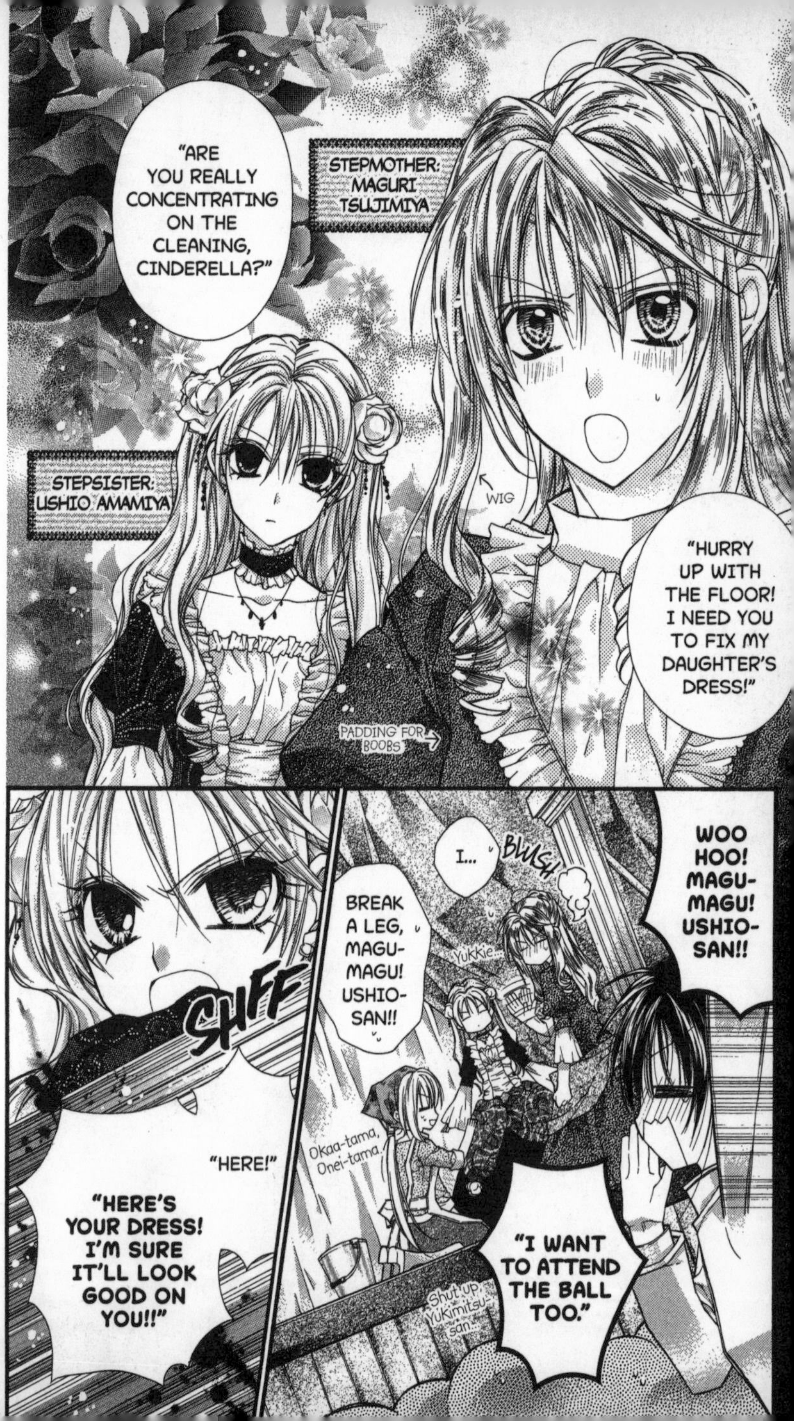
STEPMOTHER: MAGURI TSUJIMIYA
"ARE YOU REALLY CONCENTRATING ON THE CLEANING, CINDERELLA?"
"HURRY UP WITH THE FLOOR! I NEED YOU TO FIX MY DAUGHTER'S DRESS!"
WIG
STEPSISTER: USHIO AMAMIYA
PADDING FOR BOOBS
WOO HOO! MAGU-MAGU! USHIO-SAN!!
I...
BLUSH
BREAK A LEG, MAGU-MAGU! USHIO-SAN!!
Yukkie...
Okaa-tama, Onei-tama.
"I WANT TO ATTEND THE BALL TOO."
Shut up, Yukimitsu-san...
SHFF
"HERE!"
"HERE'S YOUR DRESS! I'M SURE IT'LL LOOK GOOD ON YOU!!"

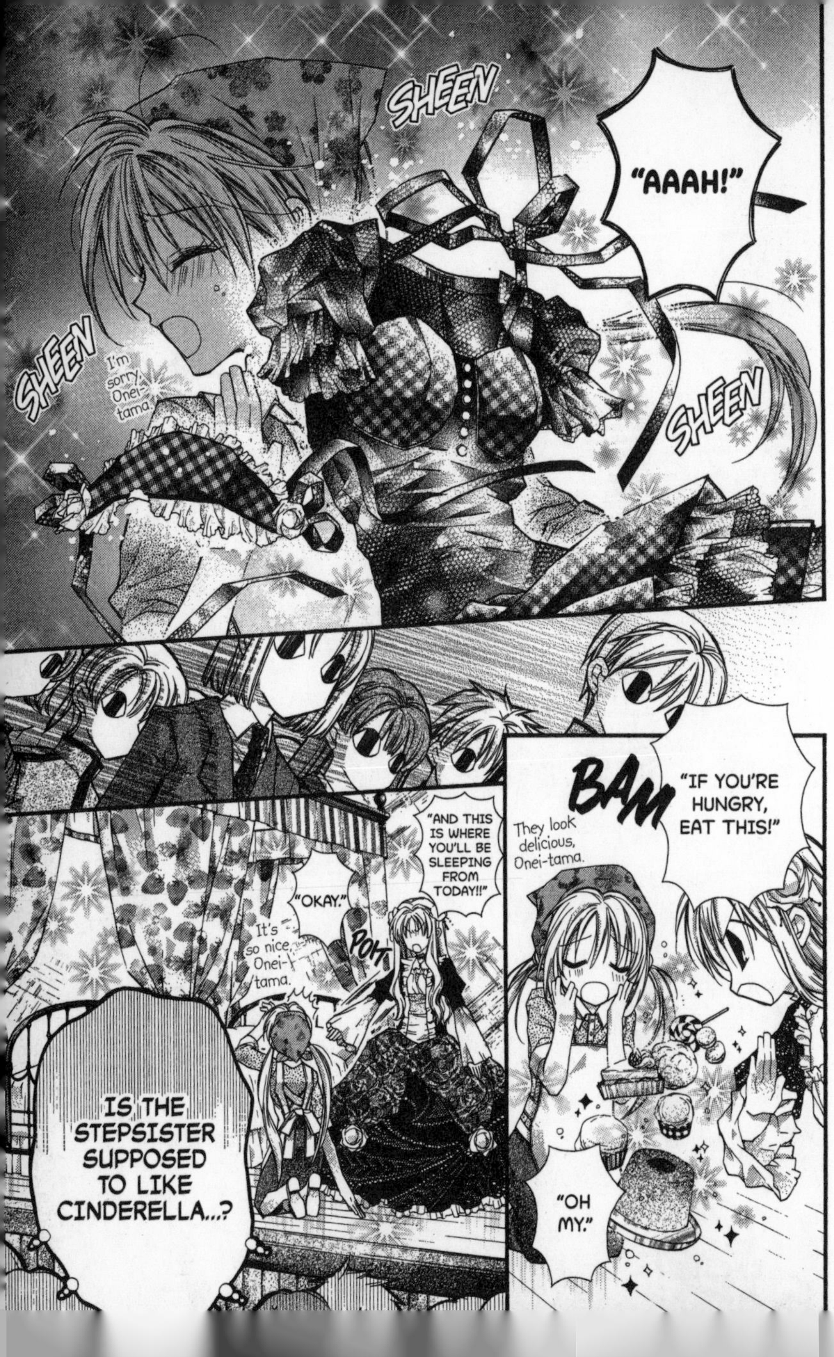
"AAAH!"
SHEEN
SHEEN
SHEEN
I'm sorry, Onei-tama.
BAM
"IF YOU'RE HUNGRY, EAT THIS!"
They look delicious, Onei-tama.
"OH MY."
"AND THIS IS WHERE YOU'LL BE SLEEPING FROM TODAY!!"
"OKAY."
It's so nice, Onei-tama.
IS THE STEPSISTER SUPPOSED TO LIKE CINDERELLA...?

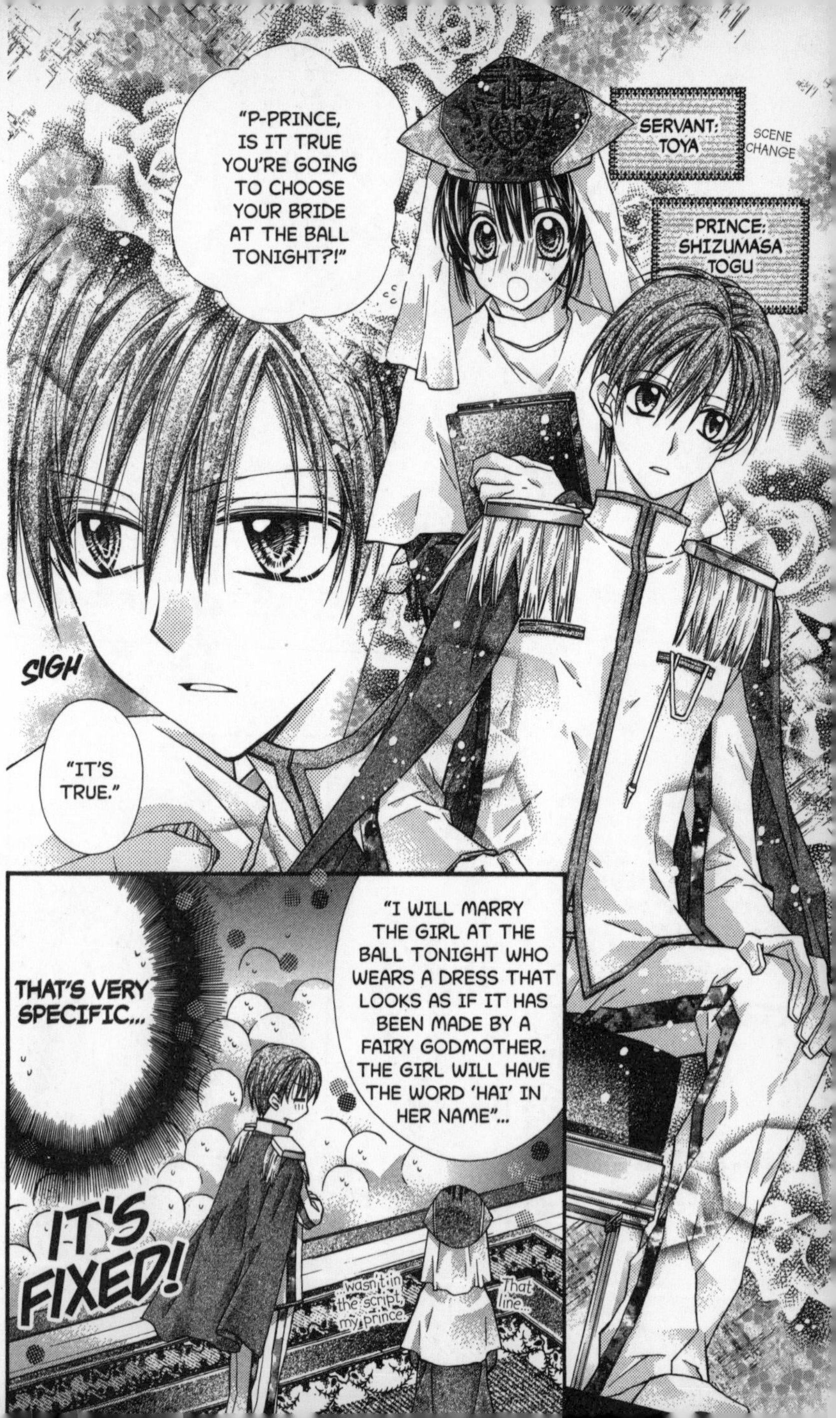
SCENE CHANGE
SERVANT: TOYA
PRINCE: SHIZUMASA TOGU
"P-PRINCE, IS IT TRUE YOU'RE GOING TO CHOOSE YOUR BRIDE AT THE BALL TONIGHT?!"
SIGH
"IT'S TRUE."
"I WILL MARRY THE GIRL AT THE BALL TONIGHT WHO WEARS A DRESS THAT LOOKS AS IF IT HAS BEEN MADE BY A FAIRY GODMOTHER. THE GIRL WILL HAVE THE WORD 'HAI' IN HER NAME"...
That line...
wasn't in the script, my prince.
THAT'S VERY SPECIFIC...
IT'S FIXED!

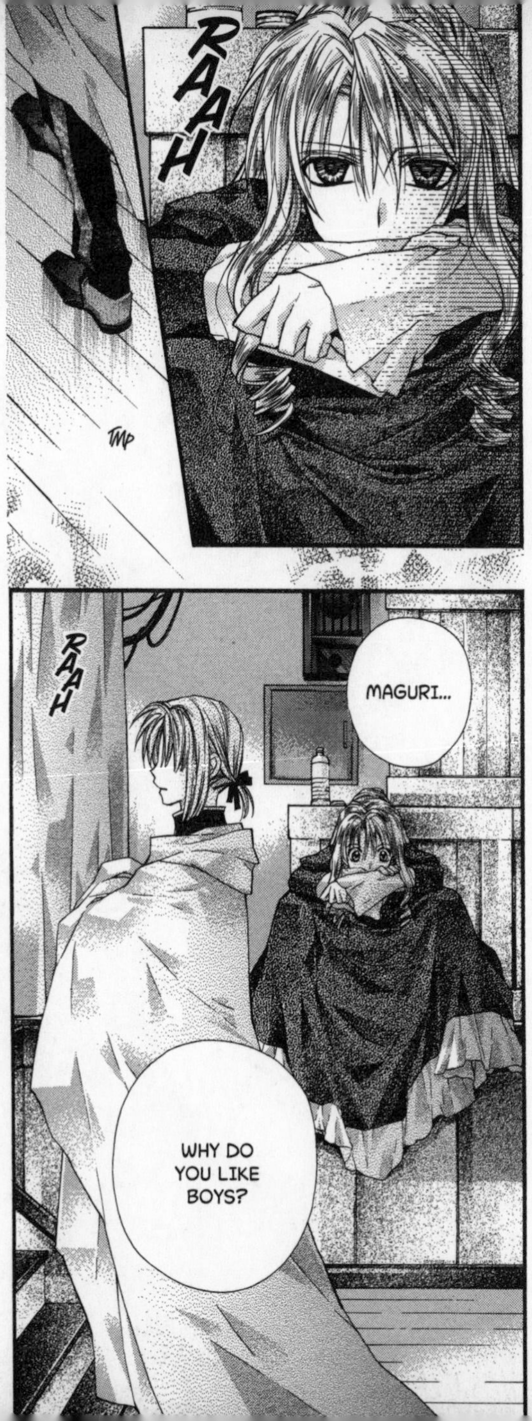
RAAAH
TMP
RAAAH
MAGURI...
WHY DO YOU LIKE BOYS?

More on the Popularity Vote

I placed all character introductions, which I uploaded to my blog, here in the manga.

And I've also added ballots written by the characters!!

I've placed those pages in this manga, so please read them. ♥

I'll place the second half in volume 7. ♥

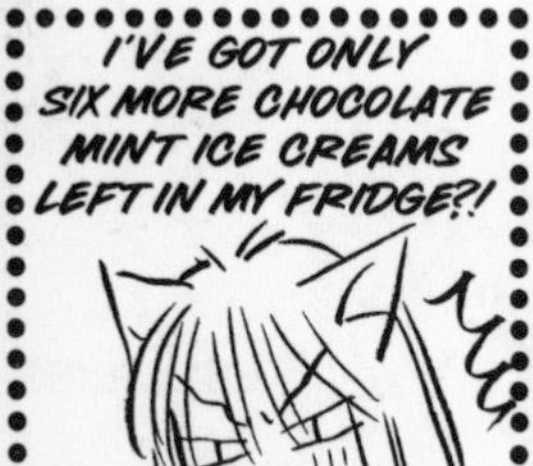
I'VE GOT ONLY SIX MORE CHOCOLATE MINT ICE CREAMS LEFT IN MY FRIDGE?!
MU

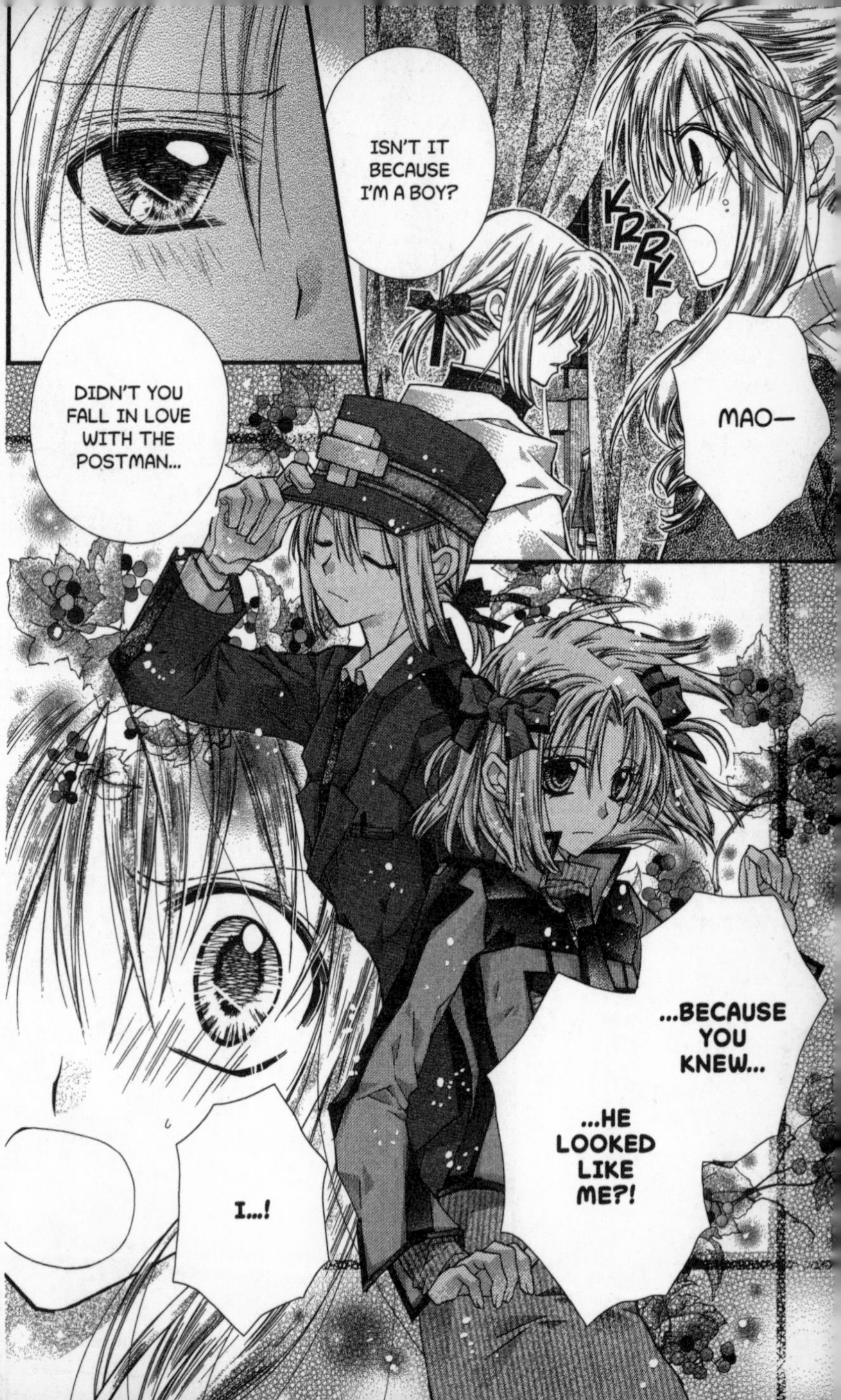
KRRK
MAO—
ISN'T IT BECAUSE I'M A BOY?
DIDN'T YOU FALL IN LOVE WITH THE POSTMAN...
...BECAUSE YOU KNEW...
...HE LOOKED LIKE ME?!
I...!

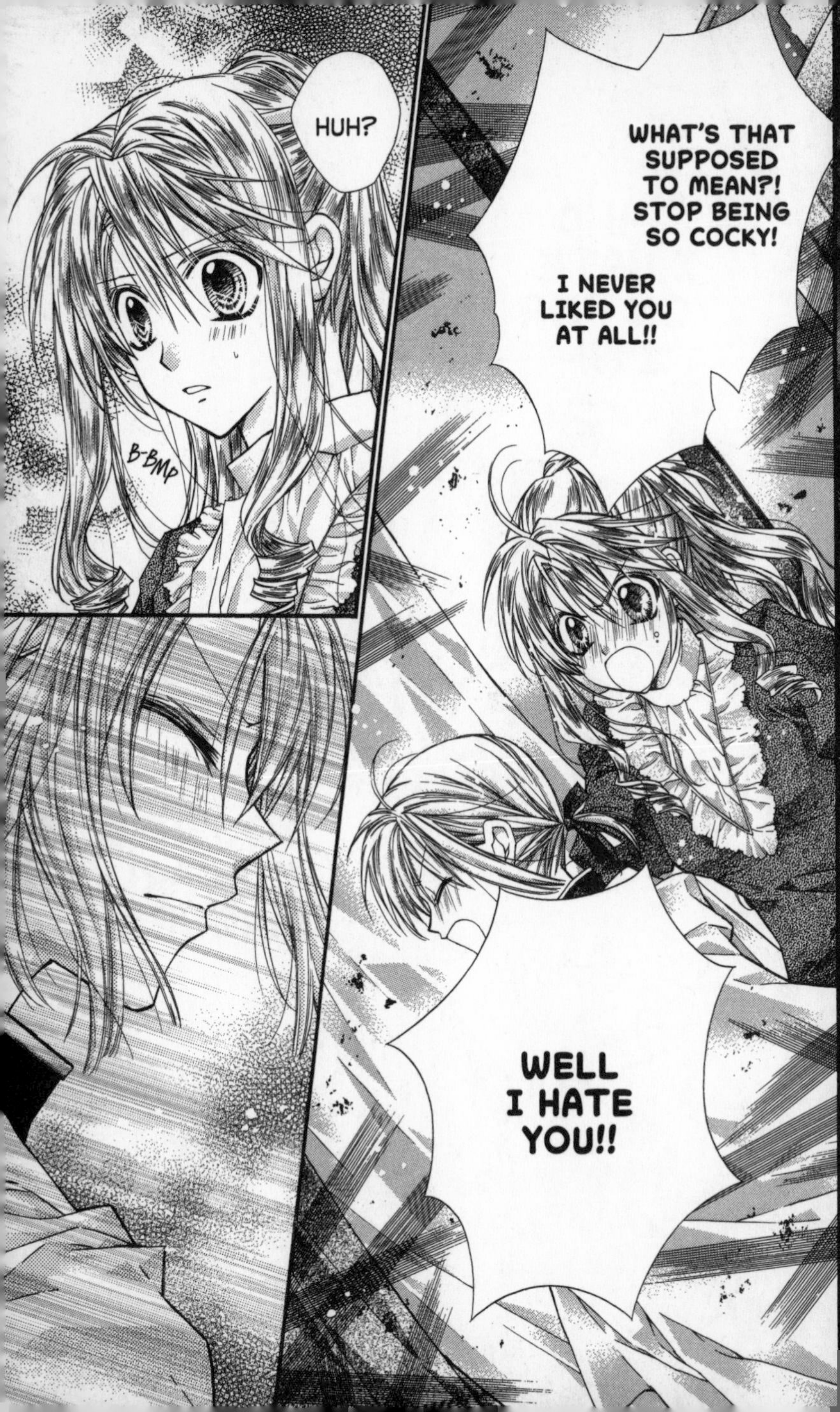
WHAT'S THAT SUPPOSED TO MEAN?! STOP BEING SO COCKY!
I NEVER LIKED YOU AT ALL!!
WELL I HATE YOU!!
HUH?
B-BMP

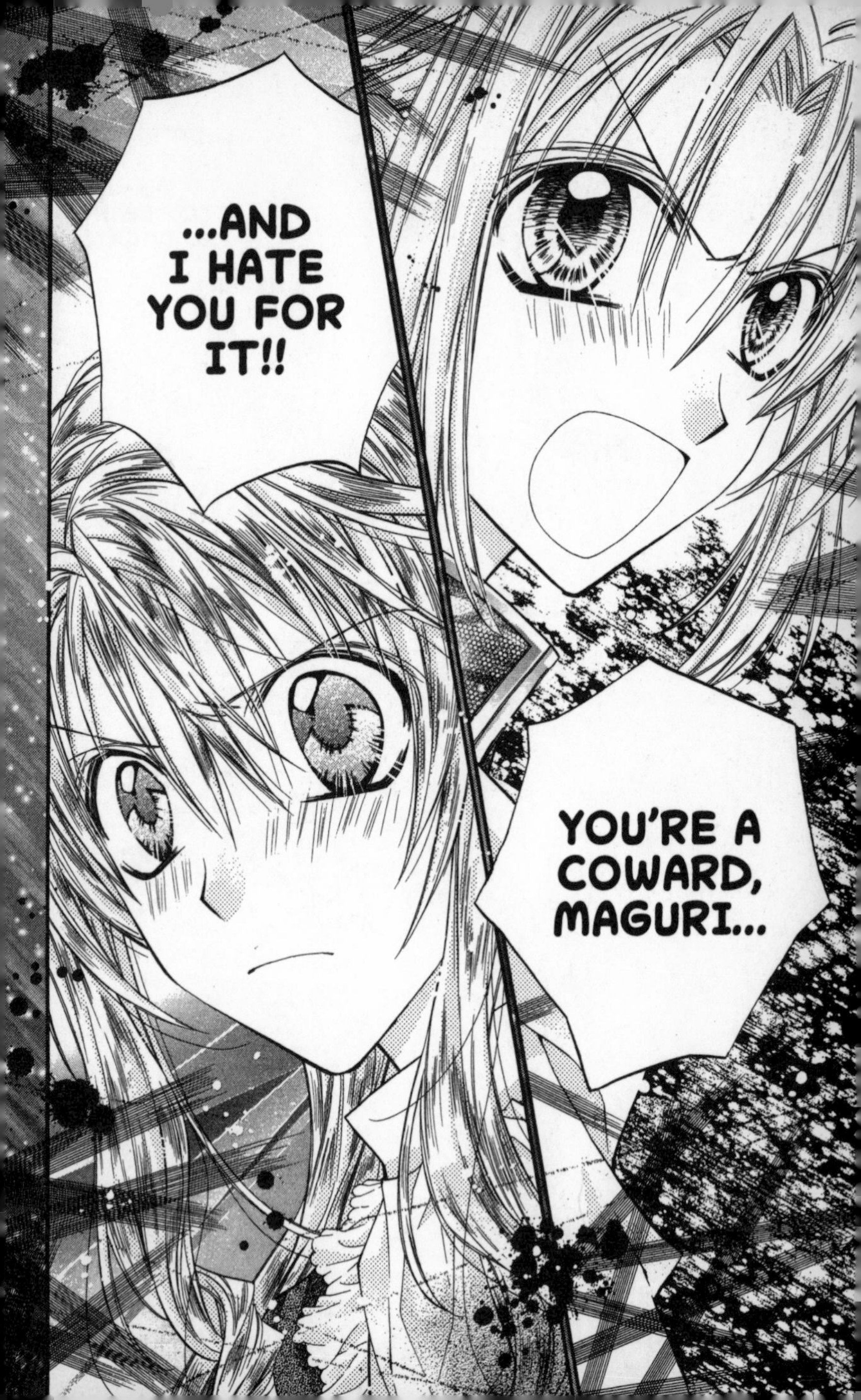
YOU'RE A COWARD, MAGURI...
...AND I HATE YOU FOR IT!!

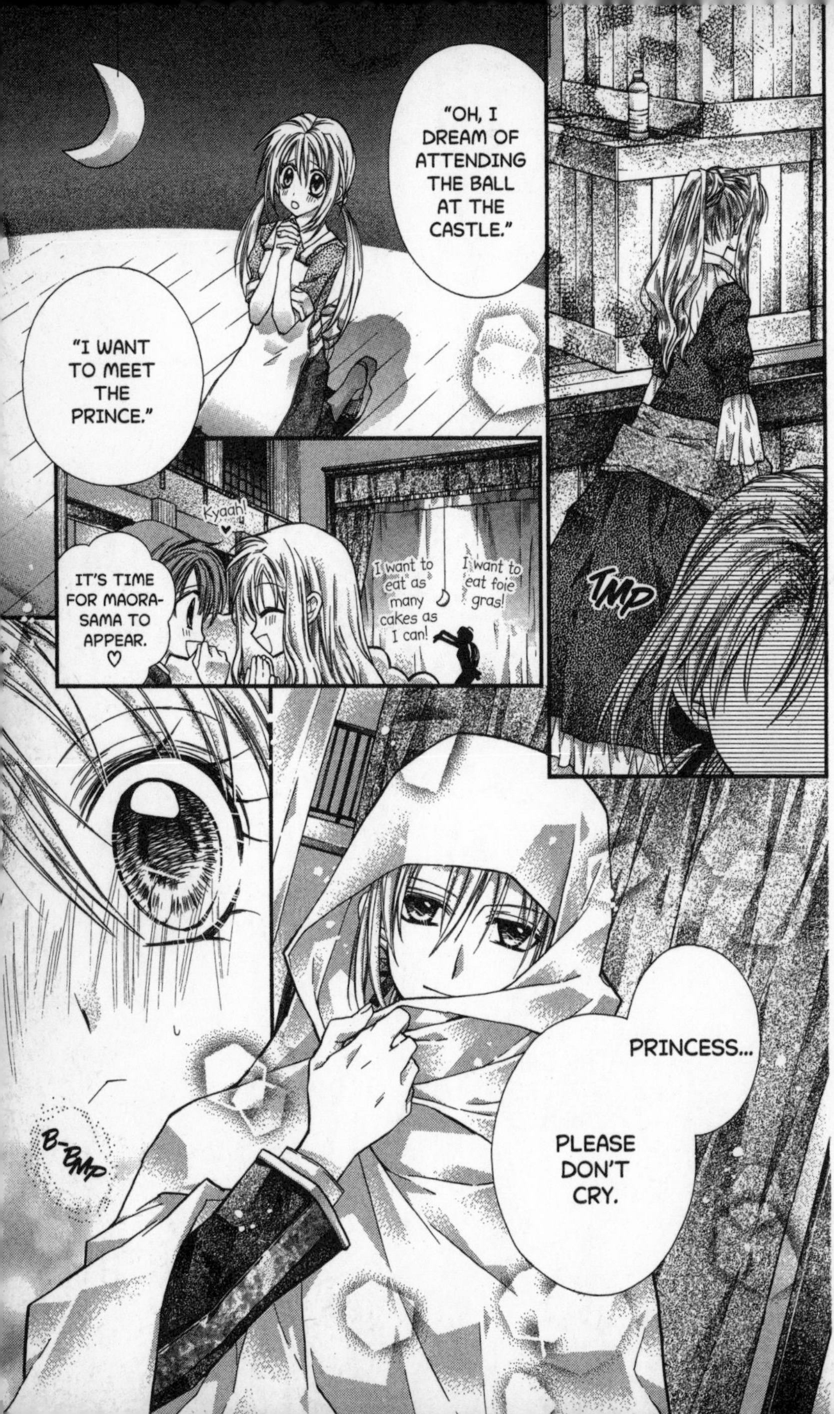
"OH, I DREAM OF ATTENDING THE BALL AT THE CASTLE."
"I WANT TO MEET THE PRINCE."
Kyaah!
IT'S TIME FOR MAORA-SAMA TO APPEAR. ♡
I want to eat foie gras!
I want to eat as many cakes as I can!
TMP
PRINCESS...
PLEASE DON'T CRY.
B-BMP

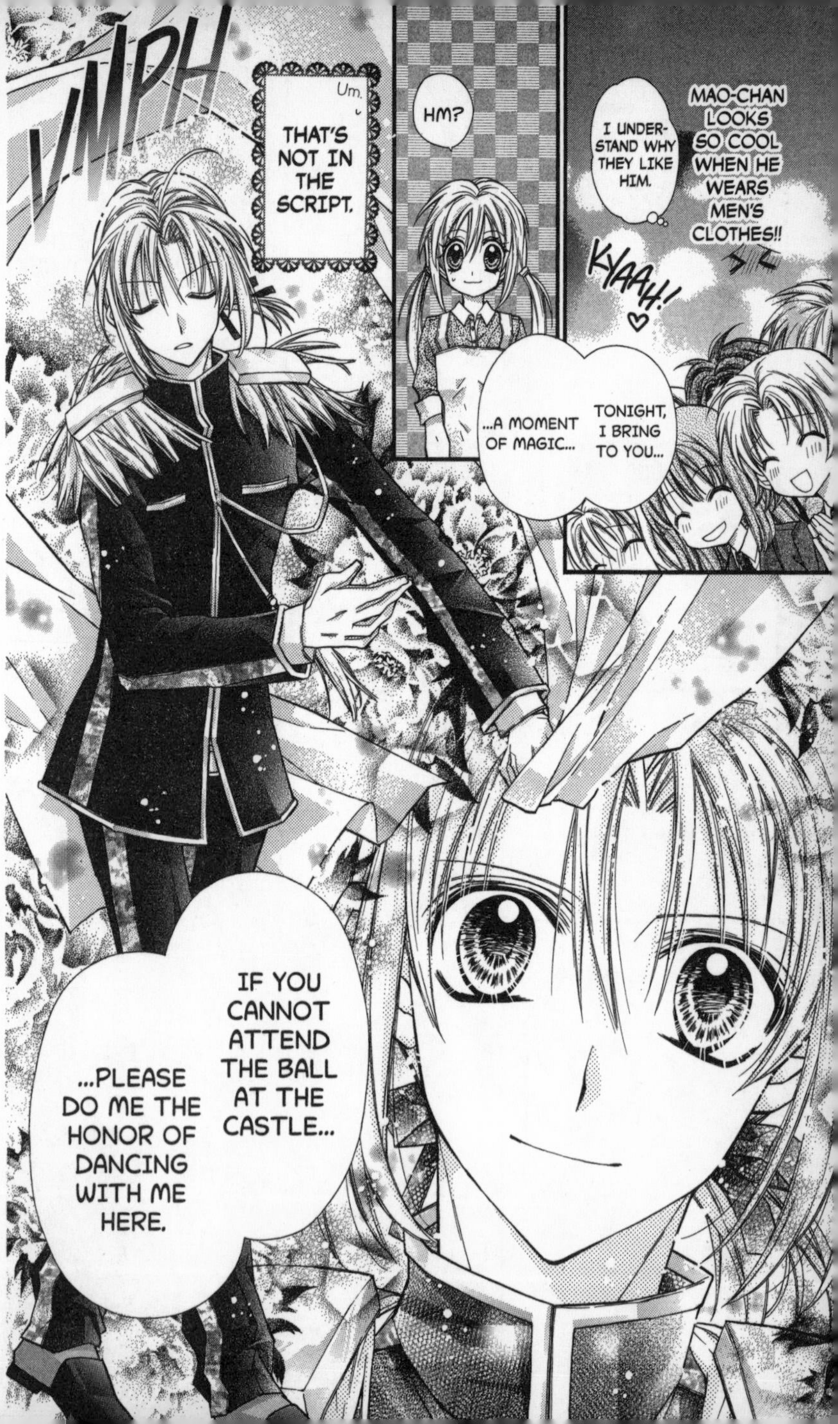

MAO-CHAN LOOKS SO COOL WHEN HE WEARS MEN'S CLOTHES!!
KYAAH!!
I UNDERSTAND WHY THEY LIKE HIM.
HM?
Um.
THAT'S NOT IN THE SCRIPT.
VMPH
TONIGHT, I BRING TO YOU...
...A MOMENT OF MAGIC...
IF YOU CANNOT ATTEND THE BALL AT THE CASTLE...
...PLEASE DO ME THE HONOR OF DANCING WITH ME HERE.

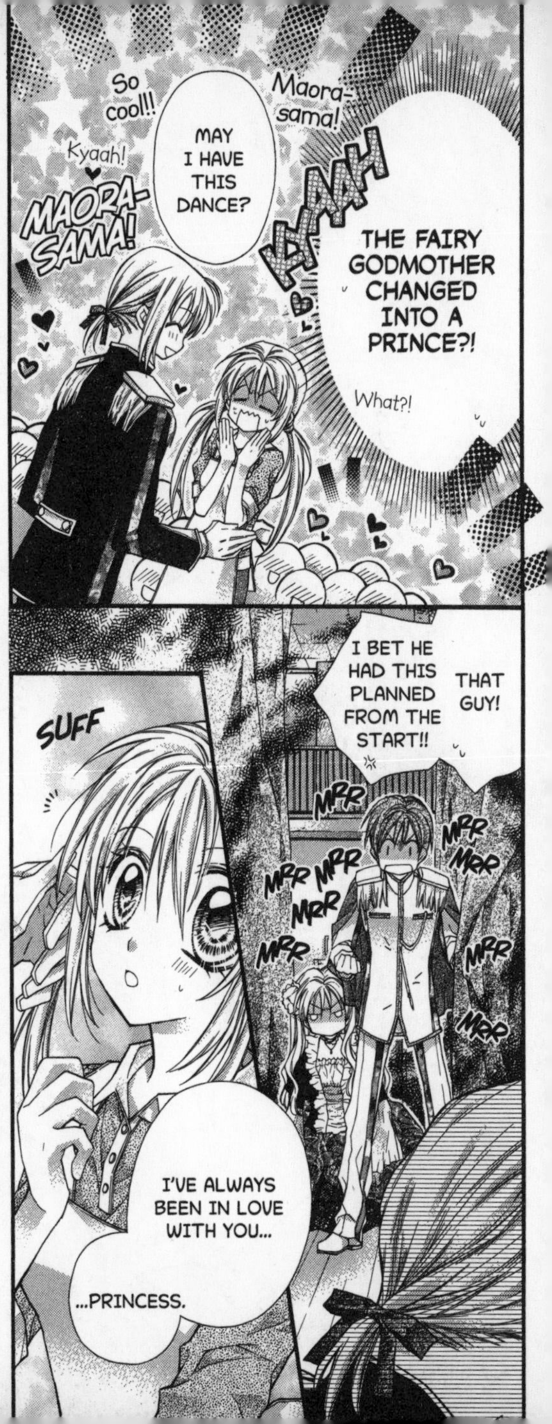
THE FAIRY GODMOTHER CHANGED INTO A PRINCE?!
What?!
KYAAH
Maora-sama!
MAY I HAVE THIS DANCE?
So cool!!
Kyaah!
MAORA-SAMA!
THAT GUY!
I BET HE HAD THIS PLANNED FROM THE START!!
MRR MRR MRR MRR MRR MRR MRR MRR
SUFF
I'VE ALWAYS BEEN IN LOVE WITH YOU...
...PRINCESS.

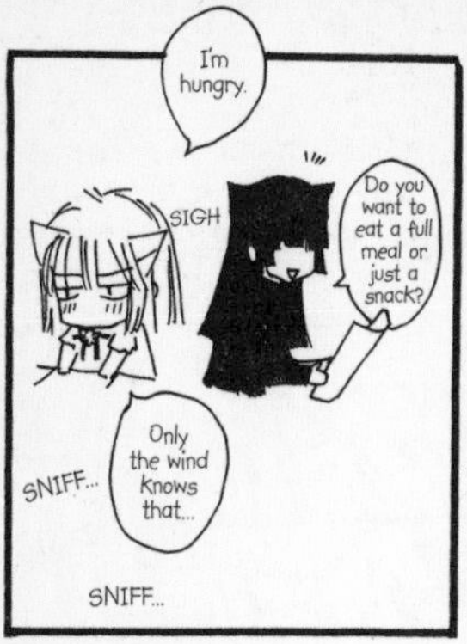
I'm hungry.
Do you want to eat a full meal or just a snack?
SIGH
Only the wind knows that...
SNIFF...
SNIFF...

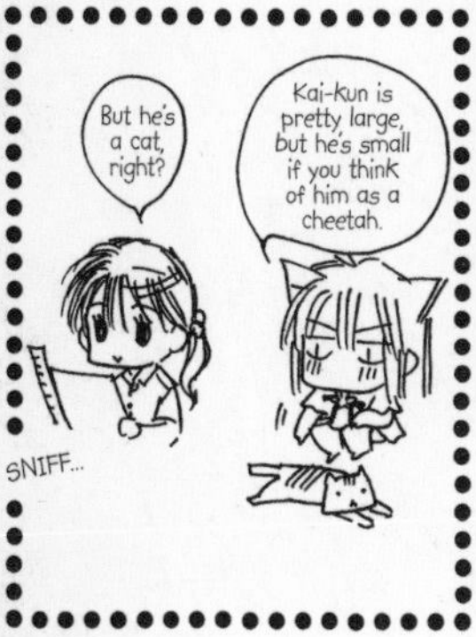
Kai-kun is pretty large, but he's small if you think of him as a cheetah.
But he's a cat, right?
SNIFF...

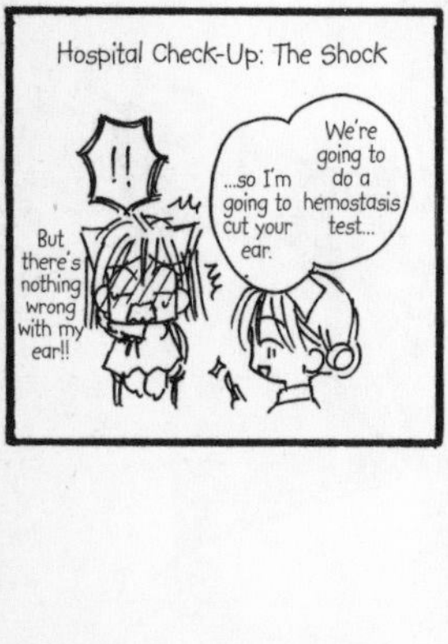
Hospital Check-Up: The Shock
We're going to do a hemostasis test...
...so I'm going to cut your ear.
!!
But there's nothing wrong with my ear!!

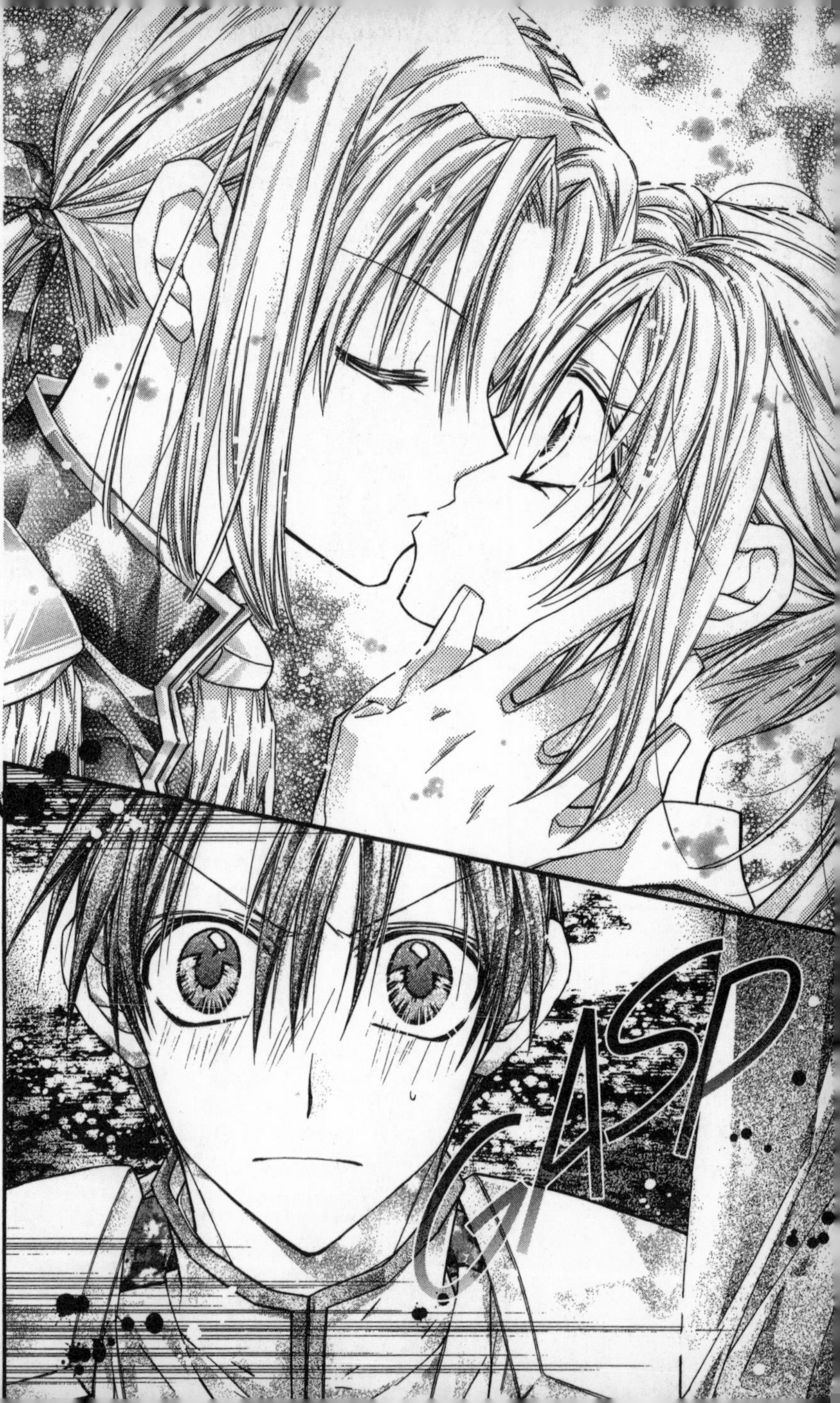
GASP

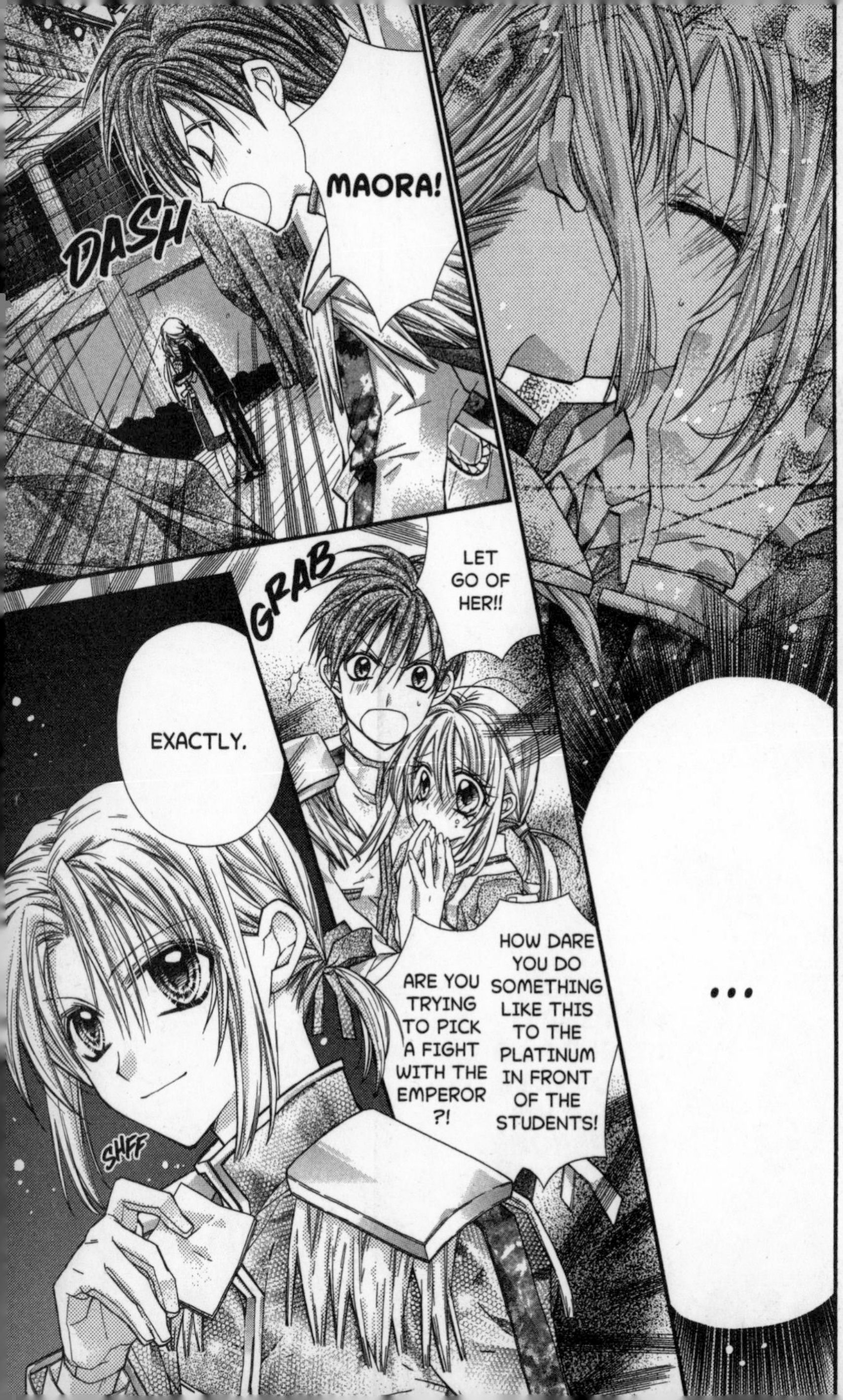
...
MAORA!
DASH
GRAB
LET GO OF HER!!
HOW DARE YOU DO SOMETHING LIKE THIS TO THE PLATINUM IN FRONT OF THE STUDENTS!
ARE YOU TRYING TO PICK A FIGHT WITH THE EMPEROR ?!
EXACTLY.
SHFF

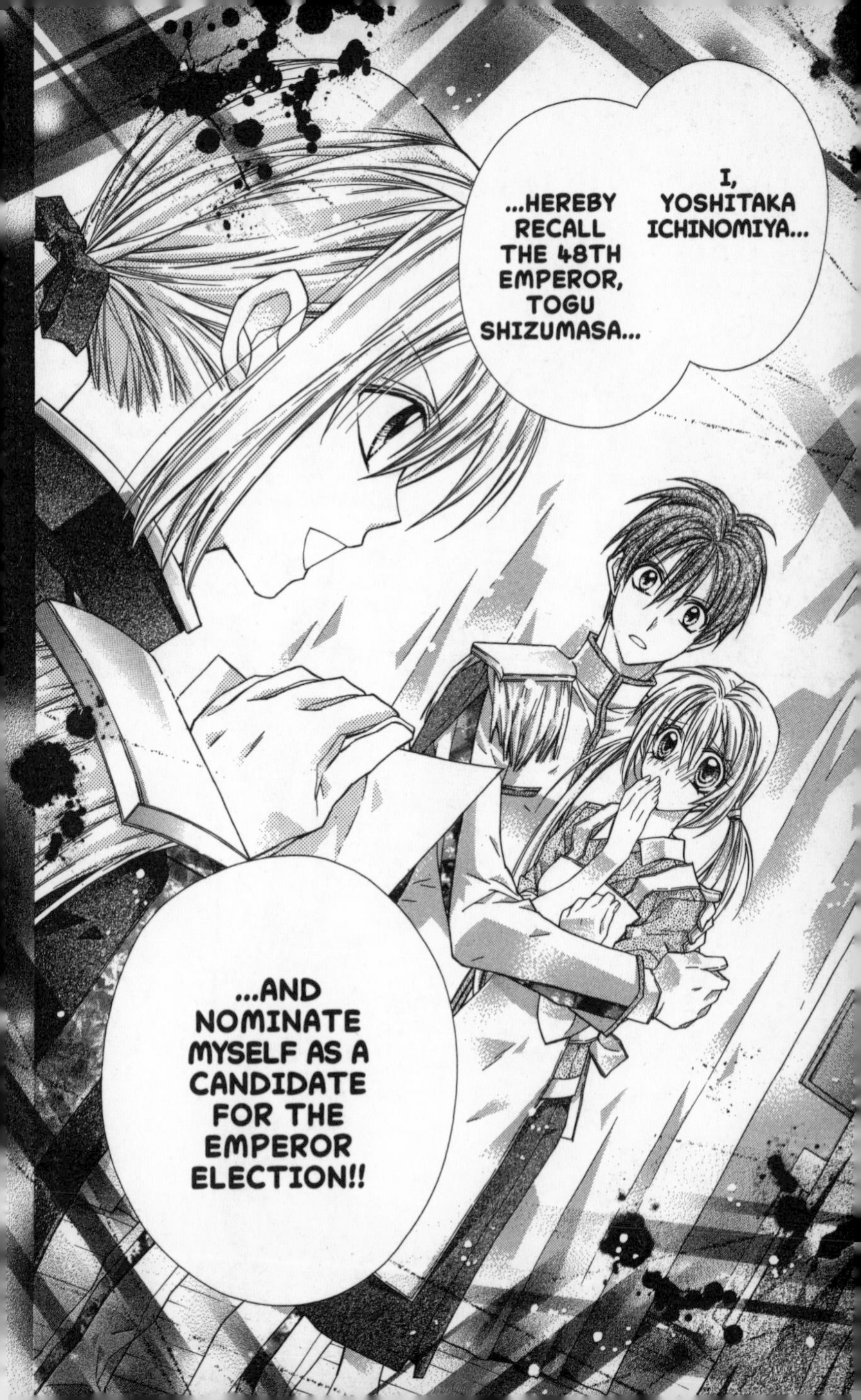
I, YOSHITAKA ICHINOMIYA...
...HEREBY RECALL THE 48TH EMPEROR, TOGU SHIZUMASA...
...AND NOMINATE MYSELF AS A CANDIDATE FOR THE EMPEROR ELECTION!!

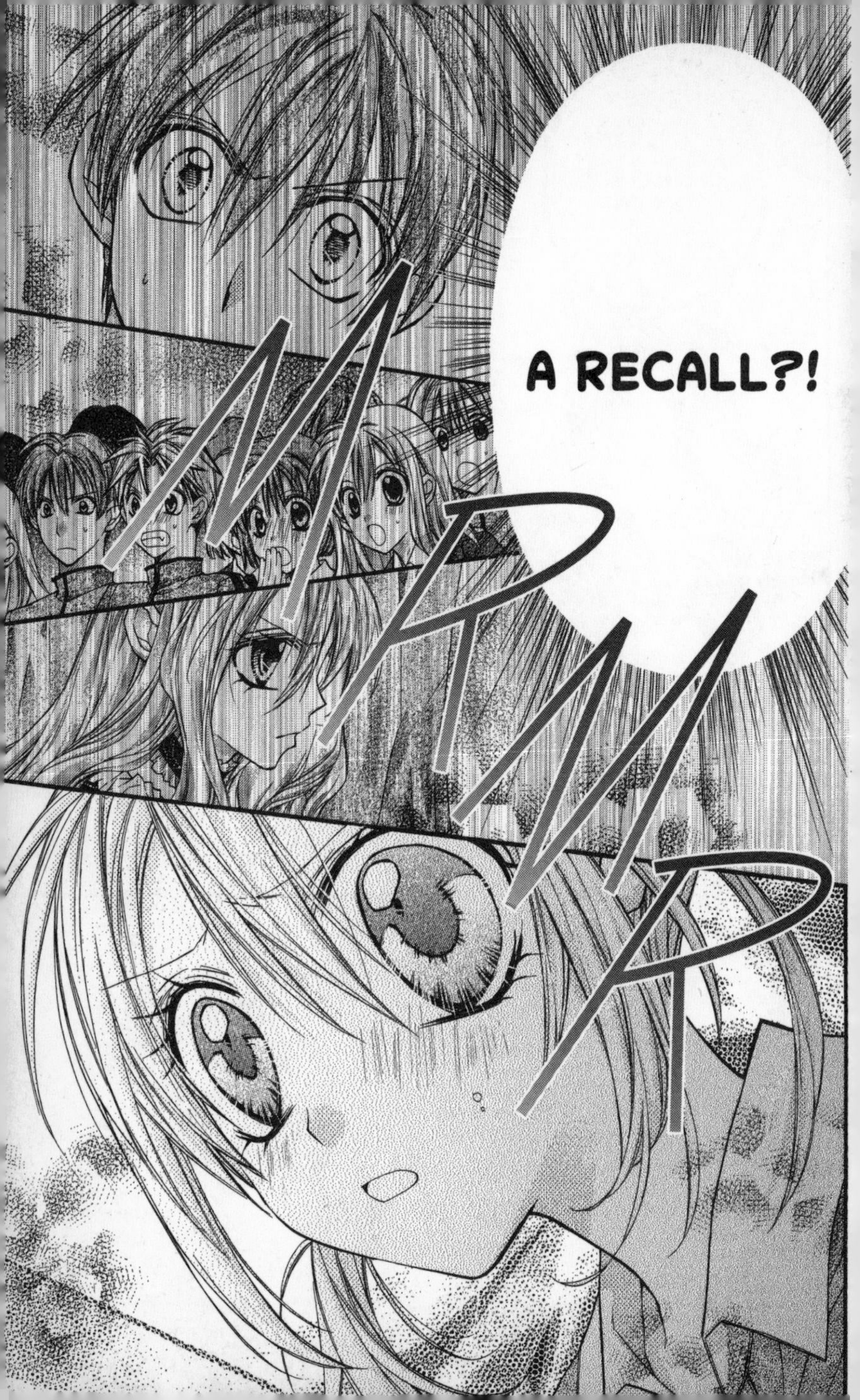
A RECALL?!

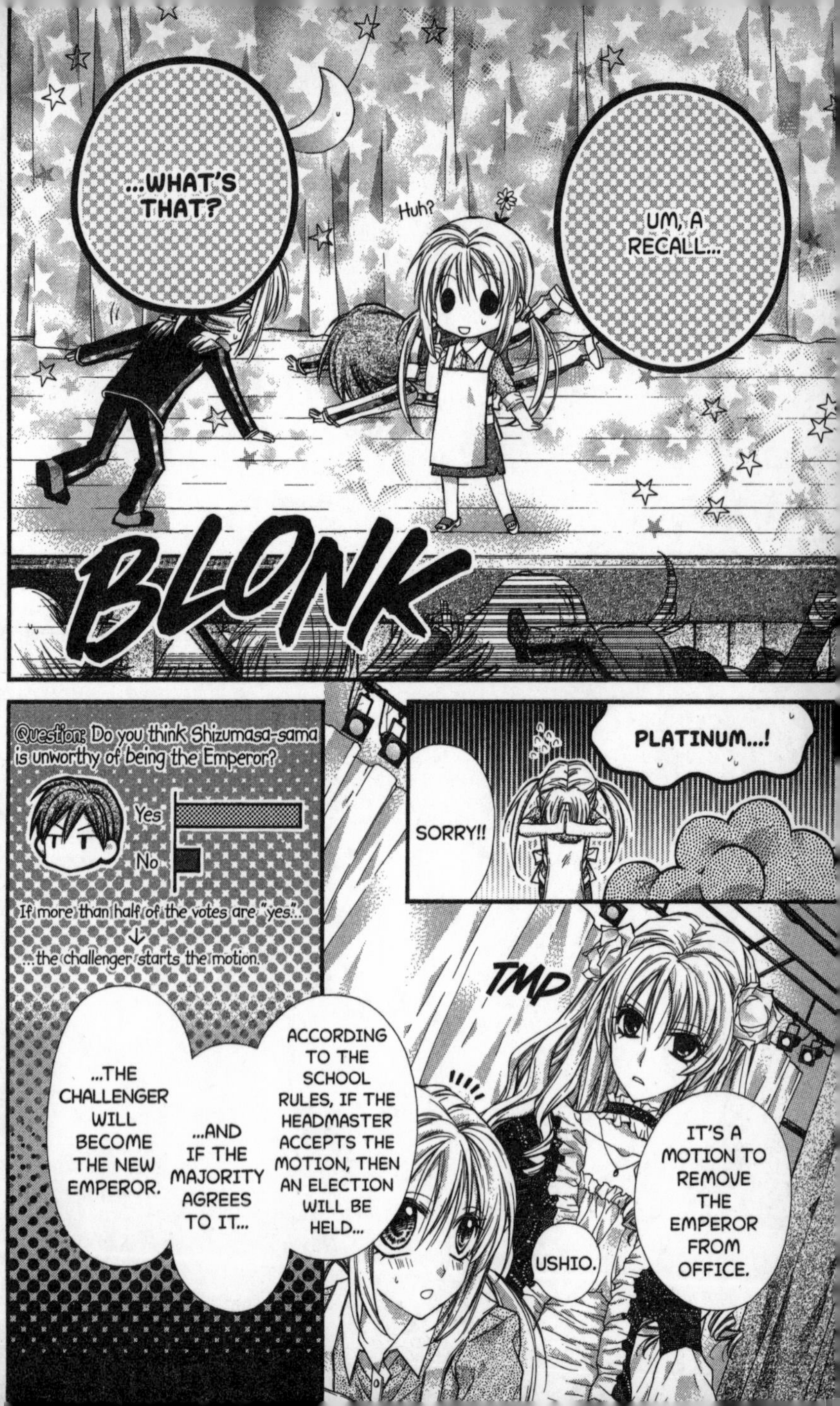

...WHAT'S THAT?
Huh?
UM, A RECALL...
BLONK
PLATINUM...!
SORRY!!
TMP
USHIO.
IT'S A MOTION TO REMOVE THE EMPEROR FROM OFFICE.
ACCORDING TO THE SCHOOL RULES, IF THE HEADMASTER ACCEPTS THE MOTION, THEN AN ELECTION WILL BE HELD...
...AND IF THE MAJORITY AGREES TO IT...
...THE CHALLENGER WILL BECOME THE NEW EMPEROR.
Question: Do you think Shizumasa-sama is unworthy of being the Emperor?
Yes
No
If more than half of the votes are "yes"...
...the challenger starts the motion.

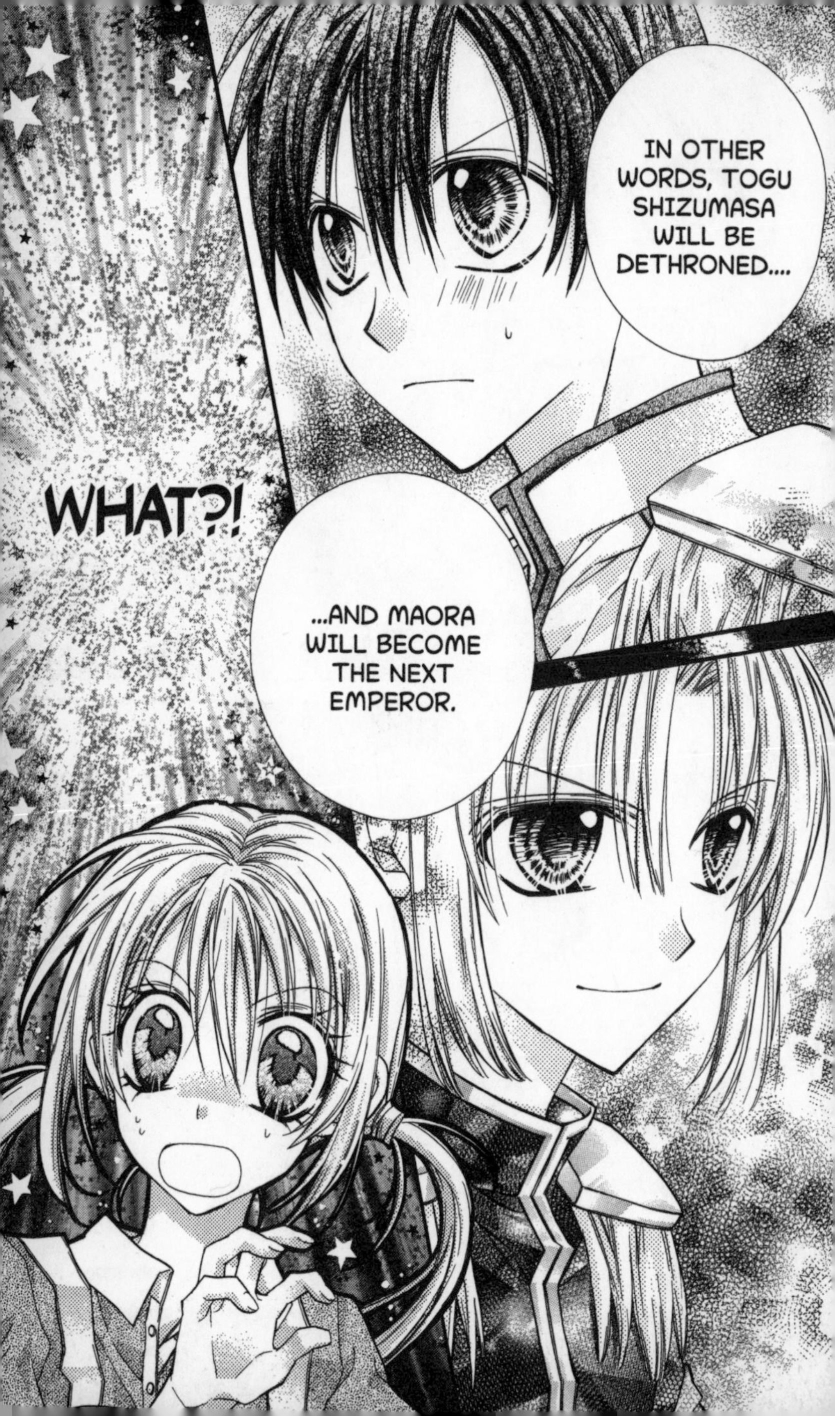
IN OTHER WORDS, TOGU SHIZUMASA WILL BE DETHRONED....
...AND MAORA WILL BECOME THE NEXT EMPEROR.
WHAT?!

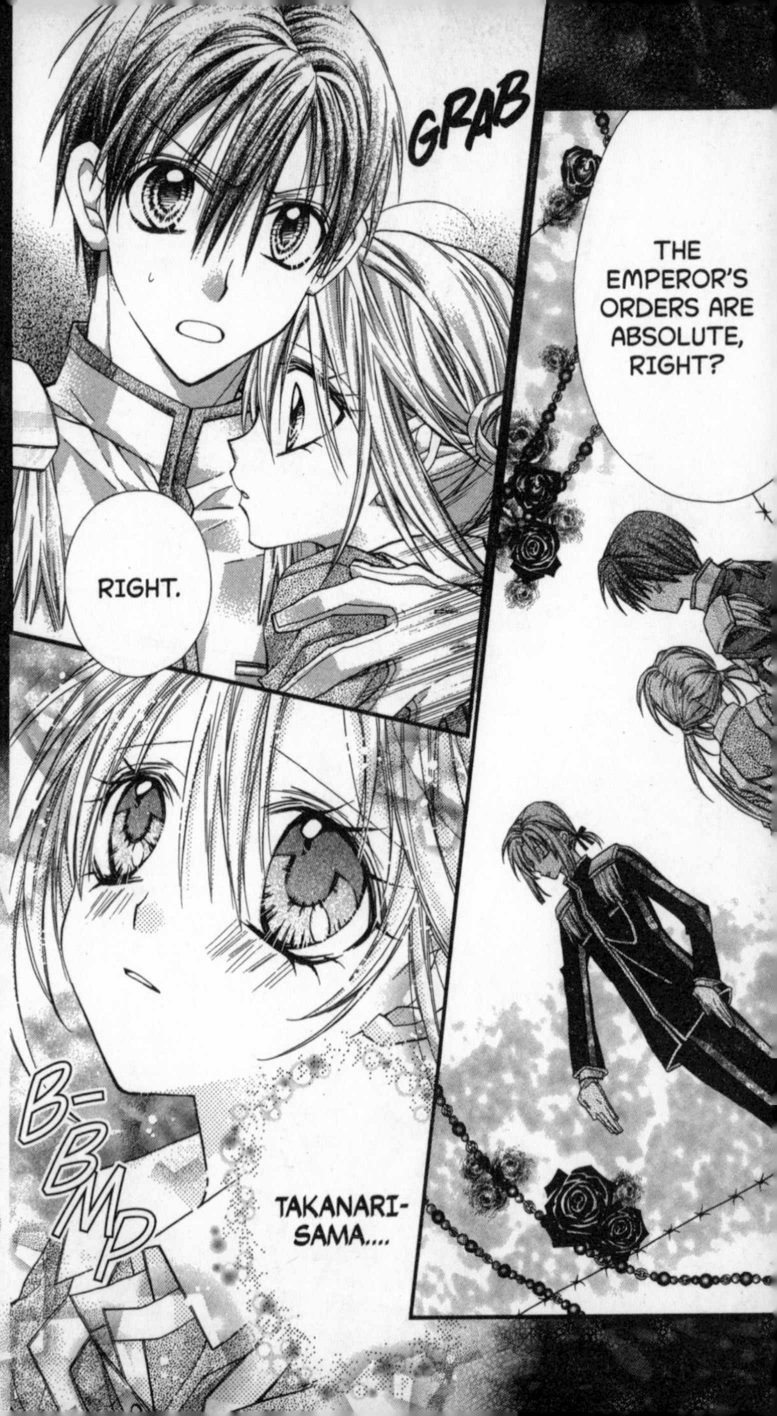
THE EMPEROR'S ORDERS ARE ABSOLUTE, RIGHT?
GRAB
RIGHT.
B-BMP
TAKANARI-SAMA....

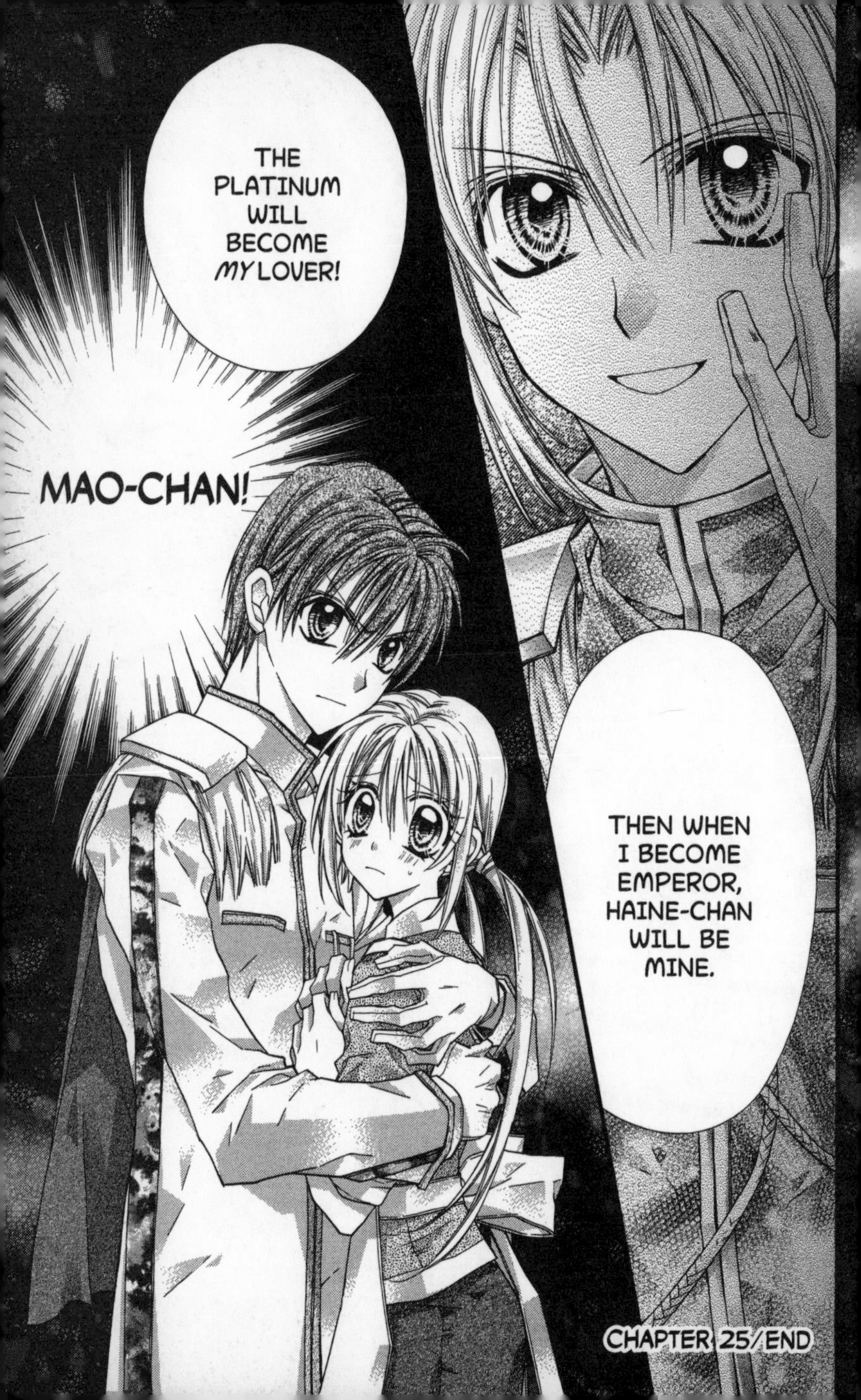
THE PLATINUM WILL BECOME *MY* LOVER!
MAO-CHAN!
THEN WHEN I BECOME EMPEROR, HAINE-CHAN WILL BE MINE.
CHAPTER 25/END

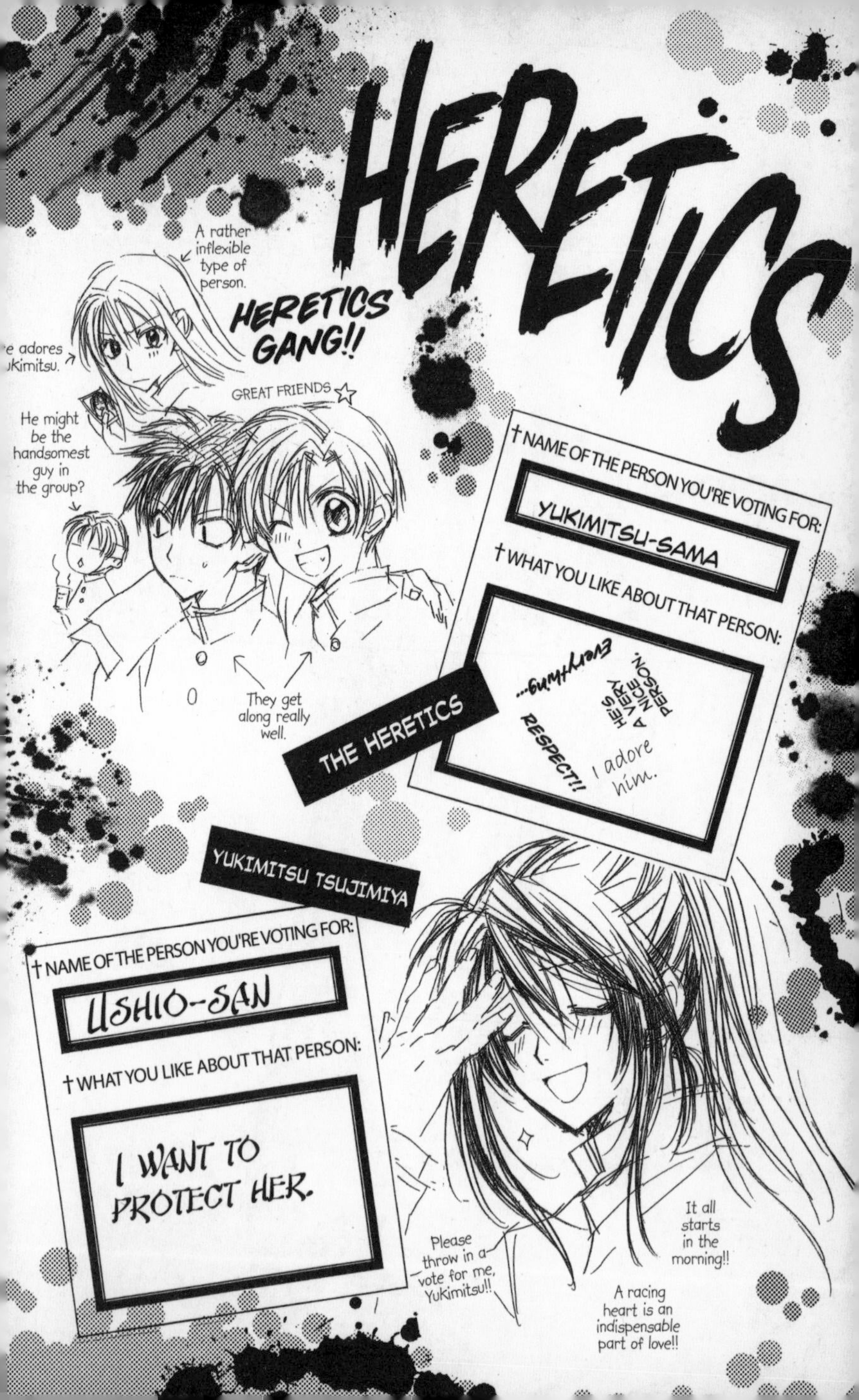
HERETICS
†NAME OF THE PERSON YOU'RE VOTING FOR:
YUKIMITSU-SAMA
†WHAT YOU LIKE ABOUT THAT PERSON:
Everything...
HE'S A VERY NICE PERSON.
RESPECT!!
I adore him.
THE HERETICS
HERETICS GANG!!
A rather inflexible type of person.
e adores
ukimitsu.
GREAT FRIENDS ☆
He might be the handsomest guy in the group?
They get along really well.
YUKIMITSU TSUJIMIYA
†NAME OF THE PERSON YOU'RE VOTING FOR:
USHIO-SAN
†WHAT YOU LIKE ABOUT THAT PERSON:
I WANT TO PROTECT HER.
It all starts in the morning!!
Please throw in a vote for me, Yukimitsu!!
A racing heart is an indispensable part of love!!

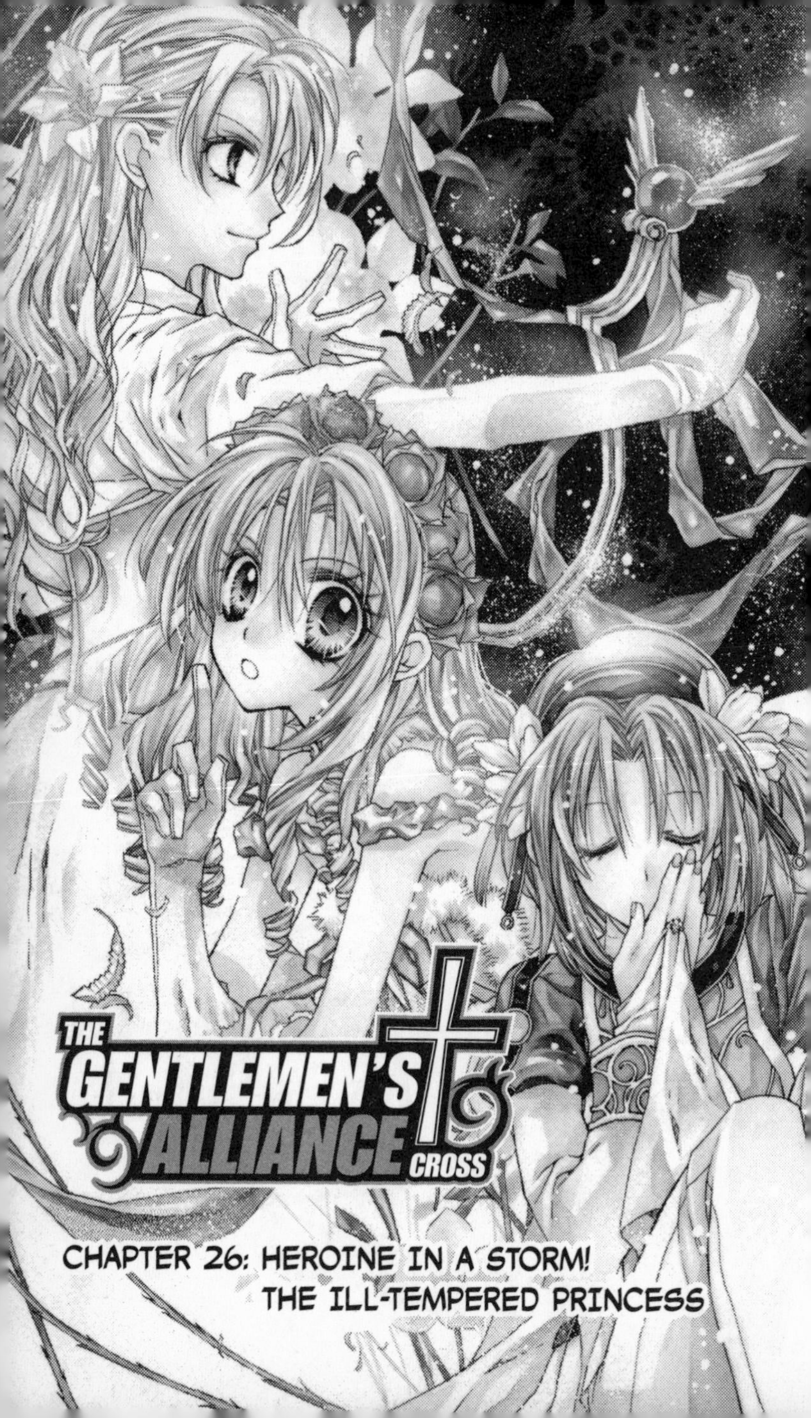
THE GENTLEMEN'S ALLIANCE CROSS
CHAPTER 26: HEROINE IN A STORM! THE ILL-TEMPERED PRINCESS

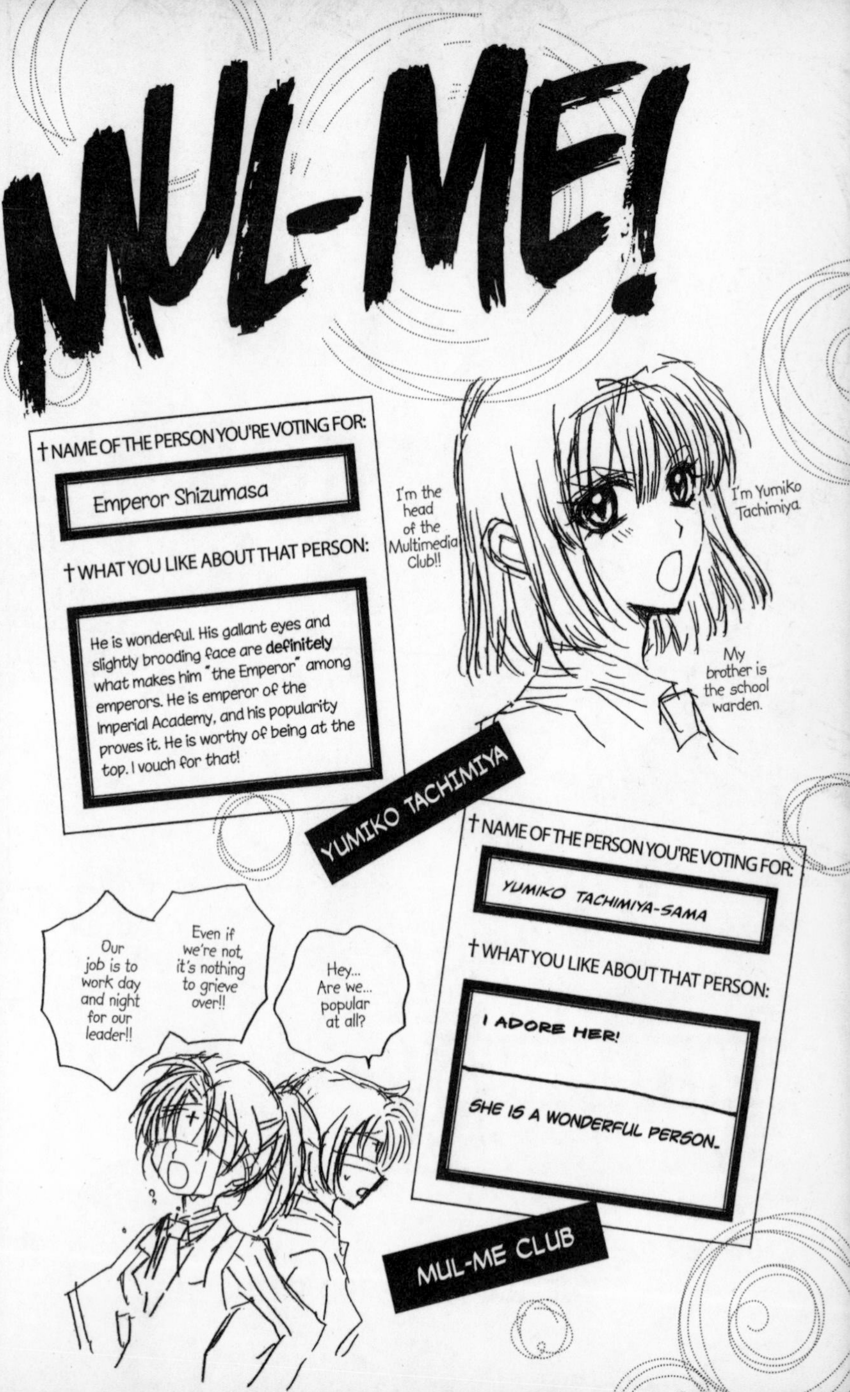

MUL-ME!

† NAME OF THE PERSON YOU'RE VOTING FOR:

Emperor Shizumasa

† WHAT YOU LIKE ABOUT THAT PERSON:

He is wonderful. His gallant eyes and slightly brooding face are **definitely** what makes him "the Emperor" among emperors. He is emperor of the Imperial Academy, and his popularity proves it. He is worthy of being at the top. I vouch for that!

YUMIKO TACHIMIYA

I'm the head of the Multimedia Club!!

I'm Yumiko Tachimiya.

My brother is the school warden.

Our job is to work day and night for our leader!!

Even if we're not, it's nothing to grieve over!!

Hey... Are we... popular at all?

† NAME OF THE PERSON YOU'RE VOTING FOR:

YUMIKO TACHIMIYA-SAMA

† WHAT YOU LIKE ABOUT THAT PERSON:

I ADORE HER!

SHE IS A WONDERFUL PERSON.

MUL-ME CLUB

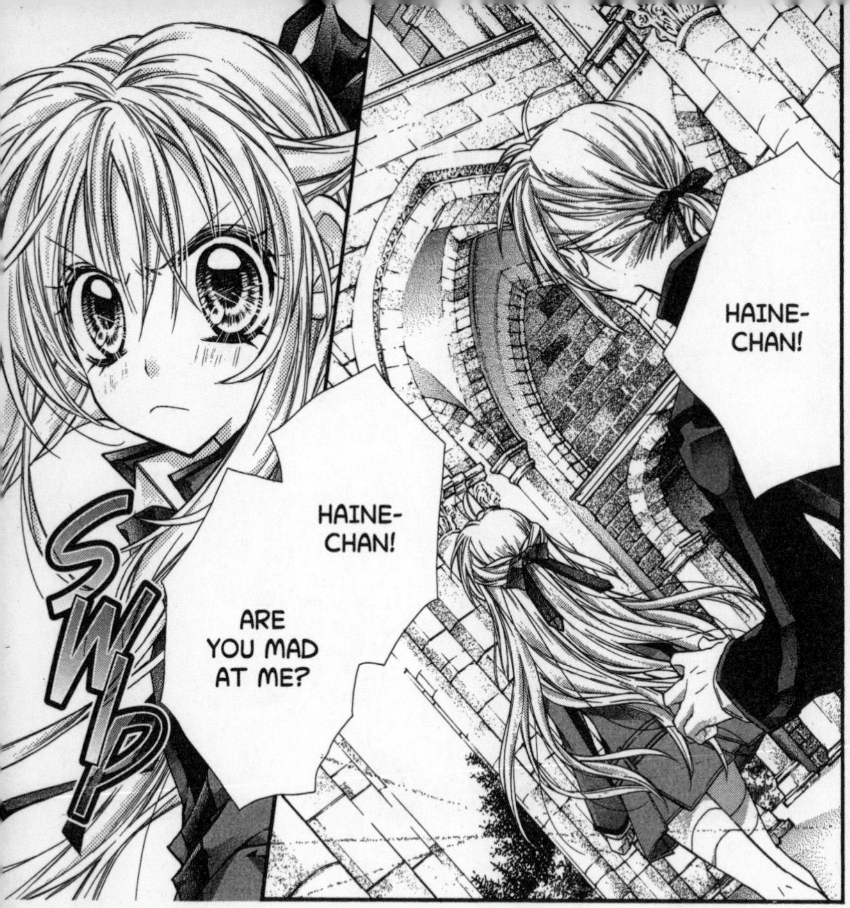
HAINE-CHAN!
HAINE-CHAN!
ARE YOU MAD AT ME?
SWIP

Chapter 26: Heroine in a Storm! The Ill-Tempered Princess

※I'm giving away the story. Lead-in I'll kiss you when I fall in love...☆

It's been a while since I drew a fantasy-like image for the chapter title page.♪
I drew it while I listened to a song called "Kaze no Fantasia."
I think the nicest thing about the illustration is the fact that Ushio-chan looks different in it.

When my supervisor was checking the rough draft, I was asked, "Why is Haine-chan so angry?" This stuck in my head, and that's how I came up with the title for this chapter. I think she's got every right to be angry. Even I felt annoyed with Maguri. It must be hard for Haine-chan since she's a victim in this case.

By the way, the thing at the end is a wooden sword. (I'm sorry that it's a little hard to distinguish)

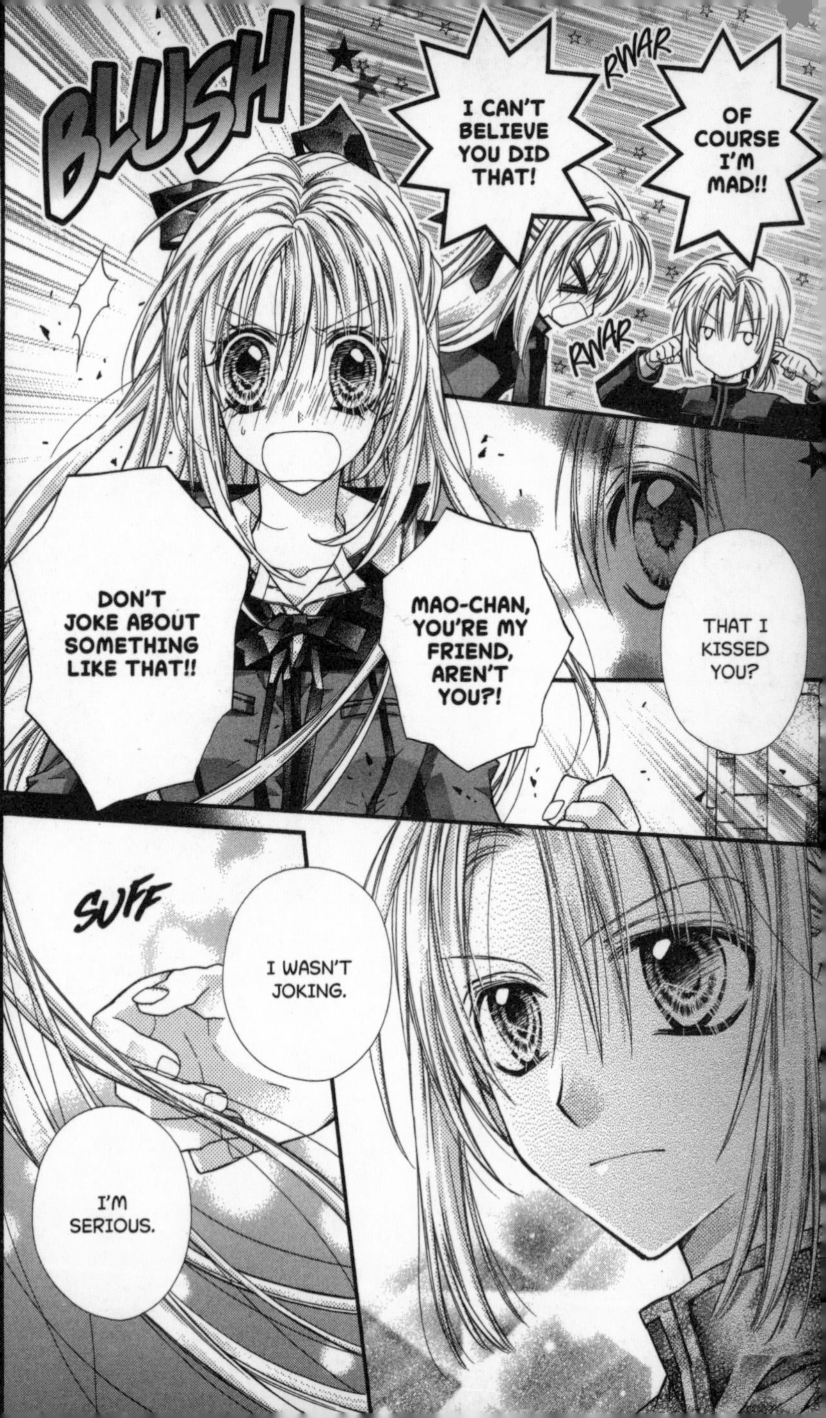
OF COURSE I'M MAD!!
RWAR
I CAN'T BELIEVE YOU DID THAT!
RWAR
THAT I KISSED YOU?
BLUSH
MAO-CHAN, YOU'RE MY FRIEND, AREN'T YOU?!
DON'T JOKE ABOUT SOMETHING LIKE THAT!!
I WASN'T JOKING.
SUFF
I'M SERIOUS.

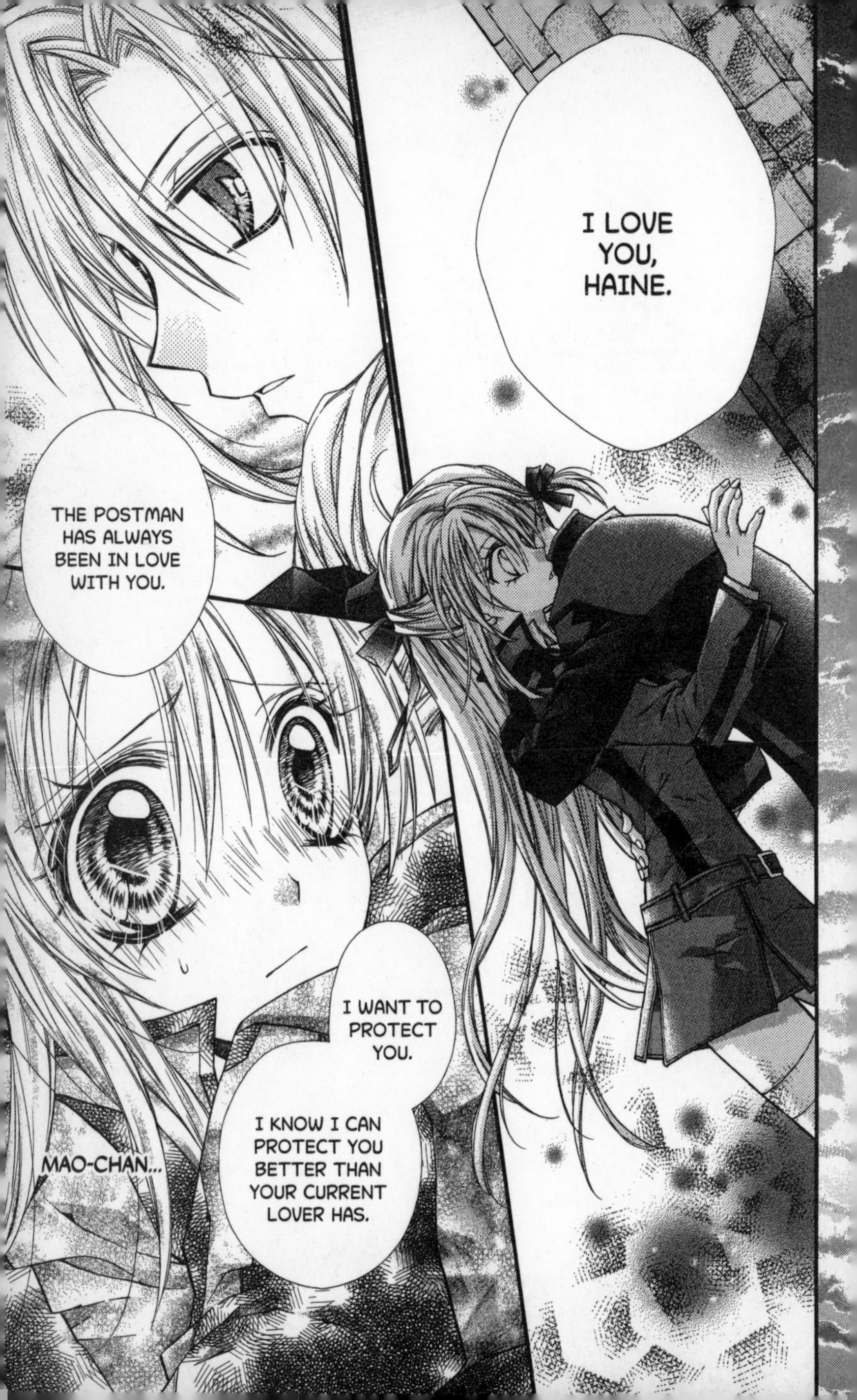

I LOVE YOU, HAINE.
THE POSTMAN HAS ALWAYS BEEN IN LOVE WITH YOU.
I WANT TO PROTECT YOU.
I KNOW I CAN PROTECT YOU BETTER THAN YOUR CURRENT LOVER HAS.
MAO-CHAN...

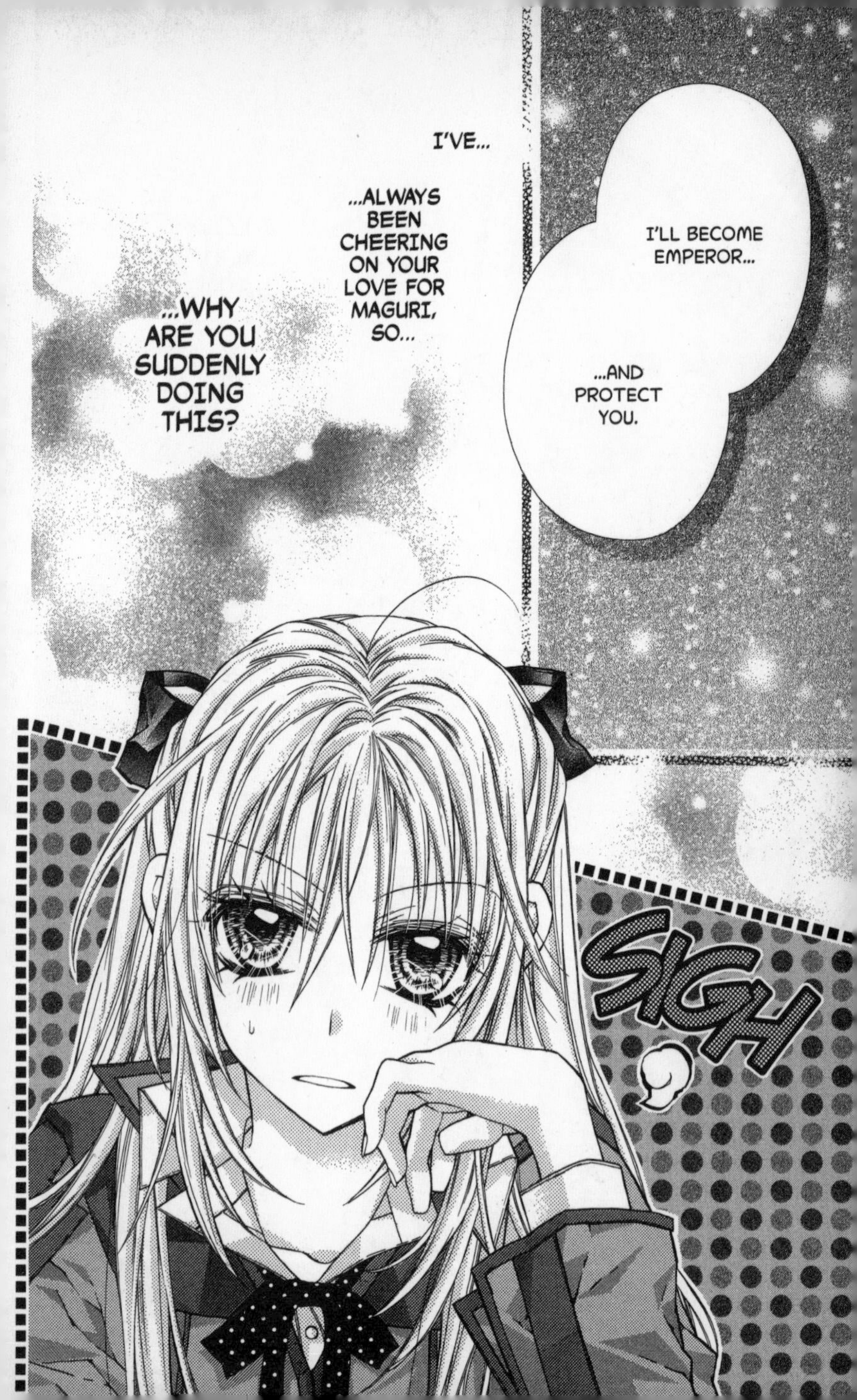
I'LL BECOME EMPEROR...
...AND PROTECT YOU.
I'VE...
...ALWAYS BEEN CHEERING ON YOUR LOVE FOR MAGURI, SO...
...WHY ARE YOU SUDDENLY DOING THIS?
SIGH

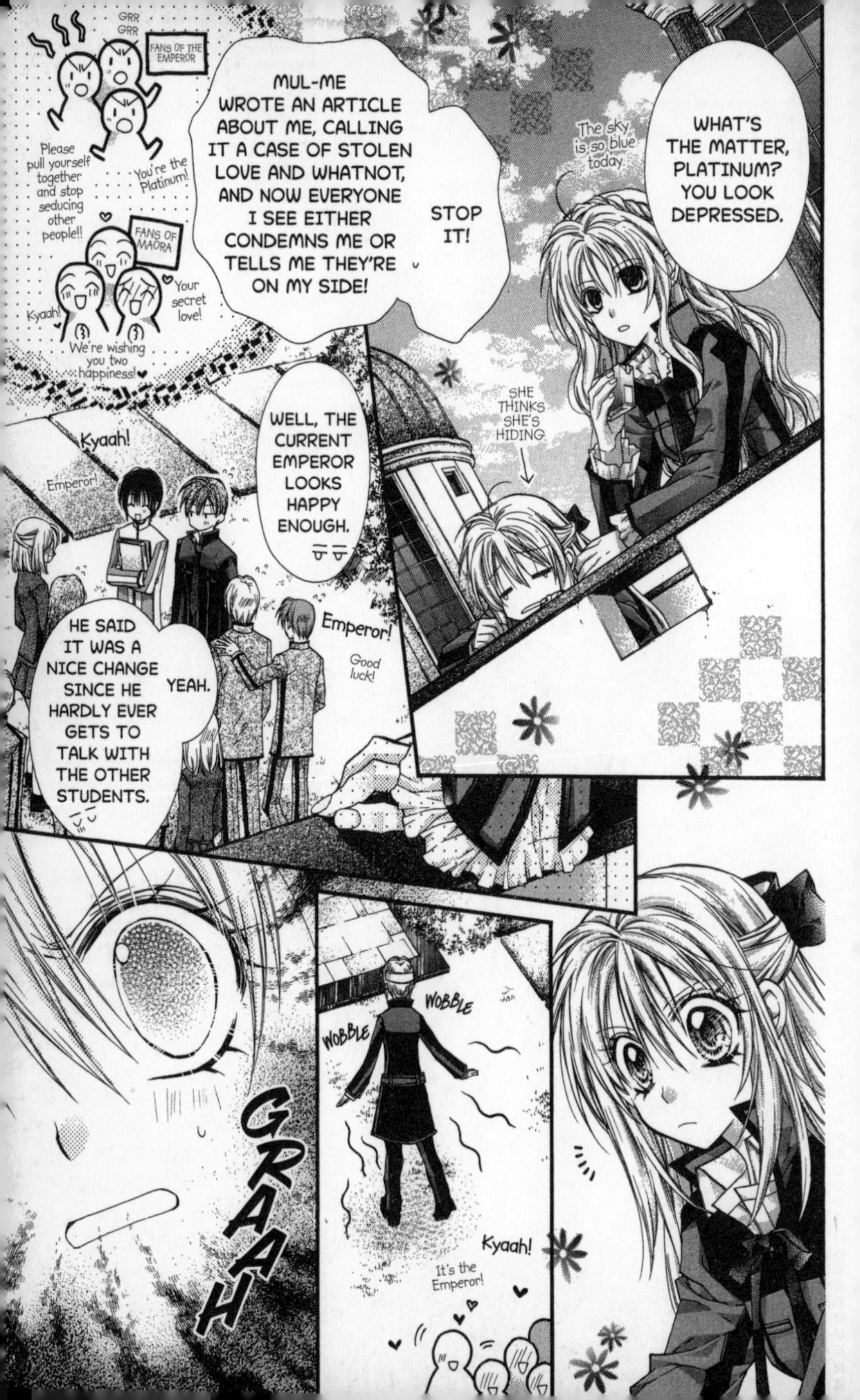
WHAT'S THE MATTER, PLATINUM? YOU LOOK DEPRESSED.
The sky is so blue today.
SHE THINKS SHE'S HIDING.
STOP IT!
MUL-ME WROTE AN ARTICLE ABOUT ME, CALLING IT A CASE OF STOLEN LOVE AND WHATNOT, AND NOW EVERYONE I SEE EITHER CONDEMNS ME OR TELLS ME THEY'RE ON MY SIDE!
GRR GRR
FANS OF THE EMPEROR
You're the Platinum!
Please pull yourself together and stop seducing other people!!
FANS OF MAORA
Your secret love!
Kyaah!
We're wishing you two happiness!
WELL, THE CURRENT EMPEROR LOOKS HAPPY ENOUGH.
Emperor!
Good luck!
Kyaah!
Emperor!
YEAH.
HE SAID IT WAS A NICE CHANGE SINCE HE HARDLY EVER GETS TO TALK WITH THE OTHER STUDENTS.
WOBBLE
WOBBLE
Kyaah!
It's the Emperor!
GRAAAH

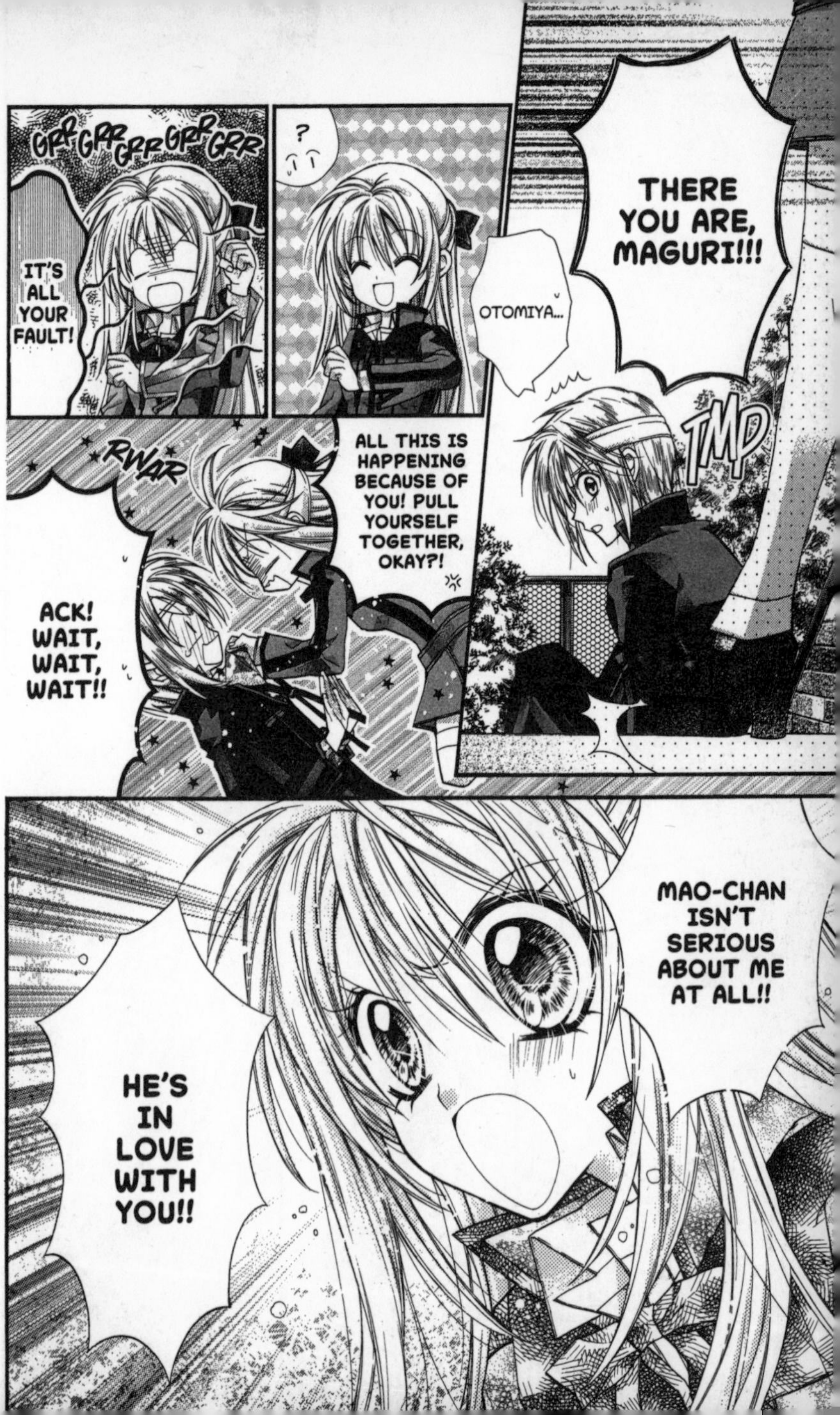
THERE YOU ARE, MAGURI!!!
OTOMIYA...
TMP
?
GRR GRR GRR GRR GRR
IT'S ALL YOUR FAULT!
ALL THIS IS HAPPENING BECAUSE OF YOU! PULL YOURSELF TOGETHER, OKAY?!
RWAR
ACK! WAIT, WAIT, WAIT!!
MAO-CHAN ISN'T SERIOUS ABOUT ME AT ALL!!
HE'S IN LOVE WITH YOU!!

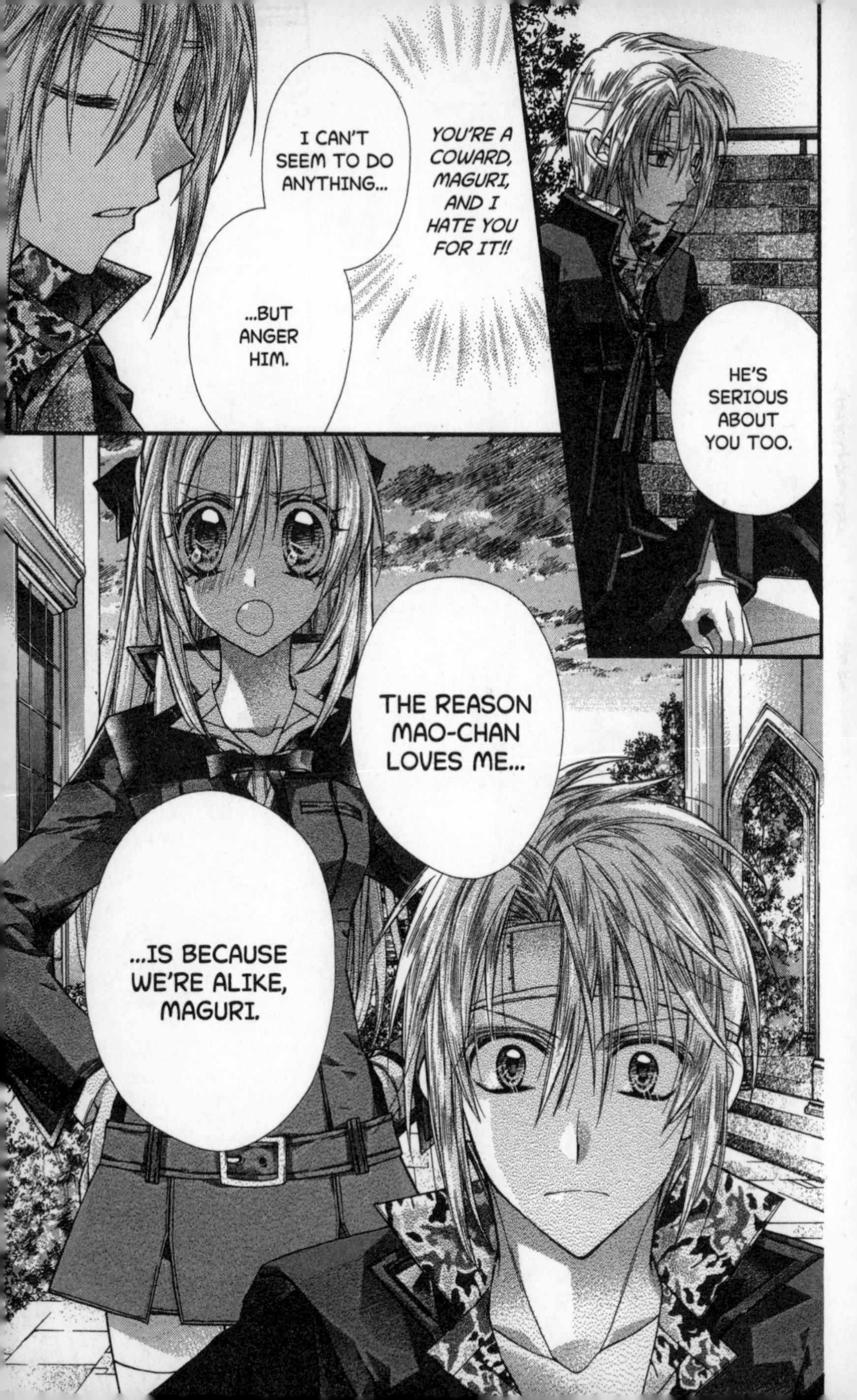
HE'S SERIOUS ABOUT YOU TOO.
YOU'RE A COWARD, MAGURI, AND I HATE YOU FOR IT!!
I CAN'T SEEM TO DO ANYTHING...
...BUT ANGER HIM.
THE REASON MAO-CHAN LOVES ME...
...IS BECAUSE WE'RE ALIKE, MAGURI.

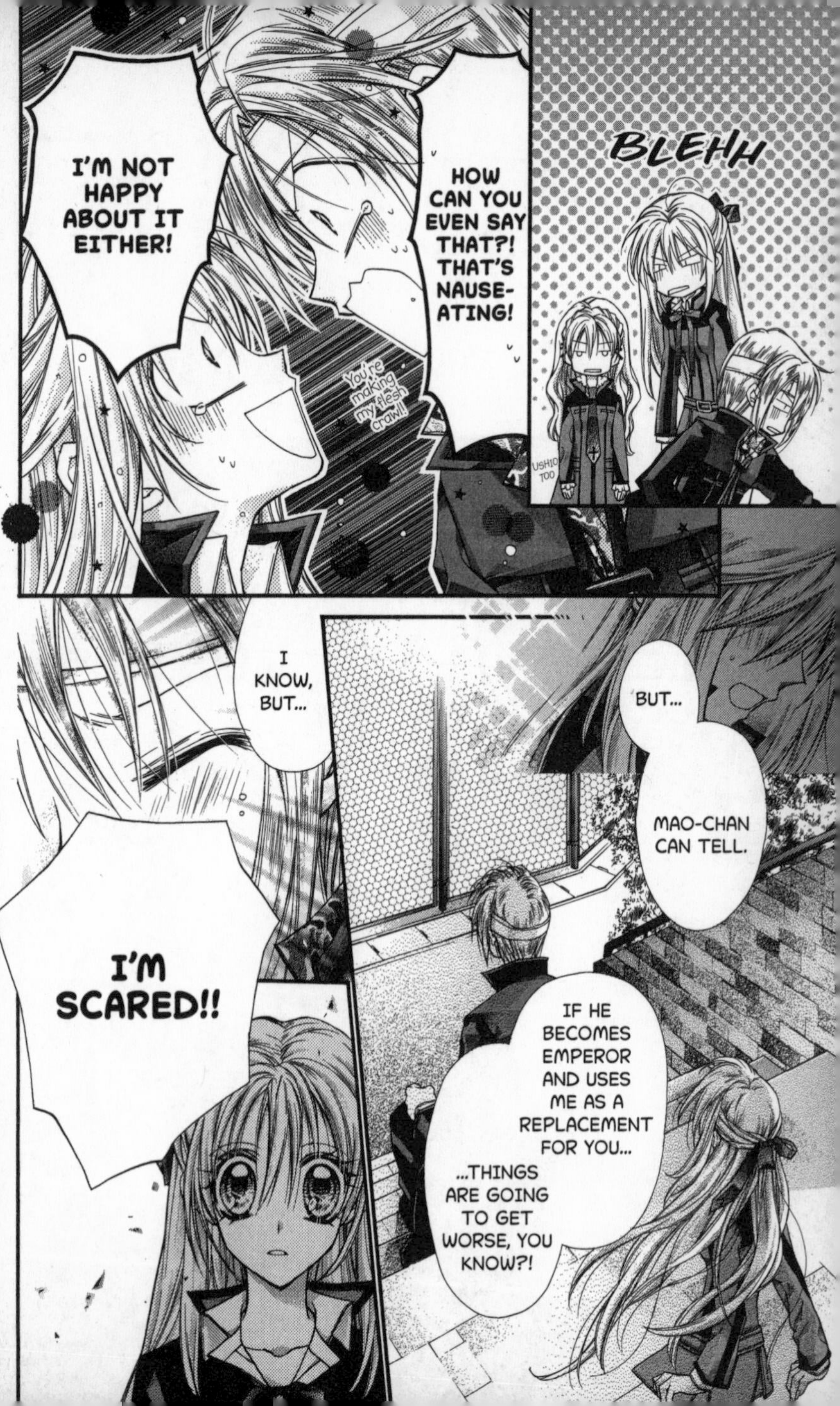
BLEHH
USHIO TOO
HOW CAN YOU EVEN SAY THAT?! THAT'S NAUSE-ATING!
I'M NOT HAPPY ABOUT IT EITHER!
You're making my flesh crawl!
BUT...
MAO-CHAN CAN TELL.
IF HE BECOMES EMPEROR AND USES ME AS A REPLACEMENT FOR YOU...
...THINGS ARE GOING TO GET WORSE, YOU KNOW?!
I KNOW, BUT...
I'M SCARED!!

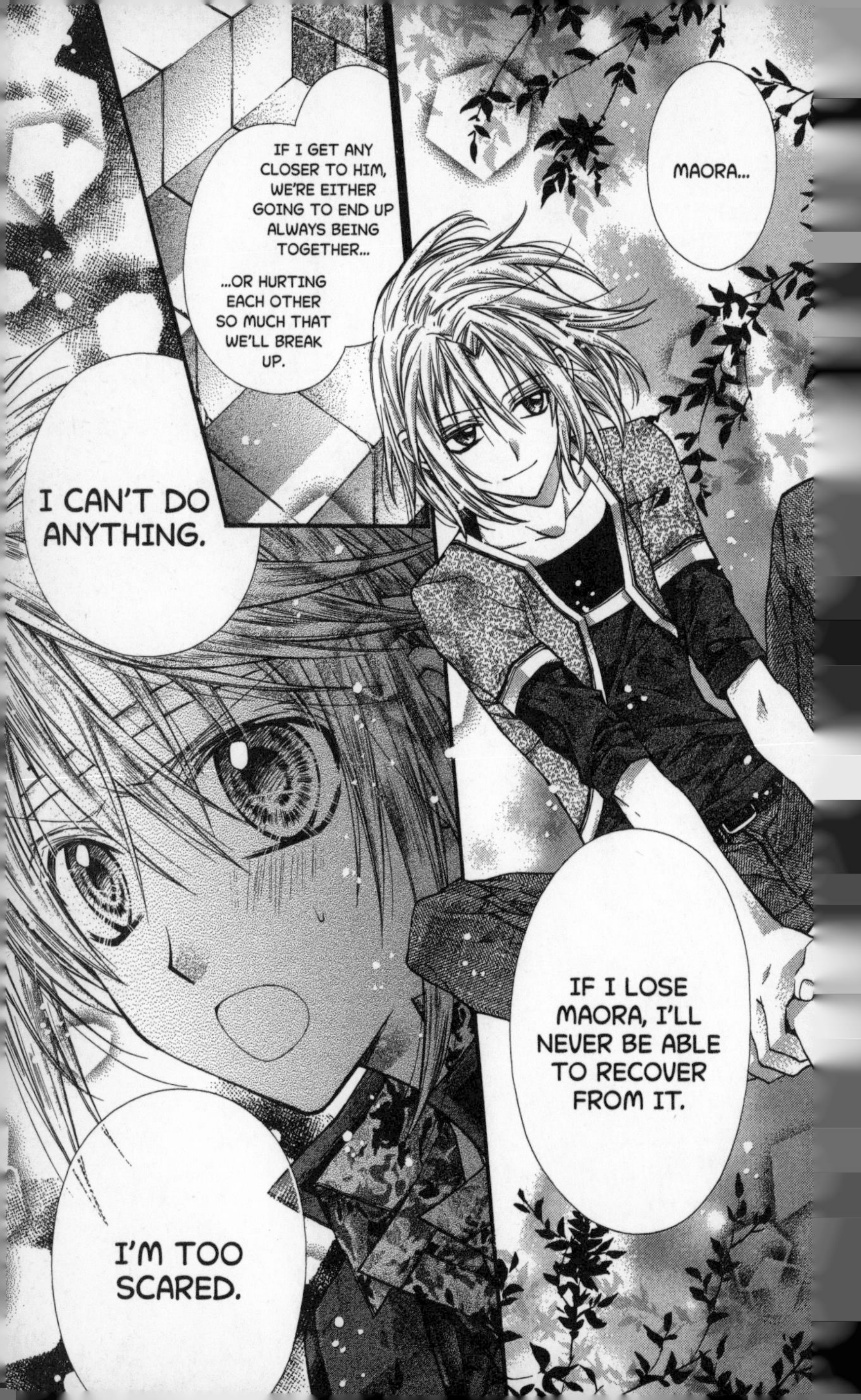
MAORA...
IF I GET ANY CLOSER TO HIM, WE'RE EITHER GOING TO END UP ALWAYS BEING TOGETHER...
...OR HURTING EACH OTHER SO MUCH THAT WE'LL BREAK UP.
I CAN'T DO ANYTHING.
IF I LOSE MAORA, I'LL NEVER BE ABLE TO RECOVER FROM IT.
I'M TOO SCARED.

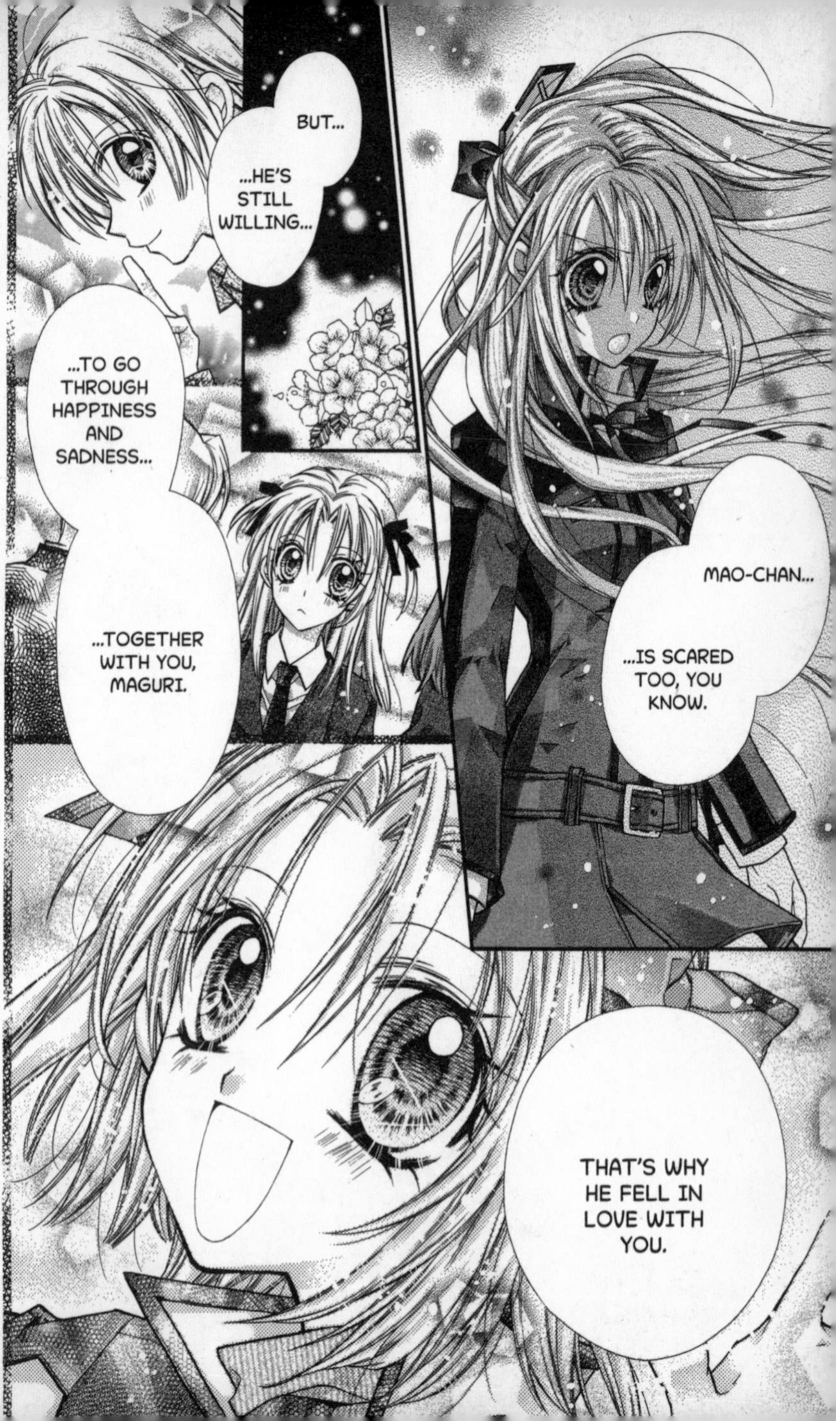
MAO-CHAN...
...IS SCARED TOO, YOU KNOW.
BUT...
...HE'S STILL WILLING...
...TO GO THROUGH HAPPINESS AND SADNESS...
...TOGETHER WITH YOU, MAGURI.
THAT'S WHY HE FELL IN LOVE WITH YOU.

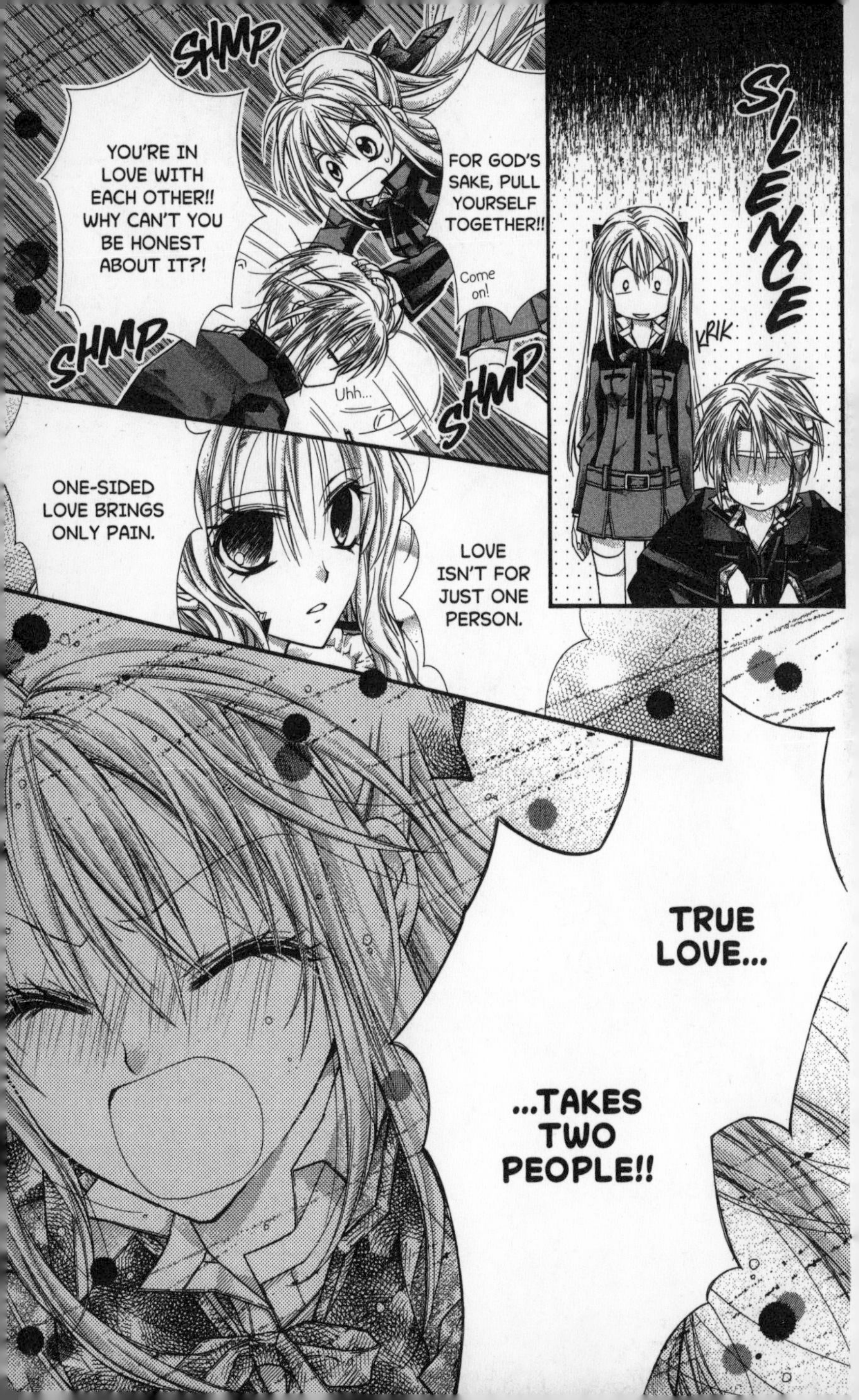
SILENCE
KRIK
SHMP
FOR GOD'S SAKE, PULL YOURSELF TOGETHER!!
YOU'RE IN LOVE WITH EACH OTHER!! WHY CAN'T YOU BE HONEST ABOUT IT?!
Come on!
SHMP
SHMP
Uhh...
LOVE ISN'T FOR JUST ONE PERSON.
ONE-SIDED LOVE BRINGS ONLY PAIN.
TRUE LOVE...
...TAKES TWO PEOPLE!!

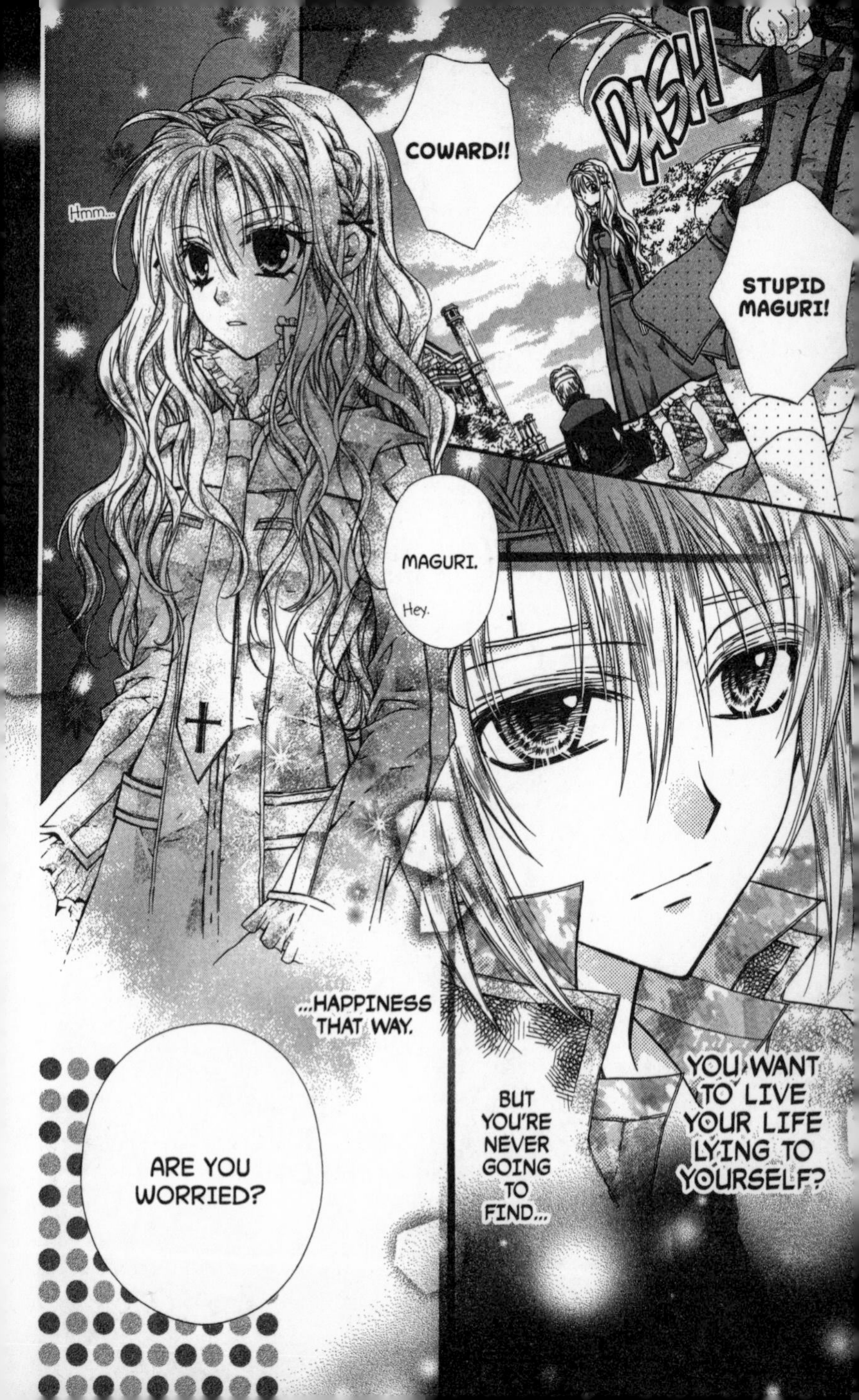
DASH
STUPID MAGURI!
COWARD!!
MAGURI.
Hey.
YOU WANT TO LIVE YOUR LIFE LYING TO YOURSELF?
BUT YOU'RE NEVER GOING TO FIND...
...HAPPINESS THAT WAY.
Hmm...
ARE YOU WORRIED?

HUH?
THAT I MIGHT LOSE IN THE ELECTION.
OH NO!! I HAVEN'T THOUGHT ABOUT THAT AT ALL!!
DON'T WORRY, I'M NOT GOING TO LET ANYBODY ELSE HAVE YOU.
BLUSH
Eh, I happen to belong to Shizumasa-sama.

I forgot to eat...
...my ice cream dessert!!
BOING

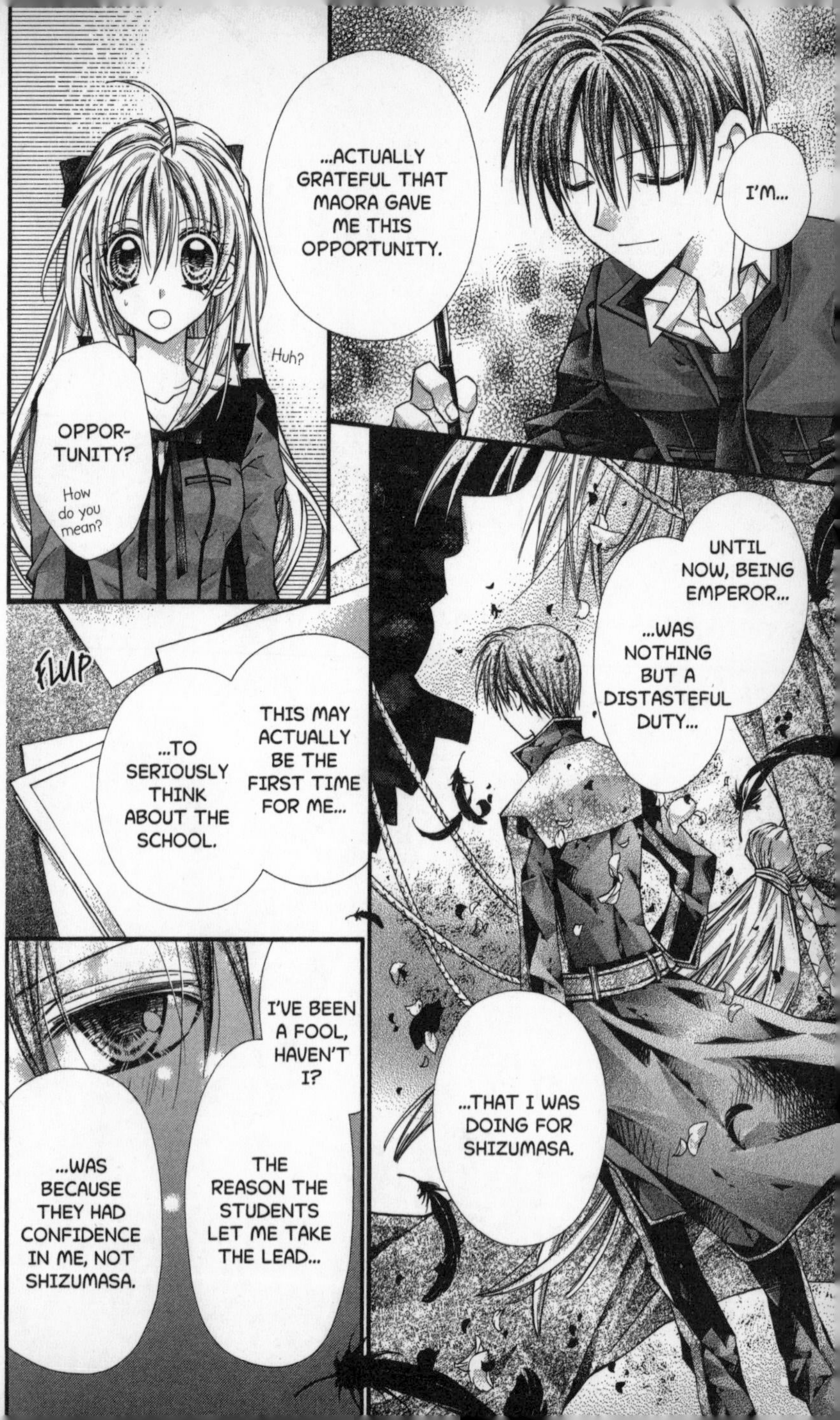
I'M...
...ACTUALLY GRATEFUL THAT MAORA GAVE ME THIS OPPORTUNITY.
Huh?
OPPOR-TUNITY?
How do you mean?
UNTIL NOW, BEING EMPEROR...
...WAS NOTHING BUT A DISTASTEFUL DUTY...
...THAT I WAS DOING FOR SHIZUMASA.
FLUP
THIS MAY ACTUALLY BE THE FIRST TIME FOR ME...
...TO SERIOUSLY THINK ABOUT THE SCHOOL.
I'VE BEEN A FOOL, HAVEN'T I?
THE REASON THE STUDENTS LET ME TAKE THE LEAD...
...WAS BECAUSE THEY HAD CONFIDENCE IN ME, NOT SHIZUMASA.

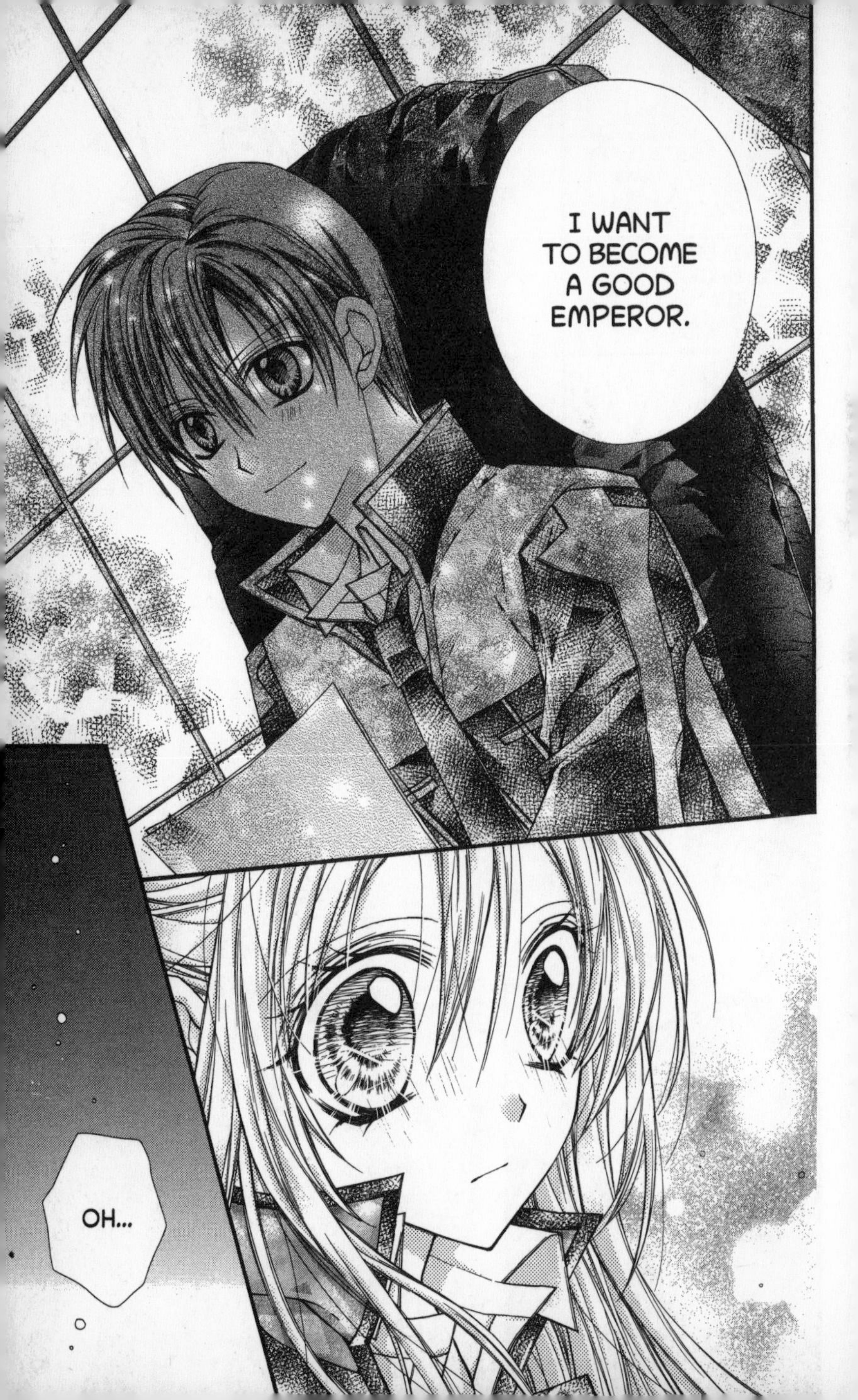
I WANT TO BECOME A GOOD EMPEROR.
OH...

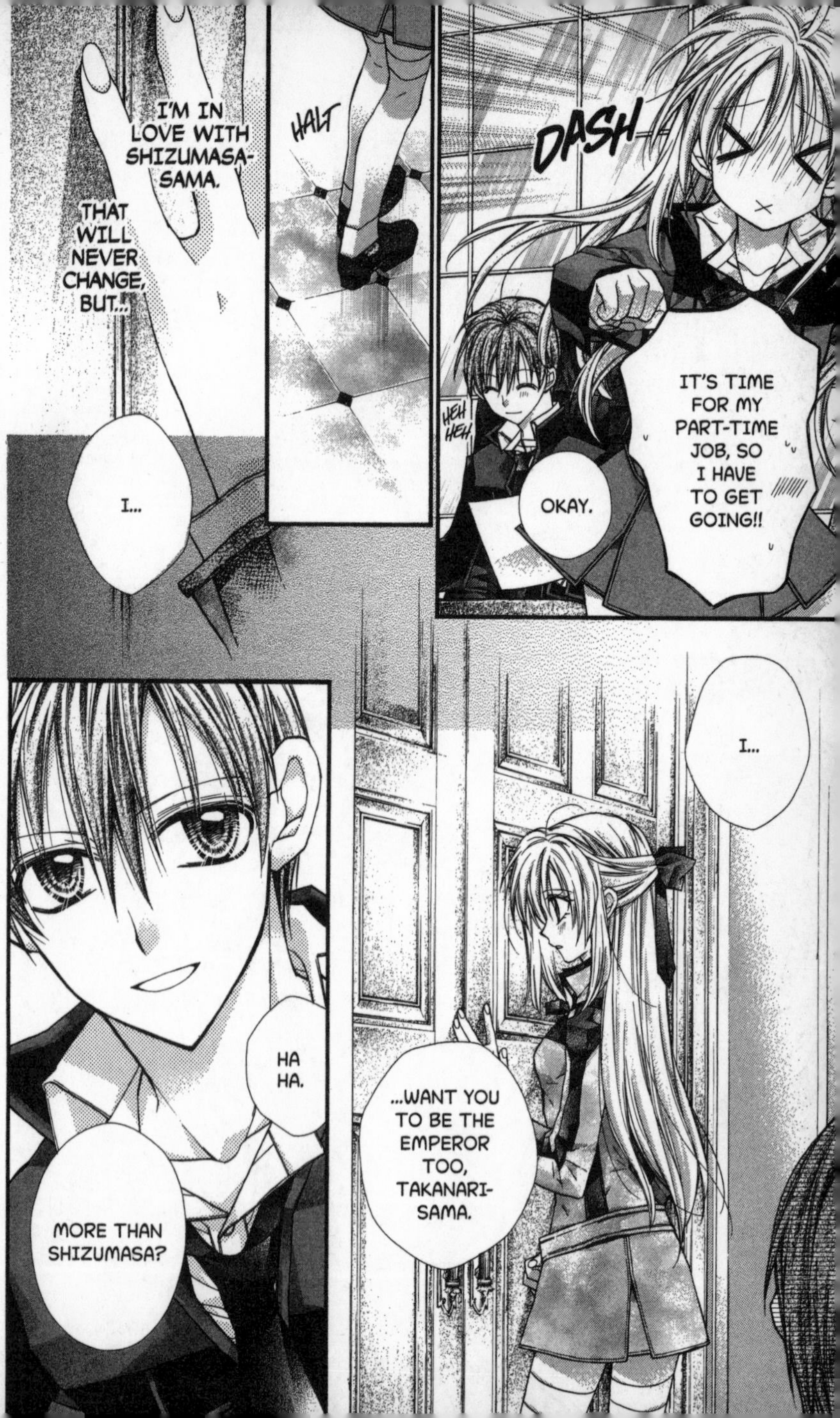
DASH
IT'S TIME FOR MY PART-TIME JOB, SO I HAVE TO GET GOING!!
HEH HEH
OKAY.
HALT
I'M IN LOVE WITH SHIZUMASA-SAMA.
THAT WILL NEVER CHANGE, BUT...
I...
I...
...WANT YOU TO BE THE EMPEROR TOO, TAKANARI-SAMA.
HA HA.
MORE THAN SHIZUMASA?

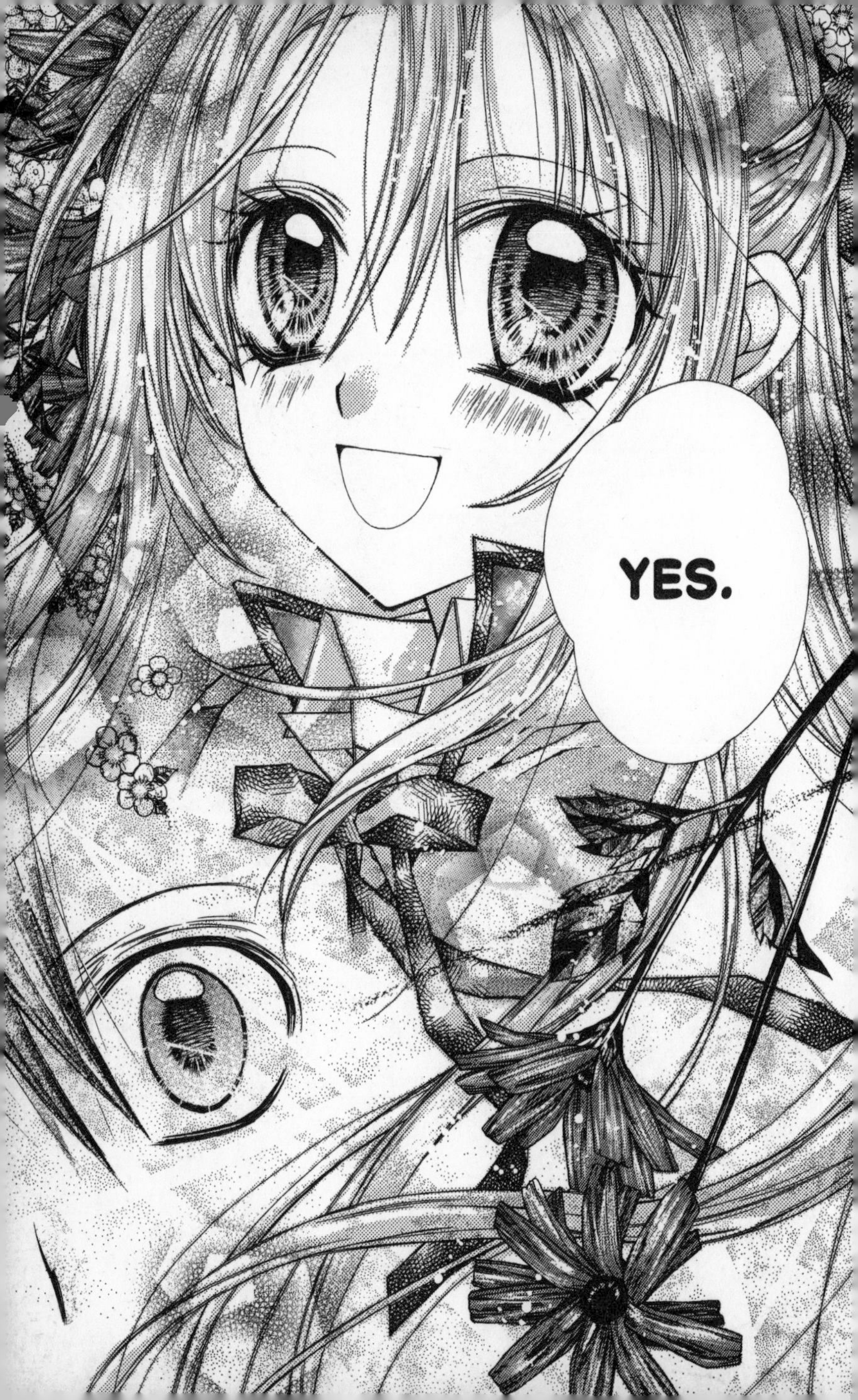
YES.

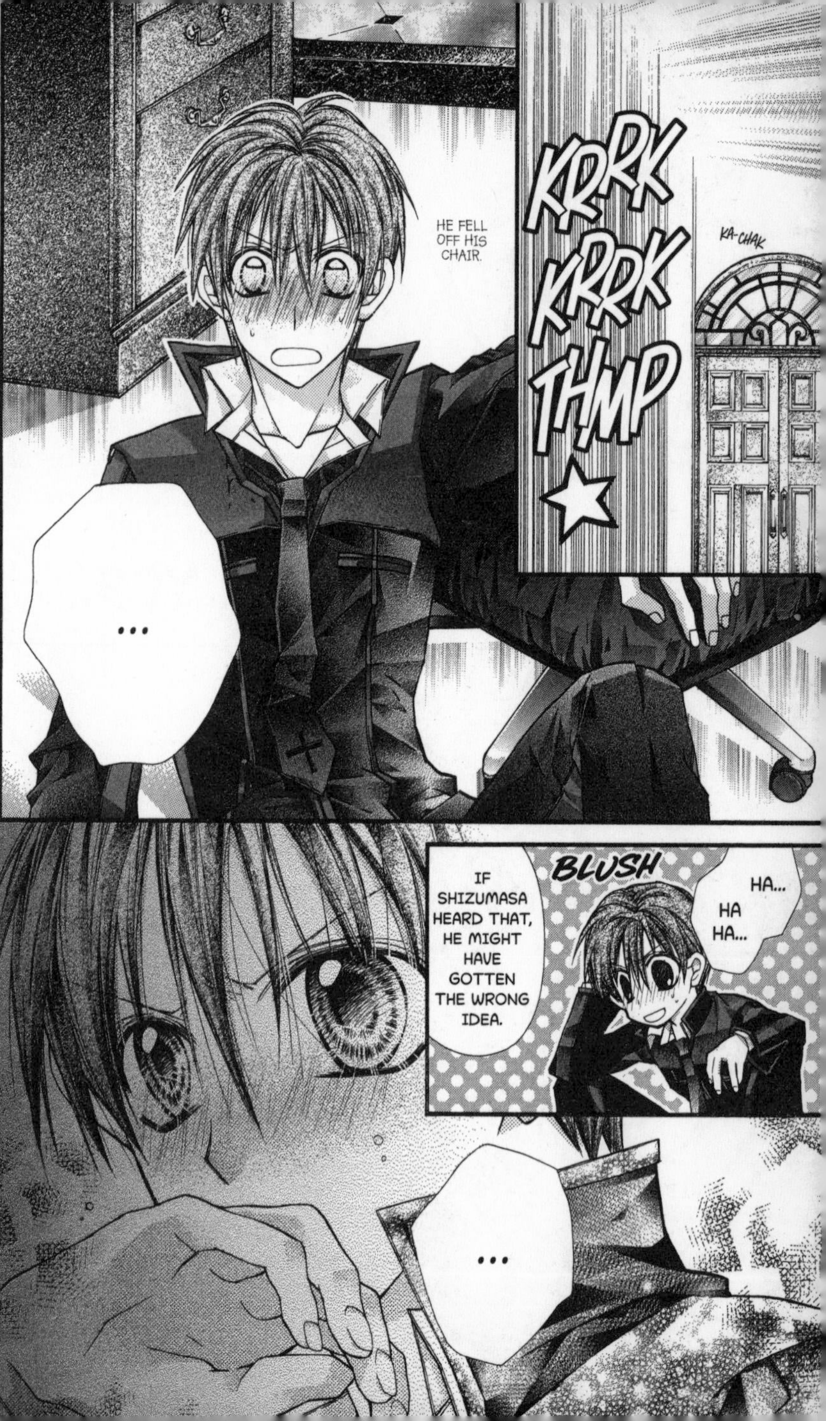
KA-CHAK
KRRK KRRK THMP
HE FELL OFF HIS CHAIR.
...
HA... HA HA...
BLUSH
IF SHIZUMASA HEARD THAT, HE MIGHT HAVE GOTTEN THE WRONG IDEA.
...

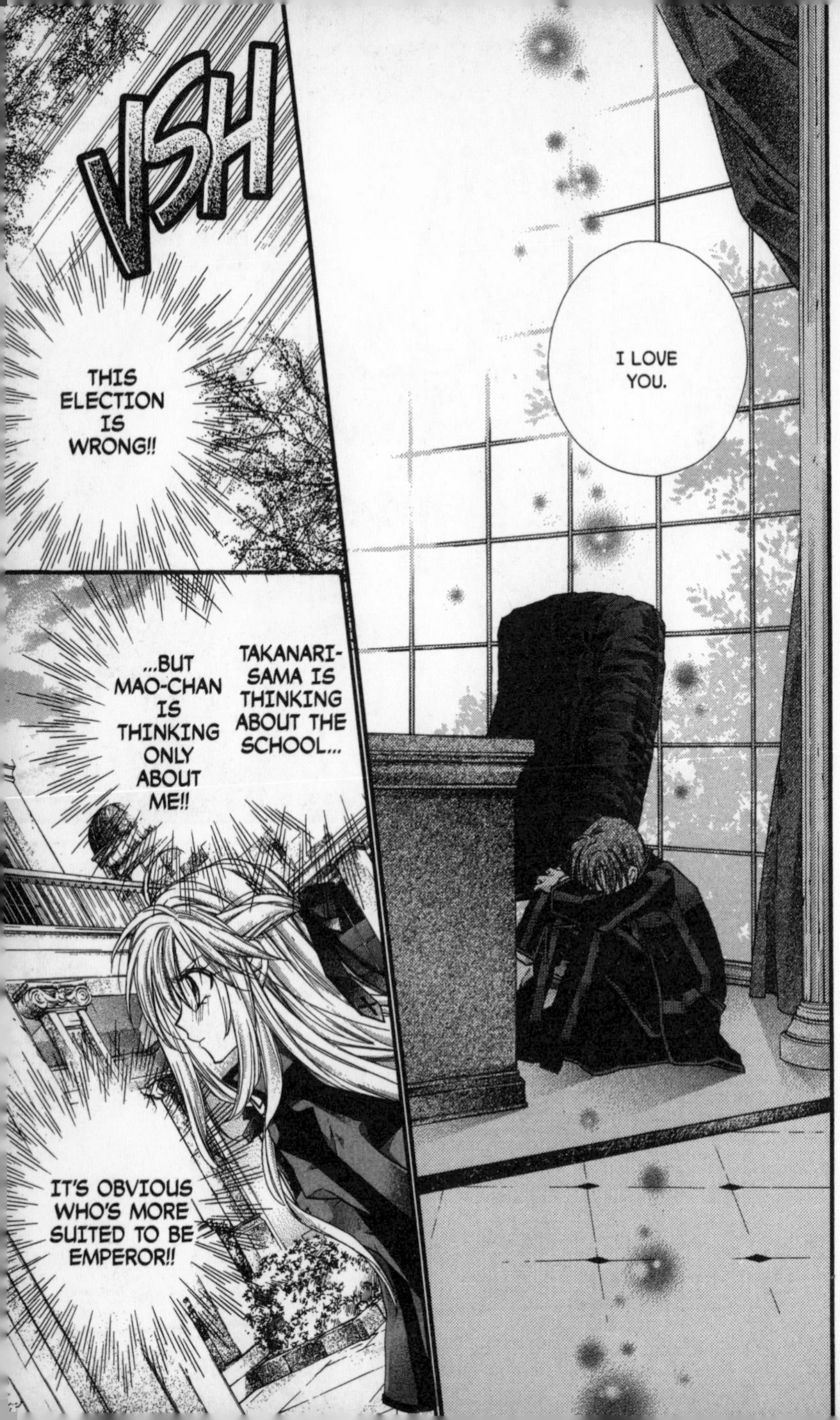
I LOVE YOU.
VSH
THIS ELECTION IS WRONG!!
TAKANARI-SAMA IS THINKING ABOUT THE SCHOOL...
...BUT MAO-CHAN IS THINKING ONLY ABOUT ME!!
IT'S OBVIOUS WHO'S MORE SUITED TO BE EMPEROR!!

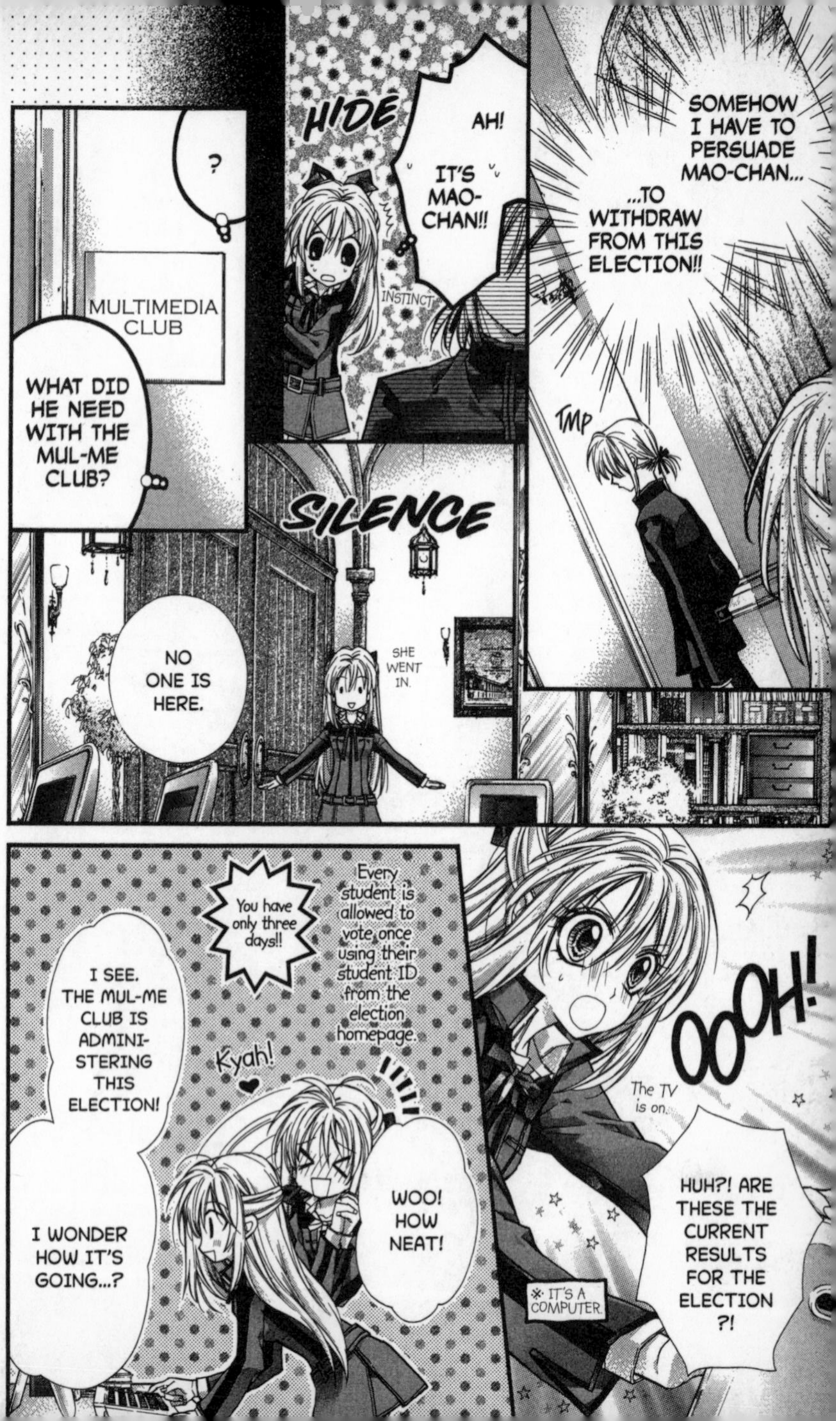
SOMEHOW I HAVE TO PERSUADE MAO-CHAN...
...TO WITHDRAW FROM THIS ELECTION!!
TMP
HIDE
AH!
IT'S MAO-CHAN!!
INSTINCT
?
MULTIMEDIA CLUB
WHAT DID HE NEED WITH THE MUL-ME CLUB?
SILENCE
SHE WENT IN.
NO ONE IS HERE.
OOOH!
The TV is on.
HUH?! ARE THESE THE CURRENT RESULTS FOR THE ELECTION?!
※IT'S A COMPUTER.
Every student is allowed to vote once using their student ID from the election homepage.
You have only three days!!
I SEE. THE MUL-ME CLUB IS ADMINISTERING THIS ELECTION!
Kyah!
WOO! HOW NEAT!
I WONDER HOW IT'S GOING...?

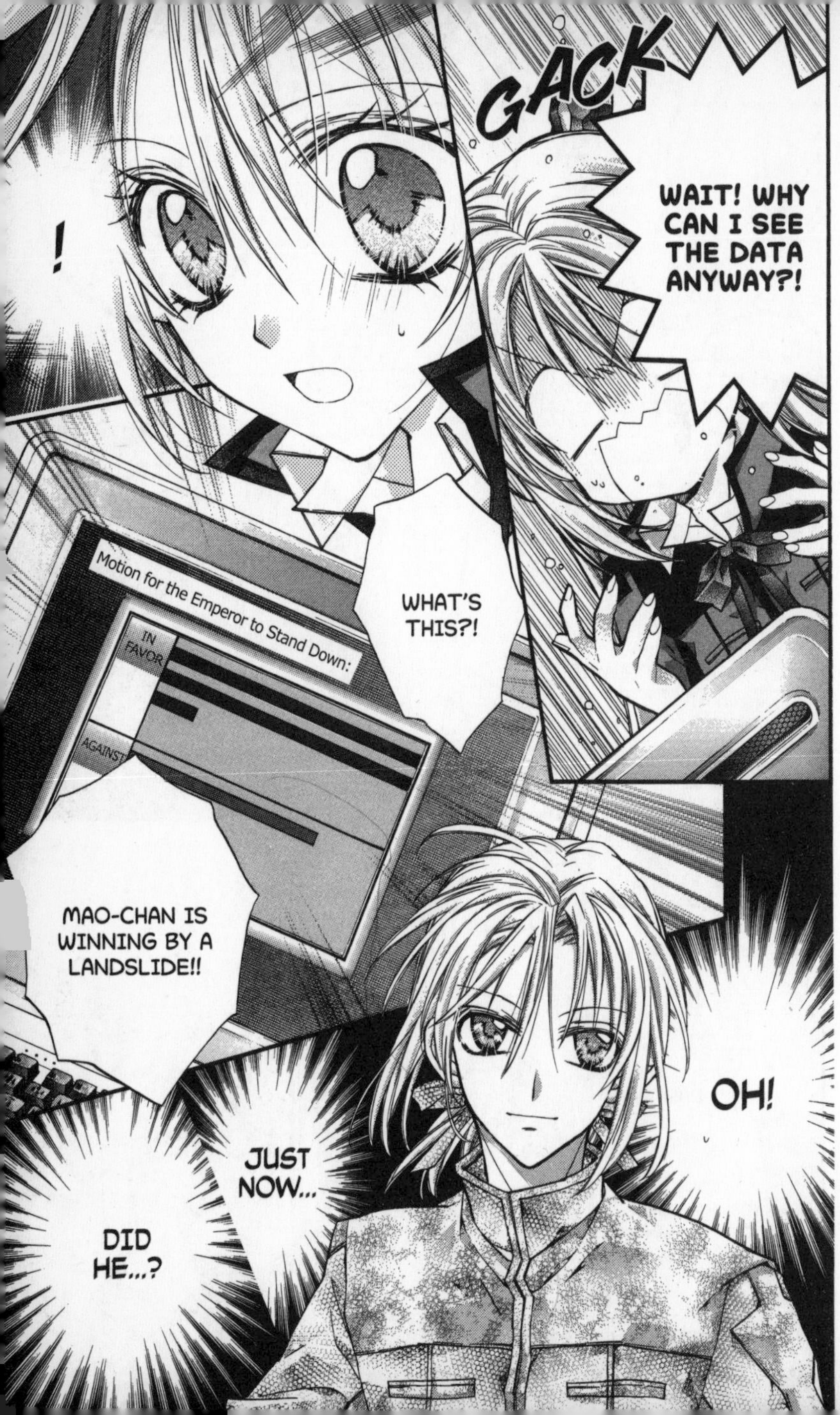
GACK
WAIT! WHY CAN I SEE THE DATA ANYWAY?!
!
WHAT'S THIS?!
Motion for the Emperor to Stand Down:
IN FAVOR
AGAINST
MAO-CHAN IS WINNING BY A LANDSLIDE!!
OH!
JUST NOW...
DID HE...?

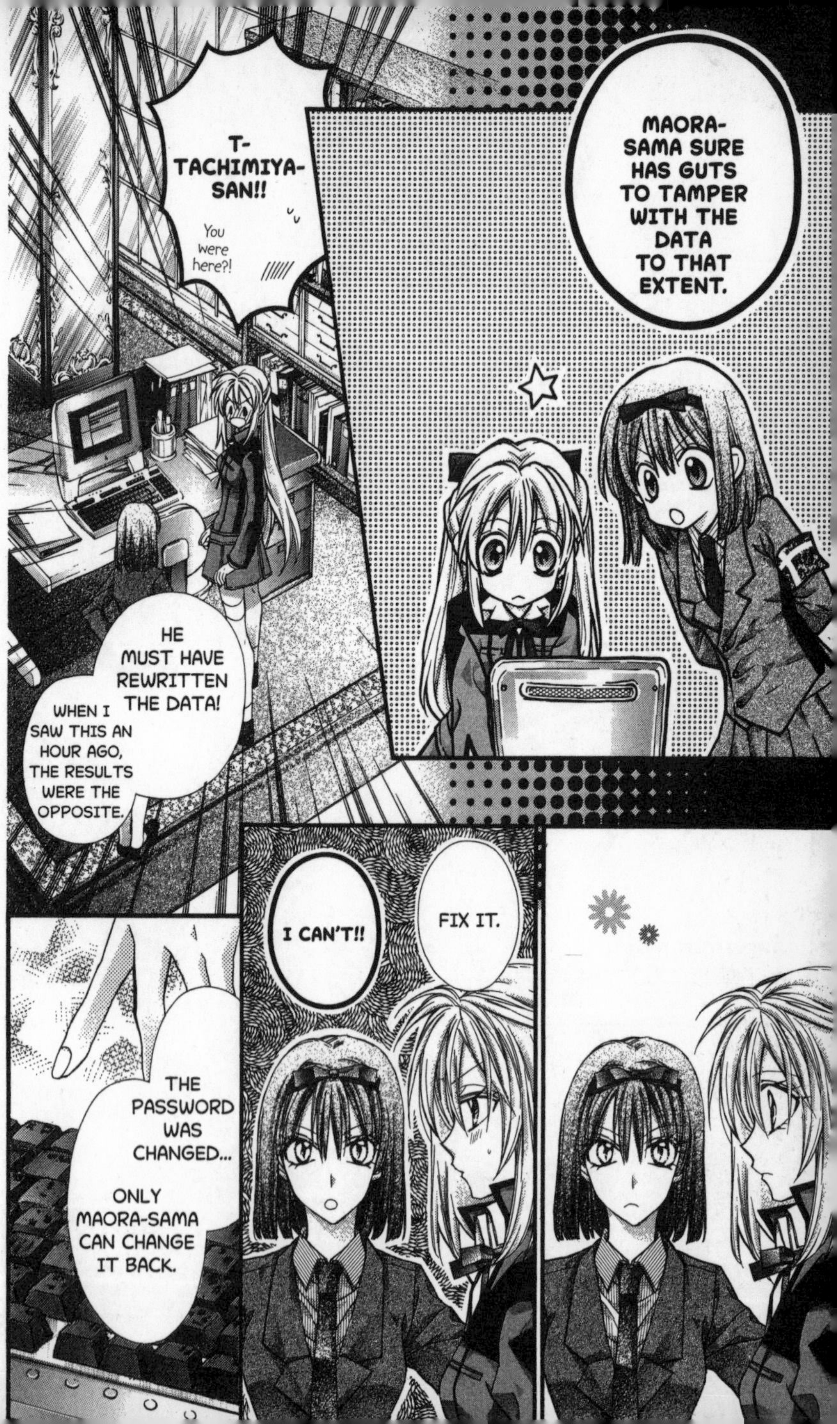
MAORA-SAMA SURE HAS GUTS TO TAMPER WITH THE DATA TO THAT EXTENT.
T-TACHIMIYA-SAN!!
You were here?!
HE MUST HAVE REWRITTEN THE DATA!
WHEN I SAW THIS AN HOUR AGO, THE RESULTS WERE THE OPPOSITE.
FIX IT.
I CAN'T!!
THE PASSWORD WAS CHANGED...
ONLY MAORA-SAMA CAN CHANGE IT BACK.

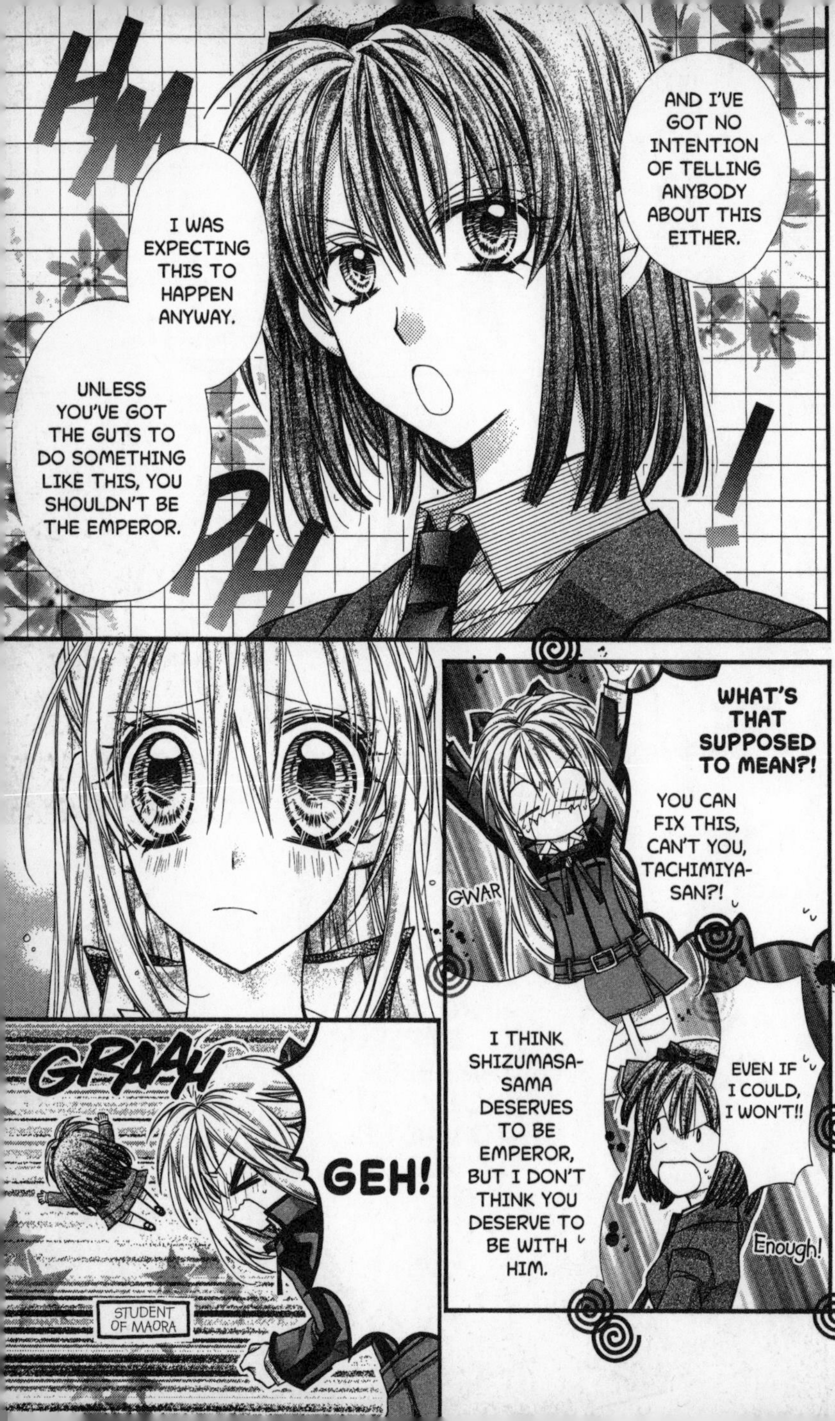
AND I'VE GOT NO INTENTION OF TELLING ANYBODY ABOUT THIS EITHER.
HM
I WAS EXPECTING THIS TO HAPPEN ANYWAY.
UNLESS YOU'VE GOT THE GUTS TO DO SOMETHING LIKE THIS, YOU SHOULDN'T BE THE EMPEROR.
PH
!
WHAT'S THAT SUPPOSED TO MEAN?!
YOU CAN FIX THIS, CAN'T YOU, TACHIMIYA-SAN?!
GWAR
EVEN IF I COULD, I WON'T!!
I THINK SHIZUMASA-SAMA DESERVES TO BE EMPEROR, BUT I DON'T THINK YOU DESERVE TO BE WITH HIM.
Enough!
GRAAH
GEH!
STUDENT OF MAORA

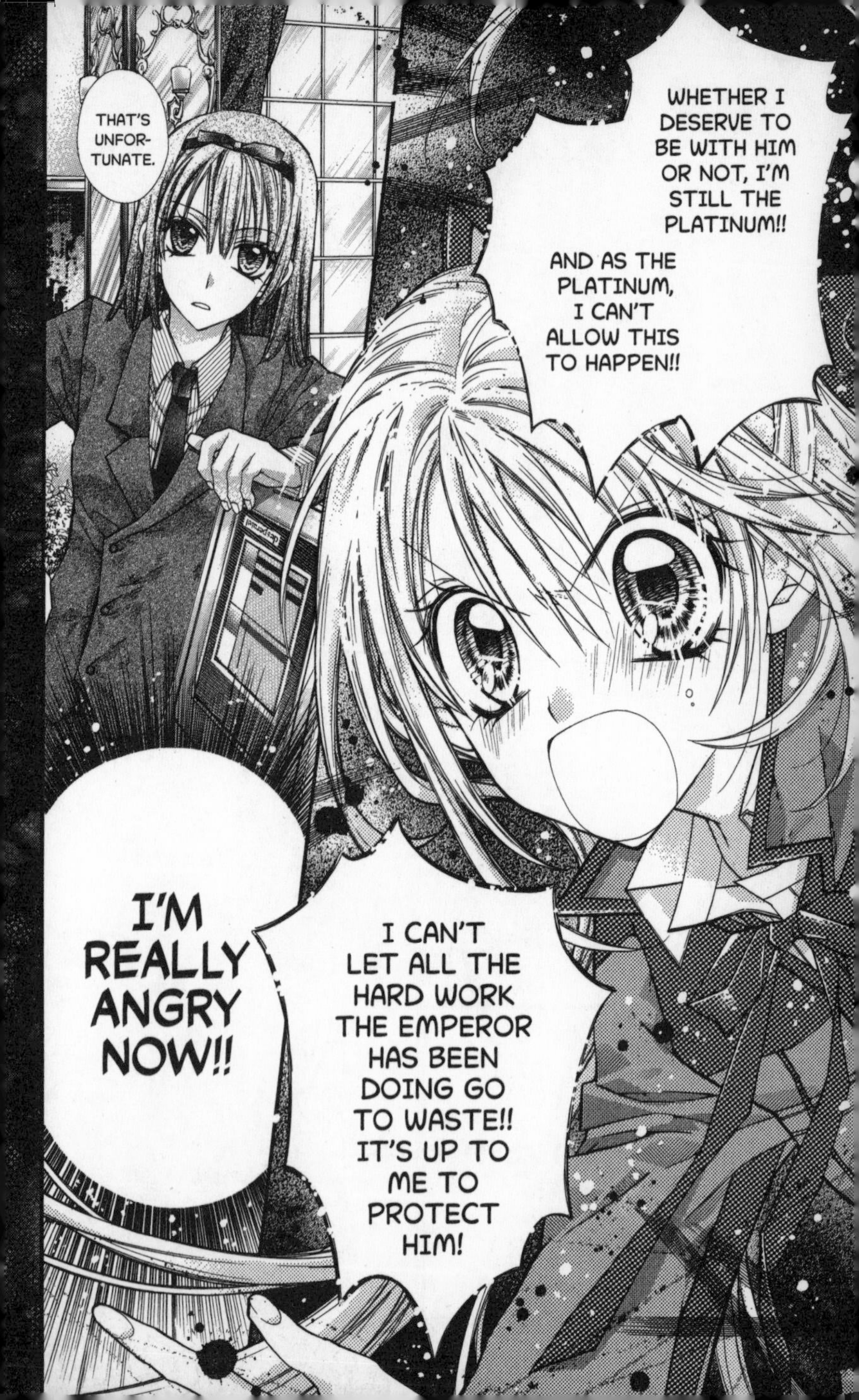
WHETHER I DESERVE TO BE WITH HIM OR NOT, I'M STILL THE PLATINUM!!
AND AS THE PLATINUM, I CAN'T ALLOW THIS TO HAPPEN!!
THAT'S UNFOR-TUNATE.
I CAN'T LET ALL THE HARD WORK THE EMPEROR HAS BEEN DOING GO TO WASTE!! IT'S UP TO ME TO PROTECT HIM!
I'M REALLY ANGRY NOW!!

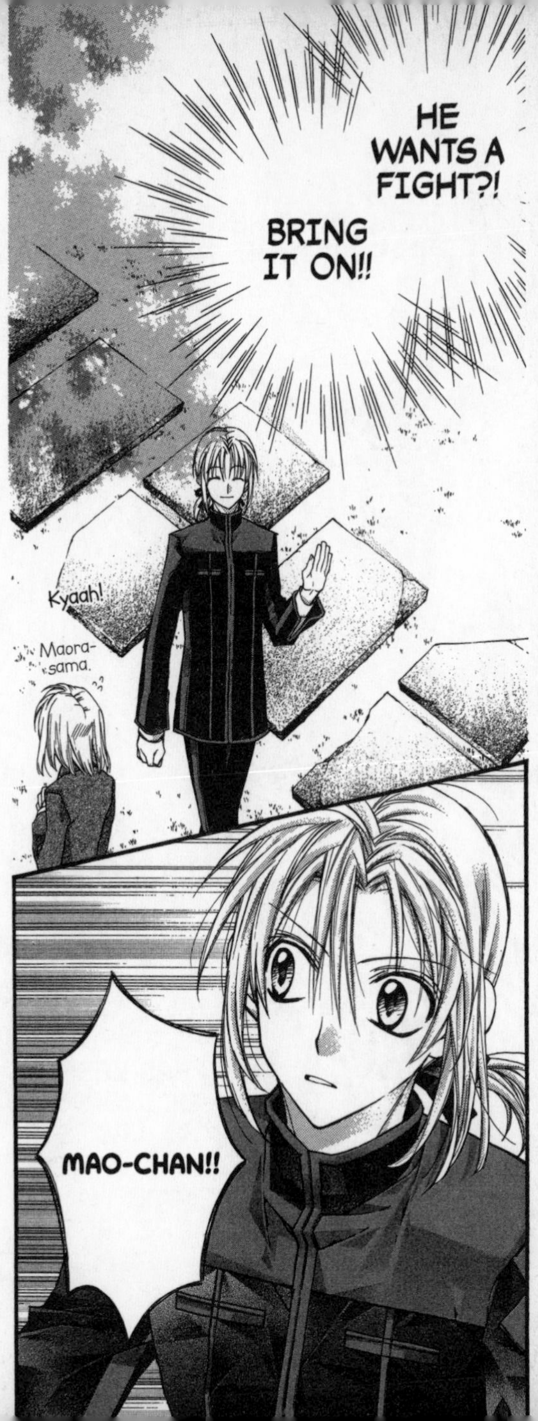
HE WANTS A FIGHT?!
BRING IT ON!!
Kyaah!
Maora-sama.
MAO-CHAN!!

Special Thanks☆

- Minase-san
- Saori
- Nakame
- Miwa-chan
- Hina-chan
- Yuko-chan
- Ibuki-chan
- Negami-san
- Sakura-chan
- Mamiko
- Takebuchi-san
- Konako
- Yamagata-san
- Arai-san

Ammonite Ltd.

Shueisha's Ribon
Editorial Department

Supervisors

O-sama
Y-sama

Riku & Kai

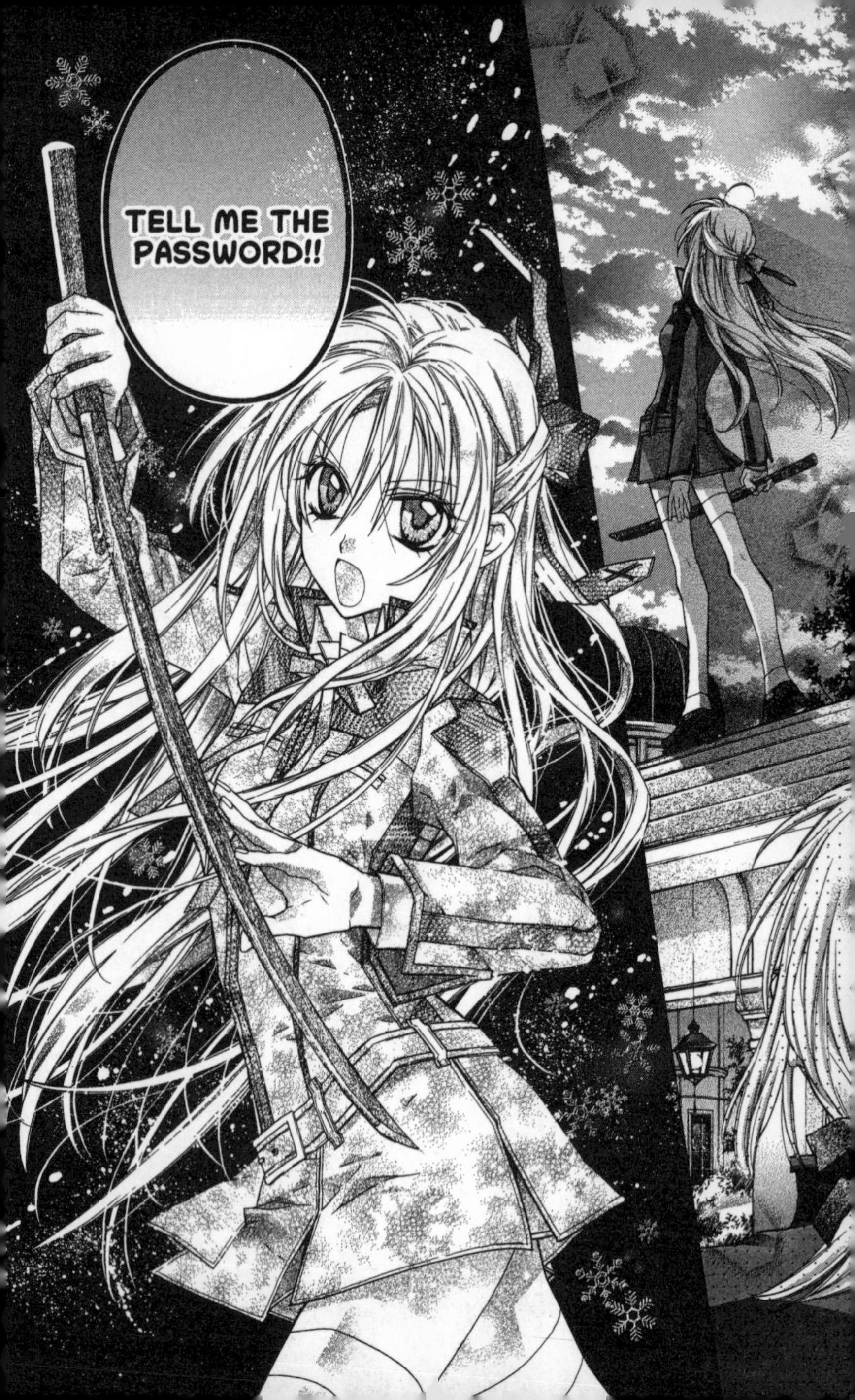
TELL ME THE PASSWORD!!

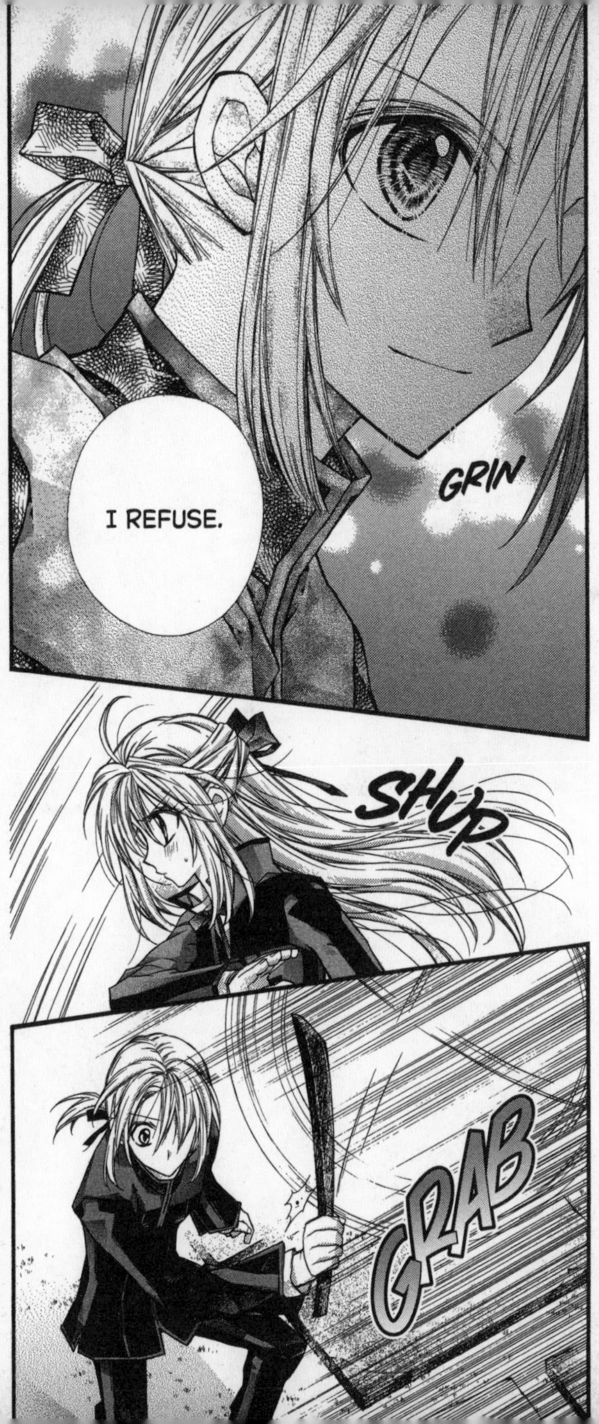
I REFUSE.
GRIN
SHUP
GRAB
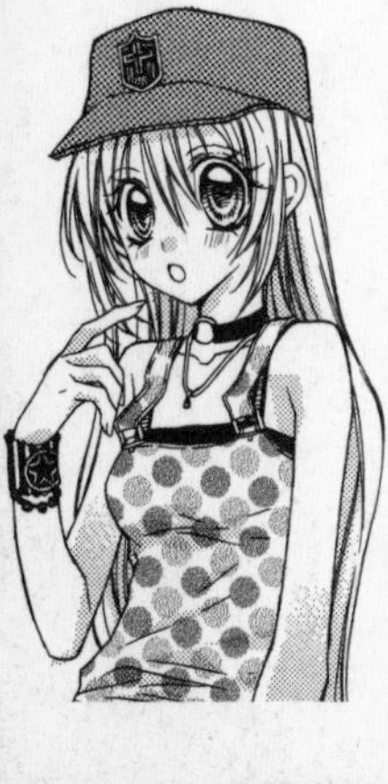

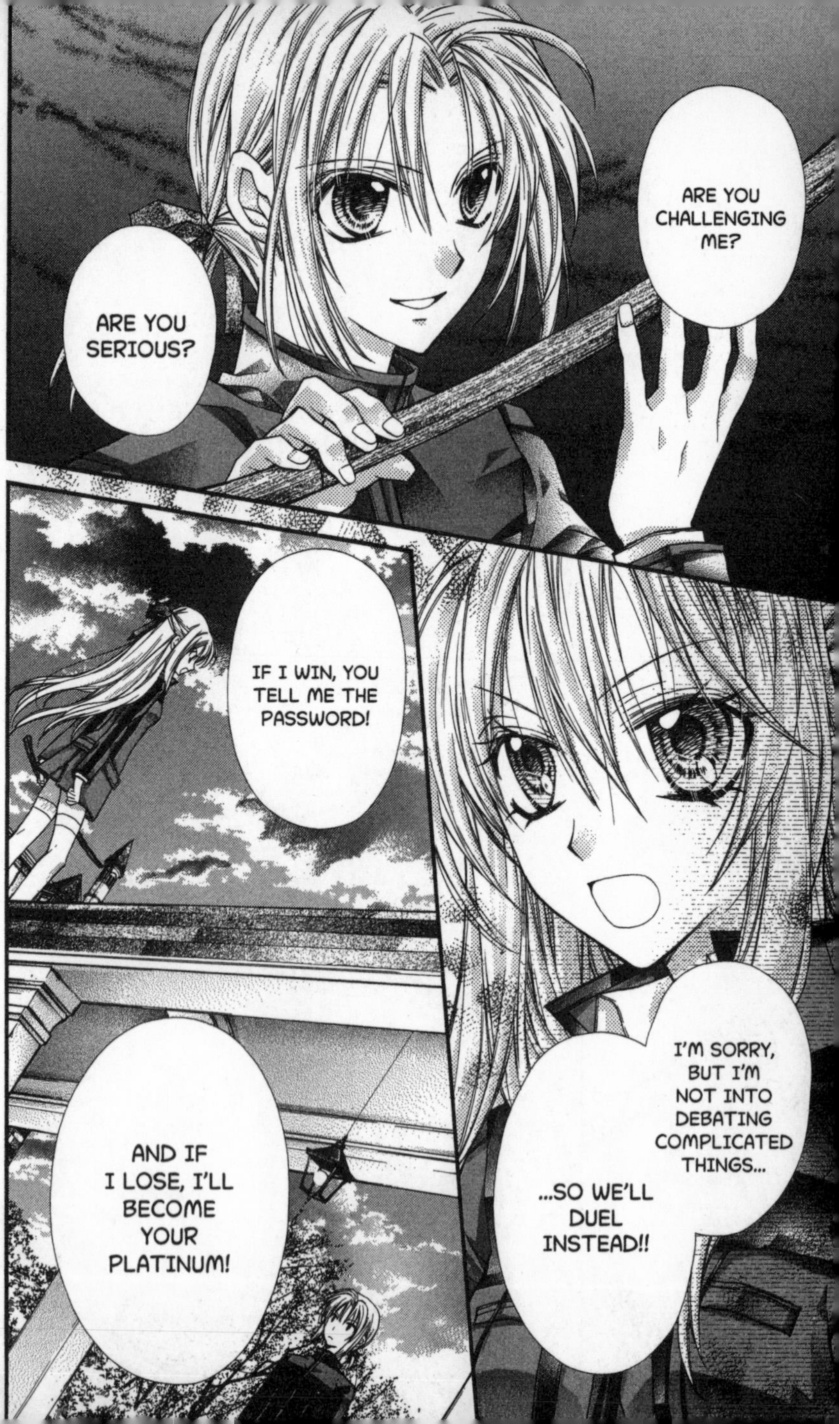
ARE YOU CHALLENGING ME?
ARE YOU SERIOUS?
I'M SORRY, BUT I'M NOT INTO DEBATING COMPLICATED THINGS...
...SO WE'LL DUEL INSTEAD!!
IF I WIN, YOU TELL ME THE PASSWORD!
AND IF I LOSE, I'LL BECOME YOUR PLATINUM!

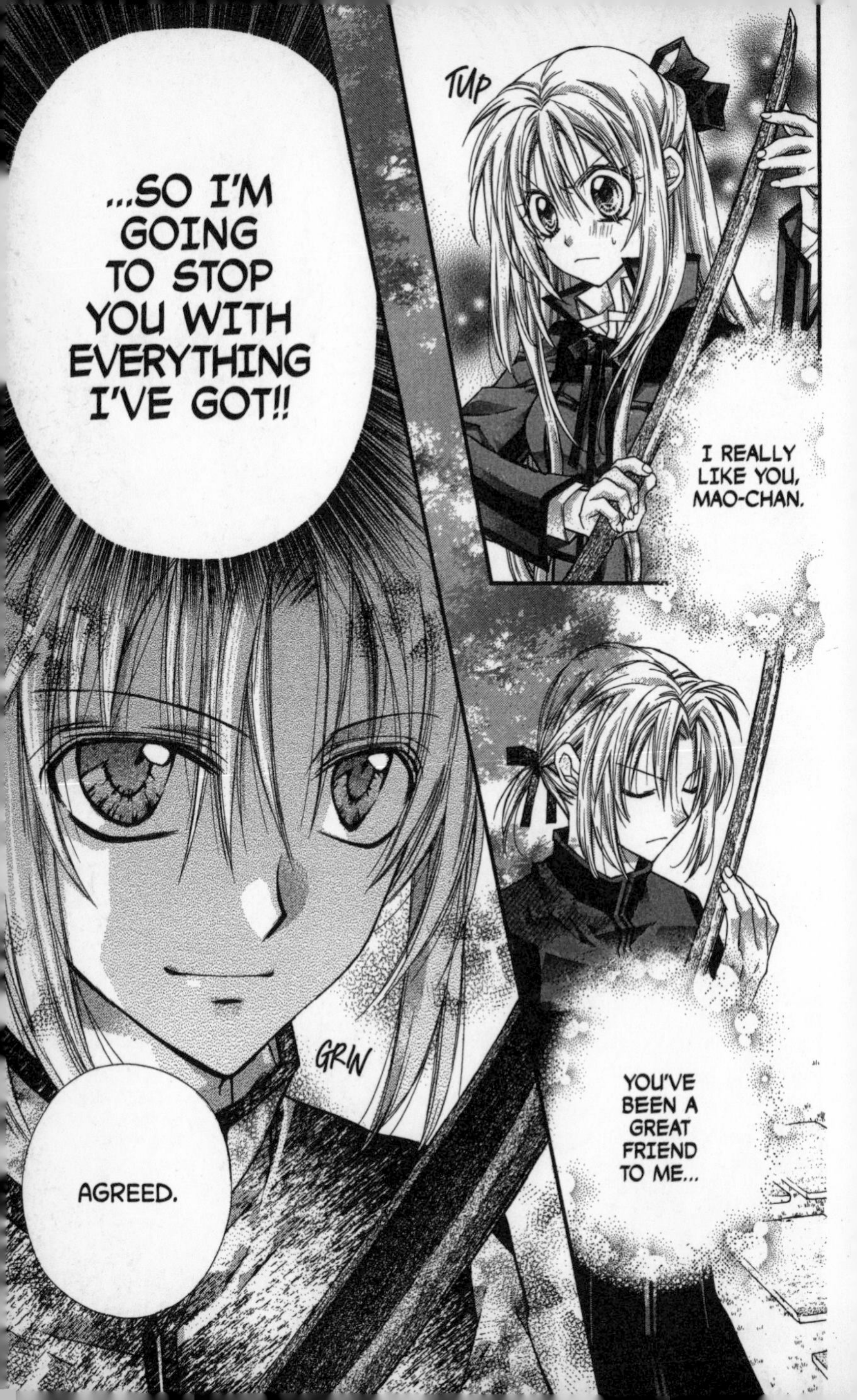
TUP
I REALLY LIKE YOU, MAO-CHAN.
YOU'VE BEEN A GREAT FRIEND TO ME...
...SO I'M GOING TO STOP YOU WITH EVERYTHING I'VE GOT!!
GRIN
AGREED.

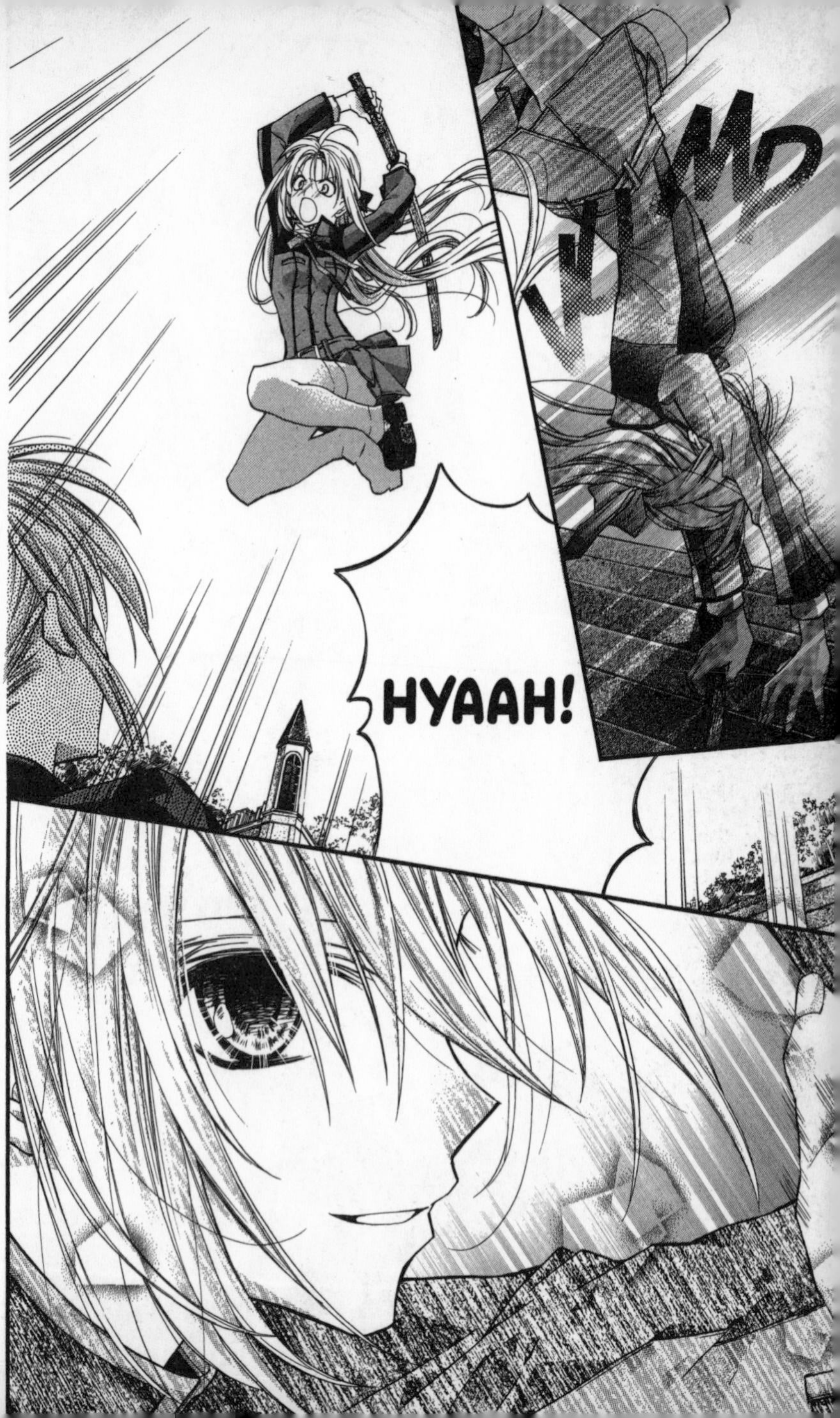
HYAAH!

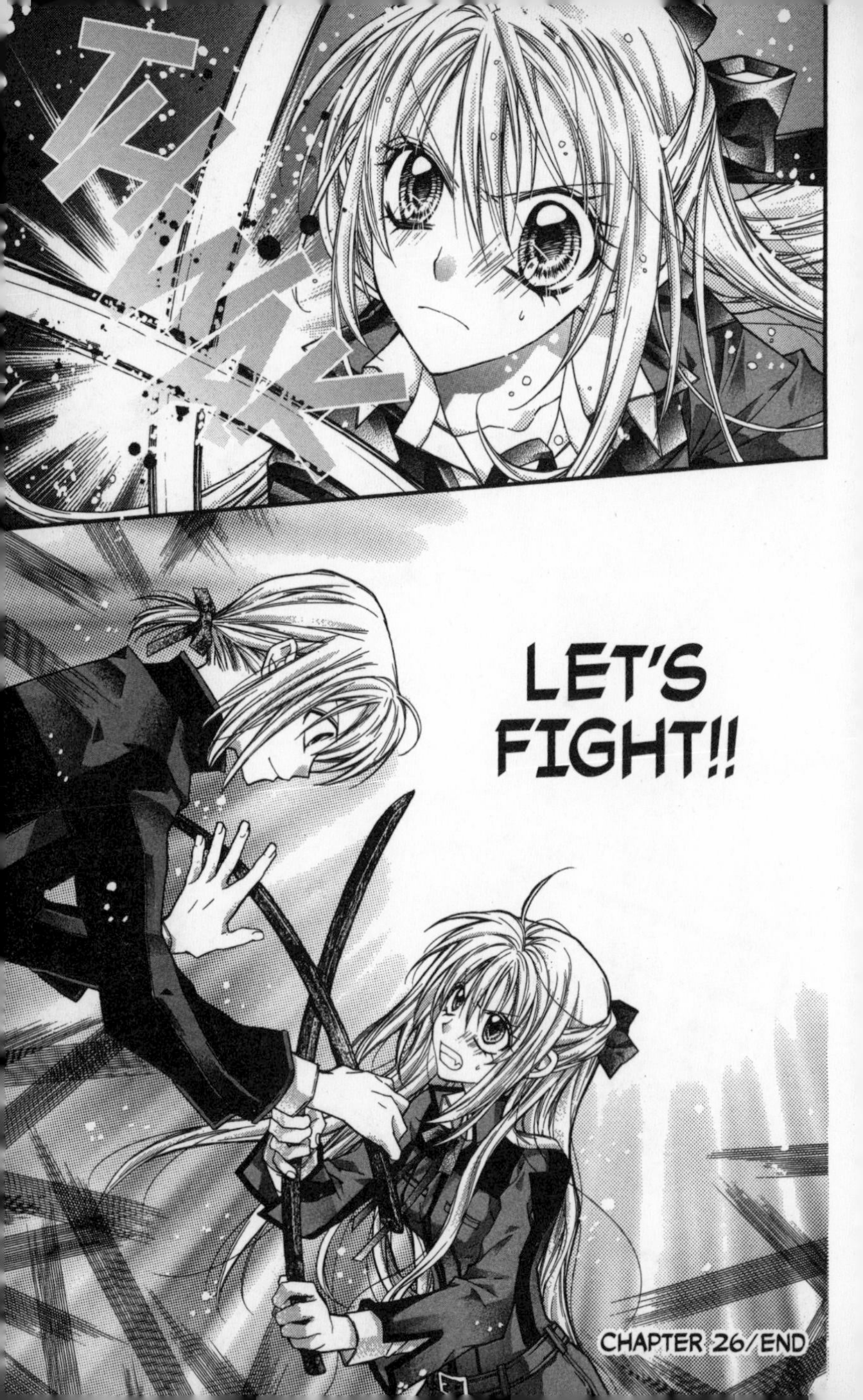
LET'S FIGHT!!
CHAPTER 26/END

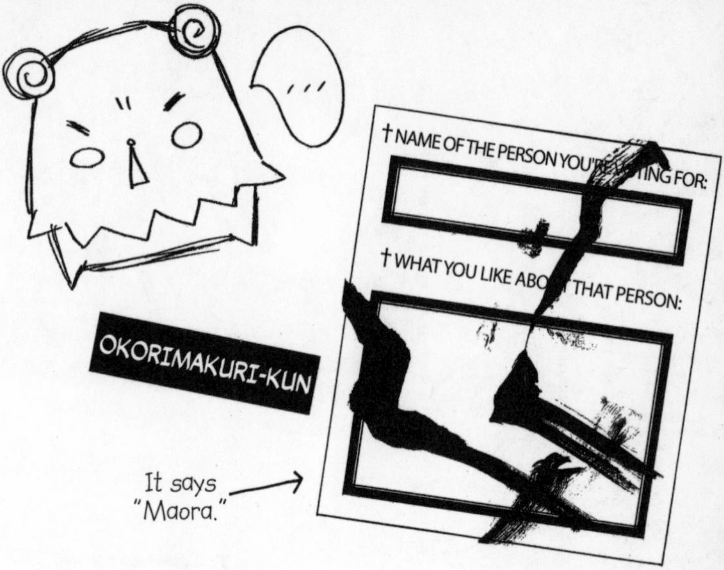

...
† NAME OF THE PERSON YOU'
TING FOR:
† WHAT YOU LIKE ABO
THAT PERSON:
OKORIMAKURI-KUN
It says "Maora."

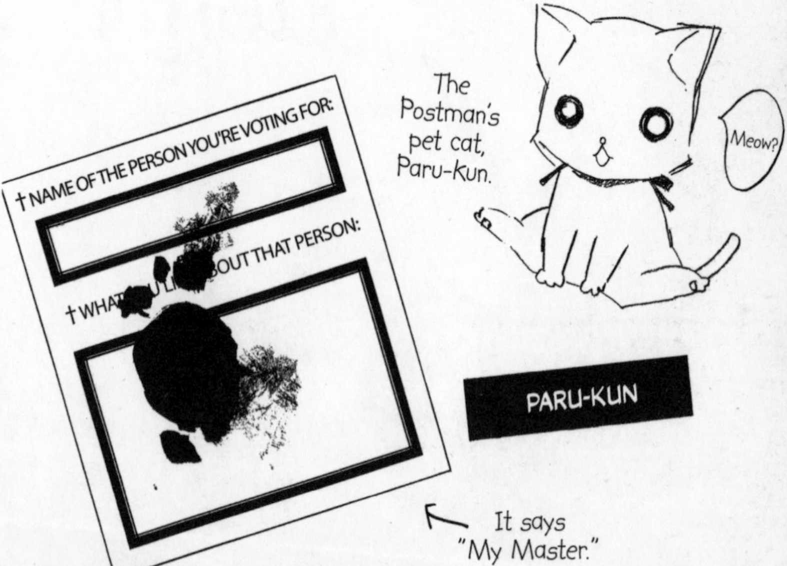

Meow?
The Postman's pet cat, Paru-Kun.
PARU-KUN
† NAME OF THE PERSON YOU'RE VOTING FOR:
† WHA
OUT THAT PERSON:
It says "My Master."

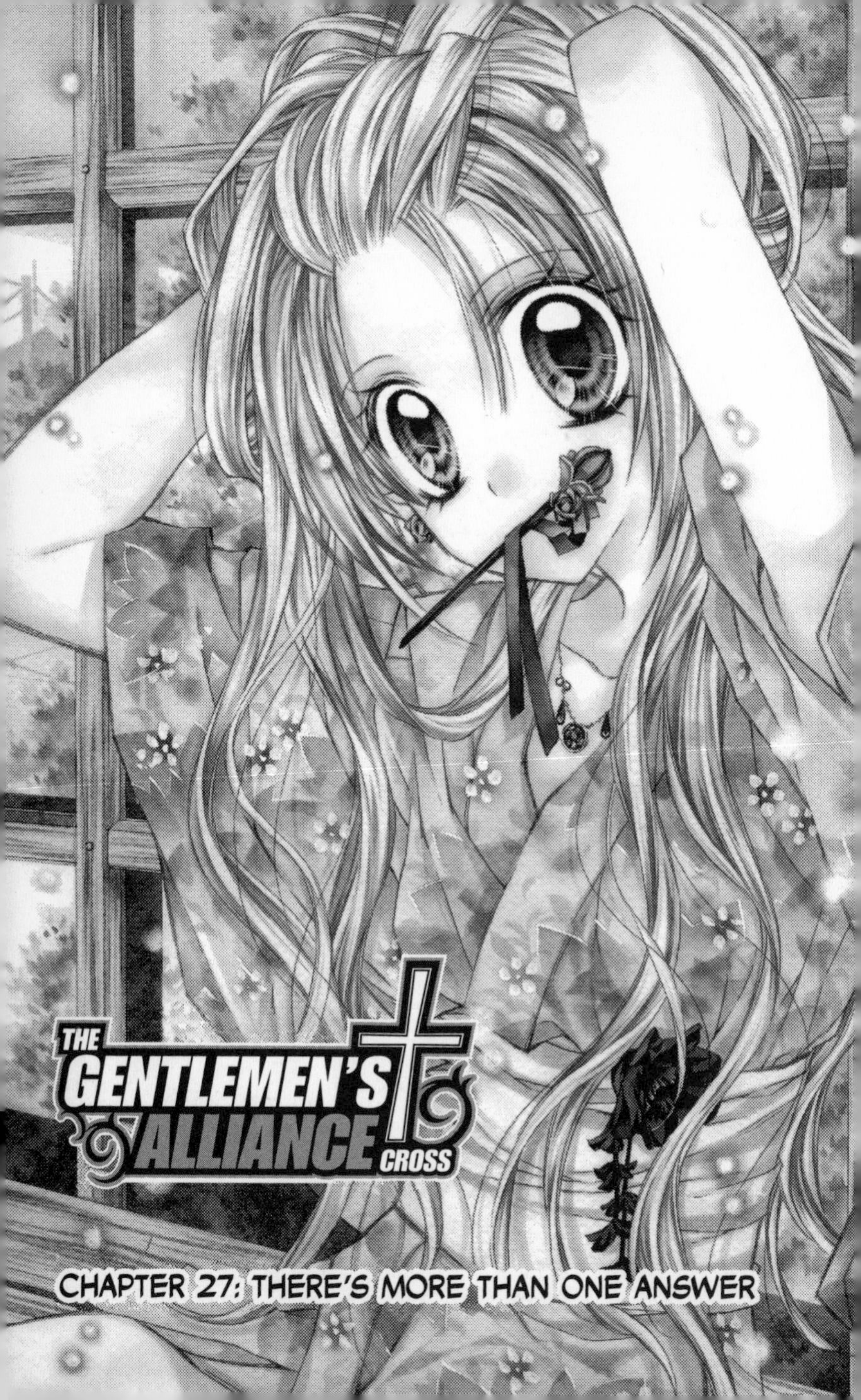
THE GENTLEMEN'S ALLIANCE CROSS
CHAPTER 27: THERE'S MORE THAN ONE ANSWER

Special Guest!

Currently serializing the very popular *High Score* in *Ribon!!*

Chinami Tsuyama-sensei ☆

The Maguri & Maora she drew on the FAX she sent to me was so cute that I even asked her to ink it for me!!

♢ **Thank you very much! It's so cute!!** ♢

I love Chinami-san as well as her manga!!

I hope we get the chance to go out to eat again.

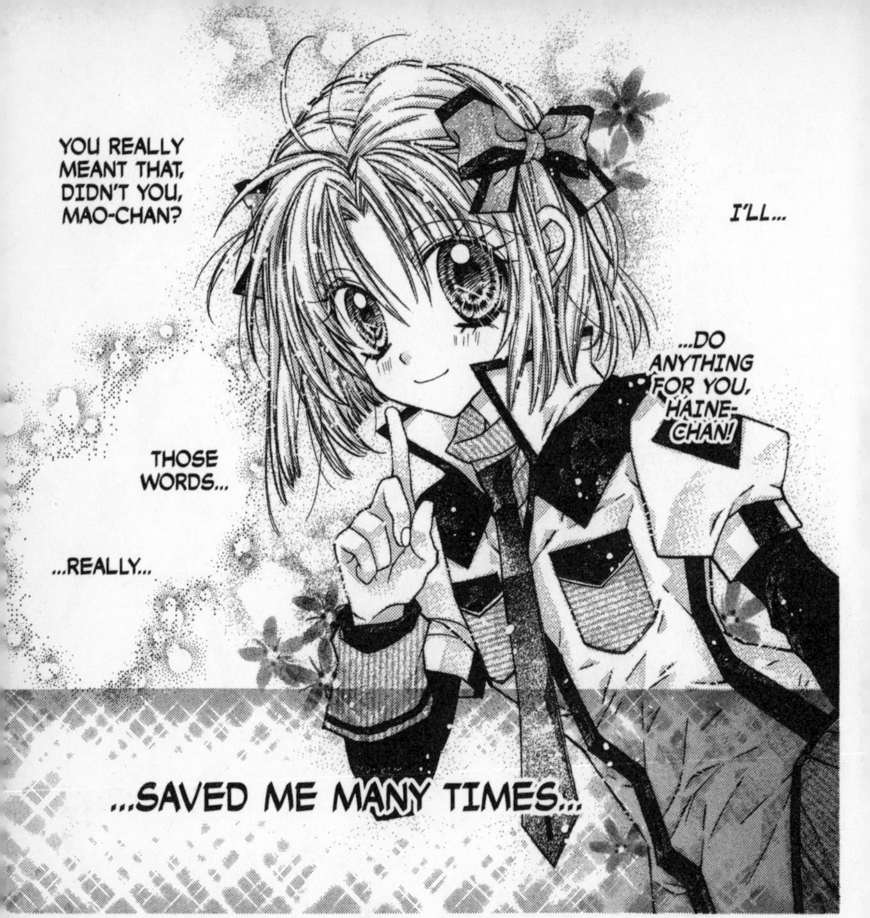
I'LL...
...DO ANYTHING FOR YOU, HAINE-CHAN!
YOU REALLY MEANT THAT, DIDN'T YOU, MAO-CHAN?
THOSE WORDS...
...REALLY...
...SAVED ME MANY TIMES...

Chapter 27: There's More than One Answer

※I'm giving away the story.

Lead-in: Won't you look at me with those eyes of yours...?

The person I paid most attention to in this chapter is Tachimiya-san. I really like Tachimiya-san!! How do I put it... I like people who can distinguish between the feelings of "dislike" and "will not accept." She's the type of person who dislikes Haine, but she is willing to accept and understand the fact that a lot of nice people support Haine. It's nice. Not that I'd like to become friends with her or anything, but...

It's just natural for Maguri and Mao-chan to be together. They feel at home with each other. But I am still unsure whether it is right or not for their wish to come true. So I'd like to watch over them and see for myself.

I like the illustration on page 169 of the manga where they're all drinking tea with milk (though I can't drink tea with milk). Ushio-chan and Takanari are thinking, "It's too sweet!" but they are keeping quiet about it... That's love.

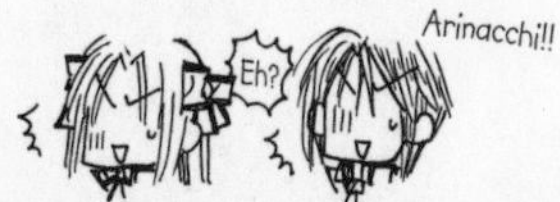
Arinacchi!!
Eh?

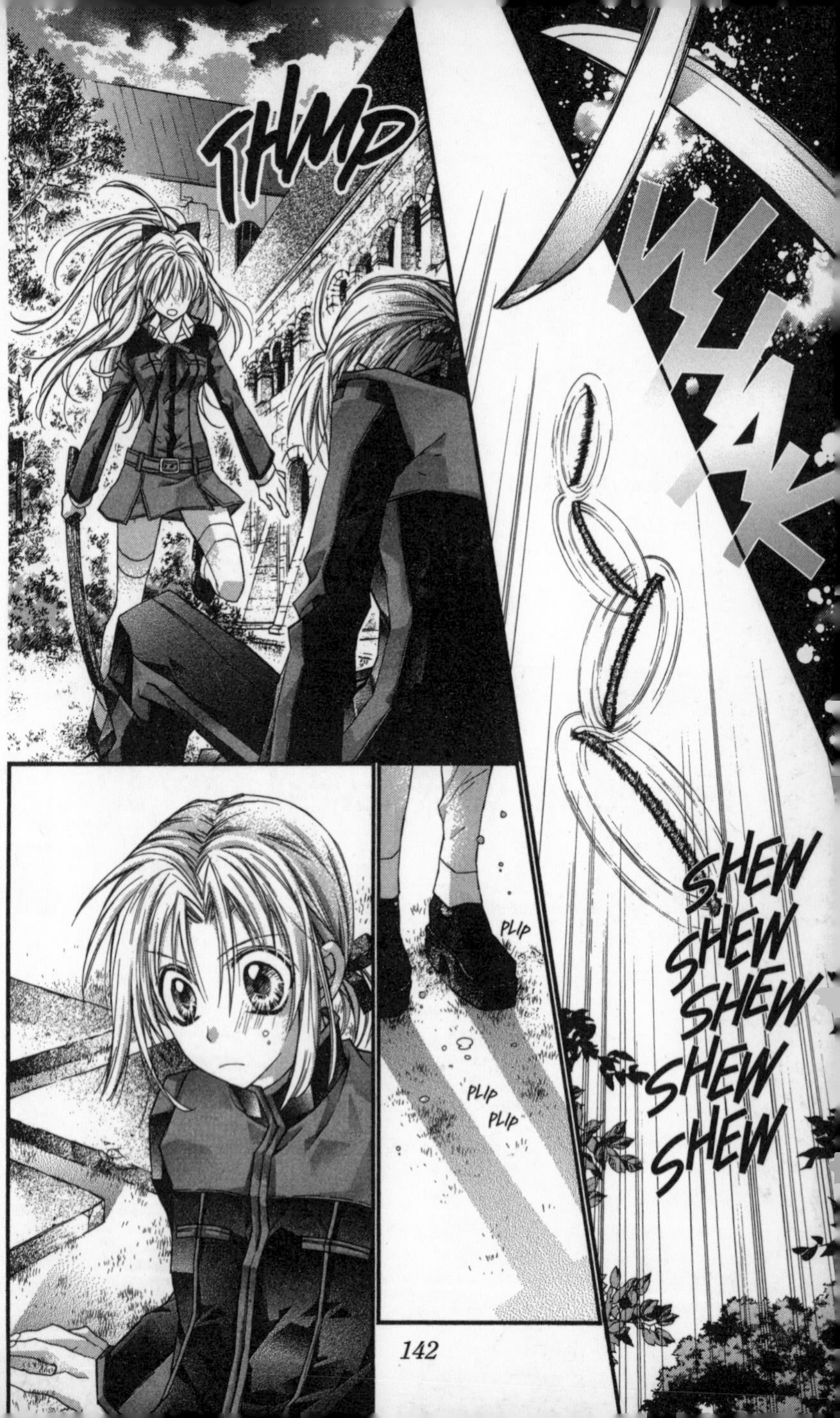
WHAM
SHEW
SHEW
SHEW
SHEW
SHEW
THMD
PLIP
PLIP
PLIP

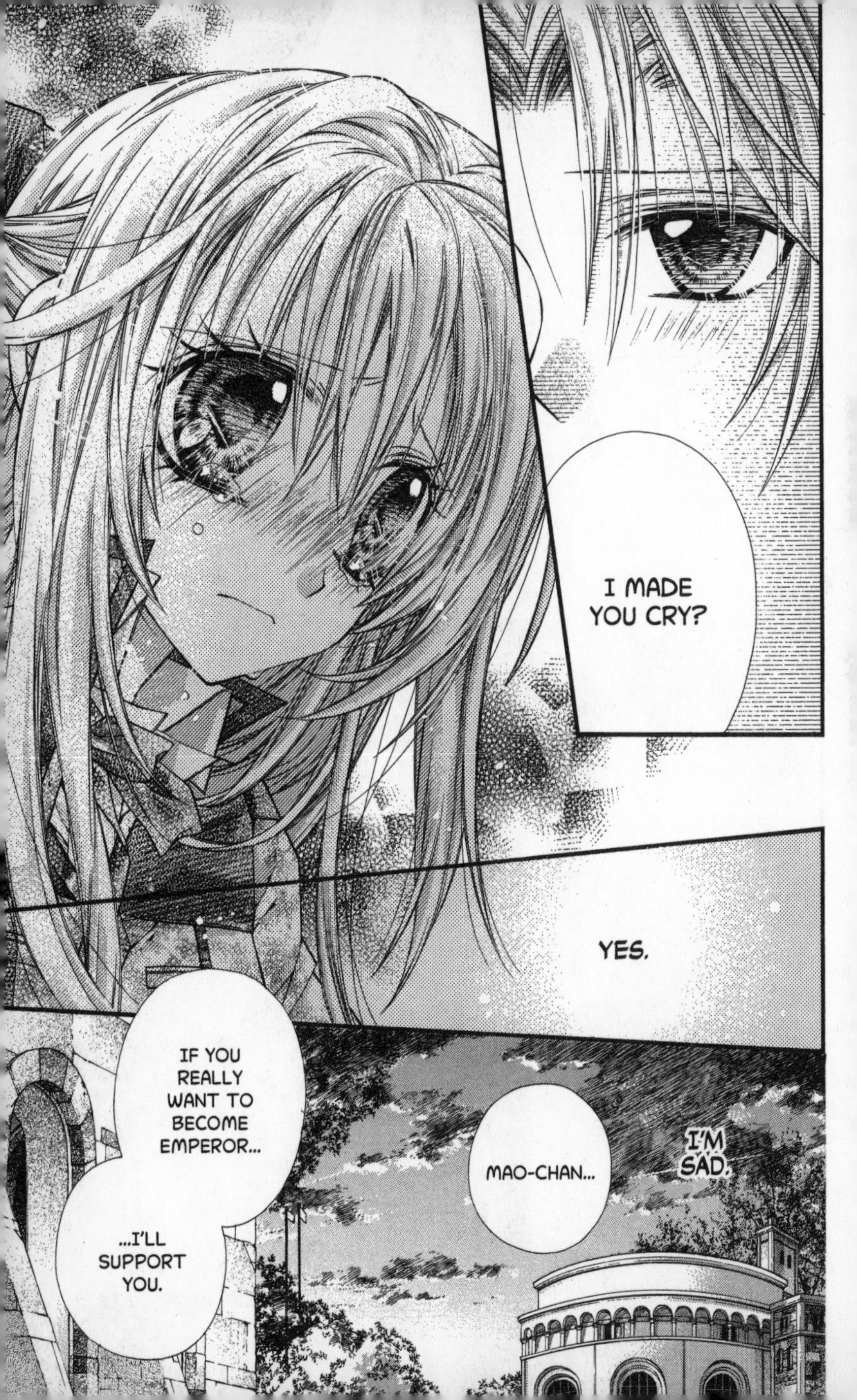
I MADE YOU CRY?
YES.
I'M SAD.
MAO-CHAN...
IF YOU REALLY WANT TO BECOME EMPEROR...
...I'LL SUPPORT YOU.

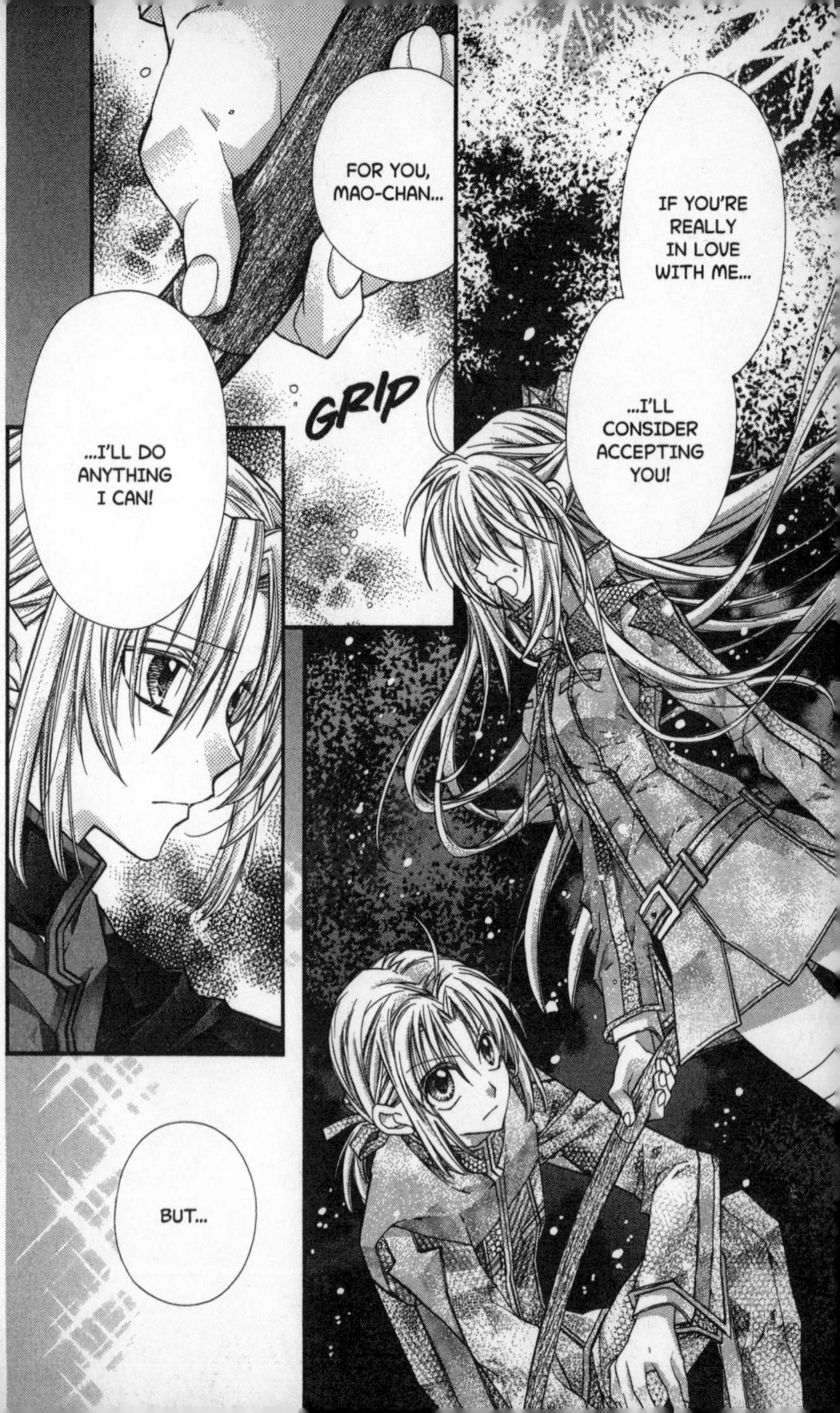
IF YOU'RE REALLY IN LOVE WITH ME...
...I'LL CONSIDER ACCEPTING YOU!
FOR YOU, MAO-CHAN...
GRIP
...I'LL DO ANYTHING I CAN!
BUT...

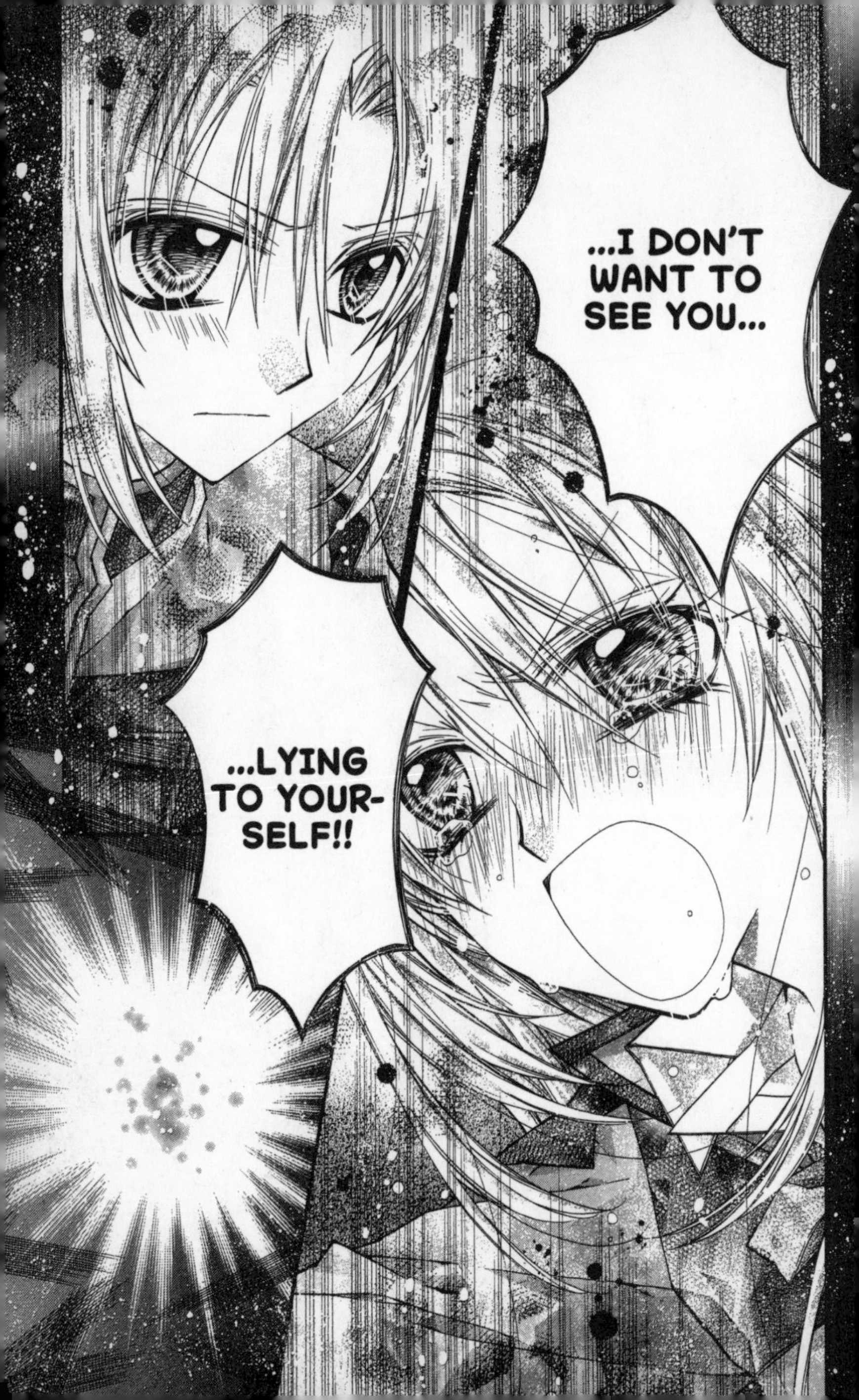
...I DON'T WANT TO SEE YOU...
...LYING TO YOURSELF!!

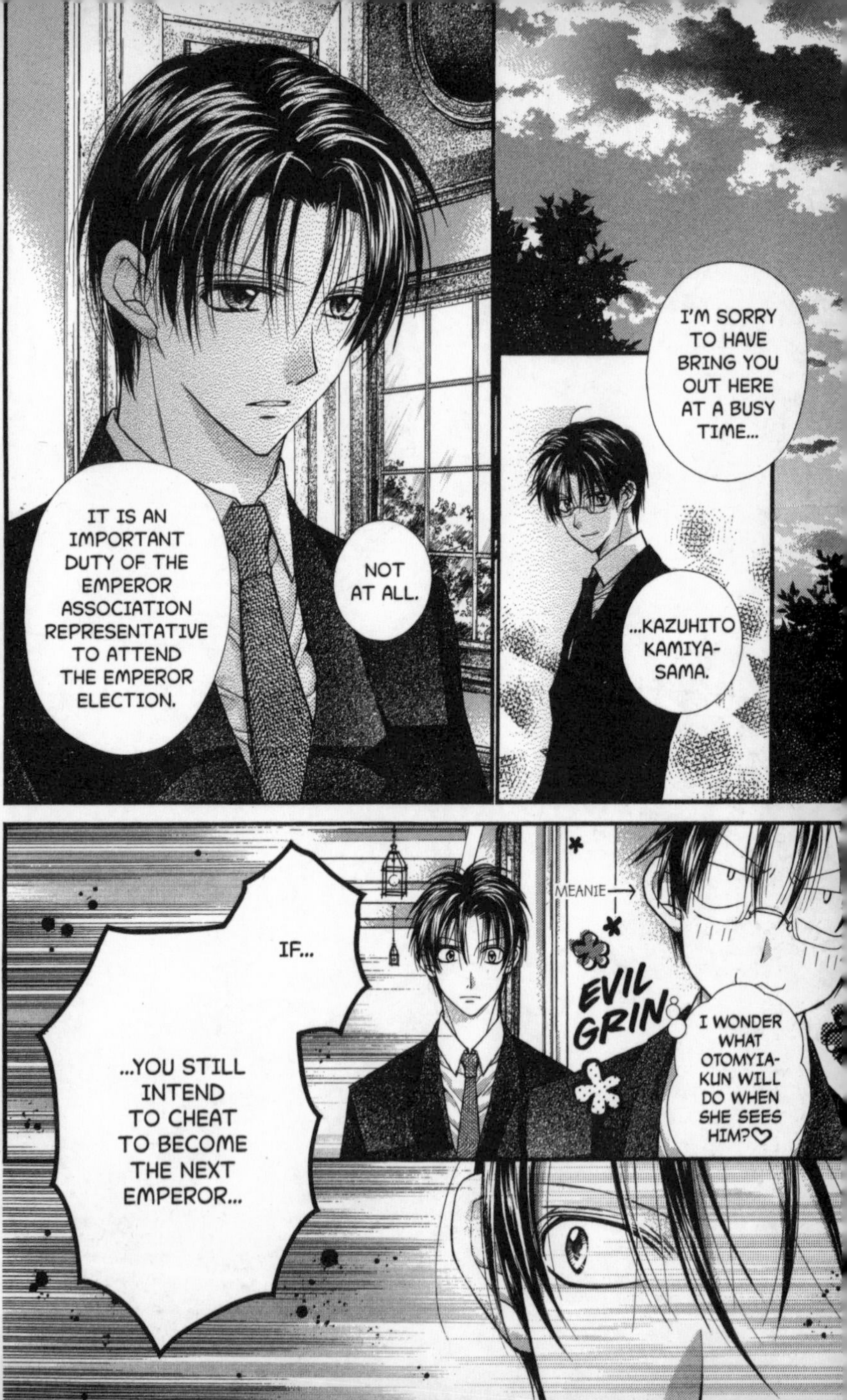
I'M SORRY TO HAVE BRING YOU OUT HERE AT A BUSY TIME...
...KAZUHITO KAMIYA-SAMA.
NOT AT ALL.
IT IS AN IMPORTANT DUTY OF THE EMPEROR ASSOCIATION REPRESENTATIVE TO ATTEND THE EMPEROR ELECTION.
MEANIE
EVIL GRIN
I WONDER WHAT OTOMYIA-KUN WILL DO WHEN SHE SEES HIM?♡
IF...
...YOU STILL INTEND TO CHEAT TO BECOME THE NEXT EMPEROR...

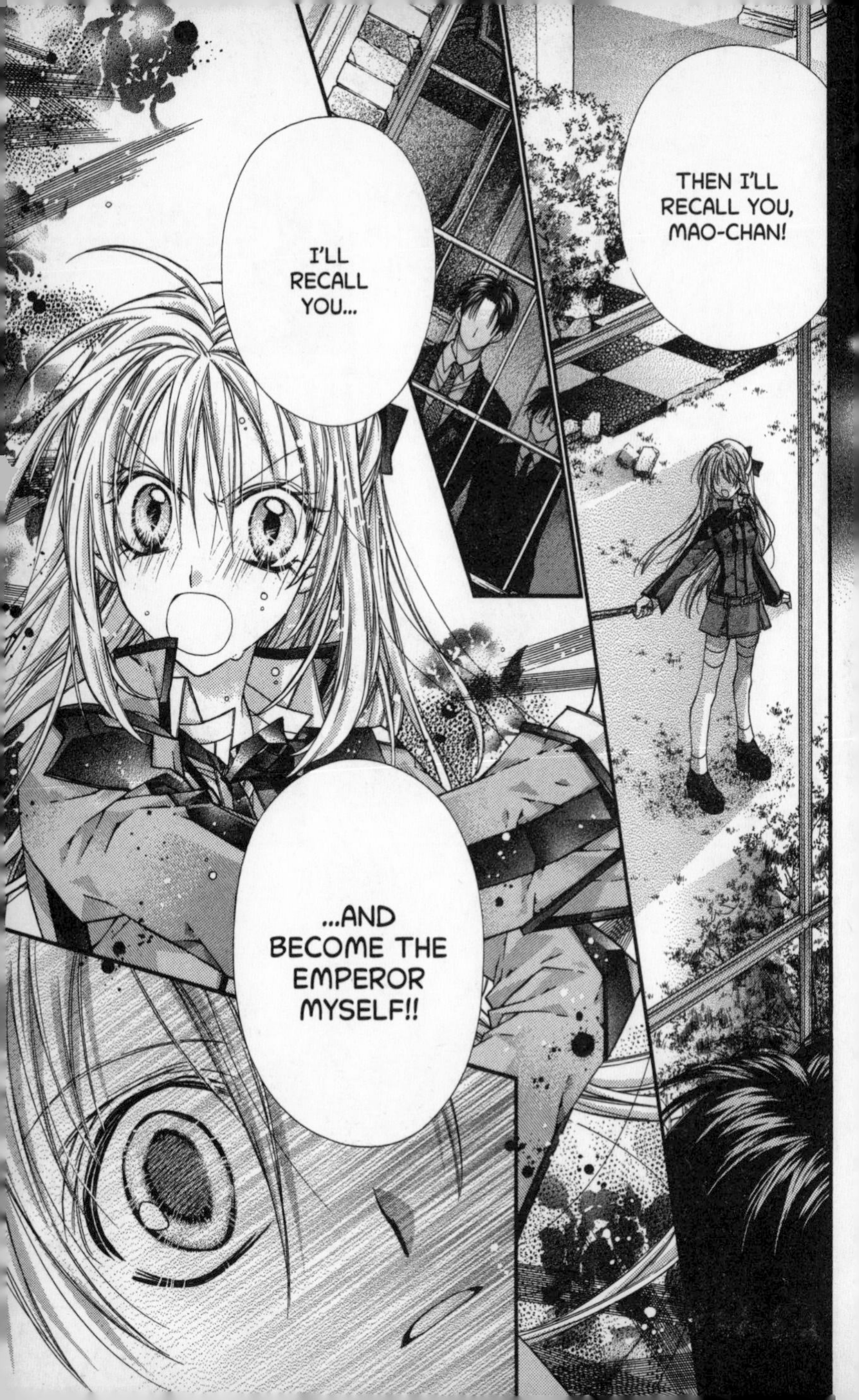
THEN I'LL RECALL YOU, MAO-CHAN!
I'LL RECALL YOU...
...AND BECOME THE EMPEROR MYSELF!!

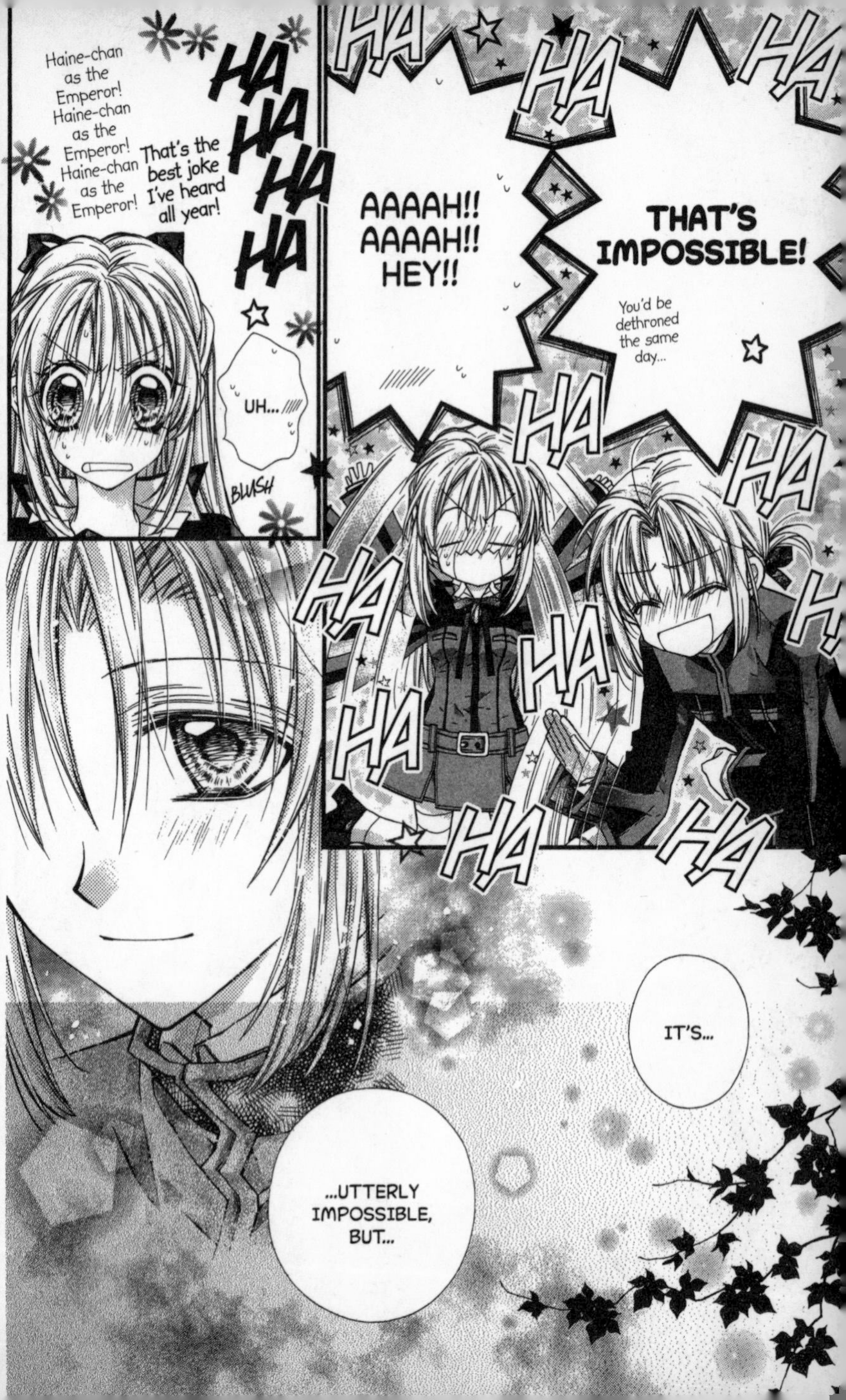
HA HA HA
THAT'S IMPOSSIBLE!
You'd be dethroned the same day...
AAAAH!! AAAAH!! HEY!!
HA HA HA HA HA HA HA HA
HA HA HA HA HA
That's the best joke I've heard all year!
Haine-chan as the Emperor! Haine-chan as the Emperor! Haine-chan as the Emperor!
UH...
BLUSH
IT'S...
...UTTERLY IMPOSSIBLE, BUT...

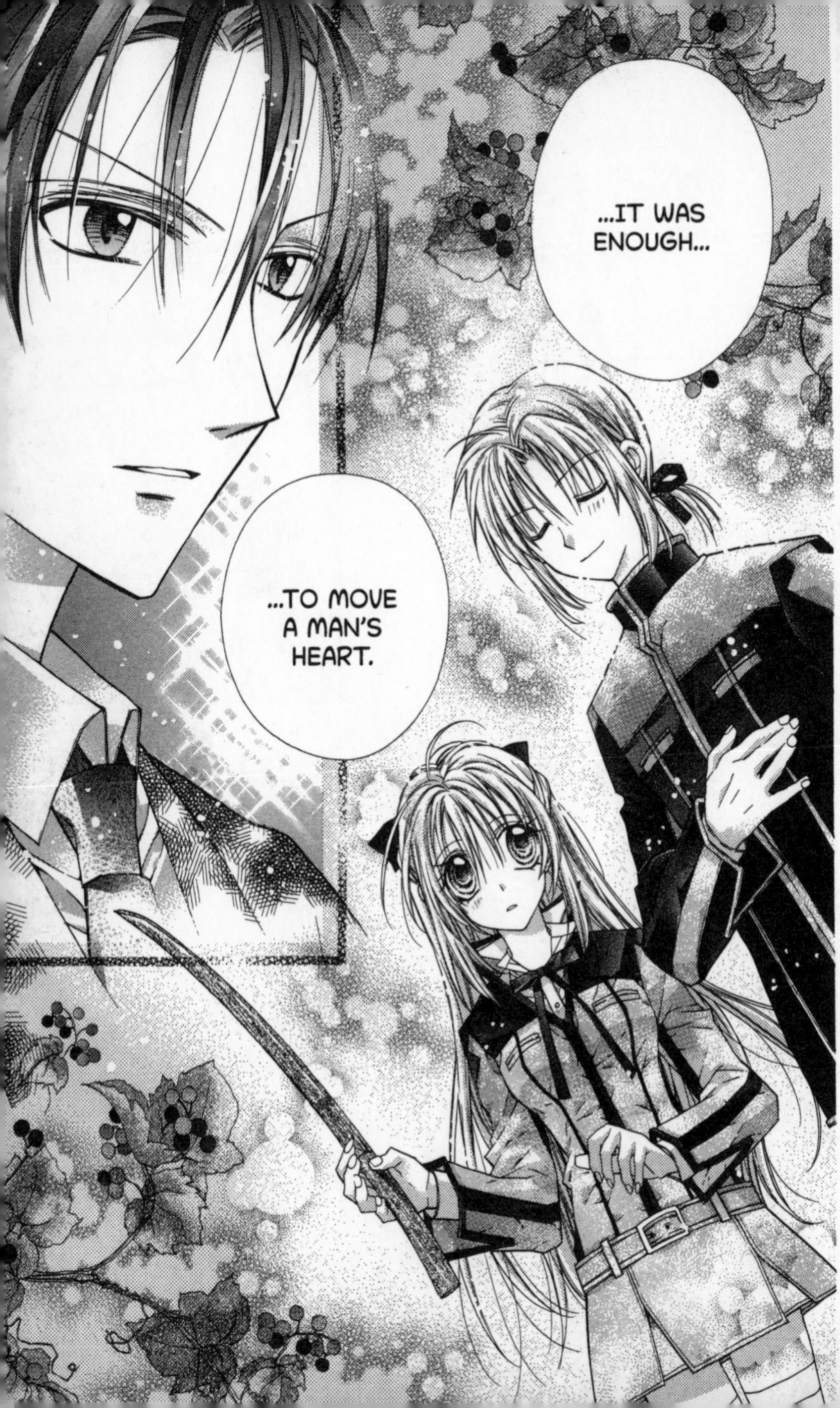
...IT WAS ENOUGH...
...TO MOVE A MAN'S HEART.

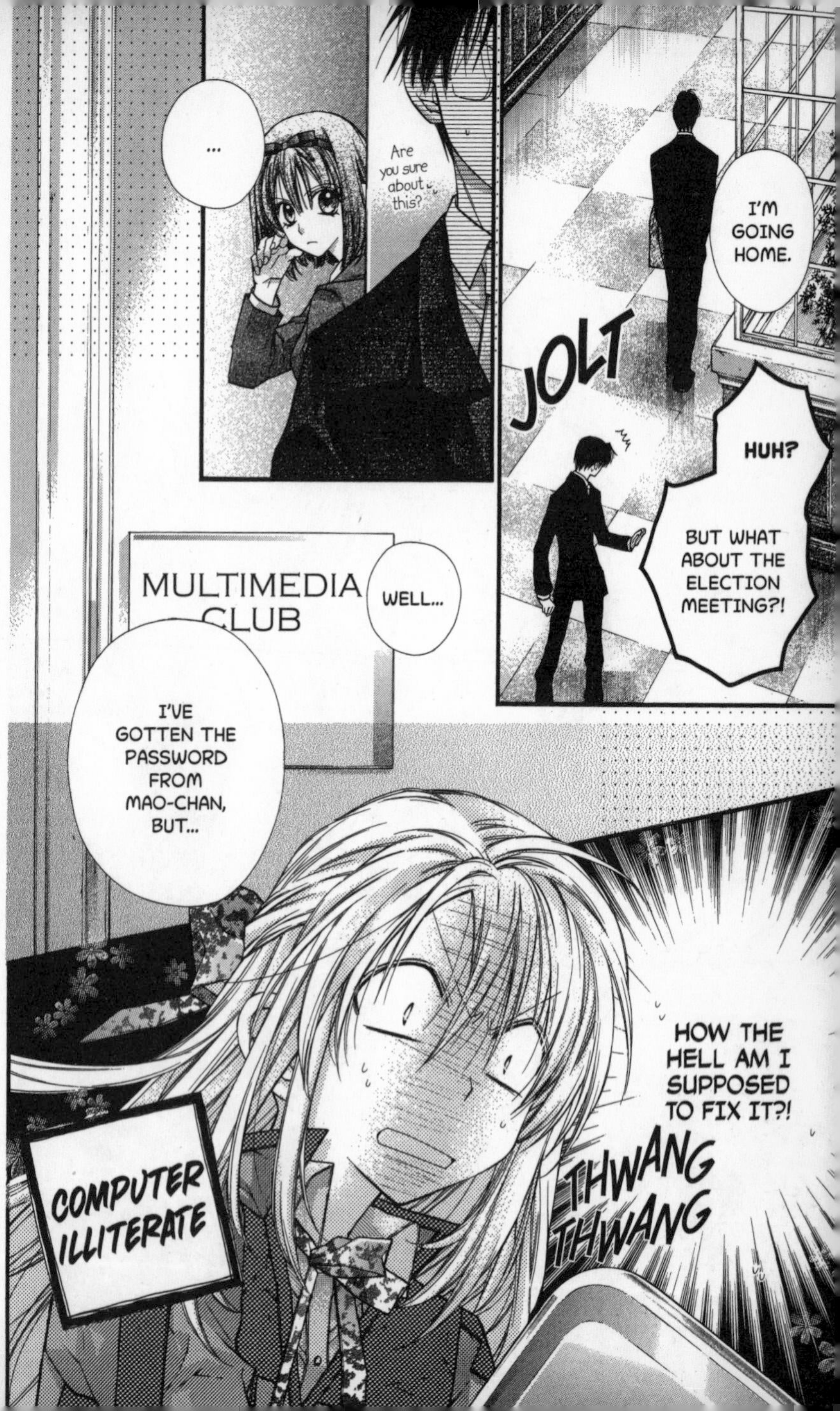
I'M GOING HOME.
JOLT
HUH?
BUT WHAT ABOUT THE ELECTION MEETING?!
Are you sure about this?
...
MULTIMEDIA CLUB
WELL...
I'VE GOTTEN THE PASSWORD FROM MAO-CHAN, BUT...
HOW THE HELL AM I SUPPOSED TO FIX IT?!
THWANG THWANG
COMPUTER ILLITERATE

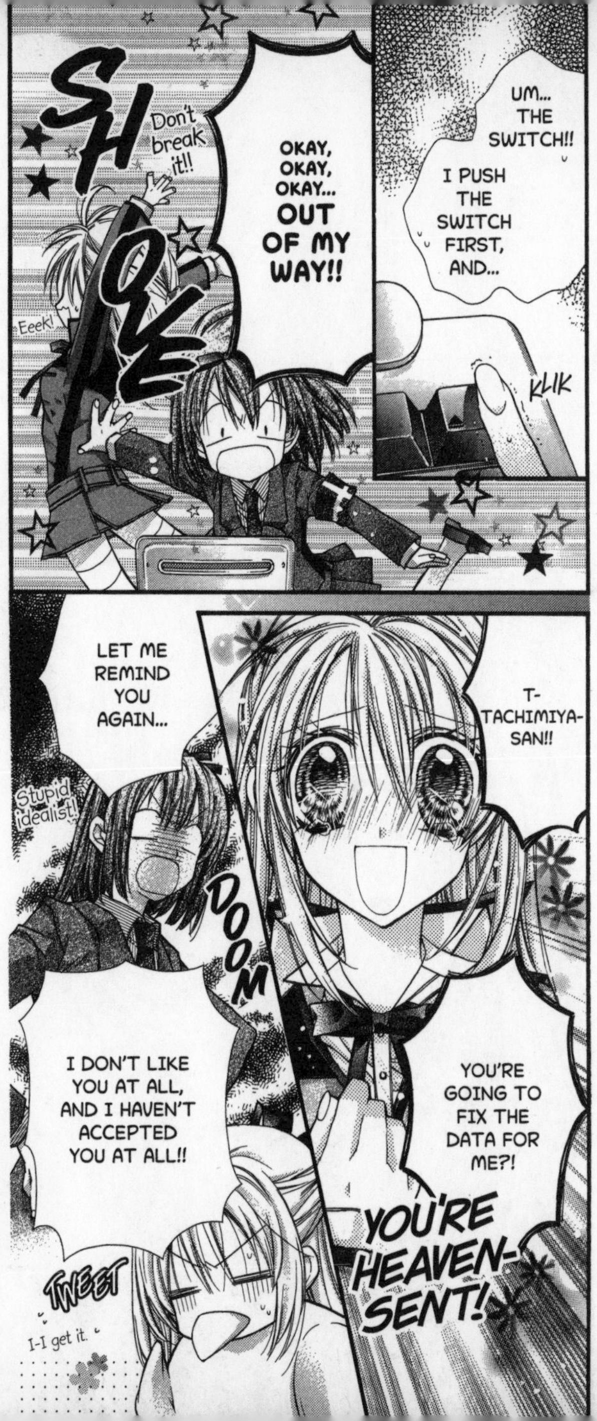
UM... THE SWITCH!!
I PUSH THE SWITCH FIRST, AND...
KLIK
OKAY, OKAY, OKAY... OUT OF MY WAY!!
SHOVE
Don't break it!!
Eeek!
T-TACHIMIYA-SAN!!
YOU'RE GOING TO FIX THE DATA FOR ME?!
YOU'RE HEAVEN-SENT!
LET ME REMIND YOU AGAIN...
Stupid idealist!
DOOM
I DON'T LIKE YOU AT ALL, AND I HAVEN'T ACCEPTED YOU AT ALL!!
TWEET
I-I get it.
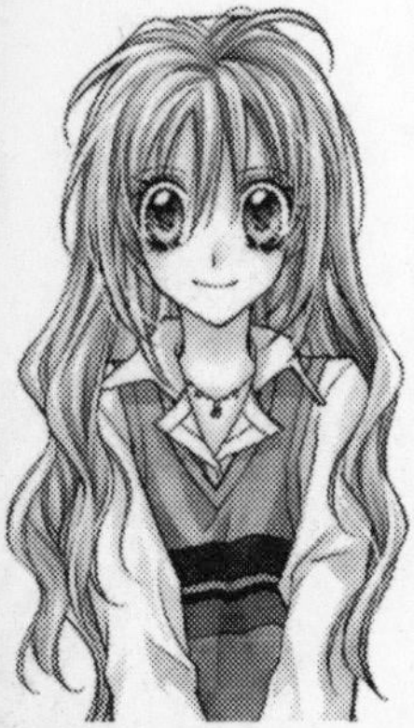

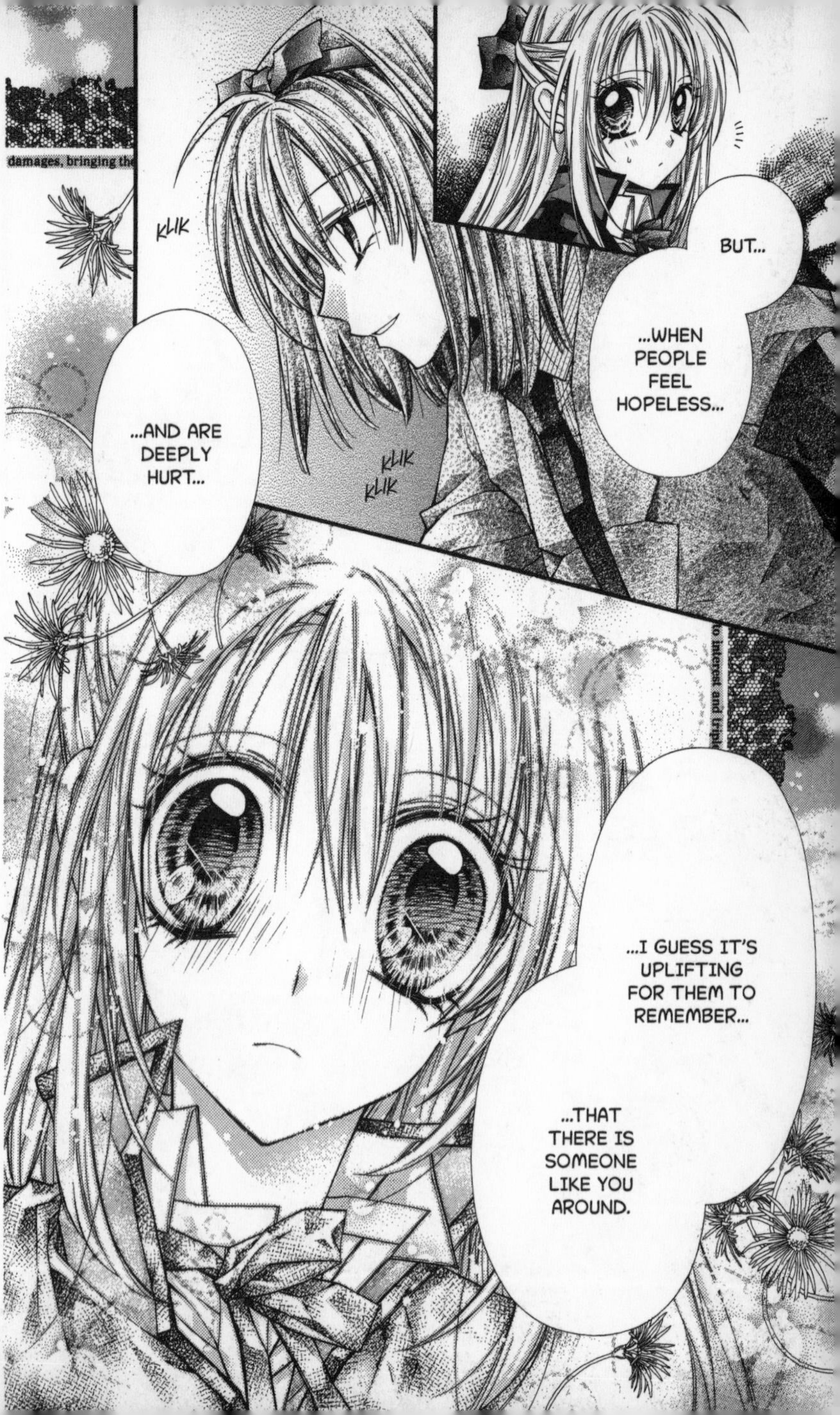
BUT...
...WHEN PEOPLE FEEL HOPELESS...
KLIK
...AND ARE DEEPLY HURT...
KLIK KLIK
...I GUESS IT'S UPLIFTING FOR THEM TO REMEMBER...
...THAT THERE IS SOMEONE LIKE YOU AROUND.

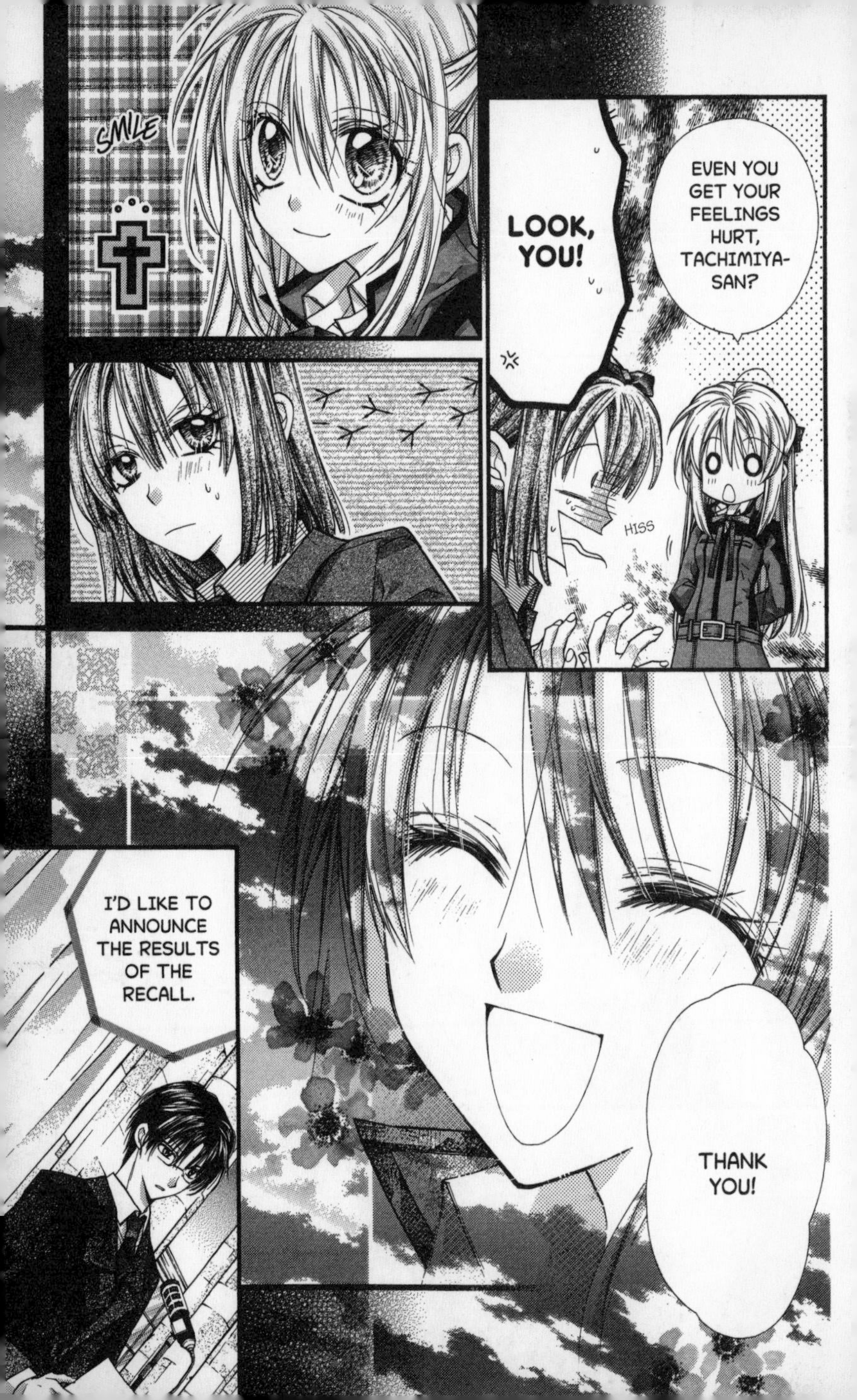
EVEN YOU GET YOUR FEELINGS HURT, TACHIMIYA-SAN?
LOOK, YOU!
HISS
SMILE
THANK YOU!
I'D LIKE TO ANNOUNCE THE RESULTS OF THE RECALL.

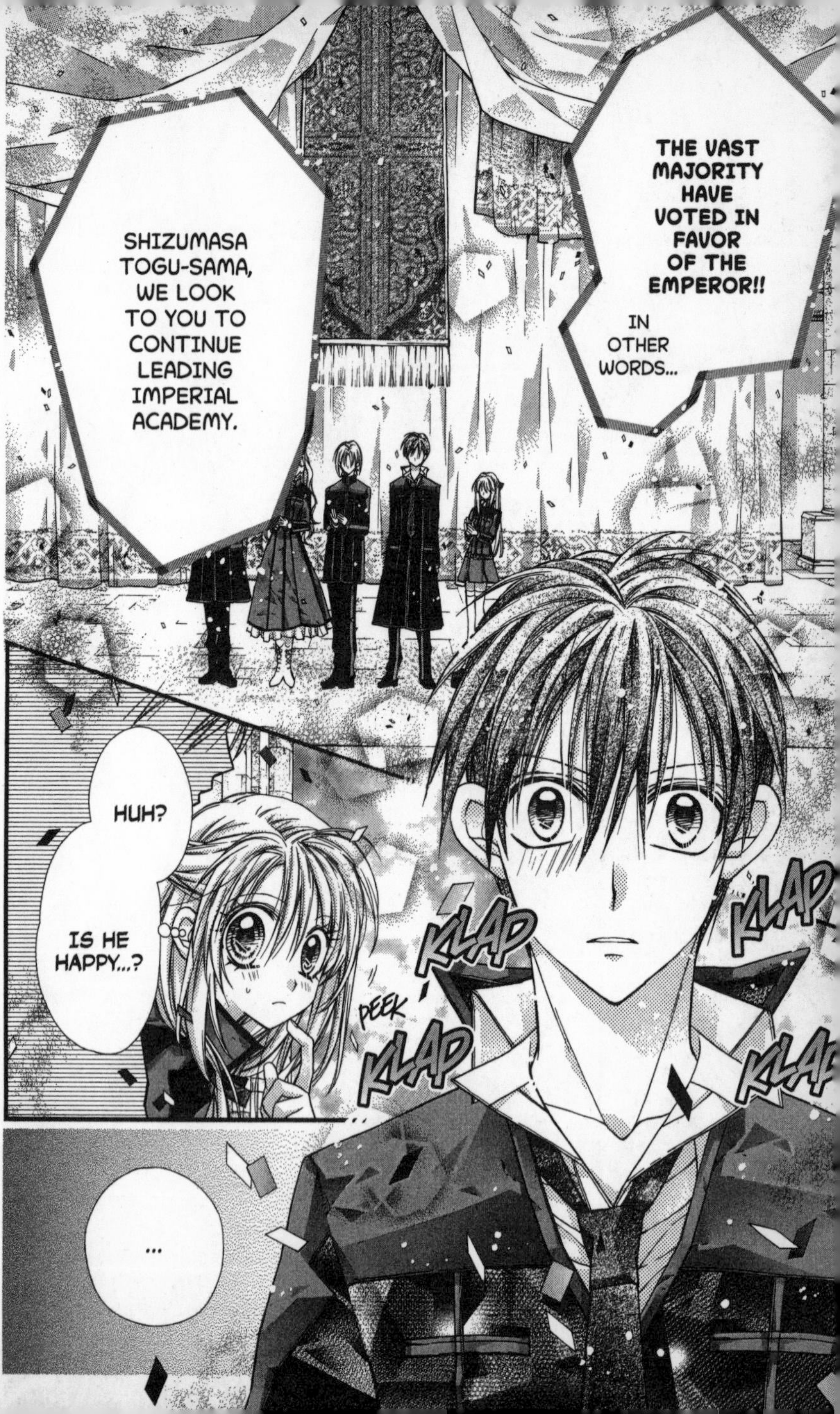
THE VAST MAJORITY HAVE VOTED IN FAVOR OF THE EMPEROR!!
IN OTHER WORDS...
SHIZUMASA TOGU-SAMA, WE LOOK TO YOU TO CONTINUE LEADING IMPERIAL ACADEMY.
KLAP
KLAP
KLAP
KLAP
PEEK
HUH?
IS HE HAPPY...?
...

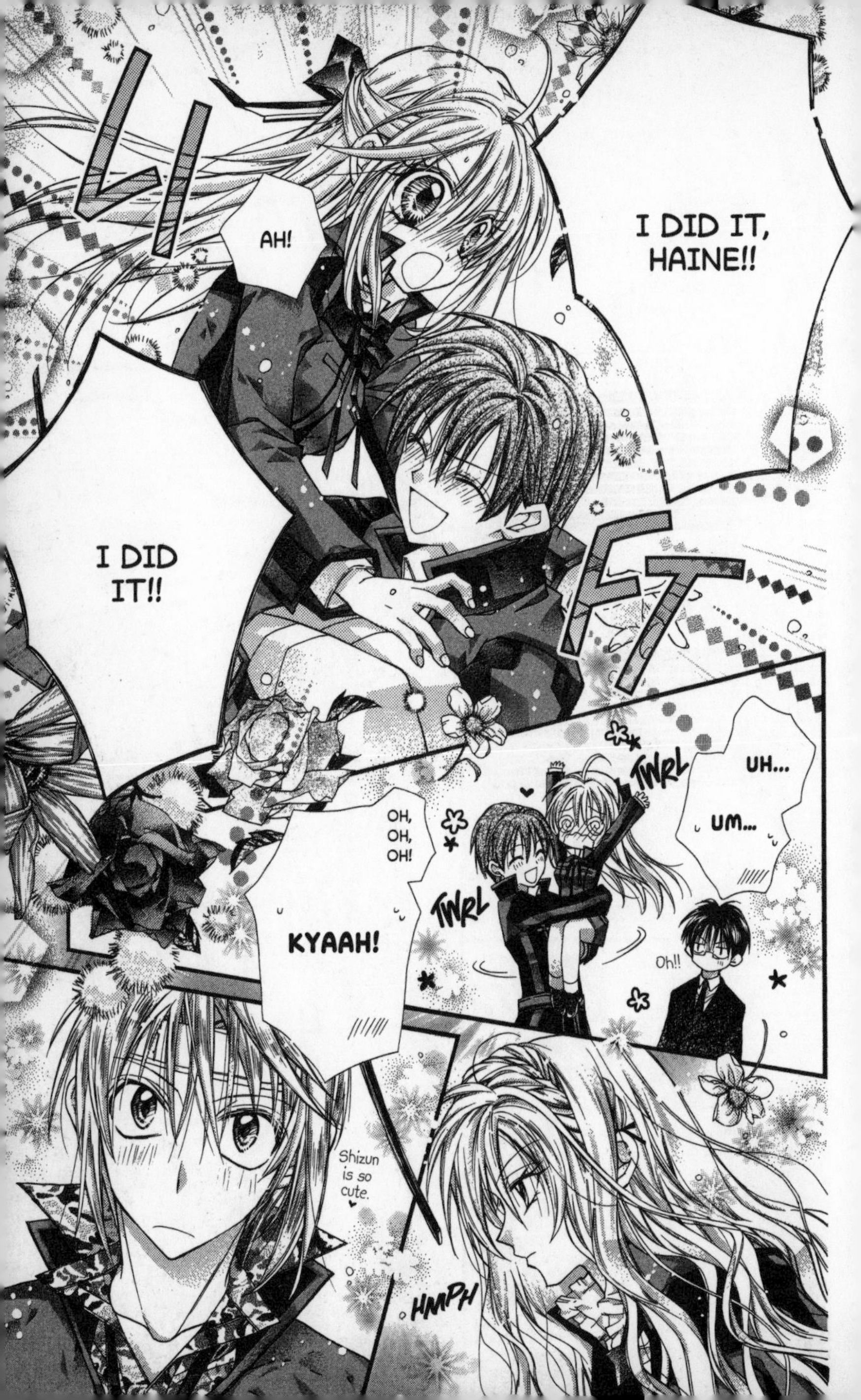
I DID IT, HAINE!!
AH!
I DID IT!!
UH...
UM...
TWRL
OH, OH, OH!
TWRL
Oh!!
KYAAH!
HMPH
Shizun is so cute.

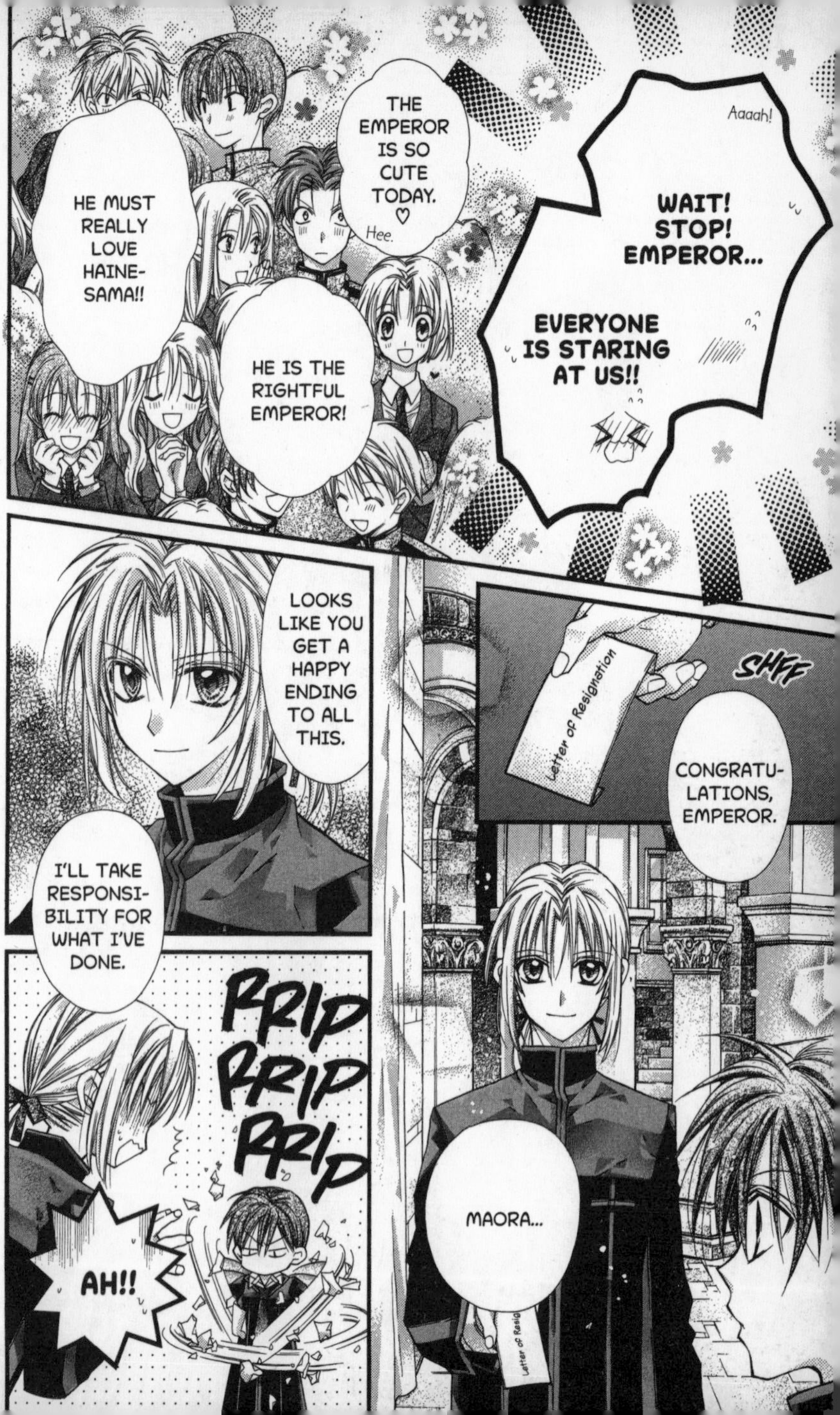

Aaaah!
WAIT! STOP! EMPEROR...
EVERYONE IS STARING AT US!!
THE EMPEROR IS SO CUTE TODAY. ♥
Hee.
HE MUST REALLY LOVE HAINE-SAMA!!
HE IS THE RIGHTFUL EMPEROR!
Letter of Resignation
SHFF
CONGRATULATIONS, EMPEROR.
MAORA...
Letter of Resig
LOOKS LIKE YOU GET A HAPPY ENDING TO ALL THIS.
I'LL TAKE RESPONSIBILITY FOR WHAT I'VE DONE.
RRIP RRIP RRIP
AH!!

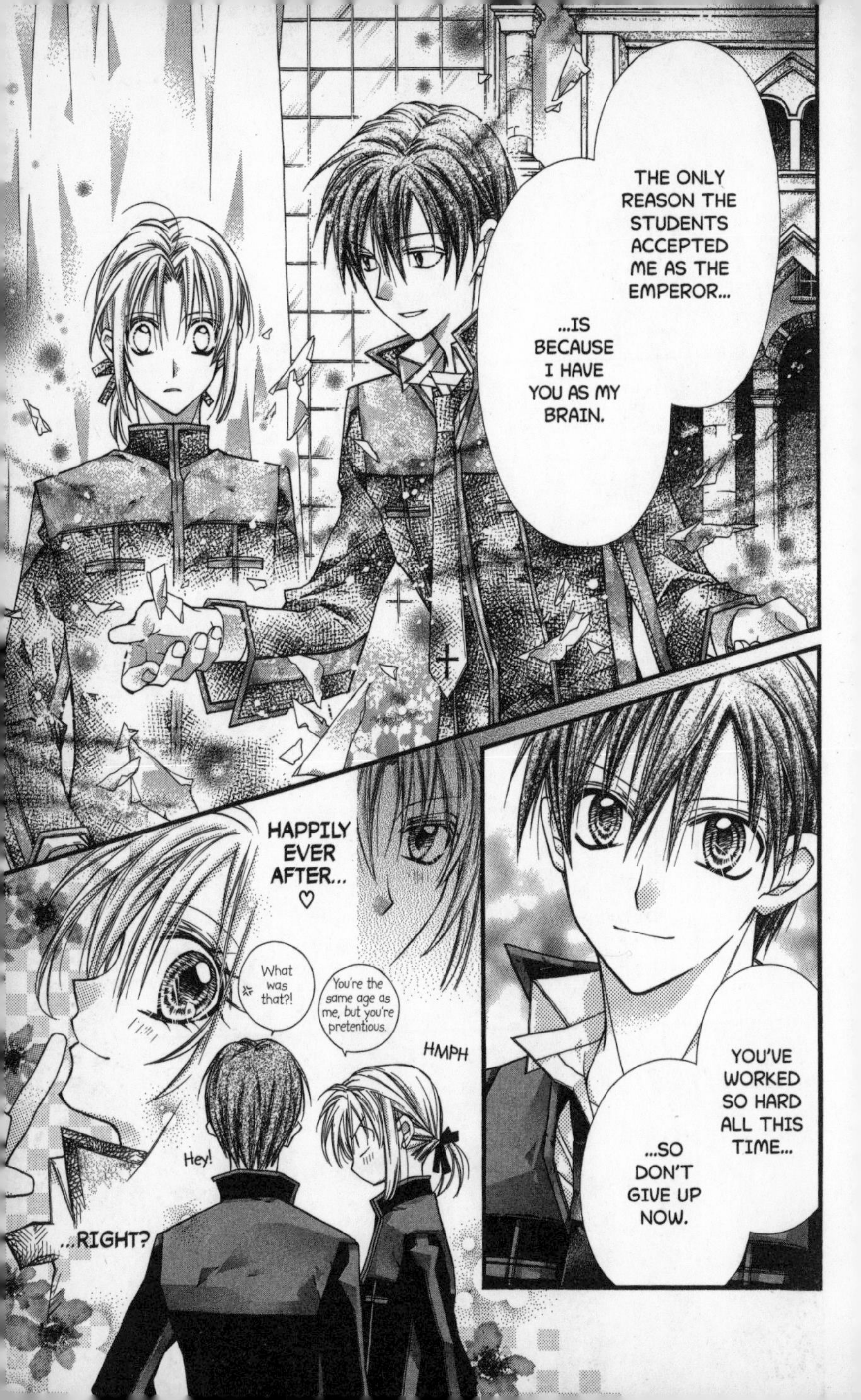
THE ONLY REASON THE STUDENTS ACCEPTED ME AS THE EMPEROR...
...IS BECAUSE I HAVE YOU AS MY BRAIN.
YOU'VE WORKED SO HARD ALL THIS TIME...
...SO DON'T GIVE UP NOW.
HAPPILY EVER AFTER... ♡
HMPH
You're the same age as me, but you're pretentious.
What was that?!
Hey!
...RIGHT?

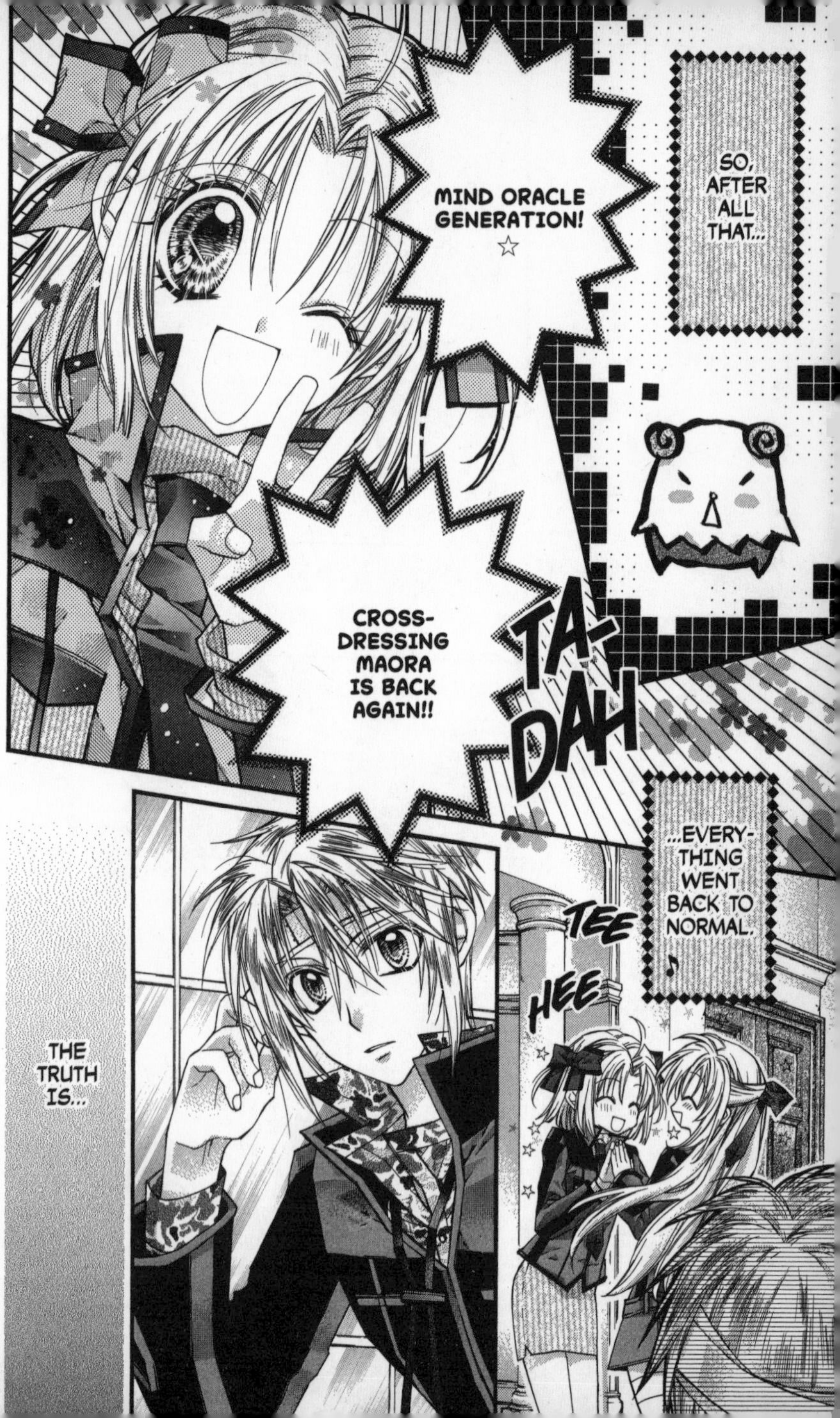
SO, AFTER ALL THAT...
MIND ORACLE GENERATION! ☆
CROSS-DRESSING MAORA IS BACK AGAIN!!
TA-DAH
...EVERYTHING WENT BACK TO NORMAL. ♪
TEE HEE
THE TRUTH IS...

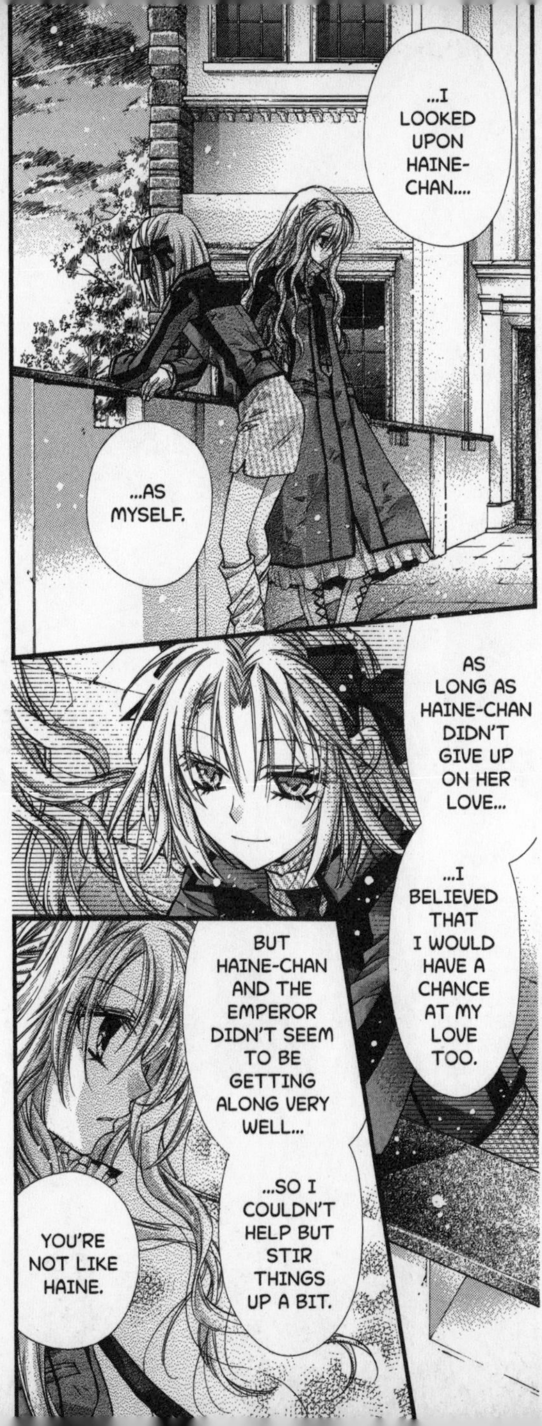
...I LOOKED UPON HAINE-CHAN....
...AS MYSELF.
AS LONG AS HAINE-CHAN DIDN'T GIVE UP ON HER LOVE...
...I BELIEVED THAT I WOULD HAVE A CHANCE AT MY LOVE TOO.
BUT HAINE-CHAN AND THE EMPEROR DIDN'T SEEM TO BE GETTING ALONG VERY WELL...
...SO I COULDN'T HELP BUT STIR THINGS UP A BIT.
YOU'RE NOT LIKE HAINE.

Continuation

Well then, see you in the next volume!

I'm sorry I haven't written a lot in the sidebars again.
(Please enjoy the popularity vote pages instead.)

I promise I'll try to write more next time.

The cover illustration for *Gentleman's Alliance †* volume 7 is...

...the Togu butlers and the attendant (Senri, Toya, and Kiriaki).

I thought about just using Senri, but then I would've had to draw Toya and Kiriaki together. That just didn't seem to click.

So it'll be those three!!!

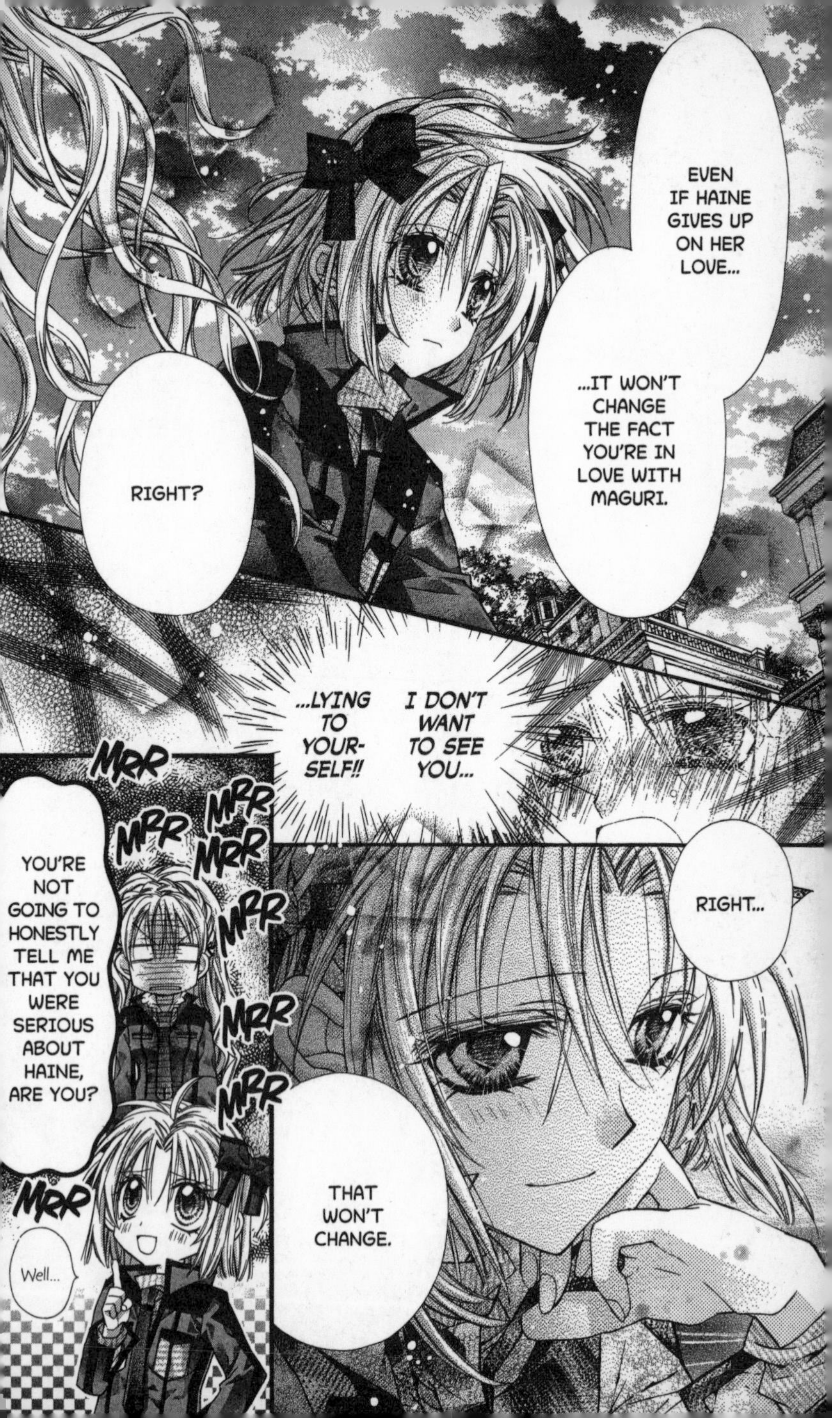
EVEN IF HAINE GIVES UP ON HER LOVE...
...IT WON'T CHANGE THE FACT YOU'RE IN LOVE WITH MAGURI.
RIGHT?
I DON'T WANT TO SEE YOU...
...LYING TO YOURSELF!!
RIGHT...
THAT WON'T CHANGE.
MRR
MRR MRR
MRR
MRR
MRR
MRR
MRR
YOU'RE NOT GOING TO HONESTLY TELL ME THAT YOU WERE SERIOUS ABOUT HAINE, ARE YOU?
Well...

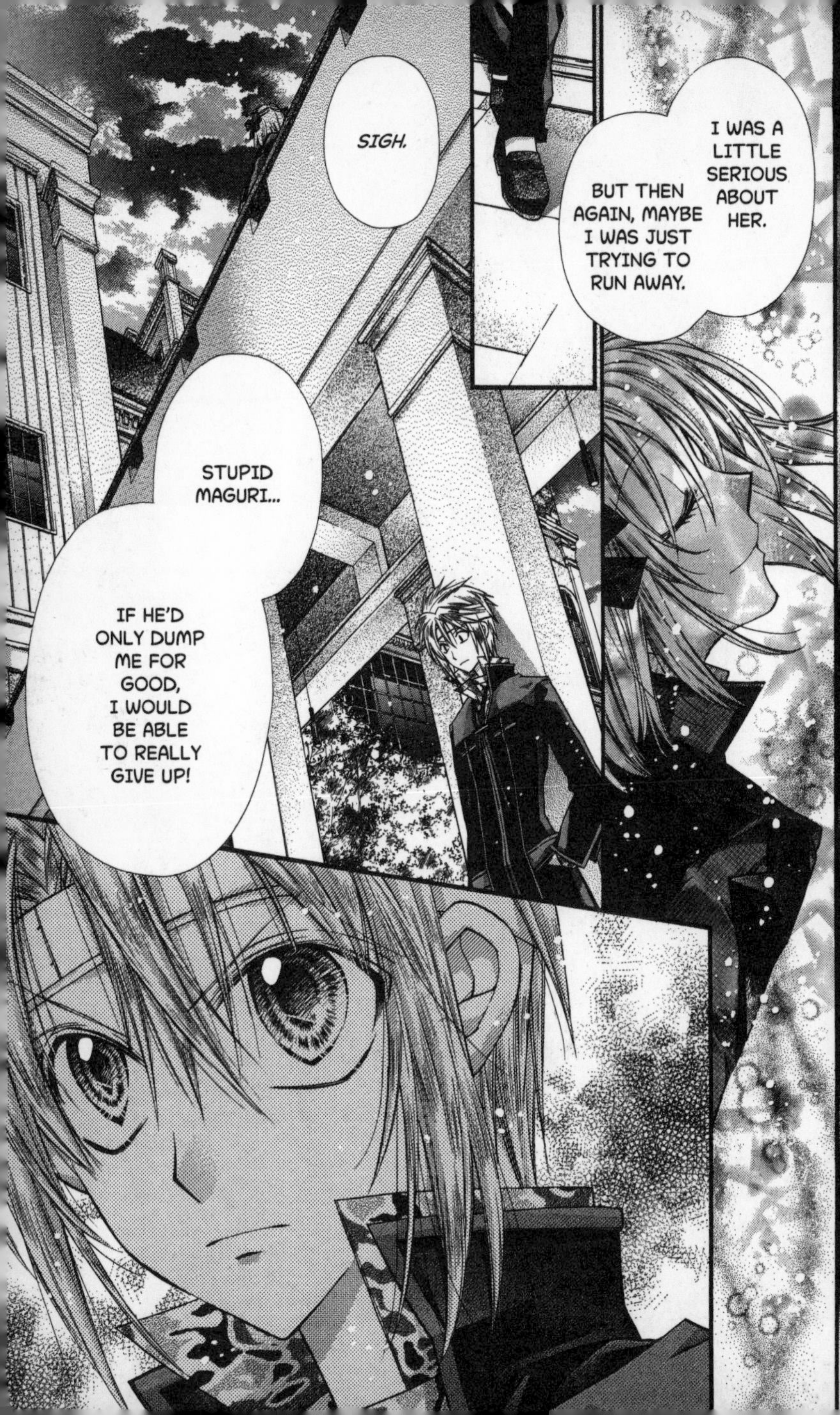
I WAS A LITTLE SERIOUS ABOUT HER.
BUT THEN AGAIN, MAYBE I WAS JUST TRYING TO RUN AWAY.
SIGH.
STUPID MAGURI...
IF HE'D ONLY DUMP ME FOR GOOD, I WOULD BE ABLE TO REALLY GIVE UP!

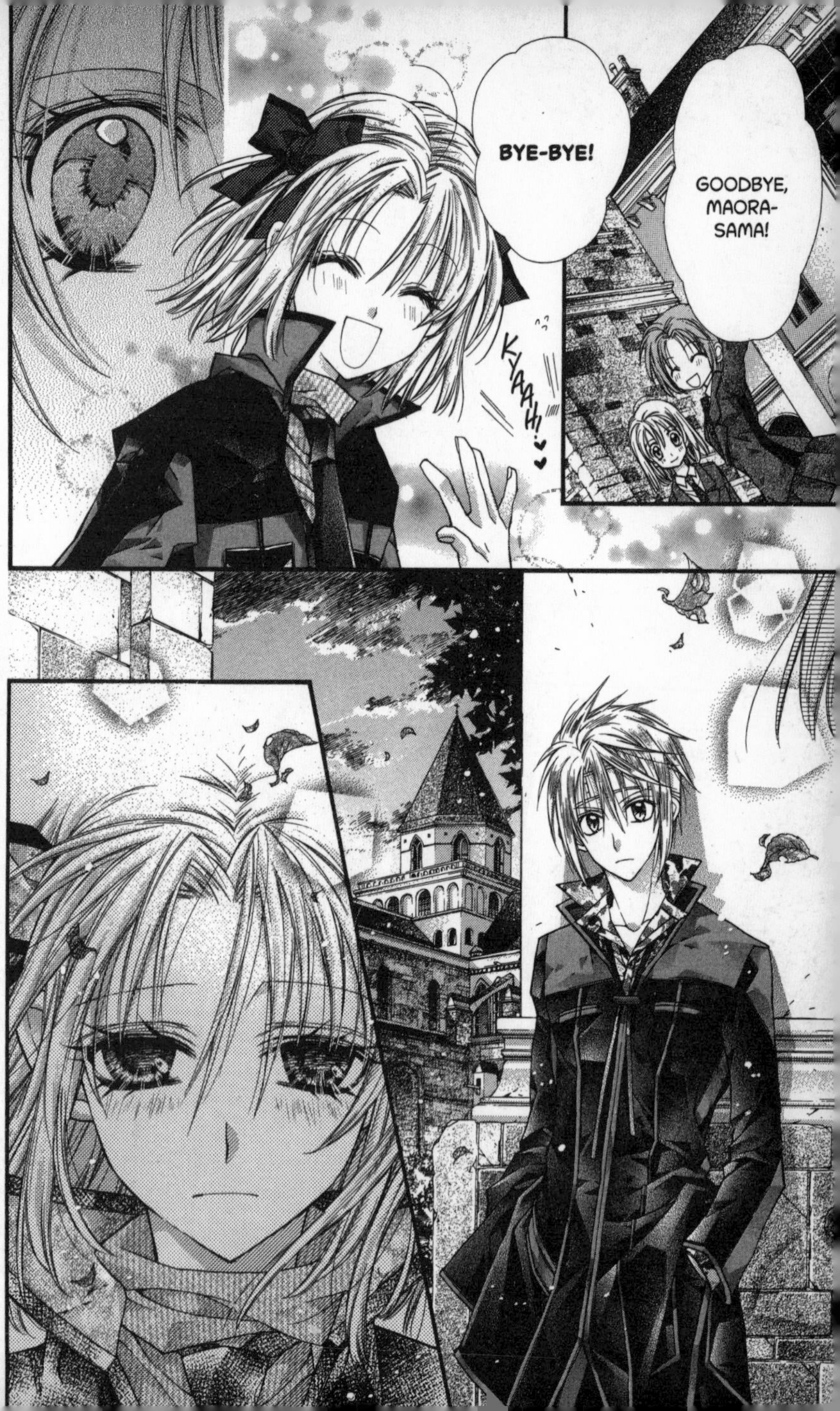
GOODBYE, MAORA-SAMA!
BYE-BYE!
KYAAAH!

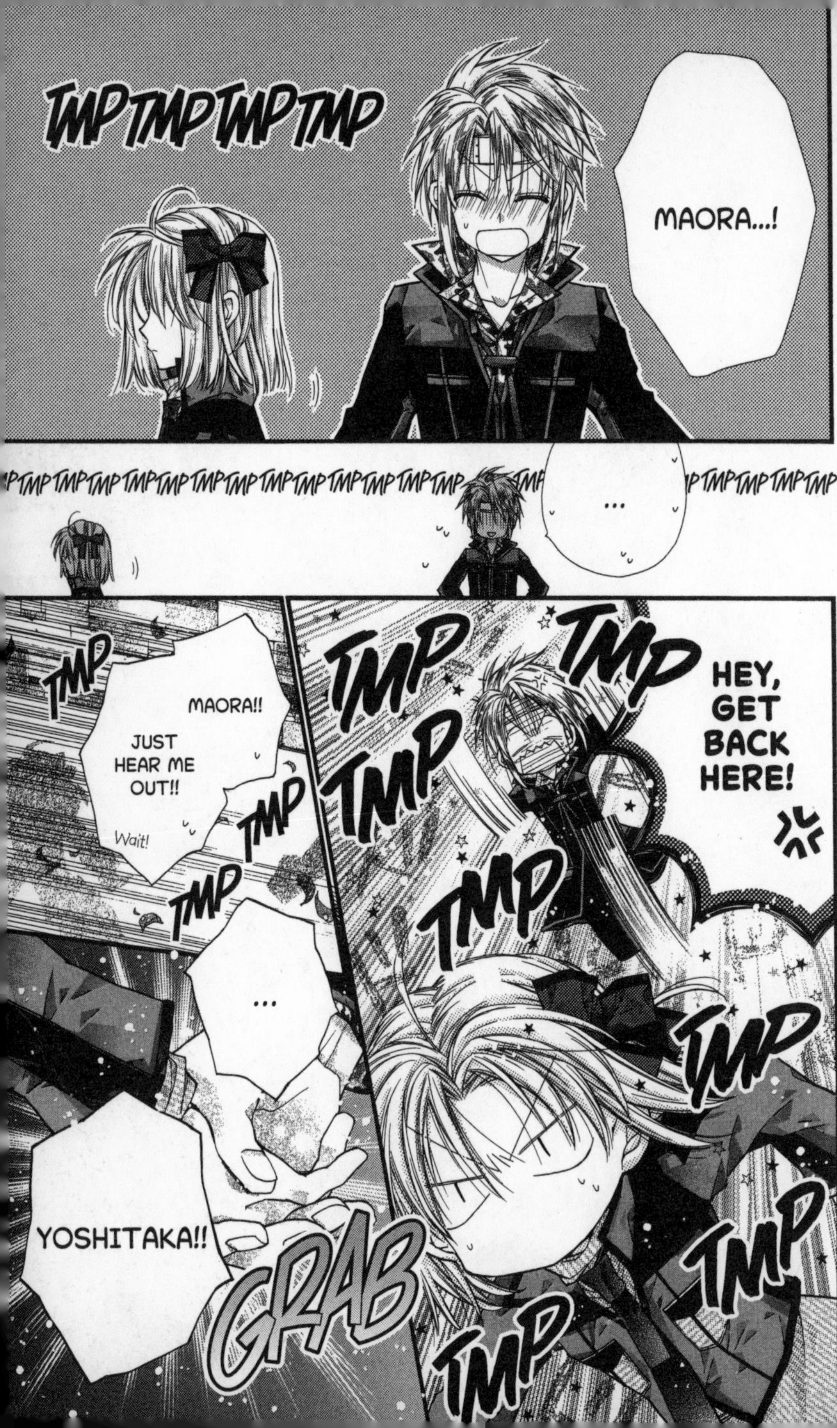
MAORA...!
TMP TMP TMP TMP
TMP TMP TMP TMP TMP TMP TMP TMP TMP TMP TMP TMP TMP TMP TMP TMP TMP TMP TMP TMP
...
HEY, GET BACK HERE!
TMP
TMP
TMP
TMP
TMP
TMP
TMP
TMP
MAORA!!
JUST HEAR ME OUT!!
Wait!
TMP
TMP
TMP
...
YOSHITAKA!!
GRAB

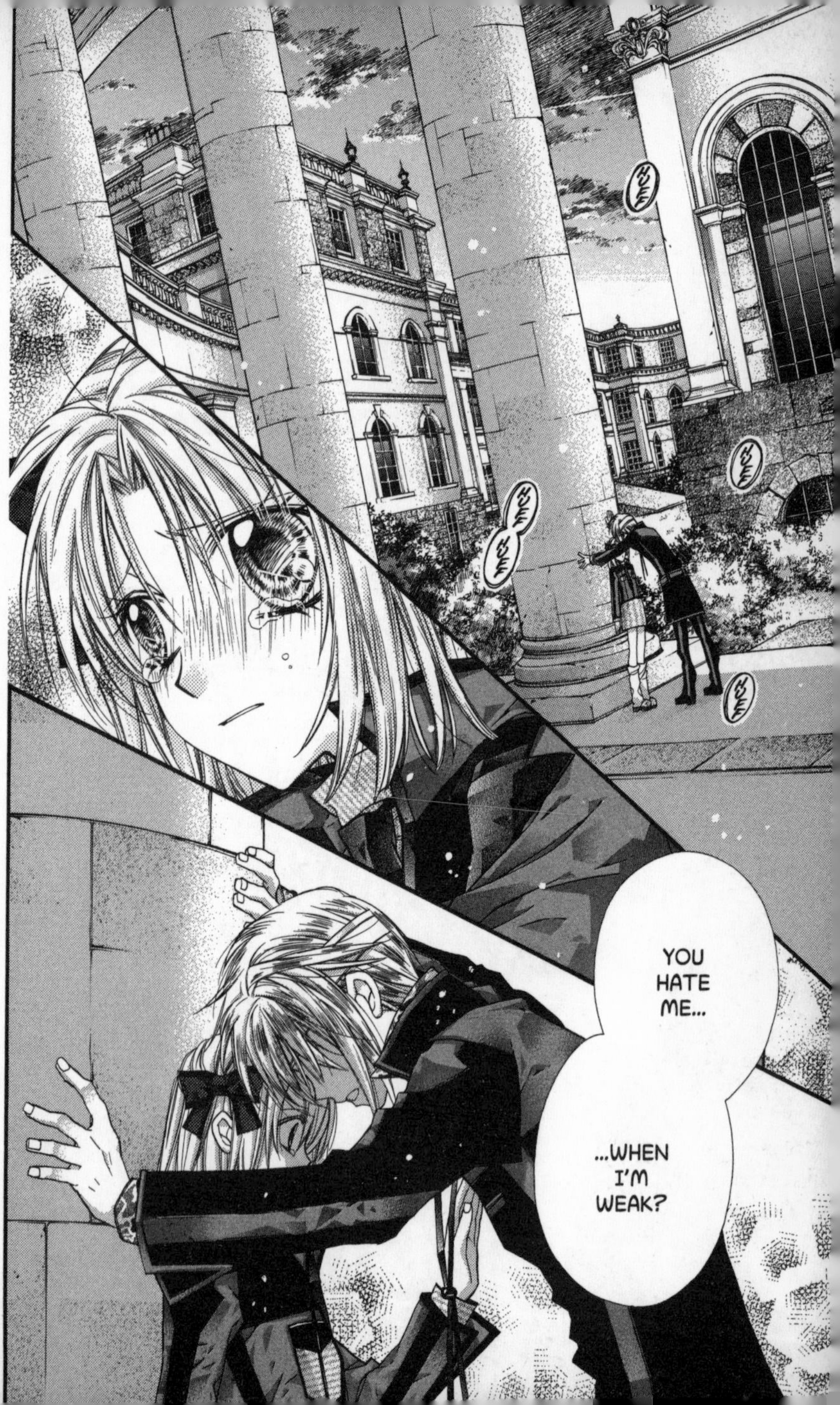
HUFF
HUFF
HUFF HUFF
HUFF
YOU HATE ME...
...WHEN I'M WEAK?

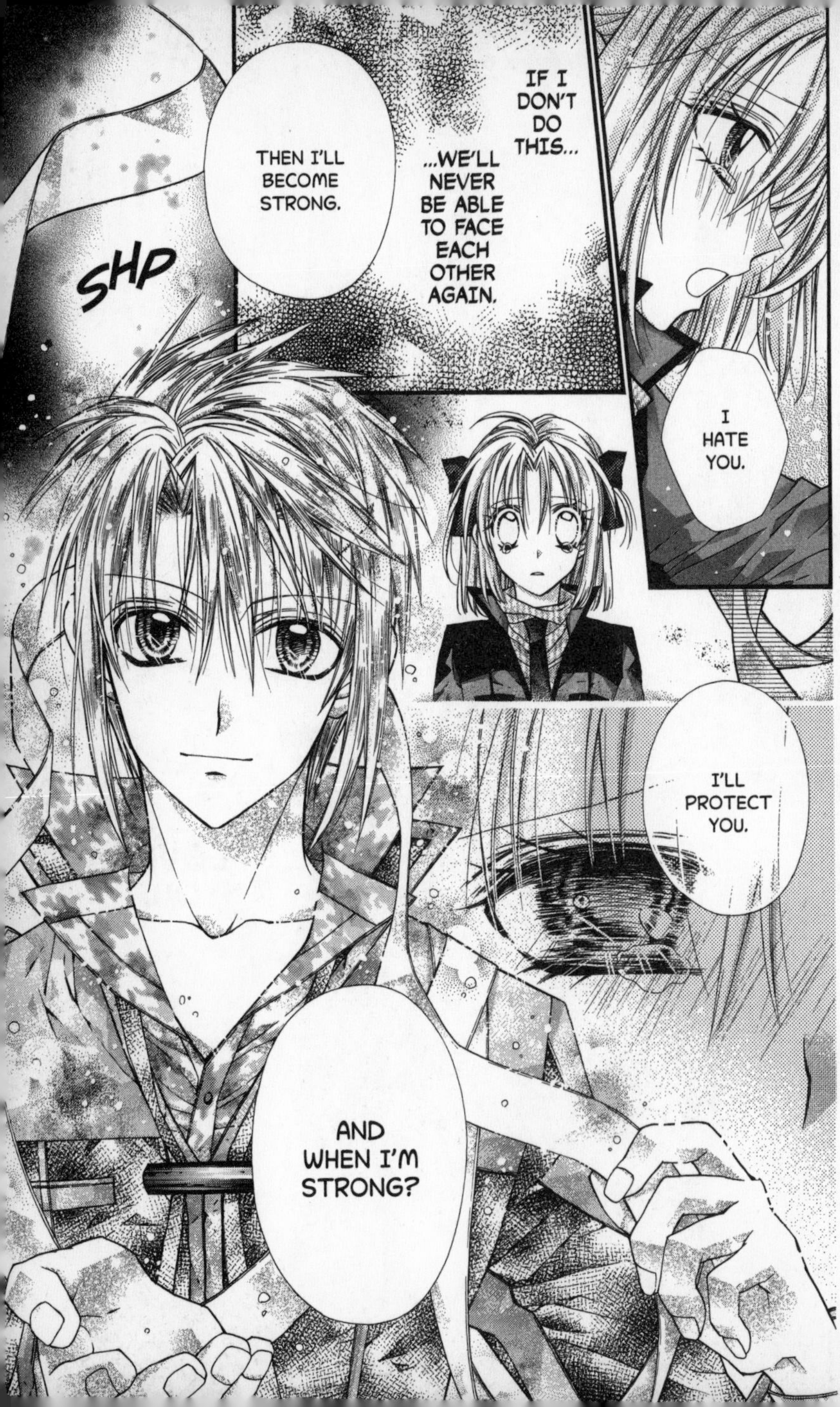
I HATE YOU.
IF I DON'T DO THIS...
...WE'LL NEVER BE ABLE TO FACE EACH OTHER AGAIN.
THEN I'LL BECOME STRONG.
SHP
I'LL PROTECT YOU.
AND WHEN I'M STRONG?

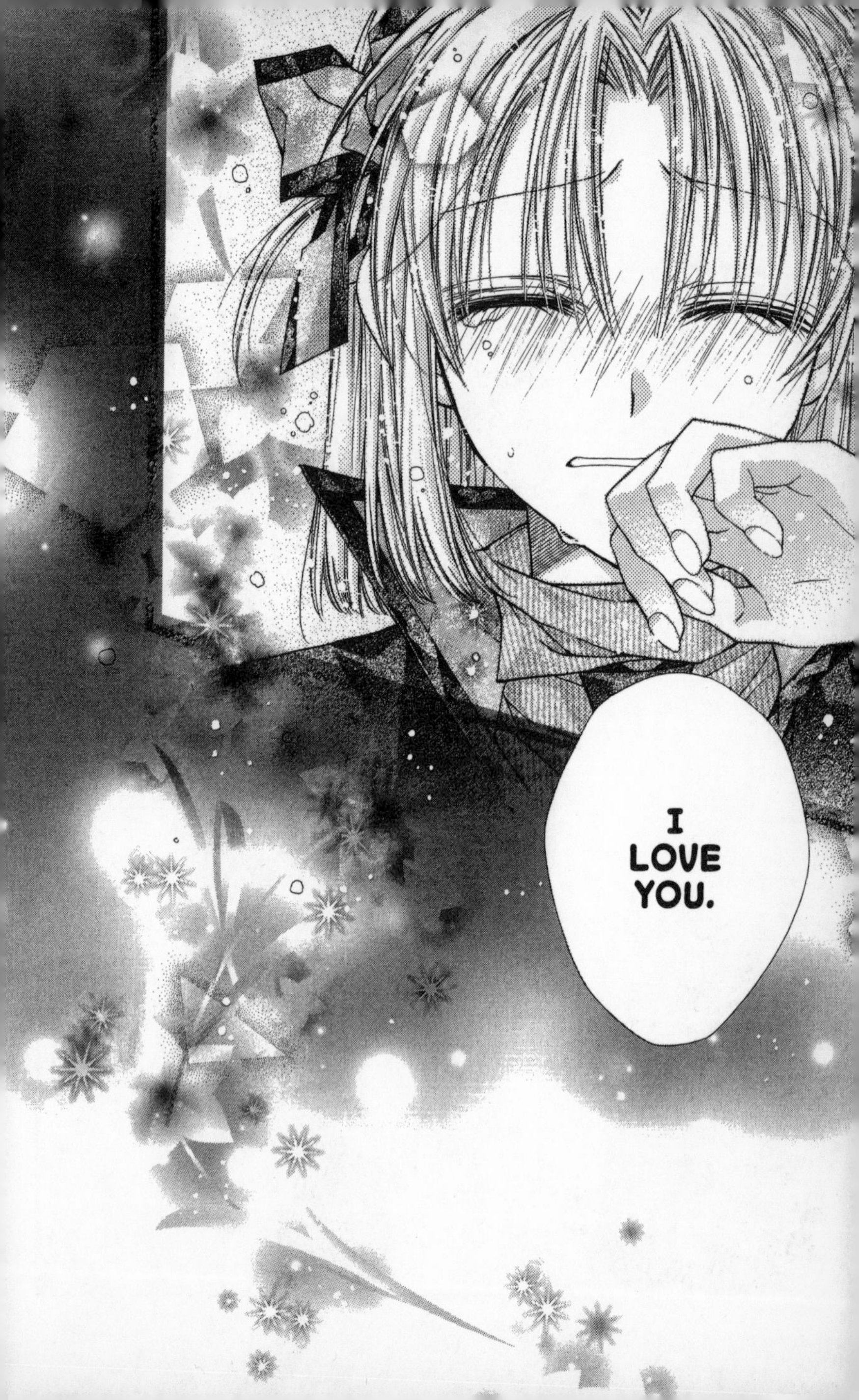
I LOVE YOU.

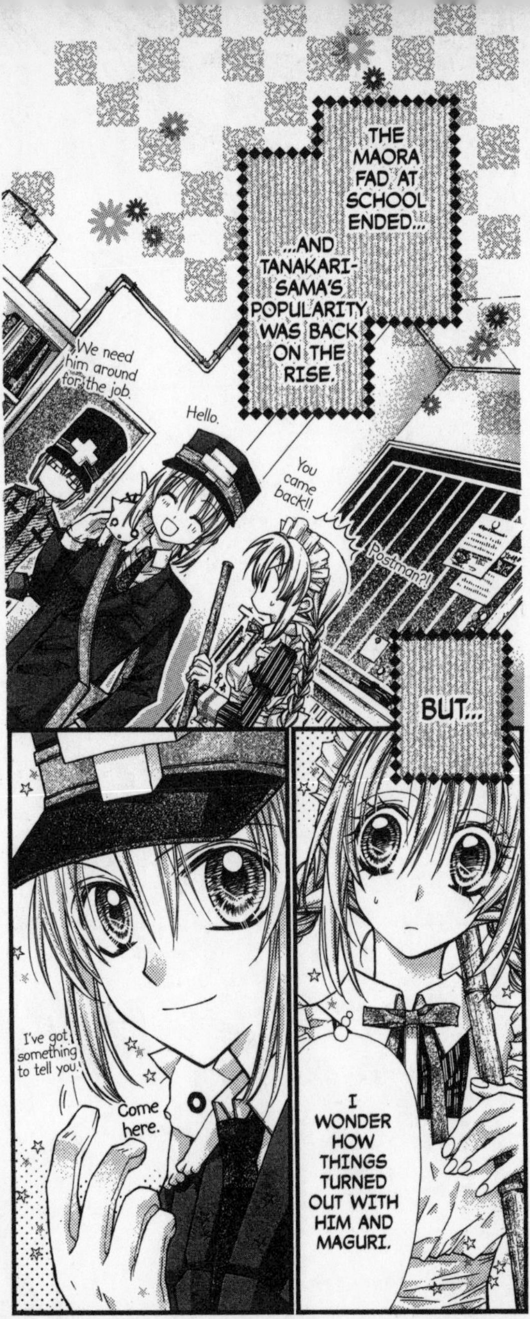
THE MAORA FAD AT SCHOOL ENDED...
...AND TANAKARI-SAMA'S POPULARITY WAS BACK ON THE RISE.
You came back!!
Postman?!
Hello.
We need him around for the job.
BUT...
I WONDER HOW THINGS TURNED OUT WITH HIM AND MAGURI.
I've got something to tell you.
Come here.

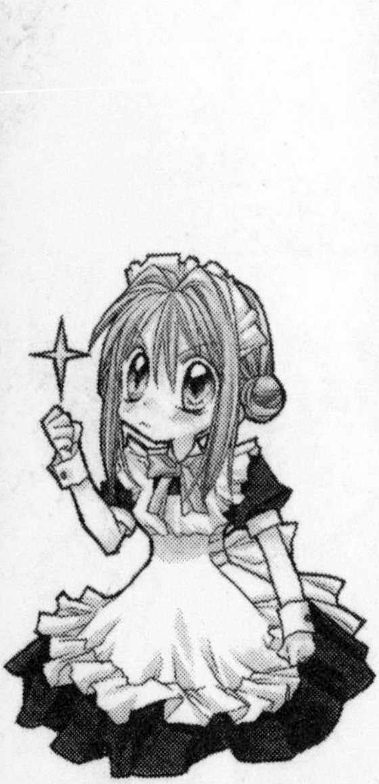

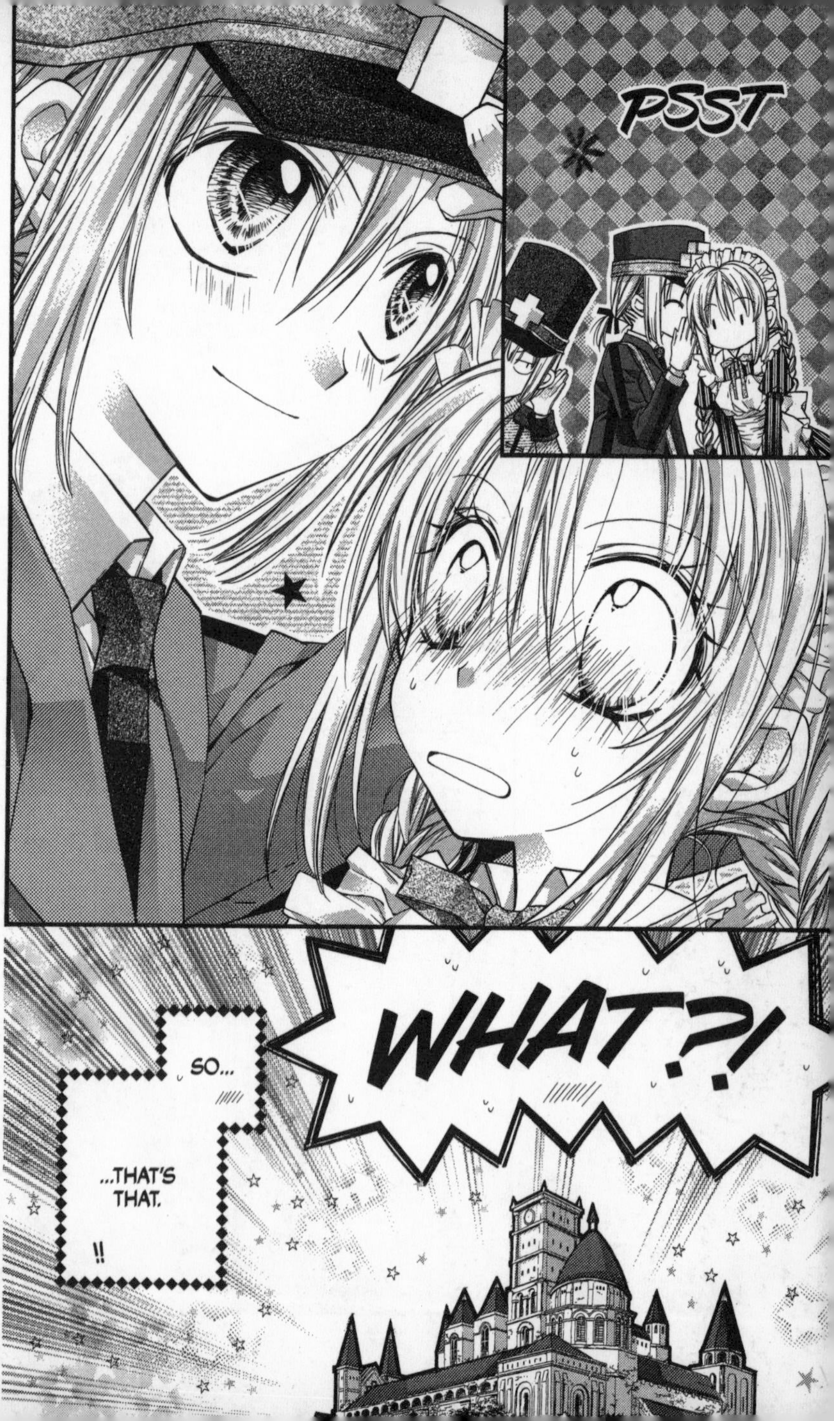
PSST
WHAT?!
SO...
...THAT'S THAT.
!!

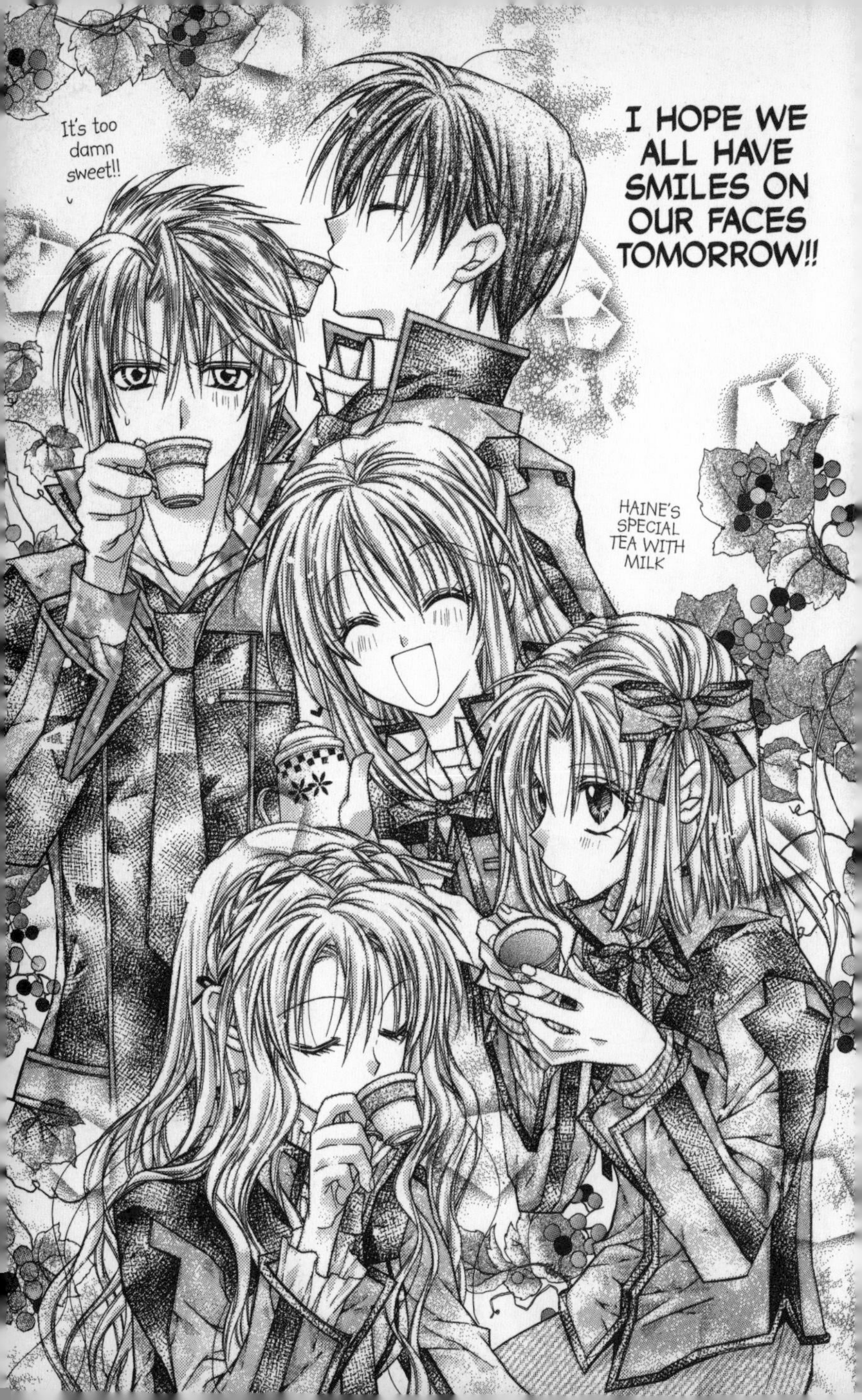
I HOPE WE ALL HAVE SMILES ON OUR FACES TOMORROW!!
It's too damn sweet!!
HAINE'S SPECIAL TEA WITH MILK

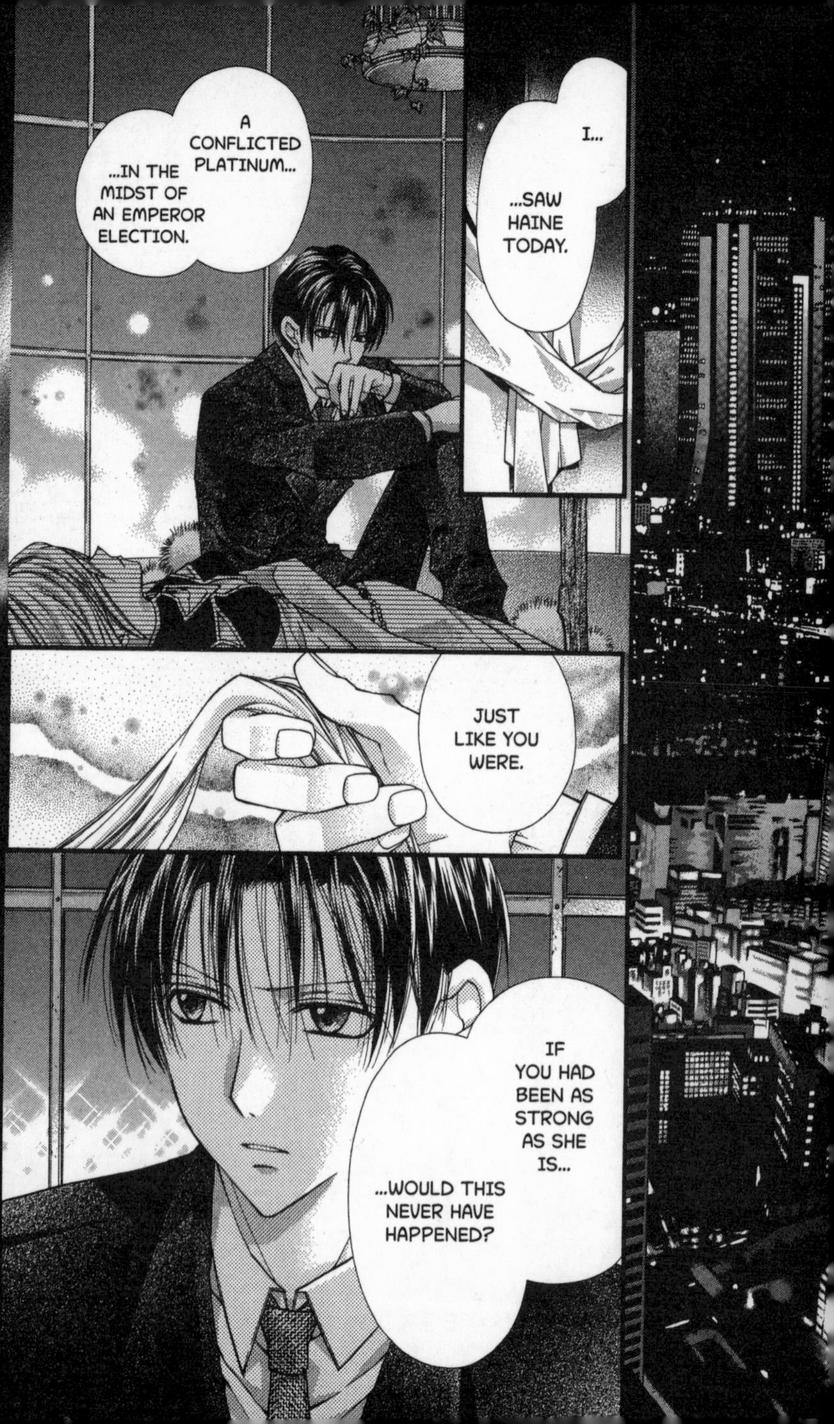
I...
...SAW HAINE TODAY.
A CONFLICTED PLATINUM...
...IN THE MIDST OF AN EMPEROR ELECTION.
JUST LIKE YOU WERE.
IF YOU HAD BEEN AS STRONG AS SHE IS...
...WOULD THIS NEVER HAVE HAPPENED?

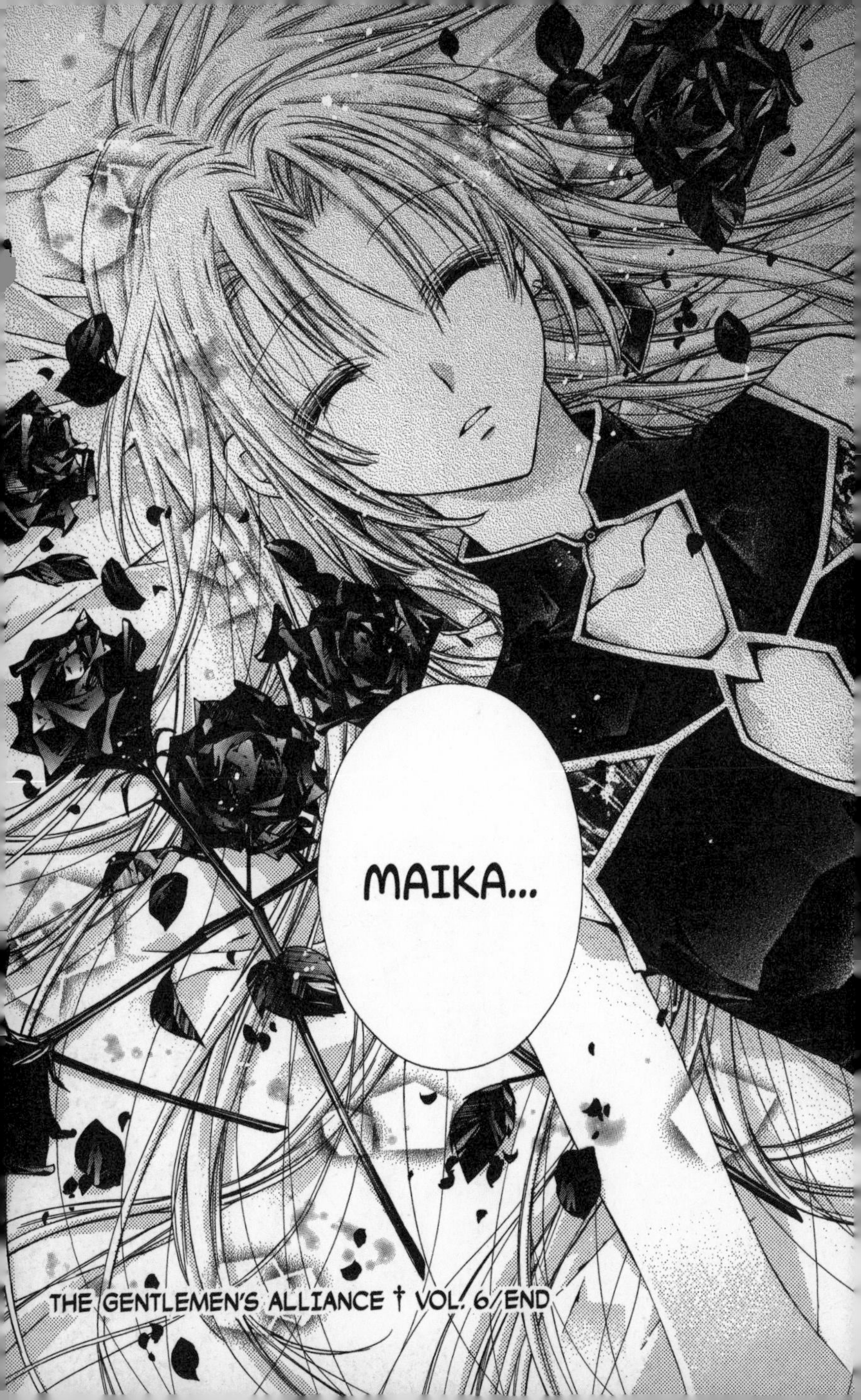
MAIKA...
THE GENTLEMEN'S ALLIANCE † VOL. 6/END

Maguri and
I made out
yesterday.
☆

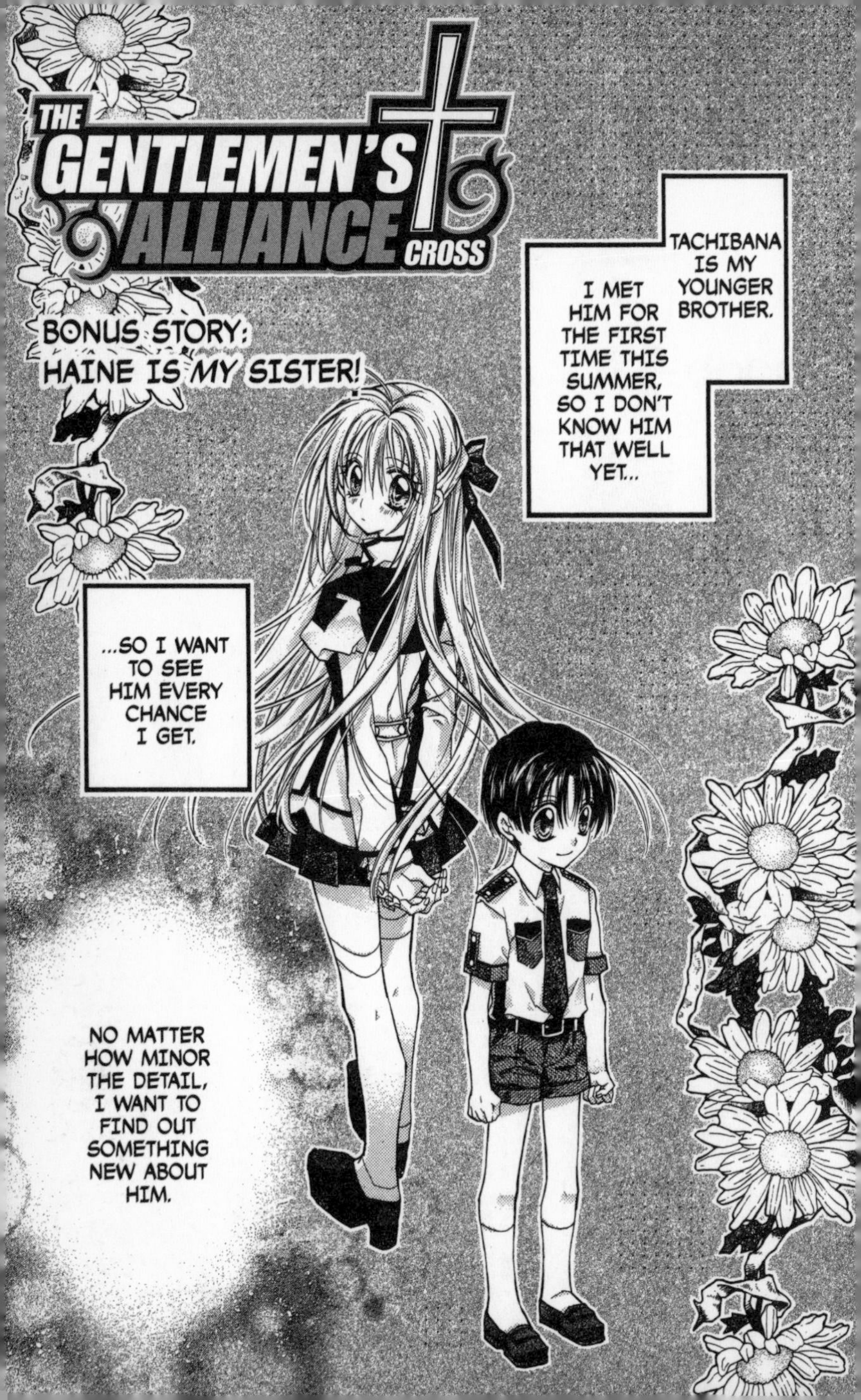
THE GENTLEMEN'S ALLIANCE CROSS
BONUS STORY: HAINE IS MY SISTER!
TACHIBANA IS MY YOUNGER BROTHER.
I MET HIM FOR THE FIRST TIME THIS SUMMER, SO I DON'T KNOW HIM THAT WELL YET...
...SO I WANT TO SEE HIM EVERY CHANCE I GET.
NO MATTER HOW MINOR THE DETAIL, I WANT TO FIND OUT SOMETHING NEW ABOUT HIM.

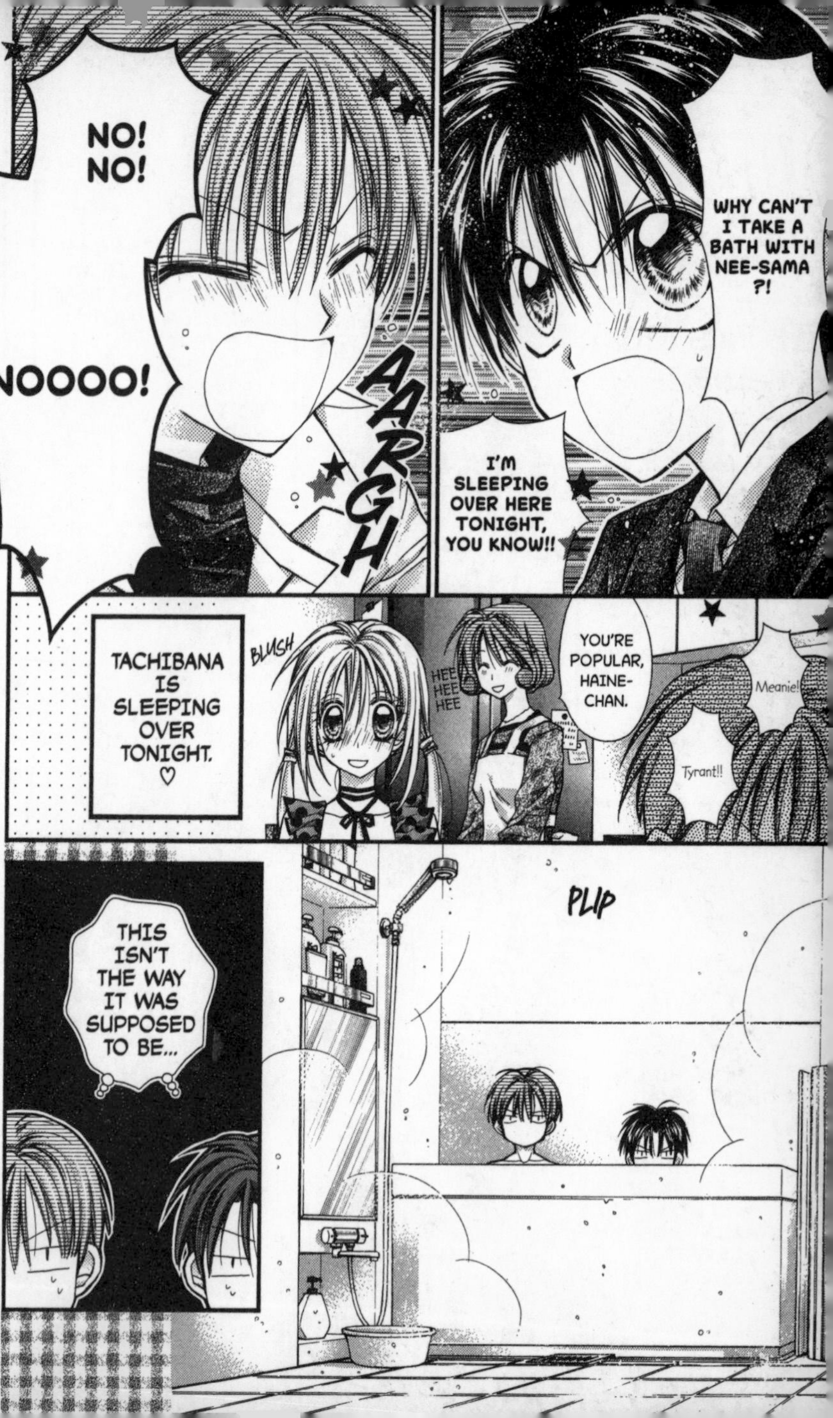
WHY CAN'T I TAKE A BATH WITH NEE-SAMA ?!
I'M SLEEPING OVER HERE TONIGHT, YOU KNOW!!
AARGH
NO! NO!
NOOOO!
Meanie!
Tyrant!!
YOU'RE POPULAR, HAINE-CHAN.
HEE HEE HEE
BLUSH
TACHIBANA IS SLEEPING OVER TONIGHT. ♡
PLIP
THIS ISN'T THE WAY IT WAS SUPPOSED TO BE...

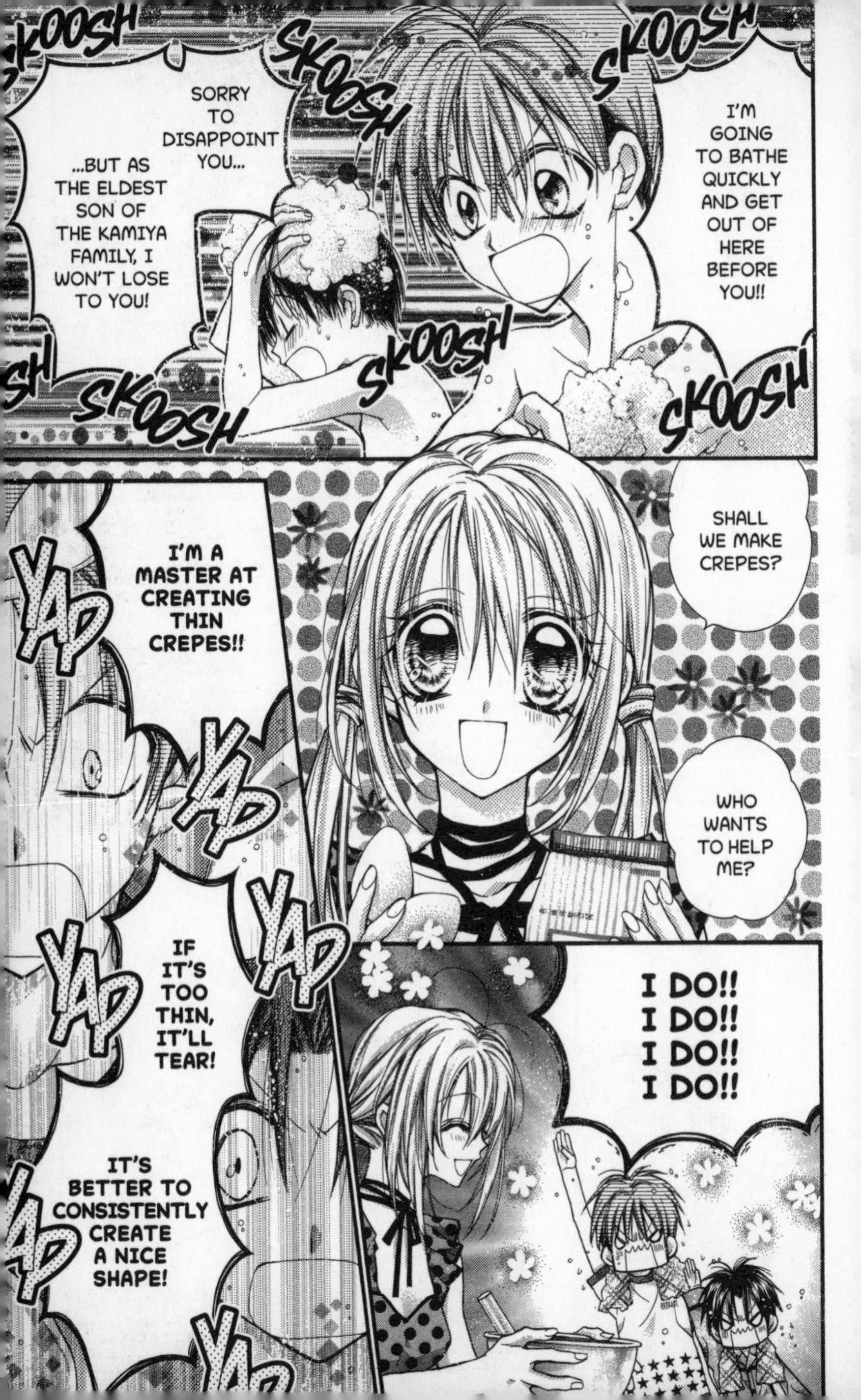
SKOOSH
SKOOSH
I'M GOING TO BATHE QUICKLY AND GET OUT OF HERE BEFORE YOU!!
SKOOSH
SORRY TO DISAPPOINT YOU...
...BUT AS THE ELDEST SON OF THE KAMIYA FAMILY, I WON'T LOSE TO YOU!
SKOOSH
SKOOSH
SKOOSH
SHALL WE MAKE CREPES?
WHO WANTS TO HELP ME?
I DO!! I DO!! I DO!! I DO!!
I'M A MASTER AT CREATING THIN CREPES!!
YAP
YAP
IF IT'S TOO THIN, IT'LL TEAR!
YAP
YAP
IT'S BETTER TO CONSISTENTLY CREATE A NICE SHAPE!

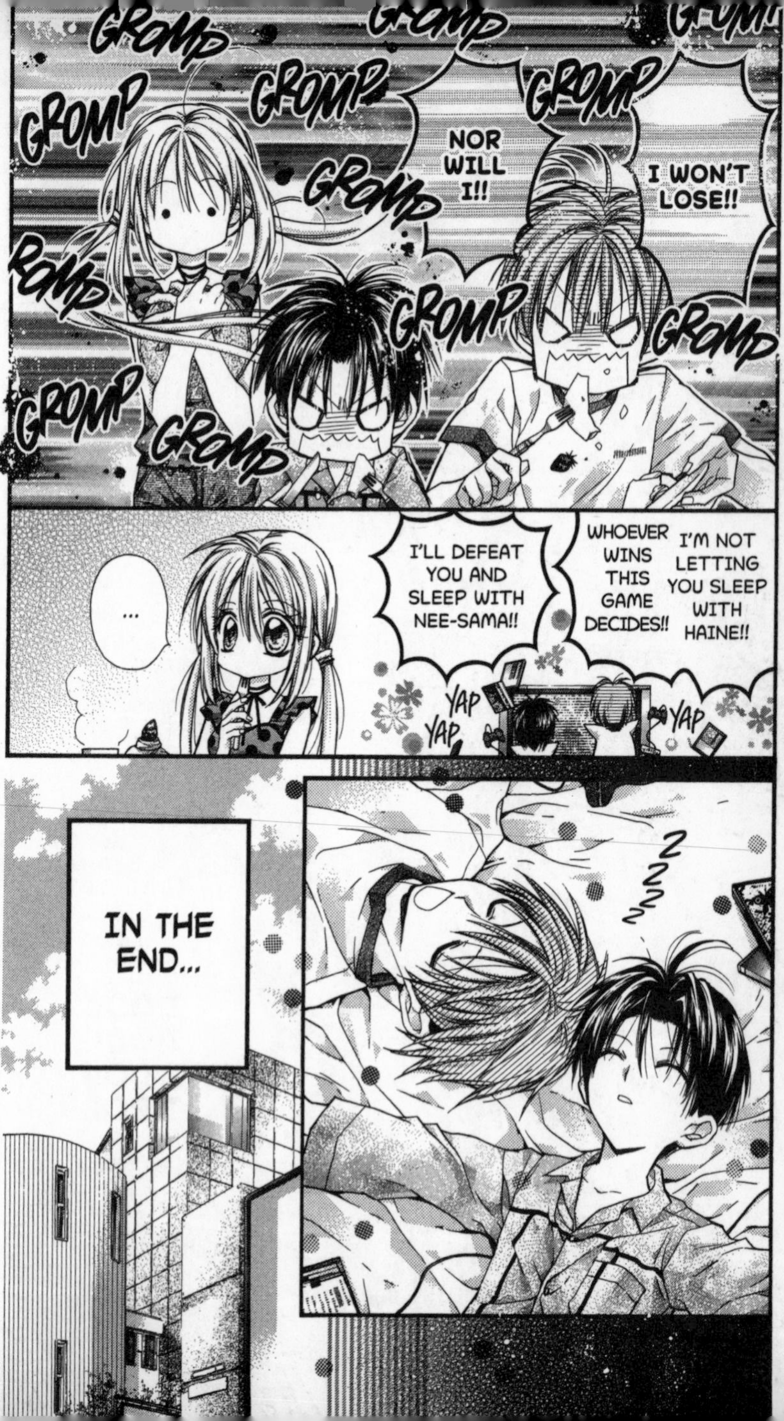
GROMP
GROMP
I WON'T LOSE!!
NOR WILL I!!
GROMP
GROMP
GROMP
GROMP
GROMP
GROMP
GROMP
I'M NOT LETTING YOU SLEEP WITH HAINE!!
WHOEVER WINS THIS GAME DECIDES!!
I'LL DEFEAT YOU AND SLEEP WITH NEE-SAMA!!
YAP
YAP
YAP
...
ZZZZ
IN THE END...

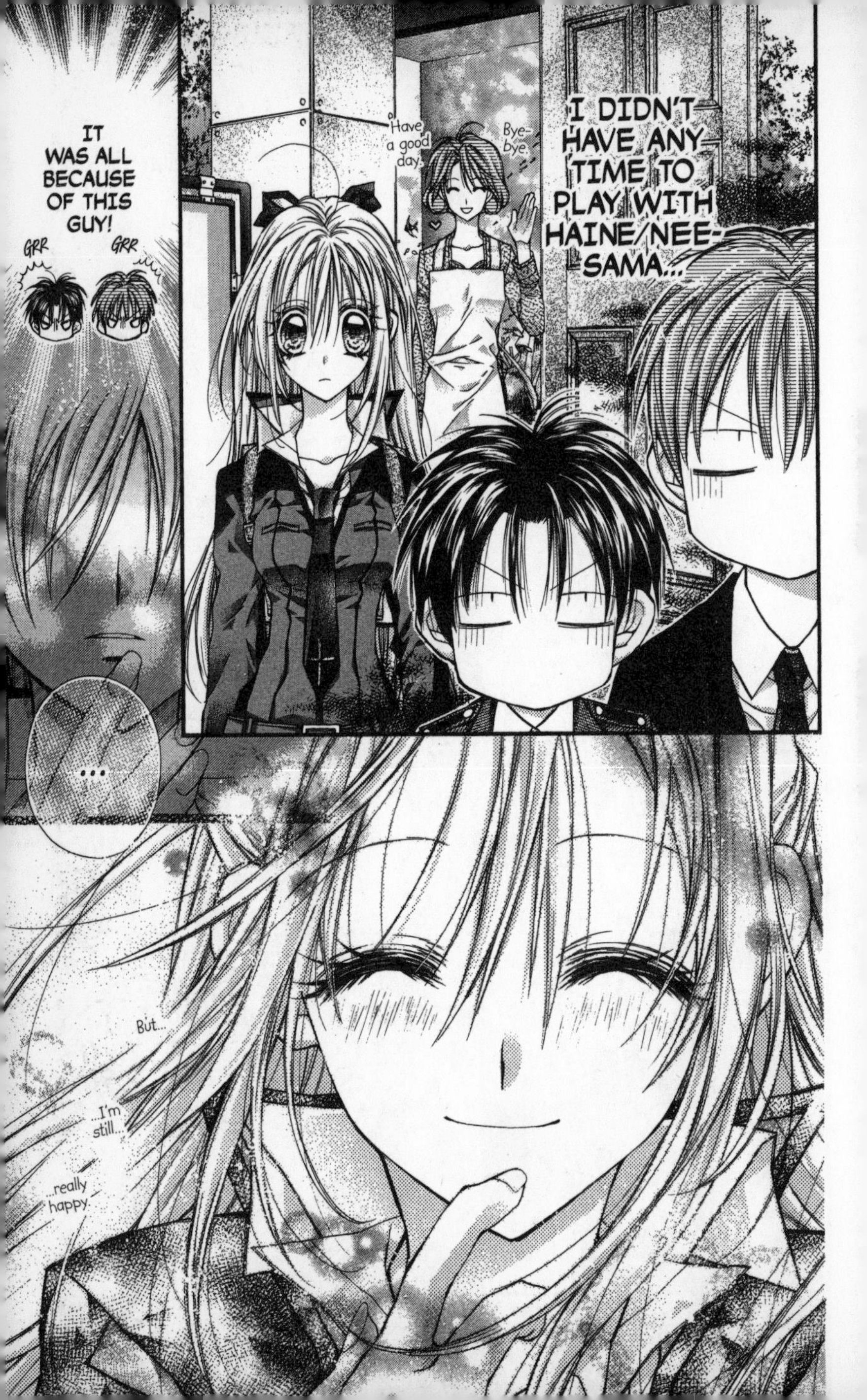
I DIDN'T HAVE ANY TIME TO PLAY WITH HAINE/NEE-SAMA...
Bye-bye.
Have a good day.
IT WAS ALL BECAUSE OF THIS GUY!
GRR
GRR
...
But...
...I'm still...
...really happy.

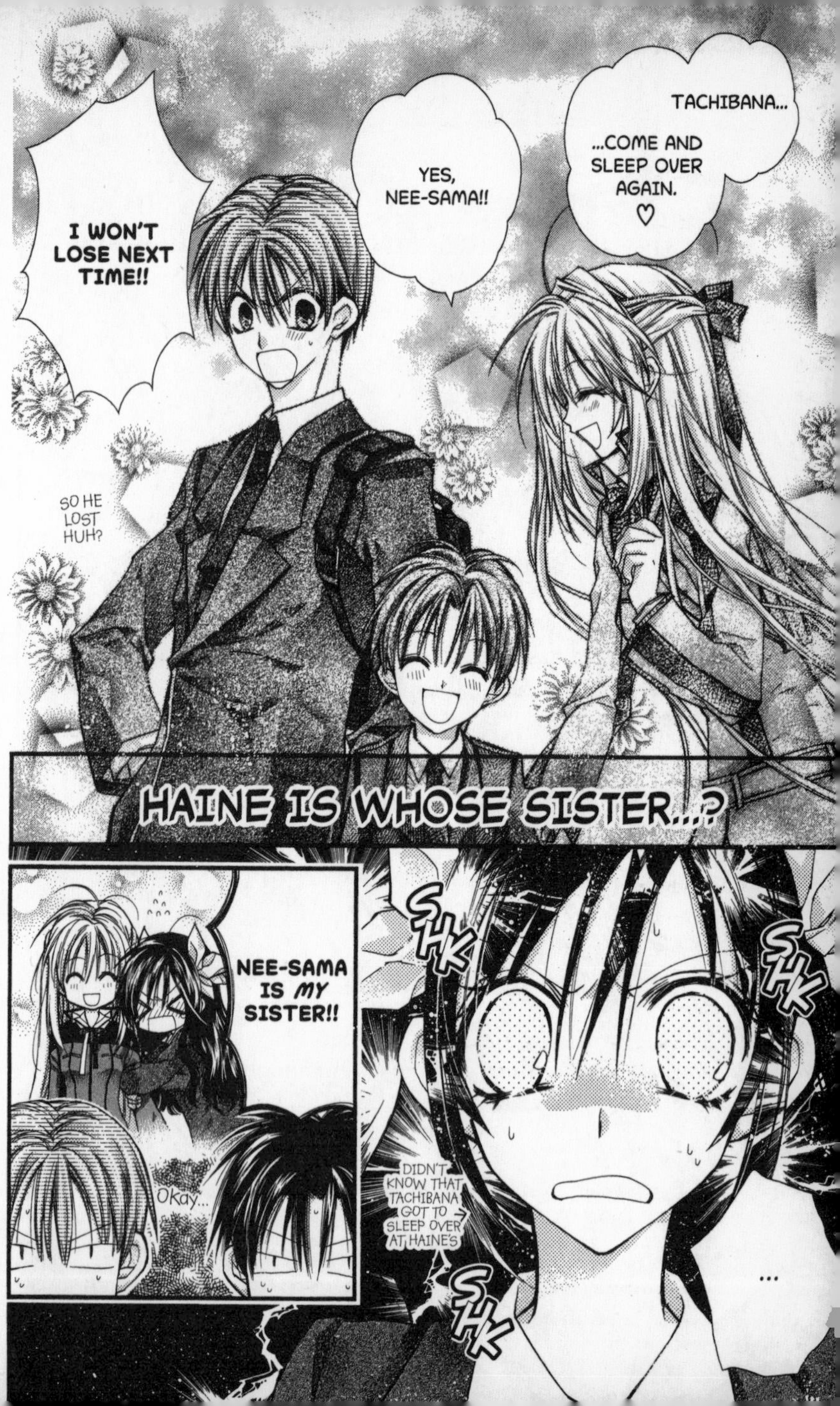
TACHIBANA... ...COME AND SLEEP OVER AGAIN. ♡
YES, NEE-SAMA!!
I WON'T LOSE NEXT TIME!!
SO HE LOST HUH?
HAINE IS WHOSE SISTER...?
SHK
SHK
DIDN'T KNOW THAT TACHIBANA GOT TO SLEEP OVER AT HAINE'S
...
SHK
NEE-SAMA IS *MY* SISTER!!
Okay...

NOTES ON THE TEXT

PAGE 5:

O-shi

The suffix -shi is like -san but it's more formal. It's used when you are talking about someone, but not to them directly.

PAGE 6:

Nii-san

Nii-san means "older brother."

PAGE 13:

Geh! It's a farewell party for the seniors, not you!

In the Japanese version, there's a pun with yosen-kai, or "farewell party," and yosen, or "elimination round."

PAGE 14:

Mind Oracle Generation!

This is a spell that Maora uses. It's possibly from a TV anime he watched as a child.

Maya, it's my destiny.

This is another allusion to Glass Mask (see volume 1).

PAGE 23:

Konkon's graduation concert!

Konkon is Asami Konno. She was a member of Morning Musume and left the group in July 2007.

PAGE 24:

Special Move: Bumpkin Crawl Stroke!

People from the countryside are often thought not to know how to swim the Australian crawl properly.

PAGE 83:

Could this be that popular period that comes around once in a lifetime?!

There is a saying among young Japanese people that everyone has a time in their life when they are unusually popular with the opposite sex. It usually lasts from a few months to a year.

PAGE 86:

Magu-Magu!
"Magu-Magu" is Yukimitsu's nickname for his younger brother. Maguri calls Yukimitsu "Yukkie."

Okaa-tama, Onei-tama
This is a cutsey way of saying "Mommy" and "Older Sister."

PAGE 106:

Mul-me
Mul-me is an abbreviation for "Multimedia Club." The Japanese abbreviation is *marume*.

PAGE 112:

It's all your fault!
In the top left panels Haine raises her hand, and her expression becomes angry. This is a gag referencing a classic Japanese monster flick called *Daimajin*.

PAGE 117:

True love takes two people!!
The Japanese version uses the distinction between *koi* and *ai* (both mean love, but *ai* is deeper): "If you're alone, *koi* doesn't become *ai*!"

PAGE 174:

Tyrant!
Tachibana is actually calling Kusame a *masegaki*, or a young child who acts too much like an adult.

Volume 6 is all about Maora! And the cover illustration for this volume turned out to be the postman and the warden. ★ The members of the student council really are somewhat disconnected from one another, but I really want Hainekko to be the center that draws them together.

—*Arina Tanemura*

Arina Tanemura was born in Aichi, Japan. She got her start in 1996, publishing *Nibanme no Koi no Katachi* (The Style of the Second Love) in *Ribon Original* magazine. Her early work includes a collection of short stories called *Kanshaku Dama no Yuutsu* (Short-Tempered Melancholic). Two of her titles, *Kamikaze Kaito Jeanne* and *Full Moon*, were made into popular TV series. Tanemura enjoys karaoke and is a huge *Lord of the Rings* fan.

THE GENTLEMEN'S ALLIANCE † vol.6
The Shojo Beat Manga Edition

STORY & ART BY
ARINA TANEMURA

English Translation & Adaptation/Tetsuichiro Miyaki
Touch-up Art & Lettering/George Caltsoudas
Design/Amy Martin
Editor/Nancy Thistlethwaite

Editor in Chief, Books/Alvin Lu
Editor in Chief, Magazines/Marc Weidenbaum
VP of Publishing Licensing/Rika Inouye
VP of Sales/Gonzalo Ferreyra
Sr. VP of Marketing/Liza Coppola
Publisher/Hyoe Narita

Printed in Canada

Published by VIZ Media, LLC
P.O. Box 77010
San Francisco, CA 94107

Shojo Beat Manga Edition
10 9 8 7 6 5 4 3 2 1
First printing, June 2008

store.viz.com

Arina Tanemura Series

The Gentlemen's Alliance †
Haine Otomiya joins Imperial Academy in pursuit of the boy she's loved since she was a child, unaware that he has many secrets of his own.

I•O•N
Chanting the letters of her first name has always brought Ion Tsuburagi good luck—but her good-luck charm is really the result of psychic powers!

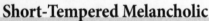

Full Moon
Mitsuki Koyama dreams of becoming a pop star, but she is dying of throat cancer. Can she live out a lifetime of dreams in just one year?

Short-Tempered Melancholic
A collection of short stories including Arina Tanemura's debut manga, "In the Style of the Second Love"!

Time Stranger Kyoko
Kyoko Suomi must find 12 holy stones and 12 telepaths to awaken her sister who has been trapped in time since birth.

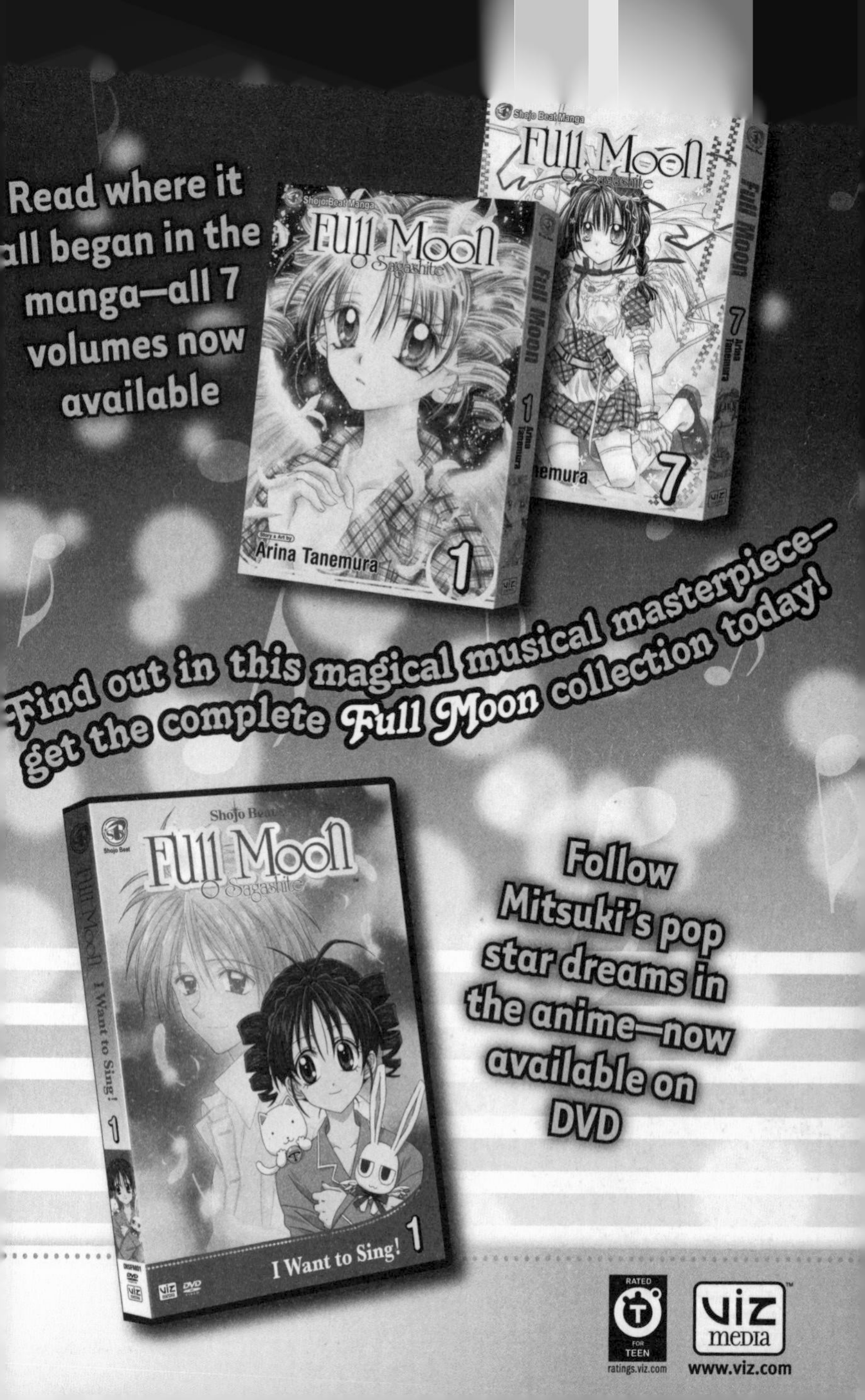

FULL MOON
O Sagashite

By Arina Tanemura
creator of *The Gentlemen's Alliance †*

Mitsuki loves singing, but a malignant throat tumor prevents her from pursuing her passion.

Can two fun-loving Shinigami give her singing career a magical jump-start?

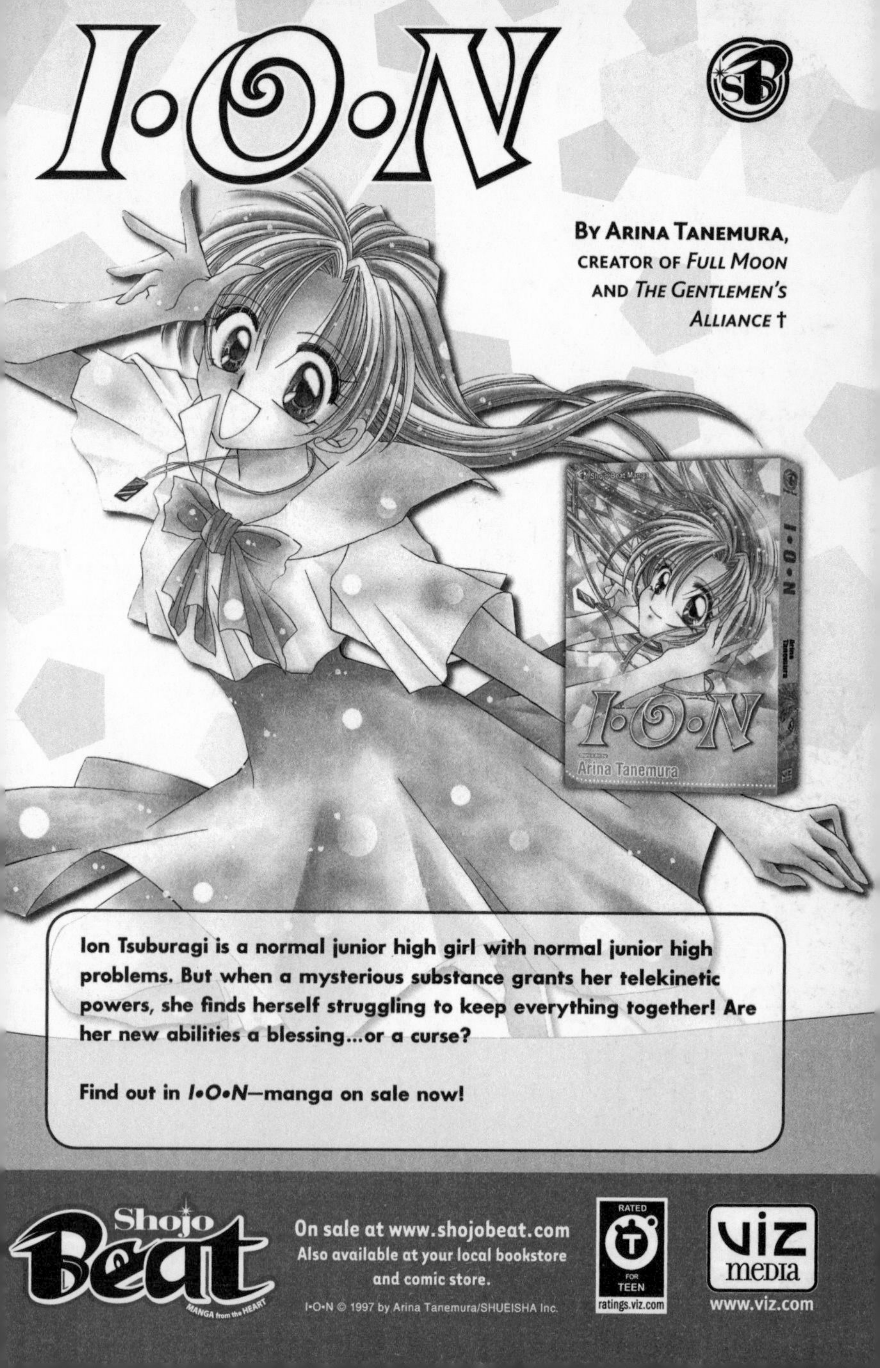
I•O•N
By Arina Tanemura, creator of Full Moon and The Gentlemen's Alliance †
Shojo Beat Manga
I•O•N
Arina Tanemura
Ion Tsuburagi is a normal junior high girl with normal junior high problems. But when a mysterious substance grants her telekinetic powers, she finds herself struggling to keep everything together! Are her new abilities a blessing...or a curse?
Find out in I•O•N—manga on sale now!
Shojo Beat
MANGA from the HEART
On sale at www.shojobeat.com
Also available at your local bookstore and comic store.
I•O•N © 1997 by Arina Tanemura/SHUEISHA Inc.
RATED
T
FOR TEEN
ratings.viz.com
viz media
www.viz.com

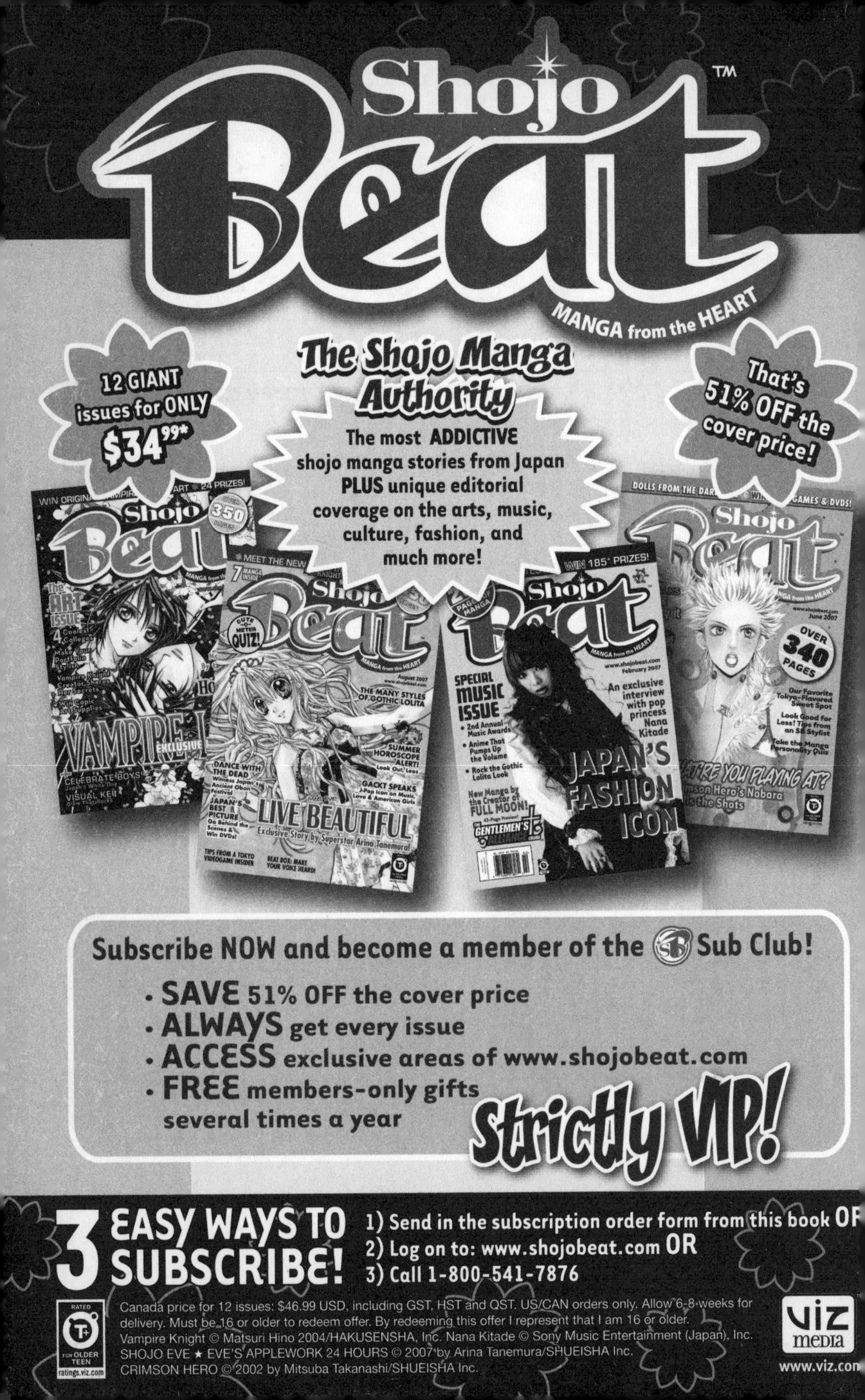
Shojo Beat™
MANGA from the HEART
The Shojo Manga Authority
12 GIANT issues for ONLY $34^99*
That's 51% OFF the cover price!
The most ADDICTIVE shojo manga stories from Japan PLUS unique editorial coverage on the arts, music, culture, fashion, and much more!
Subscribe NOW and become a member of the SB Sub Club!
• SAVE 51% OFF the cover price
• ALWAYS get every issue
• ACCESS exclusive areas of www.shojobeat.com
• FREE members-only gifts several times a year
Strictly VIP!
3 EASY WAYS TO SUBSCRIBE!
1) Send in the subscription order form from this book OR
2) Log on to: www.shojobeat.com OR
3) Call 1-800-541-7876
Canada price for 12 issues: $46.99 USD, including GST, HST and QST. US/CAN orders only. Allow 6-8 weeks for delivery. Must be 16 or older to redeem offer. By redeeming this offer I represent that I am 16 or older.
Vampire Knight © Matsuri Hino 2004/HAKUSENSHA, Inc. Nana Kitade © Sony Music Entertainment (Japan), Inc.
SHOJO EVE ★ EVE'S APPLEWORK 24 HOURS © 2007 by Arina Tanemura/SHUEISHA Inc.
CRIMSON HERO © 2002 by Mitsuba Takanashi/SHUEISHA Inc.
RATED T+ FOR OLDER TEEN ratings.viz.com
VIZ media
www.viz.com